Additions and Corrections to the W.P.A.

Inventory of Ashland County, Ohio: ASHLAND

Jana Sloan Broglin

HERITAGE BOOKS
2024

HERITAGE BOOKS

AN IMPRINT OF HERITAGE BOOKS, INC.

Books, CDs, and more—Worldwide

For our listing of thousands of titles see our website
at
www.HeritageBooks.com

Published 2024 by
HERITAGE BOOKS, INC.
Publishing Division
5810 Ruatan Street
Berwyn Heights, MD 20740

(Originally Titled)
INVENTORY OF THE COUNTY ARCHIVES OF OHIO
Prepared by
The Ohio Historical Records Survey Project
Service Division
Works Progress Administration

Columbus, Ohio
The Ohio Historical Records Survey Project
August 1942

International Standard Book Number
Paperbound: 978-0-7884-2767-1

TABLE OF CONTENTS

The Historical Records Survey Program

Sargent B. Child, National Director
Willard N. Hogan, Regional Supervisor
Francis M. Foott, State Supervisor
Lillian Kessler, District Supervisor

Service Division

Florence Kerr, Assistant Commissioner
Mary Gillett Moon, Chief Regional Supervisor
Ruth Neighbors, State Director
Beatrice Burr, District Director

WORK PROJECTS ADMINISTRATION

F.H. Dryden, Acting Commissioner
George Field, Regional Director
Carl Watson, State Administrator
Frank T. Miskell, District Manager

Sponsors

The Ohio State University

The Board of County Commissioners of Ashland County
Clayton I. Harmon
H.F. Wallett
Tom J. Stence

The Inventory of the County Archives of Ohio is one of a number of bibliographies of historical materials prepared throughout the United States by workers on the Historical Records Survey Program of the Works Projects Administration. The publication herewith presented, an inventory of the archives of Ashland County, is number three of the Ohio series.

The Historical Records Survey Program was undertaken in the winter of 1935-1936 for the purpose of providing useful employment to needy unemployed historians, lawyers, teachers, and research and clerical workers. In carrying out this objective, the project was organized to compile inventories of historical materials, particularly the unpublished government documents and records which are basic in the administration of local government, and which provide invaluable data for students of political, economic, and social history. Up to the present time more than 1700 guides, inventories, and indexes have been issued by the Survey throughout the nation. The archival guide herewith presented is intended to meet the requirements of day-to-day administration by the officials of the county, and also the needs of lawyers, business men and other citizens who require facts from the public records for the proper conduct of their affairs. The volume is so designed that it can be used by the historian in his research in un-printed sources in the same way he uses the library card catalog for printed sources.

The inventories produced by the Historical Records Survey Program attempt to do more than give merely a list of records–they attempt further to sketch in the historical background of the county or other unit of government, and to describe precisely and in detail the organization and functions of the government agencies whose records they list. The county, town, and other local inventories for the entire county will, when completed, constitute an encyclopedia of local government as well as a bibliography of local archives.

The successful conclusion of the work of the Historical Records Survey Program, even in a single county, would not be possible without the support of public officials, historical and legal specialists, and many other groups in the community. Their cooperation is greatly acknowledged.

The Survey Program was organized by Luther H. Evans, who served as Director until March 1, 1940, when he was succeeded by Sargent B. Child, who had been Field Supervisor since the inauguration of the Survey. The Survey Program operates as a nation-wide series of locally sponsored projects in the Service Division, of which Mrs. Florence Kerr, Assistant Commissioner, is in charge.

F.H. Dryden
Acting Commissioner

PREFACE
2nd Edition

In 1929 after the stock market crash along with the Great Depression which followed, President Herbert Hoover and his successor Franklin D. Roosevelt formulated relief projects; the most successful was the establishment of the Works Progress Administration (WPA).

Established as the Works Projects Administration in 1935, the WPA was the largest of the many programs developed during Roosevelt's "New Deal." In 1939, the agency's name was changed to Works Progress Administration, and continued as such until its demise in 1943.

The Federal Writers' Project, a division of the WPA (known as Federal Project Number One), created jobs for many unemployed librarians, clerks, researchers, editors, and historians. The workers went to courthouses, town halls, offices in large cities, vital statistics offices and inventoried records. Besides indexing works, many records were transcribed. One of these many projects was the *Inventory of the County Archives* which has benefitted genealogists and historians. The inventories listed the records, either by volumes or file boxes and years per record type, within the office. Although the WPA oversaw this project, the information for each volume of records may differ significantly by the information submitted.

This project was to encompass all of Ohio's eighty-eight counties although approximately thirty of these inventories have been located while others may not have been done. The original WPA volume for Ashland County contained maps showing the evolution of Ohio judicial districts and flow charts which have been omitted in this volume.

PREFACE
2nd Edition

The information herein is verbatim except for obvious spelling errors. Records listed may have met the requirement for retention and have been destroyed as per the records retention act, while other records are considered permanent records. (*See:* **https://codes.ohio.gov/ohio-revised-code** Ohio Revised Code, sections 149.31 and 149.34). Records considered "open" to the public, such as lunacy, idiotic, and juvenile cases, may be "closed" due to a revision of state laws. However, the records may be opened to family members with adequate proof of lineage.

The addresses and website section of this edition list an up-to-date location guide to each office mentioned.

Note: This series numbered the counties as they appear as listed alphabetically.

As always, contact the desired office for appointments to access the records with a minimum of 72 hours as some may be located off-site. Those records are accessible by staff only.

Jana Sloan Broglin
Fellow, Ohio Genealogical Society
Swanton, Ohio
2024

PREFACE
1st Edition

The Historical Records Survey of the Work Projects Administration began operation in Ohio in February 1936. The Project was organized and operated by the district supervisors of the Writers' Project until November 1936 when it became an independent part of the Federal Project No. 1. With termination of the Federal Projects in September 1939, the Ohio unit became the Ohio Historical Records Survey Project, sponsored by the Ohio Archaeological and Historical Society. On August 3, 1941, the Ohio Historical Records Survey Project became a unit of the Consolidated Records Assistance Project in Ohio, sponsored by the Ohio State University.

One of the purposes of the Survey in Ohio has been the preparation of complete inventories of state, county, city, and municipal records. *The Inventory of the County Archives of Ohio* will, when completed, consist of a set of 88 volumes numbered according to the position of the county name in an alphabetical list of Ohio counties. Thus, the inventory herewith presented for Ashland County is number three. The inventory of state archives and of municipal and other local records will constitute separate publications.

The principle followed in the inventory of the county records has been to place a record in the office of the origin rather than in the office of deposit. The records are arranged with those of the executive branch of government first, followed by law enforcement, fiscal, and miscellaneous agencies. Minor agencies are placed in a general arrangement according to function rather than according to constitutional or statutory responsibility to a major subdivision. The legal development of each office or agency has been treated in a prefatory section preceding the inventory of the records of the office. Although a condensed form of entry is used, information is given as to the limiting dates of all extant records, the contents of individual series, and the location of records in courthouse, statehouse, or other depository.

The Ohio Historical Records Survey was inaugurated in Summit County in May 1936. From July 1940 to February 1942 the project was under the administrative and technical supervision of Ruth Sloan. Since February 1942 the project has been under the supervision of Lillian Kessler. The wholehearted cooperation of the county officials helped to assure the thoroughness and completeness of the inventory. The Board of County Commissioners, serving as a contributing co-sponsor, made possible the publication of this volume. For the accuracy of the inventory the project personnel and Ashland County, working under the direction of William C. Hetschel, is entirely responsible. The Summit County office staff, under the immediate supervision of Florence Carnahan, arranged and edited the volume. The state office personnel, under the immediate supervision of Winifred Smith, Assistant State Supervisor, criticized and edited the volume. The duplicating and binding of the volumes was done in Cuyahoga County under the immediate supervision of Grace Clift.

The volumes comprising the *Inventory of the County Archives of Ohio* are issued in mimeographed or printed form for free distribution to state and other public officials and to public libraries in Ohio, and to a limited number of libraries outside the state. Requests for information concerning particular units of the *Inventory* should be addressed to the Ohio Historical Records Survey Project, Room 216, Clinton Building, Columbus, Ohio.

Frances M. Foott
State Supervisor
Consolidated Records Assistance Projects
Columbus, Ohio

alph. .... alphabetically
Arch. .... Archaeological
Art. .... Article
bd. .... board
bdl(s). .... bundle(s)
Bros. .... Brothers
c. .... copyrighted
CCC. .... Civilian Conservation Corps
of. .... (Confer) compare
chap(s). .... chapter(s)
Co. .... Company
comp. .... compiler
Const. .... Constitution
ct(s). .... court(s)
dist(s). .... district(s)
ed. .... edition
ed(s). .... editor(s)
Eng. .... England
et al. .... (et alii), and others
ex rel. .... (ex relations), at the instant of
et seq. .... (et sequentes, et sequentia (and the following)
G. C. .... General Code
H.B. .... House Bill
ibid. .... (Ibidem) the same reference as the last proceedings
Inc. .... Incorporated
jr. .... Junior
loc. cit. .... (loco citato) in the place sighted
Mun. .... Municipal
Nat. .... National
n. d. .... no date
n.p. .... no place of publication shown
n. pub. .... no publisher showing
n. s. .... new series
N.P. .... The Ohio *Nisi Prius Reports*
NYA. .... National Youth Administration

op. cit. . . . . (opere citato) in the work cited
p. . . . . page
passim. . . . . here and there
pt. . . . . part
pub. . . . . publisher
R. . . . . River
rep. . . . . reporter
R.S. . . . . Revised Statutes
S.B. . . . . Senate Bill
sec(s). . . . . section(s)
sic. . . . . thus, as an original copy
v. . . . . versus
vol(s) . . . . volume(s)
WPA . . . . Work Projects Administration
x . . . . by (in dimensions)
— . . . . current, to date
yrs. . . . . years
4-H . . . . (Four-H) head, hands, heart and health
& . . . . and

Each following chapter or section consists of (1) an essay describing legal status and functions of one department of county government and (2) an inventory of the records of that department.

Each record constitutes a separate entry. Entries are arranged under topical headings and subheadings. Every entry sets forth, insofar as applicable, the following:

Entry number. Entries are numbered consecutively throughout the inventory.

The exact title as it appears on the record or if the record has no title a supplied title in brackets. If the title of the record is non-descriptive, misleading, or incorrect an additional title (in capitals and lowercase letters), also enclosed in brackets, had been supplied.

Dates show inclusive years or parts of years covered by the record. Breaks in dates indicate that the record is missing or was not kept between dates shown. A dash in place of the final date indicates an open record. If no current entries have been made the date of the last entry is noted. Where no statement is made that the record was discontinued at the last date shown, it could not be definitely established that such was the case. Where no comment is made on the absence of prior and subsequent records, no definite information could be attained.

Quantity, given in chronological order wherever possible. Labeling. Numbers and letters within parentheses indicate labeling on volumes, file boxes, or other containers.

Variation in title. The current or most recent title is used but significant variations are shown with dates for which each was used.

Change of agency. Occasionally a record is discontinued as a county record and kept by some other agency.

Description. A statement of the nature and purpose of the record and of what the record shows. As the contents of a record may vary over a period of time the description may differ somewhat from the record at any one period. Wherever feasible, changes in content are shown with dates. In map and plat entries the names of author and publisher and the scale are omitted only when not available.

Arrangement. Records said to be alphabetically arranged are frequently alphabetized only as to initial letter of the surname. This is usually the case where there is a secondary arrangement.

Indexing. Self-contained indexes are described in the entry. Separate indexes constitute separate entries with cross reference to and from the record entry.

Nature of recording. Changes are indicated with dates.

Condition. No statement is made if good or excellent.

Number of pages. Averaged for the series.

Dimensions show size of volume, maps, file boxes, or other containers and are expressed in inches in every instance. The dimensions of volumes are given in order of height, width, and thickness; of file boxes in order of height, width, and depth.

Location. Rooms referred to are in the county courthouse unless some other building is specified.

Title-line cross references are used to complete series where a record is kept separately for a period of time or in other records for different periods of time. They are also used in all artificial entries which are made to show, under their proper office, records kept in the same volume or file with records of another office. In both instances, the description of the master entry shows the title and entry number of the record to which the cross reference is made. Dates shown in the description of the master entry are for the most part or parts of the record contain therein, and are shown only when they vary from those of the master entry. Artificial entries show only title, dates, and description.

Separate third-paragraph cross references from entry to entry, are used to show prior, subsequent, or related records which are not a part of the same series. If, however, both entries are under the same subject heading, no third paragraph references are made. "See also" references from subject headings refer to entries in the same department which contain records logically belonging under that heading but which have been classified under an equally appropriate heading.

Ashland County, in the north central part of Ohio, is on the dividing ridge, or watershed, between Lake Erie and the Ohio River. Neighboring counties are Huron and Lorain on the north, Medina, Wayne and Holmes on the east, Holmes and Knox on the south, and Richland and Huron on the west. Ashland is a narrow county, only 15 miles wide, but its extreme length from north to south is slightly more than 35 miles. A population of 29,785,[1] mostly decedents of people from Pennsylvania,[2] inhabit the 421 square mile area.[3] Ashland County honors Henry Clay by being named for his home in Lexington, Kentucky.

The land is divided into two principal slopes or watersheds by a range of uplands, extending in a northeasterly direction across the southern part of Clearcreek Township and the northern part of Orange and Jackson Townships. This ridge separates the streams flowing south to the Muskegon River, and north to Lake Erie.[4]

All of Ashland was covered by glaciers. The line dividing the glacial plain from the glacial plateau runs east and west through the county.[5] The surface in the southern part is hilly and rugged, in the northern, level to gently rolling. The Mohican River enters the county at Five Points and crosses Green and Hanover Townships to enter Holmes County. Most of the county is drained into this stream or one of its branches. Important ones, such as Black, Jerome, Muddy, and Lake Forks, are fed by a number of small watercourses like Katotawa and Honey Creeks. South of the divide the uplands slope gently to the south and provide excellent agricultural lands.[6] Good farm lands are found along the streams in most of the western slope of the county where the soils are clay, second bottom loam, and rich alluvium. The middle and eastern ranges are much the same, except in Hanover Township. There, the upland is more rugged, sandy, and less productive. North of the dividing range, the land dips slightly to the north and has a stiff clay soil, ideal for pastures. This is a cattle-raising section.[7]

---

1. U.S. Bureau of the Census, *16th Census of the United States, 1940, Population, First Series, Number of Inhabitants, Ohio*, 4.
2. Henry Howe, *Historical Collections of Ohio*, I, 251.
3. William A. Duff, *History of North Central Ohio*, I, 294.
4. George W. Hill, *History of Ashland County, Ohio*, 98.
5. Geological Survey of Ohio, *Report, Second Series*, III, pt. I, 519.
6. *Ibid.*, 519-522.
7. Hill, *op. cit.*, 99, 100.

Ashland County has five lakes, two a short distance southeast of Savannah, and three southwest of the village of Mifflin. The largest lake, near Savannah, covers 160 acres, and the lower, smaller one, partially drained, has an 80-acre area. The largest one near Mifflin covers approximately 50 acres, the next in size, 30 acres, and the smallest, 10 acres.[8]

In the southern part of Ashland County is a forest section of approximately 10,000 acres, one of the finest reproducing timber lands in Ohio. The oak, pine, cedar, and hemlock trees which are permitted to reach maturity before being cut, produce top quality commercial lumber. This is a practical conservation policy.

The county is limited in its subsoil production. A narrow ridge of coal lies along the south line of Hanover Township.[9] The Ohio gas belt runs through the county,[10] but is now practically exhausted.

Geologically, Ashland County evidences an early emergence from prehistoric seas. Its soils and hills are probably older than the coal and limestone ages. If these periods existed within the county, evidence of them were erased by the glaciers, or by the great northern seas which at one time flowed through the Ohio and Mississippi River valleys. That the great seas were here, is proved by large deposits of ancient shells on the surface.[11] The rock structure of the county is simple. The formations are of sandstone, freestone, fire clay, and shale. They are an eastern continuation of those in Richland County.[12] The freestone rocks are in strata, their beds ranging in thickness from three to twenty feet. The sandstone formation cropped out at a later period, and some is still found on the high land east of Ashland, commencing at Roseberry's Hill and extending south to Lake Township; also, on the elevated track of land running from Milton to Hanover Township. There were large quantities of this rock and it provided durable material for walls, bridges, and buildings.[13] The supply has been exhausted for commercial use.

---

8. Geological Survey of Ohio, *Report, Second Series*, III, pt. I, 520.
9. Hill, *op. cit.*, 99.
10. Duff, *op. cit.*, I, 39.
11. Geological Survey of Ohio, *Report, Second Series*, III, pt. I, 521,522.
12. *Ibid.*, 522, 523.
13. *Ibid.*, 523-528.

The earliest known inhabitants of the region now comprising Ashland County, were the mound-building Indians, who left earthworks as records of their existence. In the northern section is a circular embankment, 2145 feet in circumference and containing an area of approximately eight acres. This formation, now known as Gamble's Fort, is covered with trees which are equal in size to the growth in adjacent forests.[14] In addition, there are approximately 35 other earthworks within the county.[15]

Successors to mound builders were the American Indians. The tribes inhabiting this territory were the Wyandot, Erie, Mohican, and Delaware.[16] The last named built a village near the Mohican River, prior to 1783, and named it Helltown. This tribe founded Greentown in 1783, aided by Thomas Green, a New England Tory. It flourished until destroyed by American militia during the War of 1812.[17] Many of the Helltown residents were Christians, having been converted by the Moravian missionaries, and when news reached them of the massacre of some of their Moravian Brethren at Gnadenhutten, they abandoned the town.[18]

Another large Indian village, established near the present site of Jeromesville, by Mingoes under leadership of Chief Mohican John, became known as Mohican Johnstown. The tribe also established the village of Mingo Cabins a mile northeast, on the east bank of Jerome Fork. These villages were visited by Major Robert Rogers and his famous Rangers in 1761.[19]

The Greenville Treaty in 1795 left the Indians northeastern Ohio, including what is now Ashland County, as a hunting ground. They reigned supreme over the territory until 1805 when white settlement began.[20]

---

14. Duff, *op. cit.*, I, 421. Among other noted relics of the mound builders in the county are several known as forts. They are Ramsey's, in Jackson Township, Metcalf, Winbigler, and Glenn near the Jerome Fork. There is Norris Mound near Nankin, and Sprott's Mound in Clearcreek Township.
15. William C. Mills, *Archaeological Atlas of Ohio*, 3.
16. Hill, *op. cit.*, 19-23.
17. H.S. Knapp, *A History of the Pioneer and Modern Times of Ashland County*, 10-12.
18. Hill, *op. cit.*, 34.
19. Knapp, *op. cit.*, 12-14.
20. Howe, *op. cit.*, I, 532.

When white men began to infiltrate, the red men's hostility was aroused toward the invaders of their domain. This situation was aggravated by the War of 1812 when Great Britain encouraged Indian atrocities in her fight with America. Massacres were committed in and around Greentown, which was definitely pro-British. The commander of the American troops at Mansfield received orders to evict the inhabitants of the village before more outrages were committed. Consequently the Mingoes abandoned their homes under escort of soldiers. Their village was set afire.[21]

About five miles north of Greentown lived the Zimmer (Seymour) family and their neighbor, a German name Martin Ruffner. A party of Mingoes cruelly massacred Ruffner and the members of the Zimmer family who were in the cabin. This act aroused the entire countryside; all outlying districts were warned to seek protection within the blockhouse. After a few days, James Copus, another early settler, returned from the blockhouse with his wife, their seven children, and a protective detail of nine soldiers. Early on September 15, 1812, while the family prepared breakfast and the soldiers washed at a nearby spring, a band of Indians attempted to storm the cabin. Copus and several soldiers were killed, but after five hours of relentless fighting, the red men withdrew. Seventy years after this affray, September 15, 1882, two monuments were dedicated on the site of the massacre.[22]

Meanwhile people were settling permanently in Ashland County. One of the first was Alexander Finley, who in 1809, came to what is now known as Tylertown, about five miles north of Loudonville.[23] James Loudon Priest, of Crawford County, Pennsylvania, in 1810, settled with his family on the banks of Lake Fork.[24]

---

21. Samuel Riddle, *History of Ashland County Pioneer Historical Society*, 102, 103.
22. Riddle, *op. cit.*, 91-98.
23. Hill, *op. cit.*, 76, 144. The eccentric John Chapman, better known as Johnny Appleseed, a character who dressed in rags, traveled through several states of the northwest planting apple orchards, arrived in Ashland County in 1806. In one instance he was known to buy land. He received a deed from Alexander Finley for part of a quarter section, but with his customary indifference to such matters, Johnny failed to record the deed and lost the property. *Harper's New Monthly Magazine*, XVIII, November, 1871, pp. 830-835. For a number of years Johnny lived in a cabin near Perrysville. A.J. Baughman, *History of Ashland County, Ohio*, III.
24. Knapp, *op. cit.*, 379.

Priest and Stephen Butler platted the village of Loudonville in 1814. In that year Vachel Metcalf and Amos Norris arrived in what is now Orange Township and bought land adjoining the present village of Orange. Probably they were the first settlers of the township.[25] Many other pioneers cleared land on the Black Fork of the Mohican, among them being Nathan Odell, Joshua Cram, and John Newell.[26]

At the end of the War for Independence several states continued to claim title to territory north and west of the Ohio River. Virginia and Connecticut acquired their titles by colonial charters.[27] In 1784 Congress asked the states having territorial claims in the Northwest cede all lands to the national government as an aid in the payment of the debts incurred during the Revolution. Virginia released her claims in that year and Connecticut tendered all her territory except 12 counties in northeastern Ohio which came to be called the Connecticut reserve, and is known now as the Western Reserve.[28] All the territory now comprising Ashland County was included in the claim of Virginia except Troy, Sullivan, and Ruggles Townships which were part of the Connecticut Reserve.[29]

Prior to 1805, all the territory of present-day Ashland County was used by the Indians as free hunting ground. Part of the area remained in their possession until 1818, when it was purchased by the United States Land Office at Wooster, Ohio.[30] In 1796 it became a part of what is now Wayne County, Michigan, with its seat of justice at Detroit.[31] Twelve years later various sections of Ashland territory were made a part of Knox County with the seat of government at Mt. Vernon.[32]

---

25. Hill, *op. cit.*, 201.
26. Baughman, *op. cit.*, 48. Other early settlers who took up land in different sections of what was now to become Ashland County were Hugh McGuire, Thomas Smith, Samuel Burns, Daniel Campbell, Andrew Mason, Michael Riddle, and John Naylor. Baughman, *op. cit.*, 32. One of the prominent settlers of Orange Township was Joshua Thomas. Duff, *op. cit.*, 295-297.
27. Benjamin Perley Poore, *Federal and State Constitutions and other Organic Laws of the United States*, I, 182-184; 252-257.
28. *United States Statutes at Large*, I, 485. The counties were Erie, Huron, Lorain, Medina, Cuyahoga, Lake, Geauga, Portage, Ashtabula, Trumbull, most of Mahoning and Summit, and later, part of Ashland. Roseboom and Weisenburger, *History of Ohio*, 93.
29. Roseboom and Weisenburger, *op. cit.*, 72, 93.
30. Howe, *op. cit.*, I, 532.
31. Salmon P. Chase, ed., *Statutes of Ohio*, III, 2096.
32. *Laws of Ohio*, VI, 22.

The following year Huron County was formed, with jurisdiction over part of what is now Ashland.[33] In 1822 Lorain County was formed and in five years it annexed two future Ashland Townships.[34]

The general assembly, on February 24, 1846, passed a law creating Ashland County.[35] Vermillion, Orange, Green, Hanover, parts of Monroe, Mifflin, and Clear Fork townships were taken from Richland County; Jackson, Perry, Mohican, and Lake from Wayne County; Sullivan and Troy from Lorain County, and Ruggles from Huron County.[36] The last three townships belong to the Western Reserve, and their inclusion in Ashland County was bitterly opposed as the "rape of the Firelands."[37]

Upon agreement to donate $5000 and suitable land for public buildings, the village of Ashland, in April 1846, was selected as the Ashland County seat. It received 680 more votes than Hayesville, the nearest rival.[38] On April 17, 1846, the first county election was held. Joshua Thomas of Orange Township, Edward S. Hibbard of Hanover Township, and Abner Grist of Ruggles Township were elected as the first board of commissioners.[39] The first grand jury, convened May 1846, included Hugh McGuire, Daniel Carter, Sr., George Buchanan, Christopher Mykrantz, Christian Miller, Thomas Smith, Samuel Burns, Daniel Campbell, Andrew Mason, Michael Myers, John Smurr, George McConnell, James Boots, Michael Riddle, and John Naylor.[40]

---

33. *Ibid.*, VII, 194-195.
34. *Ibid.*, 12-50.
35. *Ibid.*, XLIV, 172-175.
36. Randolph C. Downes, "Evolution of Ohio County Boundaries," *Ohio State Archaeological and Historical Quarterly*, XXXVI (1927), 433-434.
37. Duff, *op. cit.*, 296. Erie and Huron Counties, occupying the extreme western edge of the Connecticut Reserve, were called the Firelands because they were given to families who had their homes in Connecticut burned by Tories and Indians during the War for Independence. Roseboom and Weisenburger, *op. cit.*, 94. The Connecticut pioneers resented being attached to a county outside the reserve. Duff, *op. cit.*, 296.
38. Duff, *op. cit.*, 296.
39. Commissioners' Record, I (1846-1863), 1.
40. Knapp, *op. cit.*, 51, 52.

Ashland county men distinguished themselves admirably during the Civil War. An entire unit, later known as Company B, 16th Ohio, was organized in answer to President Lincoln's first call for 12,357 men from Ohio. Lorin Andrews, of Ashland, was said to be the first Ohio volunteer for the Union Army.[41]

Agriculture has remained the primary industry of Ashland County since the days of the earliest settlements. Corn, wheat, oats, potatoes, and hay were the major crops raised by the pioneers. About 1817 the production of maple sugar attained large proportions. Prices were low, but the great quantities made possible a fair profit. Jonas Crouse, Abraham Huffman, and Elisha Chilcote each produced from 1800 to 2500 pounds annually.[42]

Farming expanded in Ashland County until the 1930s when prices and the amount of crops raised decreased considerably. In 1920 the county had 2512 farms with a total value, including buildings of $22,624,276. Among crops raised were wheat, 465,322 bushels, barley, 2812 bushels, buckwheat, 1259, and potatoes, 75,420 bushels.[43] By 1930 the number of farms that dropped to 2143 with a total value of $13,333,032. In that year, 459,503 bushels of wheat, 2786 bushels of barley, 7207 bushels of buckwheat, and 108,172 bushels of potatoes were raised.[44] In 1939 the figures were wheat, 459,602 bushels, barley, 1999, buckwheat, 1900, and potatoes, 65,007. In that year there were 2336 farms with a total value of $12,191,434.[45]

---

41. Baughman, *op. cit.*, 221.
42. Baughman, *op. cit.*, 37.
43. U.S. Bureau of the Census, *Fifteenth Census of the United States, 1930, Agriculture*, II, pt. ii, 402-416, 430.
44. *Ibid.*, 416, 430, 435, 452, 460.
45. U.S. Bureau of the Census, *Sixteenth Census of the United States, 1940, Agriculture, Ohio, First Series*, 10, 46-53. Though the number of farms has increased, the land area cultivated, and the crop values have decreased. *Ibid.*, 1-10.

Lack of a favorable water route minimized the profit obtained from industry and agriculture in early Ashland County. The only method of transportation was by large wagons over the road from Wooster to Mansfield, from Mt. Vernon to Huron, Huron to Lake Erie, and Mansfield to Ashland. About 1817 flatboats were built at Perrysville and Loudonville to be sent down the Mohican River and on to New Orleans. Water transportation did not become readily accessible, however, until the building of the Ohio and Erie Canal. Farmers were able to ship their produce down the Mohican River to Brinkhaven, the terminal of a lateral connection with the main canal.[46]

The first railroad in Ashland County was built in 1849. It extended from Mansfield through Perrysville and Loudonville to Wooster. The Atlantic and Great Western, now known as the Erie, was built through the county in 1864. It made Ashland an important pioneer railroad center.[47] There are three railroad companies now operating within Ashland County, the Pennsylvania, running across the southern part of the county, the Erie, routed across the center part, and the Baltimore and Ohio, which crosses the northern section.[48]

Ashland County, in 1940, was the home of 44 manufacturing plants. A total of 2910 men and 826 women were employed during that year. The Myers and Brothers Company, of Ashland, manufacturers of pumps, was the largest user of labor. This company employs 706 men and 44 women. The Flexible Shaft Company, of Perrysville, manufacturers of busses, hearses, and ambulances, employed 476 men and 39 women.[49]

The manufacturing centers of Ashland County are Ashland and Loudonville. The former, founded in 1815 as Uniontown, is laid out on the Main Street plan with residential streets running to the outskirts at right angles. It is on the New York to Chicago line of the Erie Railroad and is served by bus line. United States Highways 42 and 250 run through the city, and state routes 58, 60, 96, and 511. It is the home of about 40 small factories, producing such articles as windmills, hydraulic pumps, paper boxes, burial vaults, hardware, rubber goods, and medicines.[50]

---

46. Baughman, *op. cit.*, 53-55.
47. Duff, *op. cit.*, I, 299.
48. Rand McNally & Co., *Commercial Atlas and Marketing Guide, 1942*, 305.
49. Ohio Department of Industrial Relations, Division of Labor Statistics, Files for 1940.
50. N.W. Ayer and Son's, *Directory of Newspapers and Periodicals*, 1940, page 711.

Loudonville, on the Mohican River, was founded in 1814 by James Loudon Priest. It is platted similarly to Ashland. Each year thousands of tourists are attracted here because of nearby Mohican State Forest Park and the Pleasant Hill Dam, an Ohio Flood Control project. It is also widely known as a manufacturing center of busses and ambulances.[51]

Miscellaneous business establishments of the county employ 565 men and 398 women. The Star Telephone Company of Ashland is the largest concern. It employs 22 men and 67 women. Retail stores number 397 with a total yearly sale of $10,306,000. They furnish employment for 990 people and have an annual payroll of $888,000. Ninety-nine people are employed in twenty-two wholesale establishments. Total sales of these concerns are $2,659,000.[52]

With the founding of manufacturing plants and the general development in industry, banking institutions were established in Ashland County. Their expansion parallels that of industry. Following the President's bank holiday of 1933, the banks of Ashland, as in other counties, were strengthened by consolidation. There are now one national and three state banks in the county. Ashland is the home of the national bank, the First National.[53] The Ashland Bank and Savings Company with a capital of $150,000, and the Farmers Bank, capital $100,000, are state banks, both located in Ashland. The third is the Farmers and Savings Bank at Loudonville. It has a capital of $100,000.[54]

Pioneer Ashland County schools were supported almost entirely by subscriptions among the parents. Settlers were not numerous enough to make possible any considerable remuneration, consequently teachers were underpaid and schools lacked proper equipment. At first a few pupils gathered in the cabin of an interested pioneer for instructions by voluntary teachers. Most of these were women from Pennsylvania, New York, and Maryland. The first schoolhouses made of round logs, were erected by citizens of the district.[55]

---

51. Ayer and Son's *op. cit.*, 733.
52. U.S. Bureau of the Census, *Sixteenth Census of the United States, 1940, Manufacturers*, I, 7-22.
53. U.S. Comptroller of the Currency, *Individual Statements of Conditions of National Banks, December 31, 1940*, 116-125.
54. Ohio Department of Commerce Division of Banks, *Thirty-third Annual Report, December 31, 1941* (unpaged).
55. Hill, *op. cit.*, 79, 80.

Some of the earliest teachers were Mrs. John Coulter, Mrs. Patrick Elliot, Sage Kellogg, and Robert Nelson.[56] Schools of the county are now divided into 11 districts. This does not include Ashland and Loudonville which are exempted districts. The schools published their own monthly newspaper, the Ashland County *School News*.[57]

Among the institutions of northern Ohio devoted to higher education is Ashland College. Founded as the Ashland Academy, in 1841, it flourished under the direction of the Reverend Robert Fulton, Professor L. Andrews, and Reverend Samuel Fulton. The academy had a splendid reputation and students from every part of the state attended. When the union school system was adopted for the county in 1850, the academy grounds and buildings were purchased by the county and merged with the new school system.[58] The Ashland College was chartered in 1878 by authority of the German Baptist Brethren. At the end of 10 years the institution was bought by the Progressive branch of the church and reorganized and incorporated as Ashland University, with the privilege of conferring university degrees.[59] Although the legal title of the institution is Ashland University, for some years it has been called Ashland College because only a Liberal Arts and Divinity School remain.[60] Degrees now conferred by the College are Bachelor of Science in Education, and Bachelor of Arts, and Bachelor of Arts in Theology. Approximately 500 students are enrolled. The admission policy is nonsectarian. Seventy-five percent of the students work in either one or two groups. The first, the industrial unit, provides financial aid for part-time work. The second group, known as the participating unit, offers the students a place in industrial, social, and professional groups for experience. The college plant consists of four buildings and an 18-acre campus.[61]

---

56. Hill *op. cit.*, 80, 81. There are 15 school buildings in present-day Ashland County. No one-room schoolhouses are in use. Buildings, sites, and equipment represent an investment of $743,935. Fifty elementary, 49 high school, and 2 special subject teachers give instructions to 1449 elementary and 807 high school students. State Department of Education, Division of Statistics, Files for 1942.
57. J.A. Caldwell, *Atlas of Ashland County, Ohio*, 5.
58. Ashland College, pub., *Ashland College, Bulletin 1941-42*, 12-20.
59. James A. Burns, *Educational History of Ohio*, 356.
60. Ashland College, *op. cit.*, 36.
61. Ohio Department of Education, Division of Statistics, Files for 1942.

Ashland County has many of the recognized religious denominations. First to be established were the First Methodists, who built a church in 1823. The Church of Christ was organized in 1836; Trinity Lutheran, 1839; First Presbyterian, 1841; Emmanuel Evangelical, 1865; United Brethren, 1867; Peace Lutheran, 1868; St. Edwards Roman Catholic, 1871; Salvation Army, 1885; Congregational, 1889; Church of the Brethren, 1914; First Church of Christ Scientist, 1920; Church of the Nazarene, 1926; Church of Christ, 1929; Christian and Missionary Alliance, 1935; Church of God, 1938; and Calvary Church, 1939. Other denominations throughout the county are the Brethren Conservative Dunkers, Disciples of Christ, Evangelical Synod North America, United Lutherans Joint Synod of Ohio, and Northern Baptist. In 1926 there were 13,609 church members. The largest membership was enjoyed by the Methodists with a total of 2193. The United Brethren had 1507, and the Joint Synod of Ohio, 1247.[62]

Ashland County has produced many famous people: The Studebakers at Pleasant Ridge, founders of the great automobile factory bearing their name; Perry Township was a home of William B. Allison, United States Senator from Iowa, and Edmond G. Ross, Senator from Kansas.[63] Charles F. Kettering, the noted inventor and scientist, was a former native of the county. Dr. Mary Fulton, pioneer missionary in China, Dr. Joseph E. Stubbs, noted educator and one time president of Nevada State University, and Peter S. Grosscup, United States Circuit Court Judge, were also former citizens of Ashland County.

---

62. U.S. Bureau of Census, *Religious Bodies*, I, 1926, 656-659.

63. Edmund Ross was born at Ashland, Ohio, in 1826 and died in Kansas in 1907. He went to Kansas as a young man and served as apprentice printer. He rose in his chosen profession and became one of the noted journalists and publishers of his time. During the Civil War he enlisted as a private and rose to the rank of Major. In 1864 he was appointed by the Governor of Kansas to fill a vacancy in the United States Senate. His work as statesman was outstanding, and at the end of the term, he was elected as United States Senator for a second term. He was a leader in the opposition to President Johnson and voted for his impeachment trial. Ross thought that the evidence failed to justify the impeachment, and even though he said it meant "looking into his political grave," he voted for acquittal.

There are several interesting historical sites within the county. In the city of Ashland are the Hubbard Homestead, once a noted station on the Underground Railroad, and the Johnny Appleseed monument.[64] The small stones in this monument were collected by Ashland County school children, whose nickels also paid for its erection.[65]

A press was established in a section now known as Ashland County before official organization of the area. The first paper, the *Mohican Advocate and Hanover Journal*, was started in Loudonville in October 1834. Next was the *Ashland Herald*, established in December 1834. Both papers were short-lived. Other papers, both Whig and Democratic, prospered for a time. The *Ashlander*, founded in 1850 by L. Jeff. Sprenger, was the direct ancestor of the present Loudonville *Press*. It later became known as the *Times*, and under that title is the present weekly newspaper of that city. At Ashland, Dr. George Hill began his *States and Union* in 1868, and four years later it became the *Press*. In 1877 came the *Gazette* of Thomas M. Beer. The *Times* and *Gazette* were consolidated in 1893, and in 1919 the *Press* merged with the *Times-Gazette*, the present weekly paper of Ashland.[66] Other papers of that city are the *Brethren Evangelist*, a weekly publication of the Brethren denomination, and the *Collegian*, weekly paper of the Ashland College.[67] In addition to the editors and publishers mentioned, other outstanding journalists of the county have been W.T. Anderson, W.H. Gates, and George Hildebrand.[68]

Ashland County is one of the Democratic strongholds of Ohio. Though it chose Abraham Lincoln in 1860, four years later the soldier candidate, George B. McClellan was favored over Lincoln. Only three times since 1860 has the county wanted a Republican president; James G. Blaine in 1884, Herbert Hoover in 1928, and Wendell Wilkie in 1940. Only twice, in 1938 and in 1940 has a Republican been preferred for governor. A Democratic nomination has been almost tantamount to election for county office. A banner year for Republicans was 1938 when they gained three county offices.[69]

---

64. Baughman, *op. cit.*, 242-245. A granite boulder monument marks the site of the shop erected by the Studebakers in 1835 at their home on Pleasant Ridge. Duff, *op. cit.*, 308.
65. Knapp, *op. cit.*, 28.
66. Osman Castle Hooper, *History of Ohio Journalism, 1797-1933*, 121.
67. Ayer and Sons, *op. cit.*, 711.
68. Hooper, *op. cit.*, 121.
69. Ohio Secretary of State, *Annual Report*, 1860, p. 17; 1864, p. 26; 1884, p. 260; 1928, p. 150; *Election Statistics*, 1938, p. 153; 1940, p. 179.

The county as a political institution and as a subdivision of the state for purposes of political and judicial administration is of ancient origin.[1] In a form substantially similar in all general features and functions it has existed in England since early times, and in America since its settlement. As the tide of migration moved westward, following the American Revolution, the institutions of seaboard states were transferred to the newer west, undergoing such alteration as best suited frontier conditions.[2]

The earliest provision for the organization of counties in what is now the state of Ohio was contained in the Ordinance of 1787, by which the governor of the Northwest Territory was directed to "lay out the parts of the district in which the indian [sic] titles shall have been extinguished into the counties and townships subject, however, to such alterations as may thereafter be made by the legislature."[3] The organization of county government, therefore, began before the organization of the state and before the adoption of a state constitution. Prior to statehood nine counties were organized. The first county lines were drawn in 1788.[4] The last county lines were altered in 1888, exactly 100 years later.[5]

---

1. Thomas Hodgkins, *From the Earliest Times to the Norman Conquest* (New York and London, 1906), 432.
2. Beverley W. Bond, Jr., *The Civilization of the Old Northwest: A Study of Political, Social, and Economic Development, 1738-1812* (New York, 1934), 58-59.
3. Clarence Edwin Carter, ed. and comp., *The Territorial Papers of the United States* (Washington, 1934), II, 44.
4. *Ibid.*, III, 279.
5. *Laws of Ohio*, LXXXV, 418; Randolph Chandler Downes, "Evolution of Ohio County Boundaries," *Ohio State Archives and Historical Quarterly*, XXXVI (1927), 449.

The establishment of local government in the Northwest Territory was one of the first concerns of Governor St. Clair. The Ordinance of 1787 furnished the framework, but details of institutions had to be constructed. All county officials, under the provisions of the Ordinance, were made appointive by the governor. St Clair, a former resident of Pennsylvania, in providing for local administration depended in a large part upon the Pennsylvania Code, which in some instances, was altered to meet the needs of pioneer communities.[6]

The provisions for local administration were, for the most part, simple and effective. In each county the court of general quarter sessions of the peace, composed of three or more justices of the peace, served as the fiscal and administrative board of the county, estimating county expenditures, appointing tax commissioners, and providing for highway and bridge construction.[7] By the end of the decade the court was authorized to enter into contracts for building or repairing the county jail and the courthouse.[8] Other county officials appointed during the territorial period included a sheriff, a coroner, a recorder, a treasurer, a license commission, and justices and clerks of the various courts.[9]

Officers having been appointed, the next step in the organization of government was the establishment of a system of local courts. Evidence seems to indicate that the judicial system for the county had been carefully planned. The court of common pleas, composed of not less than three nor more than five appointive judges, was an inferior court having limited civil jurisdiction.[10]

6.The governor and judges were given power to "adopt and publish in the district such laws of the original states" as they thought necessary and these laws were to remain in force unless disapproved by congress. In many cases the governor and judges had not adopted laws of the original states, as the Ordinance stipulated, but had passed measures that conformed in spirit. Since there was some question of the legality of these laws St. Clair, in 1795, after the lower house of congress disapproved of the laws passed at the legislative session of 1792, called a legislative session to revise the territorial code. The commission, after sitting for three months, completed Maxwell's Code, named in honor of the printer, W. Maxwell. Few changes were made in the Maxwell Code by the territorial assembly which was elected in 1798. Carter, *op. cit.*, II, 43. The minutes of the legislative assembly were reproduced in the *Ohio State Archives and Historical Quarterly*, XXX (1921), 13-53.

7. Theodore Calvin Pease, comp., *The Laws of the Northwest Territory, 1788-1880* (Illinois State Bar Association Law Series, Springfield, 1925, I), 4, 36, 37, 69-70, 467-478, 74, 77, 453, 456, 485.

8. *Ibid.*, 485

9. *Ibid.*, 8, 24-25, 61, 68-69, 197.

10. *Ibid.*, 7.

The court of general quarter sessions of the peace, besides serving as the fiscal and administrative board of the county, had jurisdiction in lesser criminal cases.[11] A probate court, composed of a single judge, was given jurisdiction in probate and testamentary matters.[12] In 1795, following St. Clair's revision of the territorial code, circuit courts were established and orphans' courts were instituted.[13]

In the meantime the local government was further developed by the organization of civil townships. The governor and judges adopted a law from the Pennsylvania Code requiring the justices of the court of quarter sessions to divide each county into townships and appoint in each township a constable to serve specifically in his township and in the county, a clerk, and one or more overseers of the poor.[14]

The territory entered the second stage of administration when, in 1798, the population having reached the requisite 5000 the governor ordered the election of a representative assembly.[15] The system of local government continued as established by the governor and judges, and the transition was achieved without a disturbance of local administration.

The admission of Ohio as a state did not, in the main, materially affect county organization and administration. The system of local government having been organized by the governor and judges and the legislature of the Northwest Territory, the basic offices were continued. Except for the provision for the election of a county sheriff and a county coroner in each county, two officials of utmost importance in pioneer communities, the constitution was silent on such matters as titles, number, and duties of officials.[16]

---

11. *Ibid.*, 4-7.
12. *Ibid.*, 9.
13. *Ibid.*, 157, 181-188.
14. Pease, *op. cit.*, 37-41, 338. The system of local governmental administration was a result of sectional compromise, since it combined the county system of the southern and middle states with the element of the New England town. Dwight G. McCarthy, *The Territorial Governors of the Old Northwest: A Study in Territorial Administration* (Iowa City, 1910), 53-54.
15. Carter, *op. cit.*, III, 514-515.
16. *Ohio Const. 1802*, Art. VI, sec. 1.

It devolved, therefore, upon the legislature to confer powers upon the county. In 1804 the legislature made provision for a board of county commissioners, composed of three members elected for a three-year term.[17] The board of county commissioners, supplanting the court of general quarter sessions, became the administrative and fiscal board of the county. In 1803 the legislature, recognizing the need for a more adequate system of land records, provided for recorder to be appointed by the court of common pleas for a seven-year term and for a surveyor to be appointed by the court of common pleas.[18] Another act authorized the appointment of a county treasurer by the associate judges, a later one provided for his appointment by the county commissioners.[19]

The legislature also provided during its first session for a prosecuting attorney to be appointed by the supreme court to prosecute cases on behalf of the state.[20] In 1805 the appointing power was transferred to the court of common pleas.[21]

A new office was created in 1820, that of county auditor. The auditor, first appointed by the legislature, had as his duty the preparation of the tax duplicate.[22] The county board of revision was established in 1825, for the purpose of correcting some of the inequalities of assessments. The first board of revisions or equalization, as it was sometimes called, was composed of the county commissioners, the auditor, and the assessor.[23]

The judicial power of the state in matters of law and equity was vested in the supreme court, the court of common pleas, and the justices' courts. The articles of the constitution provided for a court of common pleas to be composed of a president and associate justices. The members of the court, appointed by a joint ballot on both houses of the general assembly, were to hold court in three judicial circuits into which the state was to be divided by the legislature.[24]

---

17. *Laws of Ohio*, II, 150.
18. *Ibid.*, I, 136, 90-93.
19. *Ibid.*, I, 97-98; II, 154.
20. *Laws of Ohio*, I, 50.
21. *Ibid.*, III, 47.
22. *Ibid.*, XVIII, 70.
23. *Ibid.*, XXIII, 68-69.
24. *Ohio Const. 1802*, Art. III, secs. 3, 8.

The court was assigned common law and chancery jurisdiction in all cases as provided by law.[25] To the court was assigned jurisdiction in probate and testamentary matters and in the appointment of guardians, functions performed during the territorial period by the probate court.[26] Finally, the court was authorized to appoint a clerk.[27]

The county offices created by the legislature were designed to transact the business of a state as yet unaffected by transformations wrought by industrialism and the problems presented by large urban areas. Aside from the maintenance of county poorhouses, the county had no functions in administration of public welfare.

As the wave of democratic philosophy swept across the country in the eighteen twenties and thirties there arose a demand not only for an extension of the franchise but also for the election of public officials. Accordingly the auditor became an elected official in 1821, the treasurer in 1827, the recorder in 1829, and the prosecuting attorney at 1833.[28]

While the legislature responded to the general demand for the election of county officials, there arose a further demand for a revision of the constitution which has failed to meet the needs of an expanding state. This movement came as a result of dissatisfaction with the judicial system which placed the burden of judicial administration upon four judges who had the task of holding court each year in all the counties.[29] Then, too, there arose a demand for the election of all public officials, for the prohibition of charters that granted special privileges, and for a limitation on the power of the legislature to create a state debt. In February 1850 the legislature, following a favorable popular vote on the proposition, called for the election of delegates to meet in convention in May.

---

25. *Ibid.*, Art. III, sec. 3.
26. *Ibid.*, Art. III, sec. 5, Pease, *op. cit.*, 9.
27. *Ohio Const. 1802*, Art. III, sec. 9.
28. *Laws of Ohio*, XIX, 116; XXV, 25-32; XXVII, 65; XXXI, 13-14.
29. J.V. Smith, rep., *Official Reports of the Debates and Proceedings of the Ohio State Convention ... held at Columbus, Commencing May 6, 1850, and at Cincinnati, Commencing December 2, 1850* (Columbus, 1851), 597 *et seq.* (Jacob) Burnet, *Notes on the Early Settlement of the North-Western Territory* (Cincinnati, 1847), 356. *See also the Ohio State Journal*, Dec. 11,1840.

The constitution drafted by the delegates, was approved by special election on June 17, 1851. The constitution of 1851, like the constitution of 1802, failed to provide a definite form of county government and administration. Aside from the constitutional provision for the election of the county treasurer, sheriff, and clerk of courts and recreating the probate court which had existed during the territorial period the organic instrument was silent on the administrative duties of the county.[30] Again all matters pertaining to county government were entrusted to the legislature. While the legislature conferred certain powers upon the county, it was limited by constitutional provision which required all laws of the general nature to be uniform throughout the state.[31]

The present administrative organization of Ohio county government presents a picture of extraordinary complexity. Each county quadrennially elects, besides the board of county commissioners, nine administrative officials: the recorder, the clerk of courts, the probate judge, the prosecuting attorney, the coroner, the sheriff, the treasurer, the auditor, and the county engineer. While these officials conduct a major portion of the county's business, there is a variety of appointive officers and boards, as well as *ex-officio* commissioners. For convenience the work of county government may be classified under the following general heads: administration, judicial system, law enforcement, finance and taxation, elections, health, public welfare, and public works.

Administration

The board of county commissioners is the central feature of the present structure of county government. The functions of this board touch either or indirectly every other branch and department. The board is the agency in whose name actions for and against the county are brought. This board is empowered to determine certain matters of policy for the conduct of county affairs such as adoption of the budget, establishment of services left optional by law, and the authorization of improvements.[32]

---

30. *Ohio Const. 1851*, Art. X, sec. 3; Art. IV, sec. 16; Art. IV, sec. 7.
31. *Ibid.*, Art. II. sec. 26.
32. G. C. sec. 2421.

Thus, in a limited sense it constitutes the legislative branch of the county. The commissioners, however, have no ordinance-making powers. The board also functions as the central administrative body although much of the administration, centered in other elective offices, is beyond its immediate control. The county auditor was originally made secretary of the board and still functions as such in a majority of the counties. Later provisions of the law permitted the board to appoint its own clerk, thus removing this duty from the auditor.[33]

Judicial system

The constitution of 1851 made significant changes in the composition of the court of common pleas. The judges, heretofore appointed by the legislature, were made elective for a term not to exceed five years. For the purpose of electing judges the state was divided into nine districts. Each district was divided into three parts, in each of which one common pleas judge was to be elected. Court was to be held in every district or county with such jurisdiction as should be provided by law.[34] The legislature provided for the districts but left the jurisdiction of the court much as it had been and earlier years of its existence.[35] The constitutional amendment of 1912 abolished the divisions and subdivisions provided by the constitution of 1851, and authorized the election of one or more common pleas judges in each county.[36]

The judicial system was extended in 1851 by the creation of district courts composed of one supreme court justice and several common pleas judges in each district.[37] For administrative purposes the nine common pleas districts were apportioned into five judicial circuits.[38] The courts were assigned original jurisdiction in the same matters as the supreme court and such appellate jurisdiction as might be provided by law.[39]

---

33. *Laws of Ohio*, XIX, 147; G. C. sec. 2566.
34. *Ohio Const. 1851*, Art. IV, secs. 3, 4, 10.
35. Willis A. Estrich, *et al.*, eds., *Ohio Jurisprudence*, XI, 827-839.
36. *Ohio Const. 1851* (Amendment), Art. IV, sec. 3.
37. *Ohio Const. 1851,* Art. IV, sec. 5.
38. *Laws of Ohio*, L, 69.
39. *Ohio Const. 1851*, Art. IV, sec. 6.

The district courts, abolished by the constitutional amendment of 1883, were superseded by the circuit courts which were given the same jurisdiction as their predecessors. The state was divided into seven circuits. In each circuit three judges were to be elected.[40] The judicial system was again altered in 1912 when, by constitutional amendment, the circuits were renamed courts of appeals.[41] The state is divided into nine appellate districts. There are three judges in each district elected by the people of the districts for a six-year term.[42]

The constitution of 1851 recreated the probate court, which, existing during the territorial period, was abolished by the first constitution, its authority and jurisdiction being then vested in the courts of common pleas. Each county has one probate judge elected by the people for a four-year term.[43] By constitutional provision, the probate judge has original jurisdiction in probate and testamentary matters, the appointment of guardians, the settlement of the accounts of executors, administrators, and guardians,[44] and the issuance of marriage licenses. An amendment to the constitution of 1912 authorized the common pleas judge, when petitioned by 10 percent of the voters in counties having a population of less than 60,000, to submit to the voters at any general election the question of combining the probate and common pleas court.[45] This combination exists in Adams, Henry, and Wyandot Counties.

Due to an increased amount of juvenile delinquency, the legislature, in 1904, authorized the judges of the court of common pleas, the probate court, and the superior and insolvency courts where established, to appoint one of their members as juvenile judge to hear cases involving neglected, dependent, and delinquent children. In counties which have a court of domestic relations the judge of that court serves in this capacity.[46]

---

40. *Ohio Const. 1851*, Art. IV, sec. 6; *Laws of Ohio*, LXXXI, 168.
41. *Ohio Const. 1851*, Art. IV, sec. 6, (Amendment, 1912).
42. G. C. sec. 1514.
43. *Laws of Ohio*, CXIV, 320; *Ohio Const. 1851*, Art. IV, sec. 7.
44. *Ohio Const. 1851*, Art. IV, sec. 8.
45. *Ibid.*, Art. IV, sec. 7 (Amendment, 1912).
46. *Laws of Ohio*, XCVII, 561-562; G. C. sec. 1532

Law Enforcement

Closely related to the courts are the agencies of law enforcement in the county. Law enforcement is conducted by four officials: the sheriff, the prosecuting attorney, the coroner, and the dog warden. These officials are concerned primarily with the enforcement of state laws, and leave the enforcement of municipal ordinances, and, in some instances, of state statutes in urban centers to municipal law enforcement agencies.

The county sheriff, whose duties have been materially curbed by municipal law-enforcement agencies and the state highway patrol, has as his duty the enforcement of state laws.[47] He serves as custodian of the county jail,[48] and as an executive agent of the courts.[49] It has been estimated that approximately one-half of the sheriff's time is devoted to duties connected with the courts. The sheriff is restricted by lack of scientific equipment which has been essential to law enforcement.[50]

The county prosecuting attorney, the most important agent in the enforcement of criminal law, is directed by law to "inquire into the commission" of crime within his county, and to prosecute on behalf of the state all complaints, suits and controversies to which the state is a party.[51] In conjunction with the state attorney general, he prosecutes in the supreme court cases arising in his county.[52] He acts also in a civil capacity as legal counsel for the commissioners and other officials.[53] The prosecuting attorney may institute proceedings against an individual, but as a rule charges must be filed against the offender before action is taken.

---

50. *The Reorganization of County Government in Ohio: Report of the Governor's Commission on County Government* (n.p., December 1934), 120 *et seq*. The sheriff system worked admirably in rural communities. From the standpoint of police administration, it is unsatisfactory in areas of dense population. In such areas there is need for a force of officers whose duty it is not merely to apprehend law violators but to prevent the infractions of the law by patrolling the territory. For an interesting discussion of some of "The Police Attack Crime," *Nat. Mun. Review*, XXLV (1935), 39-41.
51. G. C. sec. 2916.
52. G. C. sec. 2916.
53. G. C. sec. 2917.

The prosecuting attorney has certain administrative duties such as serving as a member of the county budget commission and of the board of sinking fund trustees.[54]

The county coroner has the ancient duty of determining the cause of death where death occurs under suspicious circumstances or by unlawful means,[55] the proper distribution of property found on or about the deceased,[56] and the management of the county morgue.[57] It has been suggested by authorities on county administration that the office be abolished and the duties transferred to a medical examiner appointed by the prosecuting attorney.[58]

Another law-enforcement agent existing within the county is the dog warden. This official is appointed by and is responsible to the county commissioners. No special qualifications are required for the office. The dog warden has as his duty the enforcement of the sections of General Code "relative to the licensing of dogs, the impounding and destruction of unlicensed dogs, and the payment of compensation for damages to livestock inflicted by dogs." The dog warden and his deputies, in the performance of their legal duties, have the same "police powers" as those conferred by statute upon sheriffs and police.[59] Prior to 1927 the duties now performed by the dog warden were performed by the county sheriff.[60]

Law enforcement in the county is defective in two respects: first, there is little or no co-ordination between the four agencies of the law enforcement, and second, there is little or no responsibility for neglect of duty. Evidence seems to indicate that the present inefficient and antiquated system could be corrected by consolidating all law-enforcement agencies into a county department of law enforcement under the immediate supervision of the county prosecuting attorney.[61]

---

54. *Laws of Ohio*, CXII, 399-400; CVIII, pt., I, 700-702.
55. G. C. sec. 2856.
56. G. C. secs. 2863, 2864.
57. G. C. sec. 2856-1.
58. W.F. Willoughby, *Principles of Judicial Administration* (Washington, 1929), 165-173. According to a recent act, effective June 8, 1937, only a licensed physician or a person who shall have previously served as coroner is eligible to fill the office. G. C. sec. 2856-7.
59. *Laws of Ohio*, CVIII, pt. I, 535: CXII, 348; G. C. sec. 5652-7.
60. *Laws of Ohio*, CVIII, pt. I, 535.
61. *The Reorganization of County Government*, 117-122.

The administration of criminal justice in the county has grown up in more or less hit-or-miss fashion and is for the most part unsatisfactory and extremely cumbersome. Arrests are made by the sheriff, or other police officers, who are theoretically officers of the state, but who are under little or no supervision. The accused person is brought before a local magistrate for a preliminary hearing. In the event the accused is committed, it is necessary, in most cases, to receive an indictment before a grand jury.[62]

Finance and Taxation

There are three types of financial functions performed by the county officers: tax administration, handling of fiscal affairs of the county, and the trusteeship of funds held for individuals in court procedure. The principal financial authorities are the board of county commissioners, the auditor, and the treasurer. The commissioners levy taxes, appropriate funds, and authorize payments.[63] The auditor's primary duties are the keeping of accounts, the issuance of warrants, the valuation of real estate, and the preparation of the tax list.[64] The treasurer collects taxes, receives and has custody of the county money, and disburses it upon warrant from the auditor.[65] Other functions relating to county finance are performed by the board of revision, budget commissioners, and board of sinking fund trustees.

During the early years of Ohio history, the principal sources of state and county revenue were the general property tax, the poll tax, and the fees received from licenses and permits to engage in certain kinds of business.[66]

---

62. For a criticism of the administration of criminal justice, *see* Edwin H. Sutherland, *Principles of Criminology* (Chicago, 1934), chap. xiv; Willoughby. *op. cit.*, chaps. xi, xiv, xxxvi.
63. G. C. secs. 5630, 5637, 7419.
64. G. C. secs. 2568-2570, 2573, 2583-2589.
65. G. C. secs. 2649, 2649-1, 2656, 2674.
66. An act of 1825 levied a tax on the income of attorneys, physicians, and surgeons for state purpose. Amount of tax was determined by the court of common pleas. Salmon P. Chase, comp. *The Statutes of Ohio and of the Northwest Territory, 1788-1853* (Cincinnati, 1833), 1471. This act was repealed in 1852. Maskell E. Curwen, comp. *Public Statutes at Large of the State of Ohio* (Cincinnati 1853), 1755. The poll tax was perpetually abolished by constitutional authority in 1802. *Ohio Const. 1802*, Art. VIII. sec. 23.

A tax law enacted by the first territorial legislature (1799) designated certain types of property as taxable for county purposes. All houses in towns, town lots, out-lots, all water and wind mills, ferries, cattle and horses, were put on the county tax duplicate. A tax on land, subsequently used also for county purposes, was originally devoted exclusively to the needs of the territorial government. County officials were to assist in the administration of this tax as well as that of the county levy.[67]

In the course of time many additions were made to the original list of taxables. Taxable property came to include capital employed in merchandising (1826), and by exchange brokers (1825), pleasure carriages (1825), money loaned at interest (1831), and stock in steamboats.[68] In the latter year dividends of bank, insurance, and bridge companies were also made taxable.[69] The first act of general nature directing the taxation of railroads was passed in 1851.[70] In 1862 a tax on the gross receipts of express and telegraph companies was enacted.[71] A levy on the capital stock of freight lines was authorized in 1896.[72] Subsequent enactments brought into the category of "general property" the possession of public utilities in general. By such accumulations "property," by the end of the nineteenth century, had become a much more inclusive term than it had been 100 years earlier.

County agencies became even more useful with the discovery of new tax sources. When, at the turn into the twentieth century the general property tax lost its importance as a revenue source for the state, tax on inheritance and cigarettes, then, later, on gasoline, liquid fuel, liquor, retail sales, malt, and the like, took its place.[73] County officials continued to administer the general property tax, which was devoted henceforth to the use of local governments, but they assisted in the administration of a number of those newer taxes as well.

---

67. Chase, *op. cit.*, 267-279. Previous acts of 1792 and 1795 were temporary in nature.
68. Chase, *op. cit.*, III, 1517; 1476; *Laws of Ohio*, XXIX, 272-280.
69. *Laws of Ohio*, XXIV, 302-303.
70. Curwen, *op. cit.*, 1647.
71. J.R. Sayler, comp., *The Statutes of the State of Ohio* (Cincinnati, 1876), 301.
72. *Laws of Ohio*, XCII, 89-93.
73. Ohio tax commission, *Financing State and Local Government in Ohio. 1900-1932* (mimeographed, Columbus, 1934), 2.

The assistance rendered by county officials has been extensive in the system of issuing licenses and permits. The insurance of marriage licenses began during the territorial period (1788).[74] An act to license merchants, traders, and tavern keepers was passed in 1792.[75] Ferry licenses were authorized in 1799.[76] With the passage of time, one license after another have been required until unlicensed businesses have become something of an exception rather than the rule. Even with the increasing assumption of licensing authority by the state, county officials have continued to issue certain licenses assigned to the jurisdiction long ago.[77]

Under the early law (1792) tax commissioners, appointed to annual terms by the courts of common pleas, were to list the male inhabitants above the age of 18, stocks of cattle, yearly value of improved land, and other property. Valuation of this property was made by township and village assessors, appointed annually by the court of common pleas.[78] These local assessors, who became elected in 1795, were again appointed in 1799.[79] In 1825 property valuation was assigned to a new official, the county assessor, also appointed by the court of common pleas.[80] This official, became elective in 1827, was succeeded in turn, in 1841, by township assessors to be elected annually.[81]

In conjunction with these administrators a system of real estate reappraisal was initiated. In 1846 county commissioners were directed to divide their counties into suitable districts and to appoint an assessor for each whose chief function should be to revise the valuation of real property.[82] An act of 1863 made these officers elective and provided for reappraisal every tenth year.[83] This was subsequently changed (1868) to every fifth year and in 1878 returned to the 10 year interval.[84]

---

74. Chase, *op. cit.*, I, 101.
75. Chase, *op. cit.*, I, 114-115.
76. Chase, *op. cit.*, I, 219.
77. *See* pp. xlvi, xlvii
78. *Laws of the Territory of the United States Northwest of the River Ohio* (Philadelphia and Cincinnati, 1792-96), II, 17-18.
79. Chase, *op. cit.*, I, 169, 273.
80. Chase, *op. cit.*, II, 1477.
81. Curwen, *op. cit.*, 775-779.
82. Curwen, *op. cit.*, 1269.
83. Sayler, *op. cit.*, 413.
84. Sayler, *op. cit.*, 1641; *Laws of Ohio*, LXXV, 459.

In 1913 the assistance of county officers in tax administration was temporarily dispensed with and their duties were given to state officials. The county was again made an entire assessment district but district (or county) assessors were now to be appointed by the governor. The tax commission (established in 1910) was directed to supervise and direct the assessment of real and personal property.[85] This attempt at unification of authority in the state was partially abandoned, however, in 1915, when assessment was returned to the county auditor and to elected township, village, and ward assessors.[86] In 1925 the latter officers were discontinued and the duties of assessment devolved upon the county auditor alone.[87]

The advent of the state tax commission brought no great alteration in the process of assessment. The county remains the basic unit and the county auditor continues to serve as agent of the state. Though the state commission now assesses certain forms of property, certification is made to the county auditor. For example, public utilities are now assessed by the commission and proportional shares of the revenue are apportioned to the counties which contains such property.[88] Financial institutions report directly to each county auditor the assessment of each taxable deposit.[89] Intangible property (defined in 1931) owned by individuals and corporations, not otherwise excepted, is listed and valued by the county auditor. Returns showing more than $500 of taxable income are forwarded to the commission for appraisal and certified by it back to the county auditor.[90] From these certifications of the commission, the personal property lists returned to him by individuals, and the real estate assessment for which he is personally responsible, the auditor makes up the grand duplicate of real and personal property taxes.

---

85. *Laws of Ohio*, CIII, 786-787.
86. *Ibid.*, CVI, 246 *et seq.*
87. *Ibid.*, CXI, 486-487, Revaluation of real estate was required in 1925 and every sixth year thereafter.
88. G. C. sec. 5430.
89. G. C. secs. 5411, 5412, 5412-1.
90. *Report of the Governor's Commission*, 75; G. C. secs. 5372-3, 5376, 5377.

The county continues to be the basic unit also in a matter of budgeting and the levying of taxes on property. In 1792 the courts of general quarter sessions were directed to estimate the sums needed to defray the cost of county government, specifying as nearly as possible the purposes for which such sums were necessary. This earliest of budgets was to be laid before the governor and judges and approved by the legislature. Special commissioners were to apportion or levy the tax.[91] In 1799 it became the duty of these commissioners to ascertain the probable expenses of the county as well as levy the tax – a duty which continued until refinements in administrations were made necessary because of the increasing number of taxing authorities.[92]

In order to achieve some systematic arrangement in the county fiscal system, the function of estimating expenses, or budgeting, was consolidated in recent years in the hands of a county budget commission. Since the Ohio legislature, in 1911, established a tax rate limitation, it was necessary to establish a commission vested with authority to reduce the amounts set up in the annual budgets when the overlapping districts required more than the aggregate maximum tax rate permits.[93] The county budget commission organized in 1911 was composed, for a time, of the auditor, the mayor of the largest municipality, and the prosecuting attorney. Taxing authorities in the county were directed to submit their budgets to this body through the agency of the auditor.[94] The board was authorized to make adjustments in the budgets, alterations which the taxing authority might appeal to the tax commission. The budget commission, directed in 1911 to certify its action to the auditor, were subsequently instructed by law to make such certification to the various taxing units which should themselves authorize the necessary tax levies and certify them to the auditor.[95] In 1927 the composition of this board was altered when the county treasurer replaced the mayor.[96]

---

91. Chase, *op. cit.*, I, 118-119.
92. Chase, *op. cit.*, I, 276-277.
93. G. C. sec. 5625-3. Since 1934 there has been a limitation of 10 mills on the dollar. G. C. sec. 5625-2.
94. *Laws of Ohio*, CII, 270-272.
95. G. C. sec. 5625-25.
96. *Laws of Ohio*, CXII, 399.

Early appeals against unjust assessments (1792) were heard by judges of the general territorial court, judges of the common pleas court, or justices of the general quarters sessions court.[97] After 1795 petitions for redress were directed to the county commissioners.[98] This appeal agency was superseded in 1825 by the board of equalization, composed of the commissioners, the assessors, and the auditor.[99] This agency continued to function through the following years though occasionally changes in personnel were made.[100]

With the reorganization of property administration in 1913 the function of tax revision was taken away from county officers. In each district (county) the tax commission was directed to appoint three persons for the term of three years to form a district board of complaints.[101] An act of 1915 abolished this plan, however, and returned the function of revision to the care of county officials. A board composed of the treasurer, prosecuting attorney, probate judge, and president of the board of county commissioners, was directed to appoint a county board of equalization.[102] This plan, too, was soon disposed with. An act of 1917 constituted the county treasurer, auditor, and president of the board of commissioners as a county board of revision.[103]

The history of tax collection is equally intricate. The fiscal duties of the county treasurer, who now collects the property tax, comprised, in the very early period, only the receipt and custody of revenue funds. The actual collection was performed by other agencies. Due to the fact that in earlier years there were two district tax levies–one on land for the territory and later the state, and one on other property for county purposes–tax collections involved a double operation and duplicate officials.

---

98. Chase, *op. cit.*, I, 171.
99. Chase, *op. cit.*, II, 1476-1492.
100. The county surveyor became a member at times, in 1868, for example, Sayler, *op. cit.*, 1642
101. *Laws of Ohio*, CIII, 790-791.
102. *Ibid.*, CVI, 254-256.
103. *Ibid.*, CVII, 40; G. C. secs. 5580, 5596. See also p. 184. Highest appellate jurisdiction, held originally by the general court and later (1805) by the associate judges of common pleas, was given, in 1925, to a state board of equalization composed of the state auditor and one member from each congressional district. With the establishment of the state tax commission that agency was made the body of final appeal. *Laws of Ohio*, III, 111, Chase, *op. cit.*, II, 1481; Curwen, *op. cit.*, 1784; G. C. sec. 5625-27.

The collectors of the county levy assessed in 1792 were appointed by the judge of the court of common pleas who were empowered to designate the sheriff, constable, or any other suitable person to perform this function.[104] By an act of 1795 township collectors were appointed by the commissioners and assessors.[105] From 1799 to 1805 taxes for county purposes were collected by county collectors.[106] An act of 1805 designated the township listers as collectors of the county levy but, in 1806, the commissioners were committed to appoint a county collector instead if they believed such a course to be expedient. This arrangement remained in force until 1825.[107]

The first statute of a general nature providing for a tax on land for territorial purposes was enacted in 1799. From 1799 to 1803 the collectors of the county tax were to collect the territorial tax also.[108] In 1804, however, the county sheriff was specifically designated as a collector of the state tax.[109] From 1806 to 1816 the county commissioners were again permitted to use their own discretion as to whether a county or township collector should be appointed.[110] The county collector of the land tax mentioned in the statutes from 1816 to 1825 was, in all probability, the same official who collected the county tax, though do to a lack of definite terminology it is impossible to be certain.[111]

In 1825 the arrangement for a separate tax duplicate for state and county purposes was abolished and levies for both were made on the same property. In 1827 the office of county collector, who had performed that function in the intervening period, was abolished and the treasurer, henceforth to be an elective officer, was given the duty of tax collection.[112]

---

104. Chase, *op. cit.*, I, 119.
105. Chase, *op. cit.*, I, 171.
106. Chase, *op. cit.*, I, 277.
107. Chase, *op. cit.,* I, 471, 527; II, 771, 1384, 1385.
108. Chase, *op. cit.*, I, 270.
109. Chase, *op. cit.*, I, 415.
110. Chase, *op. cit.*, I, 537, 727; II, 973.
111. Chase, *op. cit.*, II, 973, 5345, 5348-11.
112. *Laws of Ohio*, XXV, 25.

The collection of certain taxes other than that on general property is performed also by county agency. Thus, for example, inheritance taxes, authorized by the legislature in 1894, are computed by the county auditor, adjusted by the probate court, collected by the county treasurer, and distributed to the proper agency by the county auditor.[113] County auditors certify to the tax commission lists of persons licensed to engage in the business of selling cigarettes. County treasurers are the agents of the state treasurer for the sale of cigarette tax stamps.[114] The tax on wines, cordials, and beer is collected by means of the sale of stamps by county treasurers in a manner similar to that employed in collecting the cigarette tax.[115] The tax on brewers wert and malt is collected in an identical manner.[116]

The dispersal of administrative functions of county agencies is demonstrated more effectively, perhaps, in the issuance of licenses and permits which furnish a source of revenue for both the state and county. The county auditor has issued, collected, and accounted for dog licenses from 1917 to the present;[117] he has issued and the treasurer has collected the fees from cigarettes (1893—),[118] malt (1933—),[119] peddlers' (1862—),[120] and show license (1827—).[121] Hunting and fishing licenses have been issued by the clerk of courts since 1904 and 1919 respectively.[122] In addition, the clerk has issued for the court of common pleas ferry licenses (1805—),[123] auctioneers' licenses (1818—),[124] and peddlers' licenses (1810- 1862).[125] Marriage licenses, issued from 1803 to 1851 by the clerk of courts, since the latter date, have been in the jurisdiction of the probate court.[126]

---

113. G. C. secs. 5338, 5341, 5345, 5348-11.
114. G. C. secs. 5894-1 *et seq.*
115. G. C. sec. 6064- 42.
116. G. C. sec. 5545 *et seq.*
117. *Laws of Ohio*, CVII, 534.
118. Jay F. Laning, comp., *Revised Statutes of the State of Ohio* (Norwalk, 1905), 1513.
119. G. C. sec. 5545-5 *et seq.*
120. Sayler, *op. cit.*, 273; *Laws of Ohio*, LIX, 67-68; G. C. sec. 6347.
121. Chase, *op. cit.*, III, 1562; G. C. secs. 6374, 6375.
122. *Laws of Ohio*, XCVII, 474; G. C. sec. 1430.
123. *Laws of Ohio*, III, 96; VIII, 107; XXIX, 447, Ferry licenses were issued by the associate judges 1803-5, *Ibid.*, I, 94.
124. Chase, *op. cit.*, II, 1040; G. C. secs. 58 68, 5869.
125. Chase, *op. cit.*, I, 670.
126. Chase, *op. cit.*, I, 354; *Ohio Const.* 1851, Art. IV, sec. 8.

The establishment of a board of trustees of the sinking fund (1919) was a logical development in county fiscal administration. This board, composed of the auditor, treasurer, and prosecuting attorney, has as its principal function the payment of bonds issued by the county and the investment in bonds of moneys credited to the sinking fund. Bonds issued in the process of county borrowing must be recorded in the office of sinking fund trustees and signed by the auditor, as secretary of the board. The trustees certify to the board of commissioners the rate of tax necessary to provide a sinking fund for the payment of the principal and interest of the bonded indebtedness. The trustees are required to keep a full and complete record of transactions and a complete record of the funded debt of the county.[127]

Election

During the first nine decades of Ohio history the county sheriff was charged with the duty of announcing the time and place of holding elections, providing ballot boxes, ballots, and other supplies, and the township trustees were directed by law to serve as judges of the elections.[128] This system continued, with slight alterations designed to facilitate the conduct of elections and municipal centers until 1892. At that time there were created the offices of the state supervisor of elections and deputy state supervisor of elections with duties prescribed for the conduct and supervision of all elections in the state.[129] The secretary of state, designated as a state supervisor of elections, was authorized and instructed to appoint four deputy supervisors for each county, who, in turn, appointed in each precinct four judges and two clerks of elections.[130]

Under the present election law, provision is made for a chief election officer, a board of elections in each county, and judges and clerks in each precinct.

---

127. G. C. sec. 2976-18 *et seq.*

128. *Laws of Ohio*, I, 76-77; III, 331-332; VII, 113; XXIX, 44; L, 312.

129. *Ibid.*, LXXXIX, 455. This act, however did not apply to the election of school directors.

130. *Laws of Ohio*, LXXXIX, 455. In 1870 each township, exclusive of the territory embraced within the limits of the municipal corporation which was divided into wards, compose an election precinct. *See ibid.*, LXVII, 47. An act of 1891 provided for the division of precincts in which 500 or more votes had been polled. *Ibid.*, LXXXVIII, 464.

The board of elections in each county consists of four qualified electors in the county, the members of which are appointed by the secretary of state, two of such members being appointed on the first day of March in the even-numbered years to serve a four-year term.[131] In making appointments to the membership of the board, equal representation is given to the political party polling the highest and the next highest number of votes for the office of governor in the last preceding state election. In this connection provision is made for party recommendations of persons for such appointments.[132]

Under the early election laws the canvassing board was composed of the clerk of the court of common pleas and two justices of the peace called by him to his assistance.[133] This practice continued until 1892 when the board of state supervisors of elections succeeded to the duties formerly performed by both the clerk of court of common pleas and the county sheriff. The sheriff, however, continued to announce the time and place of holding elections in the county until January 1, 1930 when the board of elections assumed this historic duty.[134] The duty of canvassing the returns, under the present statutes, is performed by the board of elections. The board in each county is required, within five days after each general or special election, to canvas the returns, and to prepare abstracts of the votes cast.[135] A certified copy of the abstract is to be transmitted to the secretary of state, and another copy filed in the office of the board.[136] The board is required also to prepare and transmit to the president of the senate a separate abstract of the returns of election of governor, lieutenant governor, secretary of state, auditor of state, and attorney general.[137]

---

131. G. C. secs. 4785-6, 4785-8. *See also* p. 191.
132. G. C. sec. 4785-9. Under the Ohio election law, it is the duty of the secretary of state to appoint persons so recommended, unless he has reason to believe that such person would not be a competent member of the board.
133. *Laws of Ohio*, I, 83; III, 336-337; VII, 119-120; XXIX, 49; L, 136; LXI, 68, LXXXII, 30.
134. G. C. sec. 4785-5; *Laws of Ohio*, LXXXIX, 455; CXIII, 307. The election laws of Ohio were revised and re-codified by an act of the general assembly, passed April 5, 1929. *Laws of Ohio*, CXIII, 307-413.
135. G. C. secs. 4785-152, 4785-153.
136. G. C. sec. 4785-153.
137. *Ohio Const. 1851*, Art. III, sec. 3; G. C. sec. 4785-154.

Health

Prior to 1919 the county had few responsibilities regarding health administration. With the development of urban centers with congested areas the problem of health administration was brought to the attention of the legislature. Prior to the enactment of the present health code in 1919, jurisdiction in matters of health was vested in the cities, villages, and townships. Under the act of 1919 all villages and townships in the county were combined into a general health district under the supervision of a board appointed by the advisory council composed of the mayors of villages and chairmen of township trustees. Each city in the district is organized as a separate health district. Two general health districts or a general health district and a city health district located within such a district may combine.[138] All physicians are required to report communicable diseases to the district health commissioners who impose quarantines.[139]

The legislature has placed on the county the burden of responsibility and the treatment of tuberculosis. Any county, regardless of the size, may employee nurses, operate clinics, and care for patients in private, municipal, or county sanatorium. Any county having a population of 50,000 or more inhabitants may, with the consent of the state department of health, erect and operate sanatoriums, and two or more counties may form districts for the same purpose. The sanatoriums are operated by the county commissioners or special boards appointed by the county commissioners.[140]

Besides establishing sanatoriums for the treatment of tubercular patients, counties are authorized to operate general hospitals. The county hospital is operated by a board appointed by the county commissioners.[141] Evidence seems to indicate that the county is a proper unit for hospital administration.

---

138. *Laws of Ohio*, CVIII, pt. I, 238; CVIII, pt. ii, 1085-1086.

Public welfare

The administration of public welfare is one of the most complex and one of the most expensive functions of the county government. The administration of institutional or outdoor relief is delegated to eight boards and commissions operating independently and with little regard for efficiency.

The administration of the county home is vested in the county commissioners and a superintendent appointed from a list of names by persons eligible under civil service regulation. Employees are appointed by the superintendent.[142]

Although provision was made for the institutional care of the county's indigent as early as 1816, it was not until after the conclusion of the War between the States when hundreds of Ohio children were left homeless, that legislature enacted measures for the care of dependent children.[143] Prior to the act of 1865, the trustees of the poorhouses were authorized to apprentice dependent children. The administration of the children's home is vested in a board of trustees, appointed by the county commissioners, and a superintendent appointed by the board of trustees.[144]

The board of county visitors, an agency for the examination of county institutions, was created by the general assembly in 1882. Until 1906 the board was appointed by the court of common pleas and after that date by the probate judge.[145] The board consists of six persons appointed for terms of three years.

In 1886 counties were required by law to provide relief for indigent soldiers and sailors and their indigent wives, children, and parents.[146]

---

139. *Laws of Ohio*, CVIII, pt. ii, 1088-1089.
140. G. C. secs. 3148-1 - 3148-3. *See* p. 69.
141. G. C. secs. 3127-3138-4.
142. G. C. secs. 2522, 2523.
143. *Laws of Ohio*, III, 276; VIII, 223-224.
144. G. C. secs. 3081, 3084. *See also* p. 24.
145. *Laws of Ohio*, LXXIX, 107; XCVIII, 28; G. C. sec. 2971.
146. *Laws of Ohio*, LXXXIII, 232-234.

Soldiers' relief is administered by a commission consisting of three persons appointed by the court of common pleas or term of three years. This commission, in turn, selects township and ward committees.[147]

In 1884 the legislature made provision for a soldiers' burial committee in each county.[148] The administration of soldiers' burials is vested in committees consisting of two persons in each township and ward appointed by the county commissioners.[149]

Counties maintain a system of pensions for the needy blind. Prior to 1936 blind relief was administered in the county by the probate judge (1904-1908), by a blind relief commission appointed by the probate judge (1908-1913), and by the county commissioners (1913-1936).[150] The present system originated in 1936 when the legislature accepted the provisions of the Federal Social Security Act. Blind relief is financed by federal, state, and local funds and is administered in the state by the Ohio commission for the blind and in the county by the county commissioners, whose decisions are subject to review by the Ohio commission for the blind.[151]

Prior to 1932 the county confirmed its relief activities to the institutional care of the indigent. Outdoor relief, except for those persons lacking a legal settlement, was provided and administered by the townships and cities. With the coming of the economic depression the resources of the municipalities and townships proved inadequate for financing relief activities. Accordingly in 1932, the legislature conferred on all counties the authority to care for the poor in their own homes. Funds for such purposes were provided by the issuance of bonds and by a diversion of gasoline taxes for financing such services. While the state relief commission, created for administering state relief, is required to pass upon local relief budgets, the county relief offices, administered by the county commissioners, provide relief services in the county.

---

147. G. C. secs. 2930, 2933.
148. *Laws of Ohio*, LXXXI, 146-147.
149. G. C. sec. 2950.
150. *Laws of Ohio*, XCVII, 392-394; XCIV, 56-58; CIII, 60.
151. *Ibid.*, CXVI, pt. ii, 195-200.

Today old pensions are relieving the counties of the increased burdens of institutional relief. This system, originating in 1933, provided for persons 65 or more years of age. No person may be granted a pension if the net value of his property is in excess of $3000, or his annual income is in excess of $480.[152] The old age pension system is financed by state and federal funds and is administered by a division of the department of public welfare through county boards of aid for the aged.[153] Under the provision of the initial act the county commissioners served as *ex-officio* members of the board of aid for the aged and the county. Since May 1, 1937 the chief of the division has been required by law to appoint an advisory board in each county consisting of five members. This board, appointed for a two-year term, succeeded to the duties formally performed by county commissioners.[154]

Aid to dependent children, although provided for by the general assembly in 1913 in the form of mothers' pensions, assumed a new significance, when, in 1936, the legislature accepted the provision of the Federal Social Security Act. Aid to dependent children is financed by federal, state, and local funds. The administration of the act in the state is delegated to the department of public welfare and in Ashland County to the judge of probate court serving as *ex-officio* juvenile judge.[155]

Public Works

The responsibility for the administration of public works in the county rests with the board of county commissioners, the county engineer, and the sanitary engineer. The county commissioners, since inauguration of the county government, have had the responsibility for the authorization and financing of public works.

---

152. *Laws of Ohio*, CXV, pt. ii, 431-439; CXVI, pt. ii, 86-88, 216-221; G. C. sec. 1359-2.
153. *Ibid.*, CXV, pt. ii. 431-439
154. G. C. sec. 1359-42. *See also* p. 231.
155. *Laws of Ohio*, CXVI, pt. ii, 183-196.

With the immense development of highway improvement, occasioned by the introduction of automobiles and trucks as means of transportation, public works became one of the most important functions of the county commissioners and consequently the county engineer, who, during the first 120 years of his office, had as his principal duty the surveying of lands, received new duties and responsibilities with respect to the construction of roads, culverts, ditches, and in most cases bridges.[156] Within the last two decades the township roads, under the joint authority of the county and the township trustees, have been gradually absorbed by the county-state system of highways.[157]

The Ohio counties were formed to meet the needs of rural pioneer communities with a population spread relatively uniformly over the entire state. Recent decades have brought remarkable changes. Many sections of the state have become thoroughly industrialized, and, as a result of the change, have been forced to deal with such problems as housing, health, sanitation, police administration, scientific transportation, and sewage disposal. These problems with which the county organization has been unable to cope are rapidly taking the form of city problems.

When it is considered that in 1940, of the 1,217,250 persons in Cuyahoga County 878,336 were in Cleveland, and that of the 388,712 people in Franklin County 306,087 were in Columbus, that of the 621,987 people in Hamilton County 455,610 were in Cincinnati, and that of the 344,333 people in Lucas County 282,349 were in Toledo, it is not strange that demands have been made for a reorganization of county government to eliminate the waste and confusion occasions by overlapping jurisdictions of county and municipal functions.[158]

---

156. *Ibid.*, XCVIII, 245-247; CVIII, pt. I, 497.
157. The centralization of highway construction was guaranteed under the road law of 1915. The township trustees, at one time one of the most important agencies in local highway construction, have become a local improvement board with powers to authorize but not to supervise road construction. *Laws of Ohio*, CVI, 589-594.
158. U.S. Bureau of the Census, *16th Census of the United States, 1940, Population, First Series, Numbers of Inhabitants, Ohio*, 4, 5, 8, 9, 11. C.A. Dykstra, "Cleveland's Effort for City-County Consolidation," *Nat. Mun. Review*, VIII (1919), 551-556.

In view of the growth of large cities in the confusion occasioned by the conflict of county and municipal powers, there has been an attempt to work out a more satisfactory relationship between the two organs of local government. This took the form of a constitutional amendment, which, defeated in 1919, was placed on the ballot in 1933 by initiative petition and adopted by the electorate. The amendment provides:

"The general assembly shall provide by general law for the organization and government of counties, and may provide the general law alternative forms of county government. No alternative form shall become operative in any county until submitted to the electors thereof and approved by a majority of those voting thereon under regulations provided by law. Municipalities and townships shall have authority, with the consent of the county, to transfer to the county any other powers or to revoke the transfer of any such power, under regulations provided by general law, but the rights of initiative and referendum shall be secure to ... every measure... giving or withdrawing such consent.[159]

The constitutional amendment of 1933 altered the status of the county. Where the status of the county was formerly fixed by statute, it is now subject to local determination in the same manner as municipalities.

The arguments advance in favor of the system fall under three heads:

1. It makes possible a different form of government for urban centers where political, social, and economic conditions differ from those of rural counties.
2. It promotes efficiency and economy by the elimination of duplicate officers and employees.
3. Most efficiency by the centralization of power and responsibility.[160]

A commission on county government was appointed by Governor White in 1933 to formulate optional plans of county government for submission to legislature.[161]

---

159. *Ohio Const. 1851* (Amendment, adopted November 7, 1933), Art. X, sec. 1.

160. *Ohio State Journal*, October 9, 1933; Dykstra *loc. cit.*

161. R.C. Atkinson, "County Home Rule Developments in Ohio," *Nat. Mun. Review*, XXIII (1934), 235.

Accordingly, in 1935, the commission submitted to the legislature 10 bills embodying its recommendation as to matters of county reorganization. The major bills authorized three optional forms of county government, subject to adoption by the local electorate (1) a county manager plan, (2) the elective plan, (3) the appointive executive plan.[162] Of the 10 bills presented, two became laws. One of these authorized the transfer to the county of any local governmental activity by voluntary agreement between the county and a local subdivision within the county. This measure, of course, opened the way for the consolidation of such activities as welfare, police, and sewer construction which need unification in counties having a large urban population.[163] The other act authorized the charter county to take over health administration, non-institutional relief, and park construction.[164]

While the amendment offers and opportunity for the improvement of local government in counties in which large municipalities have developed, no use has been made of the provision.[165] At present Franklin County with a population of 388,712 has essentially the same type of county government as Vinton County with a population of 11,573.[166]

While unsuccessful attempts have been made to correct some of the defects of county administration and areas containing large urban populations, little consideration has been given to rural counties where, due to a constant decline in population, the old governmental organization has become unduly expensive and ill-suited to the needs of the population. This is particularly true in the counties located in the southeastern and northwestern portions of the state where the population has steadily declined since 1880.

---

162. R.C. Atkinson, "Ohio-Optional County Legislation," *Nat. Mun. Review*, XXIV (1935), 228.
163. *Laws of Ohio*, CXVI, 102-140.
164. *Ibid.*, XCVI, 132-135.
165. Home rule charters were submitted to the voters in Hamilton, Cuyahoga, Lucas, and Franklin Counties. Advocates of home rule attributed the defeat of these measures to politicians who saw in the scheme the destruction of the spoils system. *See* R.C. Atkinson, "Ohio– County Charter Elections," *Nat. Mun. Review*, XXIV (1935), 702-703.
166. U.S. Bureau of the Census, *16th Census of the United States, 1940, Population. First Series, Number of Inhabitants, Ohio*, 4, 5.

There is a question as to whether the services of modern government in such counties can continue to be maintained without the consolidation of contiguous territory for purpose of administration. The Ohio Constitution, from its beginning in 1802, has contained a restriction upon the legislature regarding the minimum area of counties. None could be formed with less than 400 square miles or reduce below that size.[167] With the development of modern means of transportation and communication this area is ridiculously small. The combination for administrative purposes of sparsely populated counties, having common social and economic interest would eliminate waste, overhead, and duplication of personnel.

Governmental service is constantly requiring the employment of better trained officials. Evidence seems to indicate that only by enlarging the size of the administrative area to make possible the specialization and work can the requisite degree of training and skill be secured in the performance of public service.[168]

The relation of the county to the state is also a matter of importance. As a result of radical changes in economic life, matters which were at one time a purely local interest and concern have become of state-wide importance. During recent years the old type of county organization has proved inadequate to meet the needs of modern civilization. Recognition of this fact is found in a steady growth of state control of such matters as public accounting, health and welfare administration, and law enforcement.

At the same time the county has definitely supplanted the township as the administrative unit. This is particularly noticeable in the substitution of the general health district for the township district, and the transfer of tax assessment from the township assessors to the county auditor. The county-state administration of highway maintenance in public welfare has been effected. Although many deplore in the passing of the little red schoolhouse, the substitution of the county school district for the township area has resulted in better educational advantages for children residing and rural areas.

---

167. *Ohio Const. 1802*, Art. VII, sec. 3; *Ohio Const. 1851*, Art. II, sec. 30.

168. Cf. H. Eliot Kaplan, "A Personal Program for County Service," *Nat. Mun. Review*, XXV (1936), 596-600.

It is significant that modern invention has removed the necessity for rural administrative units of such small proportions. The transfer of power from the smaller to the larger unit has arisen out of the desire for better service and economy. Little remains to justify the retention of the township.

Records System

It has been the duty of most officials since the beginning of county government to keep a record of the business of their offices. Differences in population between counties, however, forced a wide variance in the recording as evidence by the fact that several types of records were kept in the same book in some counties, and in others were kept in separate books. As indicated in detail in the office essays, preceding the records of each office, the legislature eventually prescribed not only what records were to be kept but also the content. In this field there was a remarkable advance following the adoption of the constitution of 1851. Such legislation assured some uniformity in the county records system.

There are three clerical officers who work consists mainly in the preparation and custody of records: the recorder, the clerk of courts, and the judge of the probate court. All three have some part in the recording of documents and instruments affecting the title of property and of other documents presented for record. The last two have as their principal duty the keeping of court records; the clerk of courts serves as clerk of both the court of common pleas and the court of appeals, and the probate judge keeps the records of his own court.

It is the duty of the county recorder to copy, index, and file documents authorized to be recorded in his office. The system of recording is prescribed and detailed by law. In most counties recording is done by typewriter with considerable use of printed forms. The photographic method of copying is in use in Clark, Hamilton, Lucas, Montgomery, and Summit Counties. Deeds, mortgages, plats, and leases must be copied into separate books, and indexed by direct and reverse in indexes.[169] The recorder is required, also, to prepare daily an alphabetical index to such instruments.[170]

---

169. G. C. secs. 2557, 2764.
170. G. C. secs. 2764, 2766.

The principal records of the clerk of courts are prescribed by statute. They include an appearance docket, a trial docket, an execution docket, a journal, and a complete record of proceedings, a system of indexes, and a file of original papers.[171] The clerk is responsible for a variety of nonjudicial records work of which the filing and indexing of automobile bills of sale was the major item. The bill of sale law was repealed by an act effective January 1, 1938, requiring the clerk to issue certificates of title to motor vehicles in triplicate and to file a duplicate of the certificate.[172] At present the clerk of courts may act as the agent of the state for the sale of hunting, trapping, and fishing licenses.[173] He also issues auctioneer's and ferry licenses.[174]

The office of the probate court performs the following clerical service, the recording of miscellaneous instruments, including marriage licenses[175] and certificates of physicians, surgeons, and nurses which authorize them to practice their professions in the state.[176] The court record system of the office originating in 1853 and continued by the probate code of 1931, is prescribed by statute and involves the proper keeping of papers in each case and copying materials in appropriate record books.[177] Few records are prescribed for the law enforcement agency. The county sheriff is required by law to keep at least three books: a foreign execution docket,[178] a case book,[179] and a jail register.[180] Indexes, direct and reverse, to the foreign execution docket were prescribed in 1925.[181]

---

171. G. C. secs. 2878, 2884, 2885.
172. G. C. secs. 6290-6.
173. G. C. secs. 1430, 1432.
174. G. C. secs. 5868-5869, 5947-5950.
175. *Ohio Const. 1851*, Art. IV, sec. 8.
176. *Laws of Ohio*, XCII, 45-47; XCIX, 499; CVI, 192.
177. *Ibid.*, CXIV, 321-322.
178. G. C. sec. 2837.
179. G. C. sec. 2839.
180. *Laws of Ohio*, XLI, 74; G. C. sec. 3158.
181. *Laws of Ohio*, CXI, 31.

The system of recording is prescribed by statute. The county coroner's record consists of two: a report of findings and cases of unlawful death,[182] inventory of articles found on or about the body of the deceased.[183] Such records are required by law and the contents of the records minutely prescribed.

The number and type of records kept by prosecuting attorneys in the different counties of the state vary widely. In some counties the records of the prosecuting attorney are kept on standard forms and include such records as a grand jury docket, a grand jury testimony record, and a criminal court docket. The civil records are classified as pending cases, deposed cases, foreclosures of tax liens, tax claims, opinions on schools, and letters relative to county bank deposits. However, in many counties of the state no records or files are kept and individual memoranda are disposed of by the incumbent. Since the prosecuting attorney is vested with large discretionary powers, there is need of special records and files. Such records according to authorities on judicial administration should include, among others, a permanent record of the names and addresses of witnesses, the deputy or division handling the case, and the reason for failure to prosecute, and the reason for which a *nolle prosequi* was asked and granted.

The records of financial agencies of the county government are prescribed by statute. Although records were kept in the earlier years, it was not until 1902 that the matter of keeping and the content of such records attracted the attention of the legislature. It was evident that accounts had not only been poorly kept but there had been little uniformity among the counties of the state. Accordingly, in 1902, the legislature enacted the most important and far-reaching laws on the subject. This act provided for a uniform system of accounting, auditing, and reporting, under the supervision of the newly created bureau of inspection located in the office of the auditor of state. The act further provided for the annual examination of finances of all public offices.[184]

---

182. G. C. sec. 2857.
183. G. C. sec. 2859.
184. *Laws of Ohio*, XCV, 511-515.

The governor's commission on the reorganization of county government, after studying the county records system and noting the illogical combination of administrative, judicial, and financial functions, made the following recommendation:[185]

1. County charters and optional forms of government should provide for a department of records and court service to take over the functions of the recorder and clerk of courts, the nonjudicial record work of the probate court, and the functions of the sheriff as a court officer.
2. The issuance of licenses should be transferred from the clerk of courts to the department of finance.
3. Wider use should be made of photographic process of recording in large counties.
4. Legislation should be adopted permitting the destruction of chattel mortgages and automobile bills of sale after they have ceased to have effect.
5. The requirement of three systems of indexes of cases in the clerk's office should be eliminated from the code and only the index of pending suits and living judgments should be required.
6. Provisions should be made in the rules of the common pleas court for service of process by mail and that method should be brought into general use.

Concurrently with the development of a records system, steps were taken to assure the proper restoration of damaged or dilapidated records treating of lands and surveys. The county engineer, when directed by the county commissioner, is required by law to transcribe any and all dilapidated maps and the records of plats and field notes of surveys from the records of the court of common pleas, auditor, recorder, or other officers in the state where they may be procured.[186]

---

185. *Report of Governor's Commission*, 186-187. *See also* R.E. Heiges, *The Office of Sheriff in the Rural Counties of Ohio* (Findlay, 1933), 55-56, 60-61.
186. G. C. sec. 2804.

Similarly, the county recorder, when authorized by the county commissioners, is required to transcribe from the records of the counties all deeds, mortgages, powers of attorney, and other instruments of writing, for the sale, conveyance, or encumbrance of lands, tenements, or hereditaments situated within his county.[187]

The large accumulation of county records occasioned by increasing governmental service, presents a serious problem. It is important, on the one hand, that valuable space in county courthouses and other county depositories be not cluttered up with vast quantities of useless materials. On the other hand, it is important that every precaution be taken to prevent public officials from destroying valuable public records in order to make space for current business.

Within recent years photography has become an increasingly important aid in archival administration. The Ohio Legislature, following the modern trends in recording, has enacted measures looking forward to the conservation of space in the county courthouses by permitting county officials to destroy records which have been reproduced photographically. Under this act, passed in 1937, any county official charged with keeping public records may, when a space requires it, have such records copied or reproduced by any photographic process and destroy the original papers. The original records, however, must be preserved until the time for filing legal proceedings based upon the documents shall have elapsed.[188]

While the legislature has attempted to enact legislation looking forward to the conservation a much needed space in county courthouses a significant trend is to be observed in the increasing interest which is being displayed for a department accounting archives where all noncurrent records may be properly housed, classified, listed, and made more readily accessible to those interested in consulting them.

---

187. G. C. sec. 2763.
188. G. C. sec. 32-1.

The arguments advanced in favor of such a system are: (1) that the preservation of county records should be viewed as a distinct function of the county government, (2) that the administration of county archives should be under the direction of those qualified to serve efficiently and effectively both the needs of the administration and historians, (3) that the construction of county archives buildings but noncurrent records would make available more space for current business, which, at present, is seriously curtailed.

In the field of archival administration the state, rather than the county, has been the experimental laboratory and results have been eminently successful.[189]

189. For an interesting and informative article on the administration of state archives, *see* Charles M. Gates, "The Administration of State Archives," *The Pacific Northwest Quarterly*, XXIX (January 1938) No. 1; also in *The American Archivist*, I (July 1938), 130-141.

HOUSING, CARE, AND ACCESSIBILITY OF RECORDS

In May 1846, the newly elected commissioners of Ashland County met at the office of the auditor and made the necessary arrangements for the construction of the county courthouse.[1] The first courthouse was an old stone church, which had been purchased from the Methodists, and was located near the site of the present structure.[2] Seven years later, the church was replaced by the Temple of Justice. This structure was erected in the park which is now Courthouse Square and served as the courthouse until 1928, when it was razed to make way for the construction of the present courthouse.[3] During the razing of the old structure, county records were stored in the B and V Block, corner of West Second and Church Streets, and in the Vachon Building, 121 West Second Street, these buildings having been leased to house county offices for this period.[4]

The new and present courthouse, built in 1928 and it cost of $325,000, faces Second Street between Cottage and Church Streets; the back of the courthouse is adjacent to Third Street. The building was designed by Vernon Redding and associates, and was built by Melbourne Construction Company.

The Ashland county jail, located at the corner of Main and Cottage Streets, was erected in 1886 and contains thirteen cells and the sheriff's office, the latter consisting of two rooms in which all sheriff's records are kept.

The county offices, with exceptions indicated, are located in the county courthouse. Housing conditions for each department are described in the following paragraphs.

County Commissioners. The Commissioners occupy two rooms in the southeast corner of the first floor of the courthouse. Most of the records are kept in the commissioners' office. The bound records are kept on steel shelves located along the east wall, while the unbound records are kept in steel file drawers and in the safe located along the east wall. There are some records housed in the basement storeroom, and the engineer's drafting room, and in the auditor's main office.

---

1. Commissioners' Record, I (1846-1863), 2.
2. William A. Duff, *History of North Central Ohio* (Indianapolis, 1931), I 269.
3. *Ibid.*, 296.
4. *Ibid.*

This room is quite large, and has a marble counter about four feet high separating the office from the waiting room. Ventilation and lighting conditions are good. The offices are crowded and there is little room for expansion. The records number 77 volumes, 13 file boxes, 2 bundles, and 4 cartons.

Relief administration. This department is located in the Opera House Building, corner of West Main and Center Streets, Ashland, Ohio. Records of this office are kept in steel file drawers. Ventilation and lighting conditions are good. The office is crowded and there is little room for expansion. The records number 11 file drawers and 13 file boxes.

Recorder. The recorder's office is located on the northwest corner of the first floor, and consists of two rooms. Bound records are kept on steel shelves located along the south wall, while unbound records are kept in steel file drawers located along the east end of the room. The recorder's file room is located in the northwest corner of the building. Bound records are kept on steel shelves located along the north and east walls and the unbound records are kept in steel file drawers located along the south wall. Ventilation and lighting conditions are good. Office rooms are crowded, with no room for expansion. The records number 324 volumes, 1 file drawer, 182 file boxes, 31 maps, and 3 bundles.

Clerk of Courts. The clerk of courts' office is located on the west side of the second floor, and consists of two rooms. The main office is located south of the private office. Bound and records are kept on steel shelves located along the north and east walls, and the unbound records are kept in steel file drawers located along the south and west walls. There are also various bound and unbound records which are kept in the basement storeroom safe. The clerk of courts' private office is located in the northwest corner of the building. Bound records are kept on steel shelves located along the south and east walls; unbound records are kept on steel shelves located along the south and west walls. Ventilation and lightning conditions are good. The offices are crowded and there is no room for expansion. The records number 132 volumes, 611 file boxes, and 250 documents.

Court of Common Pleas. The records of this court are kept in the clerk of courts' offices and basement storeroom. One volume, covering the years 1847-1857, is kept in the storage vault of the secretary's office. State School for the Blind, Main

Street and Parsons Avenue, Columbus, Ohio. The records number 241 volumes and 4 file boxes.

Supreme Court. Records of this court are kept in the clerk of courts' offices there are two volumes of records.

Court of appeals. This includes the defunct records of the district court and circuit court. Records are kept in the clerk of courts' offices. The records number 25 volumes.

Probate Court. Probate court is located in the southwest corner of the first floor and consists of three rooms. The probate court office is located east of the courtroom and the judge's private office. Bound records are kept on steel shelves located along the east wall, while the unbound records are kept in steel file drawers located along the south and west walls. Some records are also housed in the probate court record room located on the west side of the basement floor, east of the Aid to Dependent Children's office. The probate judge's office is located south of the courtroom. The judge's personal permanent records are housed here. The courtroom which is located south of the recorder's file room contains no records. Ventilation and lighting conditions are good. Office rooms are crowded, and there is no room for expansion. The records number 407 volumes and 820 boxes.

Juvenile Court. Records of this court are housed in the probate court office and record room. There are four volumes of juvenile court records.

Aid to Dependent Children. This office is located on the south side of the basement floor, east of the Board of Elections. All records consisting of unbound material are kept in steel file drawers, while bound and unbound records of the probate court are housed along the south and east walls. Ventilation and lighting conditions are good. The office is not overcrowded at present as there are only two volumes, four file drawers, and one file box of records.

Jury Commissioners. The jury commission has no separate office and keeps no separate records.

Grand Jury. The grand jury has no separate office and keeps no separate records.

Petit Jury. The petit jury has no separate office and keeps no separate records.

Prosecuting Attorney. The prosecuting attorney's office is located in the Winbiger Block 23 ½ West Main Street, Ashland, Ohio, and consists of two rooms. Unbound records are kept in steel file drawers located along the west wall of the main office. The prosecuting attorney's reception room houses no records. Ventilation and lighting conditions are good. The office rooms are not overcrowded at present. The prosecutor also has a reception room and private office in the courthouse, but no records are housed there. One volume and two file boxes contain all the records of this office.

Coroner. The coroner has no separate office and keeps no separate records.

Sheriff. The sheriff's office is located in the county jail at the corner of Main and Cottage Streets, Ashland, Ohio, and consists of two rooms. Some records are kept along the south wall of the main office. Other records are housed in the county jail storeroom. Ventilation and lighting conditions are good. Offices are not overcrowded at present. Two records number 24 volumes and 1 file box.

Dog Warden. The dog warden's desk is in the southwest corner of the office of the auditor's clerk. Twenty-five volumes of records are housed in the dog warden's desk drawer and one volume is carried in his briefcase.

Auditor. The auditor's office is located on the north side of the first floor, and consists of two rooms. The clerk's office is located west of the engineer's room. Bound records are kept on steel shelves located along the east wall, while the unbound records are kept in steel file drawers located along the south and west walls. The auditor's main office is located west of the clerk's office. Bound records are kept on steel racks, while the unbound records are contained in steel file drawers. Both bound and unbound records are located along the south wall of the partition separating the main office from the private office. Records are also housed in the basement storeroom and in the recorder's record room, and 4 volumes are housed in the commissioners' office. Ventilation and lighting conditions are good. These rooms are crowded, with no room for expansion. The records number 1120 volumes, 53 file drawers, 90 boxes, 37 bundles, and 2 cartons.

Treasurer. The treasurer's office is located on a north side of the first floor and consists of two rooms. The main office is located west of the auditor's main office. Bound records are kept on steel shelves located along the east and west walls. Unbound records are kept in steel file drawers located along the south side of partition under counter. There are also records housed in the basement storeroom. The treasurer's private office is partitioned off from the main office. Records are housed in a safe located in the southwest corner of the room. Ventilation and lighting conditions are good. Offices are crowded, with no room for expansion. Records number 877 volumes, 14 file boxes, 1 bundle, and 1 carton.

Budget Commissioners. Records are kept in the volumes of the Board of Revision (Minutes) in the auditor's main office and in the basement storeroom.

Board of Revision. Records are housed in the auditor's main office and in the basement storeroom. They number 3 volumes and 1 file box.

Board of Trustees of the Sinking Fund. Records are housed in the auditor's main office and number one volume.

Board of Elections. This office is located in the southwest corner of the basement floor, and consists of one room. Bound records are kept on steel racks, located on the east wall, while unbound records are kept in a steel cabinet, and in a safe located on the south and north walls. Ventilation conditions are good. The office is not overcrowded at present time. Records number 1,286 volumes, 1 folder, and 50 cardboard boxes.

Board of Education. This office is located in the southeast corner of the second floor and consists of the main office, the superintendent's office, and a storage room. All records are housed in the main office. The volume records are kept on steel shelves along the south wall, while the unbound records are housed in steel file drawers along the north and east walls and the map is hanging on the wall. Ventilation and lighting are good, but office is crowded, with no room for expansion. The records consist of 3 volumes, 14 file boxes, 10 bundles, and 1 map.

Board of Health. The board of health is located in the northwest corner of the basement floor, and consists of two rooms. The main office is located in the northwest corner of the basement. Records are housed in steel file drawers, located along the west wall. The private office is located east of the main office. There are no records housed here. Ventilation and lighting conditions are good. Offices have adequate space at present time. Records number two volumes, six file drawers, and nine file boxes.

Superintendent of the County Home. The county home is on the Haysville Road, Ashland, Ohio, and contains one office room. All the records are kept in a steel fireproof vault located along the east side of the superintendent's office. Ventilation and lighting conditions are good. The office has adequate space at present. Records number 14 volumes, 18 file boxes, and 2 bundles.

Board of Trustees of the Children's Home. The children's home is located at 1204 South Center Street, Ashland, Ohio, and contains one office room. Unbound records are kept in wooden and steel file drawers located along the west wall. Ventilation and lighting conditions are good. The office has adequate space at present. Records number six volumes and five file boxes.

Board of County Visitors. The board keeps no separate records. Their reports are kept in the commissioners' office, and the records of board appointments are kept in the probate court record room and the basement storeroom.

Soldiers' Relief Commission. The records which consist of two volumes are kept at the secretary's residence, 229 Union Street, Loudonville, Ohio.

Soldiers' Burial Committees. These committees keep no separate records.

Blind Relief Commission. These records are housed in the basement storeroom. There is only one volume of records.

Board of Aid for the Aged. This office is located in the Ashland Building and Loan Company, 122 West Main Street, Ashland, Ohio, and consists of two rooms. All records are housed in a secretary's office, except the active current records, which are housed in the director's private office. Ventilation and lighting conditions are good. The office has adequate space at present. Records number 3 volumes and 12 file boxes.

County Engineer. The engineer's department consists of two rooms on the first floor, and blueprint room on a basement floor. All records are housed in the engineer's drafting room, which is in the northeast corner of the first floor. Bound records are kept on steel shelves along the south wall, while the unbound records are housed in steel files cases along the north wall. The engineer's private office is west of the drafting room, but no records are housed here. The blueprint room is in the northeast corner of the basement, and it also contains no records. Lighting and ventilation conditions are good, but the offices are rather crowded. The engineer's records number 215 volumes, 20 file drawers, 13 file boxes, and 4 maps.

Agricultural Society. The office of this society is located in the southeast corner of the basement floor and consists of a main office and a private office. The records, however, are kept at the home of James Atterholt, secretary of the society, who resides at 613 Heltman Avenue, Ashland, Ohio. They consist of 3 volumes.

Agricultural Extension Agents. Records of this office are housed in the agricultural society office, and in the basement storeroom. Records number 2 volumes, 12 file boxes, and 1 envelope.

Basement Storeroom. This room is located on a south side of the basement floor. Early records of commissioners, clerk of courts, probate court, auditor, treasurer, blind relief commission, and agricultural extension agents are stored here on steel shelves and in steel and wooden file drawers. Ventilation and lighting conditions are inadequate. It is crowded, with no room for expansion. Records number 1134 volumes, 10 file drawers, 321 file boxes, 28 bundles, 6 cartons, 1 envelope, and 80 documents.

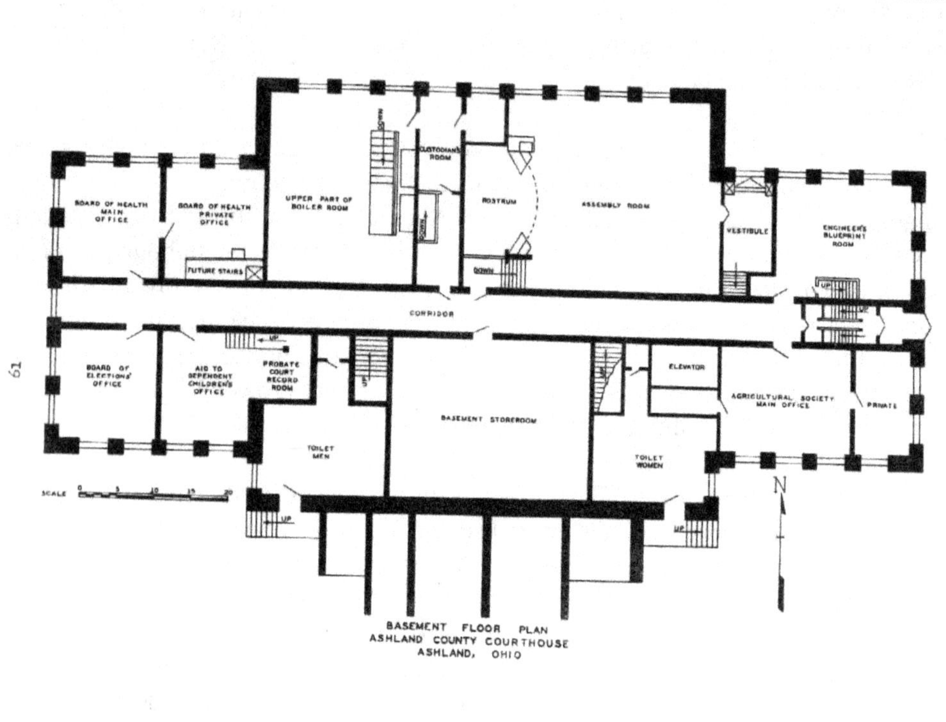

BASEMENT FLOOR PLAN
ASHLAND COUNTY COURTHOUSE
ASHLAND, OHIO

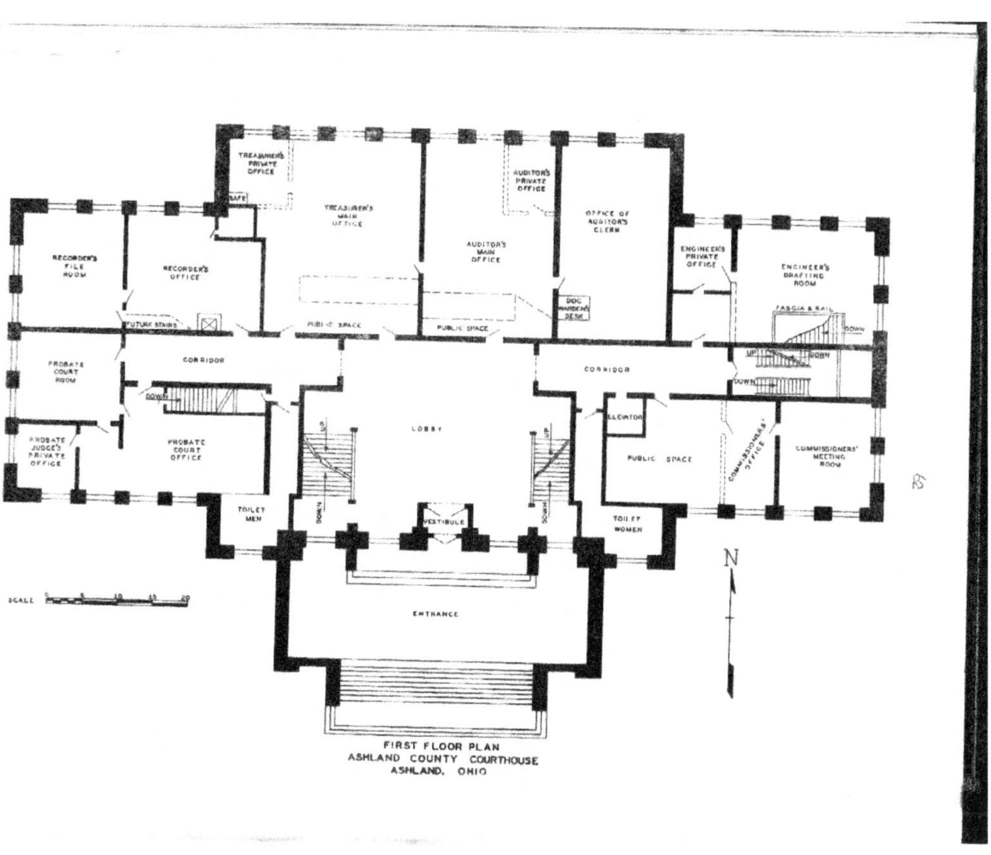

FIRST FLOOR PLAN
ASHLAND COUNTY COURTHOUSE
ASHLAND, OHIO

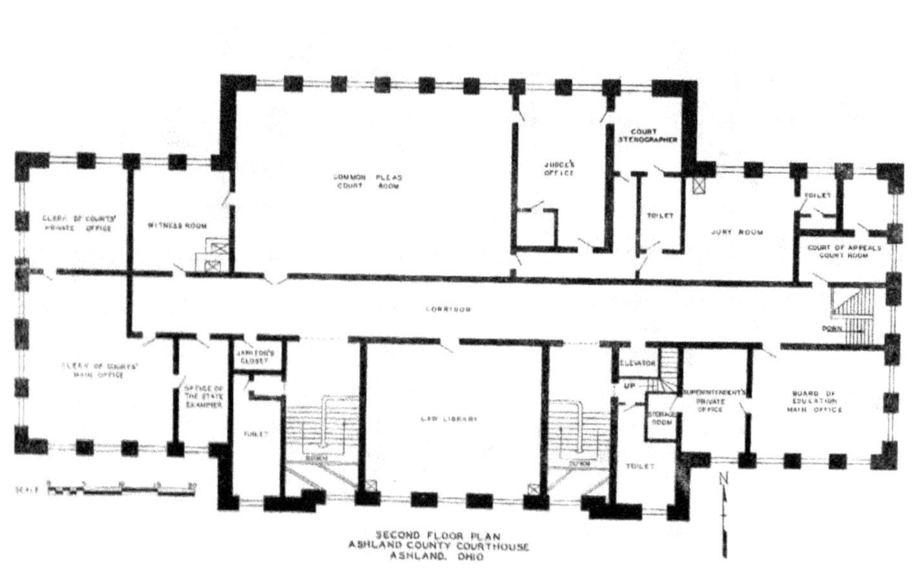

SECOND FLOOR PLAN
ASHLAND COUNTY COURTHOUSE
ASHLAND, OHIO

The governmental system established in 1802, under the first constitution of Ohio, made no provision for the office of county commissioners and its existence is due entirely to statutory enactment. The board, created in 1804, was the successor of the courts general quarter sessions of the peace, which, during the territorial period served as the representative agent of the county. The board of county commissioners consisted of three members elected for a three-year term.[1] In 1807 the commissioners were made a corporate body vested with a power to sue and be sued.[2] They were required to keep a record of their proceedings, to levy taxes for the support of the county, and to appoint a county treasurer, and to supervise the construction of bridges.[3] They were paid on a per diem basis. Moreover, during the same period (1804) they were given the task of constructing courthouses, jails, and offices for the clerk of courts, court of common pleas, the sheriff, the auditor, and the treasurer.[4] From 1805 to 1820 the commissioners were required to fix the amounts of tavern and ferry licenses and the rates for transportation by ferry.[5] Of these earlier duties the commissioners retain all but those of fixing the amount a tavern and ferry license and ferriage rates and that of appointing a county treasurer. However, since 1831 they have been authorized to examine and inspect the accounts of the county treasurer and to examine the condition of county finances.[6]

Besides the duties regarding county building construction and finance, the commissioners were given the task of constructing local highways when so authorized by legislature. During the first 30 years of Ohio history the duties of the commissioners in this respect were local in nature. But as the system of road construction expanded they were given the additional duty of converting free turnpikes into state roads.[7] Although numerous plank roads had been constructed by private companies during the 1840s, it was not until 1850 that legislature authorized incorporation for this purpose.[8]

---

1. *Laws of Ohio*, II, 150.
2. *Ibid.*, V, 97.
3. *Ibid.*, VIII, 45.
4. *Ibid.*, II, 154-157; XXIX, 315.
5. *Ibid.*, III, 96; VIII, 107; XVIII, 170.
6. *Ibid.*, XXIX 291. *See also* G. C. sec. 2644.
7. *Laws of Ohio*, XLVI, 74.
8. *Ibid.*, XLVIII, 49; L, 282.

When those companies were caught in the stringency of financial depression in 1857, the commissioners were authorized to purchase their holdings. If such transactions were made, the transfer signed by the president of the company was to be deposited with the county auditor.[9] In 1871 the commissioners, although earlier subjected to regulatory measures by the legislature, were prohibited from levying taxes for roads to exceed three and a half mills on the dollar on the taxable property in the county.[10] Later, in 1885, they were authorized to levy taxes not to exceed five mills on the dollar on all taxable property in the county for the maintenance of roads which had been damaged by excessive wear or were damaged from other causes.[11]

With the development of modern means of transportation, scientific principles were applied to road construction and maintenance. Although the county surveyor, now the county engineer, had in earlier years furnished the commissioners with estimates for bridge construction, it was not until the latter part of the nineteenth century that they were authorized to utilize his scientific knowledge in road construction.[12] At the beginning of the present century the surveyor was directed to appoint a maintenance engineer, with the consent of the commissioners, to supervise the repairing of improved roads in the county.[13]

Although the county commissioners have never been closely associated with the administration of criminal justice, their earlier duties regarding the construction the county jails qualified them, in the earlier period, for additional duties in this respect. During the middle of the nineteenth century the commissioners of Cuyahoga County were authorized to employ persons on construction work who were confined in the county jails.[14] While this provision was repealed by the criminal code adopted in 1853 other earlier functions applicable to all counties were continued. Since 1843 the commissioners have provided equipment and fixtures for places of incarceration and food and clothing for prisoners, and have appointed a jail physician.[15]

---

9. *Ibid.*, LIV, 198.
10. *Laws of Ohio*, LXXXIX, 117.
11. G. C. sec. 7419.
12. *Laws of Ohio*, LXXXIX, 172; XCVIII, 245-247. See also p. 263.
13. *Ibid.*, pt. I, 497.
14. *Ibid.*, XXXVII, 54.
15. *Ibid.*, XLI, 74; LXXXVII, 186.

Since 1869 they have been authorized to offer a reward for the detection or apprehension of any person charged with a felony in the county.[16] Since 1892 the commissioners in any county where there is no workhouse may, under certain conditions, release or parole an indigent person confined in the jail.[17] With the extension of modern crime into the rural areas in the form of small-town bank robbing, the commissioners were given the duty of furnishing motorcycles to the sheriff and his deputies in an attempt to compete with a high-powered equipment used by modern gangs. One of the latest functions in this respect is the contracting with radio stations for the broadcasting of descriptions of fleeing criminals.[18]

Besides providing for those who have violated the laws, the commissioners were given the duty caring for persons who, because of poverty or physical or mental defects, became public charges. Thus, county relief for the indigents, one of the most pressing problems of the twentieth century, was met in frontier Ohio. As early as 1805 an act, models from the territorial law, was passed which was similar in all respects to the poor laws of seventeenth century England.[19] Under the early enactments the township trustees were authorized to appoint overseers of the poor. In 1816 the county commissioners were authorized to construct "poor houses" for the care of the indigent of the county. As the system developed in succeeding decades the county was made responsible for those who had become permanently disabled, and for paupers who could not be satisfactorily cared for except at the county infirmary, now called the county home. Since 1913 they have been authorized in any county containing a city which has an infirmary, to contract with the director of public safety for the care of the county's indigent.[20]

The township trustees and officials of municipal corporations were made responsible for providing temporary relief to needy residents of the state, or the county, township, or city. In the event any person became chargeable to a township in which he had not gained legal residence, it was the duty of the overseers, later the township trustees, to remove him to the township where he was legally settled.

16. *Ibid.*, LXVI, 321.
17. *Ibid.*, LXXXIV, 408; CXIII, 203.
18. G. C. sec. 2412-1.
19. *Laws of Ohio*, III, 272.
20. G. C. sec. 2419-1.

With slight alterations, the principles of this system continued until the twentieth century.[21]

Since 1908 the commissioners have been authorized to issue warrants for the relief of the blind.[22] When the blind relief commission was abolished in 1913 its powers and duties were transferred to the county commissioners, who were authorized, on evidence furnished by a registered physician or surgeon that the applicant for blind relief might have such disability benefitted or removed by medical or surgical treatment, and with the written consent of the patient, to expend such sum as may be found necessary for the purpose.[23]

Six years later, in 1919, this allowance for blind relief was raised to $200 per person per annum, and the county commissioners were authorized to appoint such clerks as it might deem necessary to investigate applications and to serve at the pleasure of the county commissioners.[24]

In 1927 the maximum benefit for blind relief was increased to $400 per person per annum, but in the event of both a husband and wife being blind and both receiving relief, the total maximum benefit for the two was fixed at $600 per annum.[25]

In April 1936 the state accepted the provision of the federal Social Security Act approved August 14, 1935, providing federal grants for state aid to the blind. The general assembly designated the Ohio commission for the blind the administration agency in the state, and the county commissioners were made the administration agency in the county. The county commissioners were directed to appropriate the general fund of the county a sum sufficient when supplemented by federal and state grants to provide for the blind a subsistence "compatible with the decency and health," and if they failed to make such appropriations the attorney general was directed to bring *mandamus* proceedings against them.

---

21. For an excellent study of the administration of relief in Ohio prior to 1934 *see* Aileen Elizabeth Kennedy, *The Ohio Poor Law and Its Administration* (Sophonisba P. Breckinridge, ed. *Social Service Monographs*, no. 22, University of Chicago Press, Chicago, 1934).
22. *See* p. 229.
23. *Laws of Ohio*, CIII, 60; CXIX, H.B. 601.
24. *Ibid.*, CVIII, pt. I, 421-422.
25. *Laws of Ohio*, CXII, 109.

An act of 1941 amending the acts of 1936 and 1940, provides that those entitled to blind relief are persons not less than 18 years old, except those receiving aid for the aged, who have lost their sight while residents of the state, and who have resided in the state for a period of five years in the nine years immediately preceding application, the last year of which period shall have been continuous. Applications for blind relief are filed with the county commissioners who are required by statute to list such claims in their order of application in books kept for that purpose. The applicant files a duly certified statement, including a certificate from a registered physician "skilled in disease of the eye" stating to what extent the applicant's vision is impaired, and written evidence from two reputable citizens that they know the applicant to be blind and that "he has the qualifications to entitle him to the relief asked." The county commissioners may allow the examining physician a fee not to exceed $3 and may employ an additional position to examine the applicant. If after such inquiry the county commissioners are satisfied that the applicant is entitled to relief, they are directed by statute to issue an order for such some as the board finds necessary, not to exceed $40 per month, such some to be paid monthly from the fund created for that purpose. The ruling of 1913 concerning medical and surgical treatment for applicants remains in effect. Persons whose applications are denied by the county commissioners may appeal to the state department of public welfare which on its own motion may review any decision of the county commissioners. The state department of public welfare has the power to issue subpoenas, compel presentation of papers, and examined witnesses under oath.

At least once each quarter of the calendar year, oftener if directed by the state department of public welfare, the county commissioners must examine the qualifications, disabilities, and needs of all persons on the list of the blind, and may increase or decrease the amount of relief according to the budgetary requirements within the limits fixed by law. If the county commissioners remove a name from the list of the blind, they are required to notify the county auditor and the state department of public welfare as to their action.[26]

---

26. *Laws of Ohio*, CXVI, pt. ii, 195-200; CXVIII, 745-749, H.B. 601.

In Ashland County each new applicant for relief is considered carefully after a searching investigation, and after relief is granted a case, a worker employed by the commissioners makes regular inspection calls. In 1941 there were 14 persons receiving aid, the monthly grants range from $10 to $30.[27] The applicant's family need not be on relief to get this assistance. The county commissioners appropriated $2,500 to cover the cost of blind relief in a year 1941.[28]

In addition to furnishing financial aid to the civilian population, the commissioners were authorized, in 1886, to levy a tax for the relief of indigent Union soldiers, sailors, or marines of the Civil War, or if such veterans were deceased, for the dependents.[29] In 1919 the provisions of the original act were amended to include all indigent veterans of the World War.[30] The commissioners were authorized also, in 1884, to defray the funeral expenses of any honorable discharge soldier, sailor, or marine who died indigent. Ten years later the provisions of the act were extended to include the mother, wife, or widow of any soldier, sailor, or marine; and war nurses.[31]

The humanitarian duty of caring for the country's dependent and neglected children was delegated to the county commissioners. Since 1866 they have been authorized to establish and maintain children's homes. At the beginning of the present century, when the treatment of children was undergoing a remarkable change, they were authorized to place dependent and neglected children in private homes or institutions where they would receive food, clothing, and medical and dental treatment.[32] The development of the juvenile court system added new responsibilities. In order to segregate completely juvenile offenders from adults being tried in the regular criminal courts, the commissioners were authorized to provide a separate building, to be known as the "juvenile court."[33]

---

27. Commissioners' Record, XXVI (1939-1941), 574.
28. *Ibid.*, XXVI, 510.
29. *Laws of Ohio*, LXXXIII, 232. *See also* P. 227.
30. *Ibid.*, CVIII, pt. i, 633.
31. *Ibid.*, XC, 177.
32. *Ibid.*, CIX. 533.
33. *Ibid.*, CXIII, 470.

The unprecedented depression in the third decade of the twentieth century proved the antiquated, uncentralized system of relief administration entirely inadequate. As a result of the abnormal employment conditions and the crop failures following the drought of 1930, many local subdivisions of the county charged by law to administer support and medical relief to the indigent were unable to discharge the obligations. Accordingly, in 1931, the legislature passed an emergency act authorizing the county, township, and municipal taxing authorities to borrow money and issue bonds for poor relief, providing the state tax commission found that no other funds were available.[34]

During the early months of 1932 the governor, aware of the widespread suffering in the state, called the legislature into special session.[35] At this session the legislature authorized him to appoint a state relief commission composed of five members to study the relief situation. This commission was permitted to co-operate with the national, state, or local relief commission, which, in many counties, had been established and was already functioning. Since the county and township treasuries were depleted, on account of the excessive drain caused by the mounting relief load and the steady decline of tax collections, the legislature authorized an excise tax on utilities, for the year 1932-1937, to be used for relief purposes. This state tax was to be allocated to the counties on the basis of population, the tax duplicate, and the value of the utilities property in the county as of 1930. The funds allocated to each county under this act were to be credited to the "county poor relief excise fund."[36]

The county commissioners were authorized to borrow money for emergency relief and evidence such indebtedness by the issuance of negotiable bonds and notes. Upon submission of such resolution to the state tax commission, the commission was directed to estimate the amount which would probably be allocated to the county than the public utility excise taxes and was directed to calculate the total amount of bonds, the principal and interest on what might be paid out as such estimated allocation. The date of maximum maturity of such bonds was to be on or before March 15, 1938.

---

34. *Laws of Ohio*, CXIV, 11-12.
35. *See* message of the governor to the eighty-ninth general assembly in *Laws of Ohio*, CXIV, pt. ii, 6-8.
36. *Laws of Ohio*, CXIV, pt. ii, 19-20.

If, in the year 1932, additional funds were needed for poor relief, the county commissioners were authorized, should the state tax commission find that no other funds were available, to issue additional bonds in the amount not exceeding one-tenth of one percent of the general tax list and duplicate of the county. The maturity date of such additional bonds was to be on or before September 15, 1940.[37]

The proceeds of sale of such bonds were to be placed in a special fund, denominated the "emergency relief fund." No expenditures were to be made from this fund except in accordance with the method and under the uniform regulations prescribed by the state relief commission, and in no case after December 31, 1933. The county commissioners were authorized to distribute, prior to the first of March 1933, portions of the fund to the political subdivisions of the county, according to their needs for poor relief, determined by the county and set forth in such an approved budget. The money distributed to the subdivisions was to be expended in them for poor relief, including the renting of lands and the purchase of seeds for gardening by the unemployed.[38] County poor relief included mothers' pensions, soldiers' relief, temporary assistance to nonresidents, maintenance of a county and a children's home, and work and direct relief. In the townships and municipalities relief was interpreted to be the support of the poor and the burial of persons who died indigent. Each subdivision administering funds under the act was expected to require labor in exchange for relief given to any family in which resided an able-bodied wage earner.[39]

In the same year the county commissioners were designated as a board to administer the state law providing aid for the aged.[40] In February 1933 the tenure of the state relief commission was extended to March 1, 1935.[41] In the same year the legislature levied an additional stamp tax on the sale of bottled and bulk beer, malt, cosmetics, and toilet preparations to furnish additional funds for emergency relief.[42] The state treasurer was authorized to appoint the county treasurer as his deputy for the purpose of selling tax stamps to be affixed to such articles.[43]

---

37. *Ibid.*, CXIV, pt. ii, 19-21
38. *Laws of Ohio*, CXIV, pt. ii, 21, 22.
39. *Ibid.*, CXIV pt. ii, 17.
40. *Ibid.*, CXV, pt. ii, 431-439. *See also* p. 231.
41. *Ibid.*, CXV, 22.
42. *Ibid.*, CXV, 642, 6:49; CXV, pt, ii, 5, 33, 83, 177, 200, 247, 256.
43. *Ibid.*, CXV, 642.

The commissioners' duties regarding poor relief were further extended in 1935. They were authorized to provide noninstitutional support, care, assistance, or relief for the indigent in the county.[44] In 1935 the state relief commission ceased to exist by reason of the terms of the act creating it. The legislature, however, passed a measure design to co-ordinate and correlate all emergency poor relief work, activities, and administration with the Federal Emergency Relief Administration which was authorized to administer and direct the distribution and expenditure of federal funds for relief in the state. Accordingly, all powers previously vested in the state relief commission were transferred to the county commissioners. Whenever in their discretion such action was necessary in order to continue the coordinating and correlation of the state, local, and federal funds, they were authorized to appoint, with the approval of the director of finance of the state of Ohio, a representative or representatives of such emergency poor relief.[45] If such an officer were appointed, the representative succeeded to all powers and functions, which, under the act, were delegated to the county commissioners. This representative, however, was subjected to such terms and conditions in respect to auditing, examinations, and reports as were directed by the county commissioners and such federal agency. The county commissioners were directed to conduct relief activities outside limits of municipal corporations through the township trustees, insofar as practicable, and were to be guided by the recommendations of the township trustees with respect to relieve need in such political subdivisions. Again, as in 1932, the commissioners were authorized, if the state tax commission found that no other means existed to provide funds, to borrow money and issue bonds in the year 1935-1936. The maximum maturity date of such bonds was to be on or before March 1, 1944.[46] Other bonds, in addition to those secured by the counties share of the excise tax, might be issued not to exceed one-fifth of one percent of the general tax list of the county.[47]

---

44. *Ibid.*, CXVI, 571.
45. *Ibid.*, The county commissioners recommended to the state relief commission on December 30, 1935 the appointment of William G. McKee as director of emergency relief for Ashland County.
46. *Laws of Ohio*, CXVI, 571.
47. *Ibid.*, CXVI, 575.

If the county was unable to issue bonds by reason of the limitations imposed by the constitution,[48] the taxing authority of each subdivision was authorized to submit the question of issuing bonds to the electorate either at a general or special election.[49]

The year 1936 saw the re-creation of the state relief commission. Consisting of four members appointed by the governor; this body was authorized to serve until January 31, 1937. Again, as in 1932, the commission was directed to study problems of relief, to receive advice from the federal, state, and local governmental departments, to co-operate with agencies of the national and local governments and private agencies engaged in the administration or financial support of direct or indirect relief, to administer moneys appropriated to the commission for the poor relief, to examine the conduct of local governmental agencies in administering relief, and to order the distribution and payment of moneys from the state treasury.

The county commissioners were authorized to administer all advances by the state to the relief commission and were directed to operate through duly authorized agencies of townships, municipalities, and school districts. Within the appropriations made by the commissioners and subject to the rules and regulations of the state relief commission, the commissioners were instructed to appoint assistants and such other employees as were necessary.[50]

The county commissioners, like the state relief commission, were directed to co-operate with all agencies of the federal, state, and county governments and with the private agencies which were engaged in administering relief or financial support to the needy. It was made the duty of all county, township, and municipal governments administrating relief or assistance to dependents to report to the county commissioners, at their request, the names and addresses of all persons to whom they were providing aid and the amount and character of aid given.[51]

The principle of issuing bonds and securing them by the county's share of the utility taxes was continued. Moreover, there was appropriated to the state relief commission from the general revenue fund the sum of $3,000,000, which was designated as the "state relief rotary fund."

---

48. *Ohio Const. 1851*, Art. XII, sec. 2.
49. *Laws of Ohio*, CXVI, 578.
50. *Ibid.*, CXVI, pt. ii, 133-148.
51. *Laws of Ohio*, CXVI, pt. ii, 133-148, 240.

The various counties of the state which had not issued bonds and were not authorized to do so without the consent of the people, were empowered to obtain an advance from the state relief rotary fund in an amount equal to that of bonds which were permitted to be issued under the provision of this act. If the county failed to repay the total of all advances and interest at two percent before June 1936, the state relief commission was directed to refuse to make further allocations or distributions to the county.[52]

In the early months of 1937 the legislature authorized the state relief commission to serve until April 1937. Under this act the county commissioners were authorized to give temporary support and medical relief to nonresidents and to all needy persons possessing legal residence in the county. Funds may be expanded for both direct and work relief. However, all persons on relief able and competent to perform labor yet refuse to accept private employment under prevailing conditions and prevailing wages, may be dropped from the relief rolls. This ruling does not apply, however, to areas where strikes are prevalent. On the other hand, any person receiving relief in the county is permitted to engage in any business without losing this relief status. During the period of such employment he is required to forfeit the *pro rata* amount of relief received by him, but is eligible to his former relief status upon conclusion of such employment.

The county commissioners are required to file with the state relief commission a budget and a detailed statement and plan, showing how the funds received are to be expended, the purpose for which they are to be used, the nature and kind of work to be carried on, and a number of persons to be aided by such relief. Besides this, the county commissioners must file a complete analysis of their proposed expenditures, together with an estimate of all available resources, including the unencumbered proceeds of any bonds heretofore issued and the amount of bonds which the county commissioners have a right to issue without a vote of the people on the approval of the state tax commission of Ohio as authorized in 1935.

---

52. *Ibid.*, CXVI, 133-148.

Of the fund allocated to the county by the state relief commission for direct relief, the commissioners may, when they believe that the cost of the administration may be reduced, reallocate the funds on a percentage basis of relief requirements of the various subdivisions.[53]

The emergency relief measures passed during the period 1932-1937 gave the counties for the first time a centralized relief administration. All records of this work are located in the relief administration office.

The first relief director of Ashland County was appointed by the commissioners in December 1935,[54] when the state relief commission ceased to exist, and the powers previously vested in the state relief commission were transferred to the commissioners. During the years of the depression three bond issues totaling only $82,900 were issued against the excise tax expectancy,[55] the county being easily able to handle its relief load without resorting to the other extraordinary expedients permitted by depression legislation. In the year 1940 the commissioners expended $51,157 for the direct relief,[56] maintaining an average monthly role of 190 families.[57]

In addition to other forms of relief the county commissioners provided funds for aid to dependent children.[58]They are required to include in the annual tax budget an amount not less than that computed to yield a levy of fifteen one-hundredths of one mill on each dollar of the general tax list of the county. Funds are also provided by the federal and state government. If the commissioners fail to comply with the provisions of the act relative to appropriations, the state department of public welfare is directed to institute *mandamus* proceedings against them.[59]

While control over relief work has become one of the most important phases of the commissioners' work, particularly in recent years, many other responsibilities have been assigned to them. The commissioners, by the authority conferred upon them to construct public buildings, were given duties regarding educational advancement.

---

53. *Laws of Ohio*, CXVII, 13.
54. Commissioners' record, XXIV (1935-1937), 52.
55. *Ibid.*, XXI, (1932-1933), 453; XXIII (1934-1935), 8; XXV (1937-1939), 589.
56. (Auditor's) Annual Financial Reports to County Commissioners, 1940, entry 267.
57. Case History Index–Active, 1940. Entry 26.
58. *See* p. 111.
59. G. C. secs. 1359-311–1359-45; *Laws of Ohio*, CXVI, pt. ii, 188-195.

Since 1871 they have been authorized to accept the bequests for the construction of county libraries, and since 1923 to issue bonds, after receiving the approval of the voters, for the construction of libraries, or to contract with existing libraries for the use of people in the county.[60] Moreover during the same period, they were authorized to provide and maintain civic centers in the county and to employ an expert director to supervise and administer them.[61]

Other duties not closely related to the original ones have been added from decade to decade. For example, in 1850 the commissioners were authorized to subscribe for one leading newspaper of each political party in the county and cause them to be bound and deposited with the county auditor as public archives.[62]

An amendment to the original act, passed in 1923, provided for the preservation of such newspapers for a period of ten years, after which they may be removed to the Ohio State Archaeological and Historical Society library.[63] They have been authorized also to promote historical research by appropriating annually a sum not to exceed $100 to defray the expenses of compiling and publishing historical data for historical societies not incorporated for profit.[64]

During the early years of the twentieth century the commissioners were given the duty of providing facilities for county sanitation, which, in previous years have been sadly neglected. In 1917 they were authorized to lay out, establish, and maintain one or more sewer districts within the county. Since 1917 no sewer or sewer treatment works maybe constructed outside of any incorporated municipality by any person, persons, firms, or corporation until the plans have been approved by the commissioners.[65]

Then, too, during the same period the commissioners were authorized to provide facilities for the treatment of tuberculosis. In1908 they were authorized to establish a county tuberculosis hospital and in 1909 to co-operate with the commissioners of other counties with the establishment of a district tuberculosis hospital.[66]

---

60. G. C. secs. 2554, 2455; *Laws of Ohio*, CX, 242.
61. G. C. sec. 2457-4.
62. *Laws of Ohio*, XLVIII, 65.
63. *Ibid.*, CX, 4.
64. G.C. sec. 2457-1.
65. G. C. sec. 6602-1; *Laws of Ohio*, CVII, 440.
66. *Laws of Ohio*, CXIX, 62; C, 87.

Ashland county maintains no tuberculosis hospital. Patients are sent to Ohio State Sanitarium, or to Avalon and Oak Ridge Sanitariums, where the county pays the maintenance cost if a patient is indigent. Since 1917 the commissioners have been authorized to establish tuberculosis dispensaries and provide by tax levies the necessary funds for their establishment and maintenance.[67]

Finally, the county commissioners have acted in a supervisory capacity over other county officials. Since 1850 they have been authorized to compare the annual reports and statements made to them by the prosecuting attorney, the clerk of courts, the sheriff, and the treasurer; take measures to rectify errors, correct discrepancies, and report in their journal the results of such examinations. Prior to the transfer of the duties as secretary to the board the county commissioners to a full-time commissioners' clerk, appointed in 1910[68] in Ashland County under the provision of the act of 1904[69] these reports were required to be filed with the county auditor, who had custody of the commissioners official acts and proceedings.[70] In 1896 the commissioners were given their present duty of visiting hospitals, detention homes, private asylums, and any other institutions exercising a reformatory or correctional influence over individuals, and reporting on the sanitary conditions and the treatment of inmates.[71] Although these reports are required to be filed with the county prosecuting attorney and kept open to the inspection and examination of the public, they were not located in the inventory of Ashland County records.

The board of county commissioners offers a typical example of an office, which, designed primarily for the agricultural society, has expanded to meet the needs and requirements of modern society. At present the commissioners are elected for a four-year term.[72]

Ashland County, being primarily agricultural, has always been extremely conservative in its management. All bonds having so far been paid when due, no refunding of issues have ever been necessary. The county has exceeded the ten-mill limit only once in its history, in 1928, when it issued bonds to raise funds for building a new courthouse. This issue will have been liquidated in 1952.[73]

---

67. G. C. secs. 3148-1, 3153-4, 3153-5.
68. Commissioners' Record, VIII (1910-1911), 67.
69. *Laws of Ohio*, XCVII, 304.
70. G. C. sec. 2504; *Laws of Ohio*, XLVIII, 66.
71. *Laws of Ohio*, XCII, 212.
72. *Ibid.*, CVIII, pt. ii, 1300.
73. Register of Bonds, 1928, entry 271.

By the nature of its people and their needs, Ashland County tends toward a less complex county government than most. It has no county water supply or sewer system, no metropolitan park system, no county library, no planning commission, and no tuberculosis sanitarium. The county has never built a workhouse, but boards its prisoners in Toledo.[74]

Much of the work of road maintenance and repair is now delegated to the engineer, though responsibility for its performance still rest with the commissioners, who have in their charge the 263 miles of highway and 5500 bridges and culverts of Ashland County.[75] Here, as everywhere, upkeep rather than new construction constitutes by far the greater part of the work.

---

74. Commissioners' Record, XXV (1937-1939), 536-7.

75. Highway Map of Ashland County, entry 387.

Minutes

1. COMMISSIONERS' RECORD
1846—. 26 vols. (1-26).

Record of meetings and proceedings of the board of county commissioners including copies of all petitions to establish roads; copies of all resolutions passed by the board; record of appointments of certain county officials; itemized accounts of bills for payment from county funds with records of date order was issued on the county treasury for payment; reports of assessors and tax collectors; record tax levies; records of proceedings and laying out and establishing roads; fixing damages to land by construction of roads; appraising property and fixing the tax thereon; allowing appropriation for the building and improvement of roads, bridges, ditches, and culverts; appointing of land viewers; proceedings and relation to the establishment of county institutions, and organization of county commissions, boards and societies; also includes record of applications for paroles from county jail, granted or refused, 1900—, showing name of prisoner, physical description, date of application for parole, offense charged, and record of action taken on application; record of applications for blind relief, 1908—, showing name and address of applicant, medical evidence of loss of sight, and amount of award granted; emergency relief record, claims to owners of livestock injured or killed by dogs, showing name of claimant, amount asked, number of sheep killed or injured, and amount allowed by the commissioners; approval of reports of soldiers relief commission, 1884—, showing date of report, name and address of soldier or sailor, and amount of compensation granted; soldiers' burial commission reports, showing date of report name and address of soldier or sailor, date and cause of death, itemized account of burial expenses, and date approved by county commissioners; copies of the annual reports of the prosecuting attorney, clerk of courts, sheriff, and the probate judge, 1850—, showing date of report, number of cases and disposition, statistics of prisoners, and financial statement from each office; copies of the monthly financial statements from the auditor and treasurer, 1904—, showing date of report, name of each county fund, receipts and disbursements to and from each fund during the past month, balance or deficit of each fund, and totals for all county funds; copies of the weekly report of the county dog warden, 1927—, showing number of dogs seized, impounded, redeemed and destroyed; all other business before the board of county commissioners, showing date of meeting, business transaction, names of principles or subjects, and action taken. Arranged chronological by dates of meetings. 1846-1881, No index; 1882—, for index, see entry 2. 1846-1898, handwritten; 1899—, typed. Average 400 pages 18 x 12 x3. 1 volume, 1846-1867, engineer's drafting room; 7 volumes, 1863-1911, basement storeroom; 18 volumes, 1912—, Commissioners' office.

2. INDEX TO COMMISSIONERS' JOURNAL (Record)
1882—. 5 vols. (1-5).

Index to Commissioners' Record, entry 1, showing date of entry, names of principals or subjects (bills allowed, roads, bridges, ditches, contracts, and miscellaneous), and volume and page number of record. This index is not complete, some dates and subject data are missing. Arranged alphabetically by names of principles or subjects. Handwritten on printed forms. Average 200 pages 17 x 14 x 2. 3 volumes, 1882-1913, basement storeroom; 2 volumes, 1914—, Commissioners' office.

3. JOURNAL– INFIRMARY
1913—. 2 vols. (1, 2).

Minutes of county commissioners sitting as board of directors for the county home, showing date of meeting, names of members present, and action taken on business presented; record of bills submitted for approval, showing name of creditor, goods supplied or service rendered, and amount of bill. Arranged chronologically by dates of meetings. Bills indexed alphabetically by names of creditors, otherwise, no index. Handwritten and typed, some on printed forms. Average 500 pages 18 x 12 x 3. Commissioners' office.

4. MEMORANDUM OF NEW AND UNFINISHED BUSINESS
1931—. 1 file box.

Papers of memoranda concerning new and unfinished business transactions undertaken by county commissioners, showing date of memorandum, subject, and notation of completion. Arranged chronologically by dates of memoranda. No index. Handwritten on printed forms. 5 x 17 x 27. Commissioners' office.

Public improvements
(See also entry 20-a, 20-h)

Roads

5. NEW COUNTY ROADS
1924—. 1 file box.
Papers pertaining to the alteration, construction, and vacation of county roads including typewritten letters on resolutions, petitions, estimates and surveys on roads, agreements, transfer of funds, awarding of contract, claim for damages, grading, draining and graveling, resolutions, bids, instructions to bidders, estimate of costs, and correspondence, all showing date of document, name and location of road. All papers for each road improvement are filed together in separate folders, showing name of road. No index. Handwritten and typed on printed forms. 10 x 15 x 26. Commissioners' office.

6. OLD COUNTY ROADS
1923—. 1 file box. (4).
Papers pertaining to requests for improvements of old roads, showing name of township, sections of county roads, name of each road, survey data, names of petitioners, and date filed. Arranged chronologically by dates filed. No index. Handwritten. 12 x 17 x 27. Commissioners' office.

Ditches

7. DITCH RECORD
1900-1905. 3 vols. (3-5).
Record of ditches, showing copies of partitions for proposed ditch, dates of petitions, names of petitioners, and commissioners' approval or rejection; reports by county engineer of survey of proposed ditches, showing location of ditch, name of road, estimated cost, name of contractor to whom contract is let, and copy of contractor's bond. Arranged alphabetically by names of principal petitioners and chronological thereunder by dates of petitions. Handwritten on printed forms. Average 355 pages. 18 x 12 x 3. Commissioners' office.

8. MISCELLANEOUS DITCHES

1924—. 1 file box. (3).

Ditch and road papers including ditch petitions signed by petitioners and submitted to commissioners for approval, showing name of petitioners, date of petition, whether approved or rejected, location of ditch, an estimate cost for improvement; record of new and old inter-county highways, showing name and location of road, whether the new road petition or proposal to repair old road, location, whether approved, estimated cost, date of petition, names of owners of land through which road extends, and signatures and petitioners. Arranged alphabetically by names of ditches or roads and chronologically thereunder by dates of petitions. No index. Handwritten and typed on printed forms. 12 x 17 x 27. Commissioners' office.

County Buildings

9. BUILDING COMMISSION RECORD

1927—. 1 vol.

Record of all contracts entered into by county commissioners and various contractors or individuals for construction, repair or improvement of county property, or for services to be rendered, showing name of contractor or individual, authorization, date of contract, name of witnesses, location and name of project, and terms of agreement. Arranged chronologically by dates of contracts. Indexed alphabetically by names of contractors. Typed on printed forms. 250 pages. 18 x 12 x 3. Commissioners' office.

Institutions and Relief

10. BURIAL RECORD–INDIGENT SOLDIERS

1884—. 4 vols.

Record of burial of indigent soldiers, showing date of entry, name of decedent, date and cause of death, army rating, company and regiment, amount allowed for burial, itemized account of funeral expenses, name of undertaker, and signature of witnesses. Arranged chronologically by dates entered. Indexed alphabetically by names of decedents. Handwritten on printed forms. Average 200 pages. 14 x 8 x 1. 1 volume, 1884-1912, basement storeroom; 3 volumes, 1913—, Auditor's main office.

11. COMMISSIONERS' RELIEF FUND
1934-1937. 1 vol.

Record of help to needy granted by the county commissioners, including direct relief, soldiers' relief, and old age pensions, showing date of entry, name of township, name of client, type of aid granted, amount granted for medical care, drugs, rent, groceries, fuel, light, and clothing, and total amount granted over the period of relief. Arranged alphabetically by names of relief clients. No index. Handwritten. 150 pages. 11 x 8 x 2. Commissioners' office.

Financial Records

12. MONTHLY FINANCIAL STATEMENT
1927, 1929—. 3 cartons, 1 file box.

Original monthly financial statement of the county auditor to the county commissioners, showing receipts from all sources to each fund, expenditures authorized by vouchers or warrants against each fund, credit balance to each fund at beginning of report period, credit balance to each fund on date of statement, record of transfer of funds, and date of filing; includes daily statements of the county treasurer of funds and depositories (active and inactive), showing date of statement, name of county funds, names of depository, daily receipts and disbursements, outstanding warrants, credit balance to each fund, and date filed. Arranged chronologically by dates filed. No index. Handwritten and typed on printed forms. Cartons average 12.5 x 16 x 22. File boxes, 10 x 15 x 26. 3 cartons, 1927, 1929-1940, basement storeroom; 1 file box, 1941—, Commissioners' office.

13. AUDITORS DOCKET OF BILLS FILED
1904—. 11 vols. (1-11). Title varies: Record of Bills filed, 1904-1927, 10 vols.

Commissioners' docket of bills filed, showing date of bill, consecutive number, name of creditor, goods supplied or services rendered, amount of bill, date of filing, date and amount approved, date of payment, number of warrant, and remarks. Arranged chronologically by dates filed. No index. Handwritten on printed forms. Average 200 pages. 18 x 12 x 2. 10 volume, 1904-1927, basement storeroom; 1 volume, 1928—, Commissioners' office.

14. RECORD OF BILLS FILED, COUNTY HOME

1904—. 4 vols. (1, 1-3). Title varies: Record of Bills Filed, Infirmary, 1904-1916, 1 vol.; Commissioners' Journal, Infirmary, 1913-1935. 1 vol.; Commissioners' Journal, County Home, 1935-1937, 1 vol.

Commissioners' record of bills filed for operation and maintenance of county home, showing date of bill, consecutive number, name of creditor, goods supplied or services rendered, date of filing, date and amount approved, date of payment, number of warrant, and remarks. Arranged chronologically by dates filed. No index. Handwritten on printed forms. Average 200 pages. 18 x 12 x 3. 3 vols., 1904-1929, basement storeroom; 1 volume, 1929—, Commissioners' office.

Miscellaneous

15. REPORTS TO COMMISSIONERS

1850-1941. 2 bundles.

Miscellaneous reports including:

a. Original annual reports of the prosecuting attorney to the commissioners, 1850-1938, showing number of cases filed in county courts, number of cases disposed of, number of cases pending, total amount of fines and costs assessed, amount collected, total witness and juror fees per diem, mileage, and date filed; 1939—, in entry 21-u.

b. Copies of the monthly statements for justices of the peace to clerk of courts, showing date filed, names of litigants, nature of suit, amount of fines and costs assessed, amount collected, and amount paid to clerk of courts.

c. Annual financial reports of board of education to county auditor, showing date filed, name of school district, number of subdistricts, school buildings and school rooms, value of school property, number of teachers and superintendents, average monthly wages of teachers, number of pupils in each district, and average daily attendance.

Arranged by subjects and chronologically thereunder by dates filed. No index. Handwritten and typed, some on printed forms. 9 x 14 x 24. Basement storeroom.

16. DOG WARDEN REPORTS

1929-1938. 2 file boxes. Title varies: Old County Roads, 1929-1937, 1 File box. 1938— in Miscellaneous (To officers, Bonds, Probate Fees), entry 21-t.

Original reports of dog warden to county commissioners of claims for damages to livestock inflicted by dogs, showing date of report, name and address of claimant, name of township, number, kind, grade, quality, and value of animals, nature of injury, amount of damage claimed less deduction for carcasses or pelt sold or used, net damages claimed, and warden's estimate of net injury; weekly report of the dog warden to commissioners of all dogs seized, impounded, redeemed or destroyed, showing date of report, name of owner, keeper, or harborer (if known), description, sex, breed, and color of dog, address where dog is kept or harbored, date seized or impounded, date disposed of, whether sold, redeemed, or destroyed, amount of fees and costs collected, and date paid into county treasury. Arranged chronologically by dates reported. No index. Handwritten on the printed forms. 10 x 15 x 26. Commissioners' office.

17. OPINIONS
1906—. 20 vols. (1-20).

Copies of prosecuting attorney's opinions on cases as requested by county officials, showing date of opinion, name of official requesting opinion, and prosecuting attorney's recommendation. Arranged chronologically by dates of opinion. Indexed alphabetical by subjects, 1906-1920, Handwritten; 1920—, typed. Average 600 pages. 18 x 12 x 3. 2 volumes, 1906-1917, basement storeroom; 18 volumes, 1918—, Commissioners' office.

18. REQUISITIONS
1937—. 1 file box.

Requisition of the various county offices for supplies and materials issued to county commissioners for approval, showing name of office, itemized list of supplies or materials needed, remarks, signature of officer, and date of requisition. Arranged alphabetically by names of offices and chronologically thereunder by dates of requisition. No index. Handwritten. 12 x 17 x 27. Commissioners' office.

19. CORRESPONDENCE AND MISCELLANEOUS
1909—. 2 file boxes. (5, 6).

Original letters from persons desiring information regarding work, blind relief, direct relief, and aid to crippled children; also includes relief budgets and statements, road blanks, and county commissioners' monthly relief report, all showing date of correspondence or report, subject, and date filed. Arranged chronologically by dates filed. No index. Handwritten on printed forms. 12 x 17 x 27. 1 file box, 1909-1934, basement storeroom; 1 file box, 1935—, Commissioners' office.

20. MISCELLANEOUS FILE
1923—. 1 file box.

County commissioners' miscellaneous file, including:

a. Transcript of stenographers' notes of minutes of the board of county commissioners, showing information as in entry 1.

b. Original petitions to county commissioners from taxpayers for road, bridge, ditch, and culvert construction and repair, showing date of petition, date filed, type of improvement, and signatures of petitioners; also record of work completed.

c. Bids received on roads, bridges, culverts, ditches, and other work, showing date filed, type of construction or improvement, name of bidder, and total amount of bid.

d. Original contracts entered into by county commissioners and various contractors for the construction of bridges or improvements of existing structures, showing date of contract, date filed, project number, name of contractor, sureties, and county commissioners.

e. Road papers, showing date filed, directions of highways and public works improvements, location of county and state roads, name or number of road, restricted highways, and type and construction of road.

f. Contract for surface treatment of county roads, showing date filed, name or number of road, name of contractor, amount of contract, specifications to be followed, and signature of contractor, sureties to his bond, and county commissioners.

g. Summary of bids received for repair work on courthouse as ordered by county commissioners, showing date filed, kind of repair work, number and amount of bids, name of bidders, and name of bidder to whom contract is awarded.

h. Original estimates from the county engineer to the commissioners for road, bridge, ditch, and culvert construction, and other improvements, showing date filed, type of improvement, estimates for labor and material to be used on specifications set up by the engineer.

I. Agreements for joint use of private roadways, showing date filed, name of owner, location of road, amount of compensation, and signatures of commissioners and road owner.

j. Legal notice to contractors of advertisements appearing in local newspapers for bids on various county work.

k. Appointments of all offices coming under control of the county commissioners including trustees, auditor's deputies, committees, dog warden, deputies, and special officers, showing date of appointment, name and the address of appointee, term of office, date file, and amount of salary.

l. Certified statements of fees collected by coroner, showing date filed, name of payer, services rendered or goods supplied, amount paid, and record of all moneys and variables found on dead bodies.

m. Articles of agreement between managers and board of directors of county infirmary, showing date filed, articles of agreement, and signatures of the managers and board directors.

n. Original reports of inspectors of plumbing, electrical wiring, housing, and other inspectors, showing date of report, date filed, name of inspector, type of inspection, condition of item inspected, and inspector's recommendation on place inspected.

o. Record of repairs made on county property, showing date of inspection, date repairs, kind of repair, material used, labor cost, date paid, and date filed.

p. Statement of amount of money city of Ashland owes Ashland County for building rent, cost of prisoners' board, and other expenditures, showing date filed, list of expenditures, amount due, and certified for payment by commissioners.

q. Original jail agreements with other counties for board of prisoners, exchange of prisoners, and other similar items.

r. Buyers orders, showing date filed and items purchased, from whom purchased, services rendered or good supplied, amount and date paid.

s. Monthly report of county engineered to commissioners, showing all the work accomplished during each month and date filed.

t. Record of relief bond issues showing date issued, for what purpose, amount sold, numbers sold, name a purchaser denominations, rate of increase, and dates due.

u. Original bills passed for payment, showing date of bill, date filed, amount of bill, for what purpose, name of creditor, and date and amount of payment.

v. Claims or damages, showing date file, amount claimed, number and address of claimant, final disposition of claim by commissioners, and date and amount paid.

w. Monthly record of salaries paid to commissioners, showing date filed, amount paid, period covered, and names of commissioners.

x. Detailed reports of trustees of law library and miscellaneous correspondence with construction companies, old age pension bureau, state relief board, architects, and other persons, 1937—, showing date of report or statement, subject matter, and signature of correspondent or person submitting the report.

All papers of each subject are filed together in a folder. Arranged alphabetically by subjects and chronologically thereunder by dates filed. No index. Handwritten on printed forms. 12 x 14 x 18. Commissioners' office.

21. MISCELLANEOUS (to Officers, Bonds, Probate Fees)
1907—. 1 carton.

Miscellaneous papers of the commissioners' office, including:

a. Bridge transcripts and contracts, 1927—, showing date of contract or transcript, name and location of bridge, name of contractor, terms of contract, and provisions of resolutions.

b. Financial statements of auditor to county commissioners, 1929—, showing date of statement, condition of various funds, bonds, notes and indebtedness, period covered by report, and signature of county auditor.

c. Copies of annual inventory of equipment and institution furnishings by superintendent of county home to county commissioners, 1931—, showing date of inventory, itemized list, and estimated value of each item.

d. Annual report of the superintendent accounting at home to commissioners, showing all expenditures during the past year for medical services, salaries, equipment, outside relief, food, clothing, and other services or goods supplied, total number of inmates cared for, discharged, ran away, died, number sent to state institutions, and dates covered by report.

e. Miscellaneous reports of Ashland County children's home to Ohio State Division of charities and to county commissioners including the quarterly and annual reports, 1925-1927, showing a detailed account of expenditures of the home for food, fuel, forage, clothing for inmates, pay of employees, repairs and improvements to buildings, office supplies, and all other expenditures.

f. Children's home receipts from all sources showing date and amount of receipt, from whom received, and for services or goods supplied.
g. Semiannual statistical report of children's home, 1930-1936, 1938—, showing date of report, number of inmates, statistics for the year, number of inmates from other counties, list of expenditures, to whom paid, for services or goods supplied, number and amount of voucher, total amount of cash received during year, total amount on hand at close of fiscal year, and signatures of trustees.
h. Reports of board of county visitors to commissioners on various charity and penal institutions visited, 1913—, showing name and condition of institutions, names of board members, date of visit, and recommendations for improvements.
I. Copies of proceedings of board of directors of the conservancy district, 1933—, showing resolutions for transfer of funds for this conservancy district, preliminary surveys, various projects contemplated, those undertaken, location of project, drainage area, maximum capacity, minimum retention, estimated cost, relocation and reconstruction of roads in district, assessments, owners request for flood easements, request denied or ratified, land purchased, and amount paid.
j. Contracts for boarding of prisoners at the Canton Workhouse, 1927—, showing name and address of prisoner, number of days and rate per day, total cost of board of prisoner.
k. Contracts for work of county garages, 1928—, showing date, amount, purpose and date of expiration of contract, and name of contracting parties.
l. Miscellaneous assessment schedules, appraisements and auditor's statements to county commissioner of general property tax, budgets and estimated tax rates, 1928—, showing date of schedule, appraisements or statements, amount of tax rate, property value, and signature of auditor.
m. Bids of depositories for county funds, 1928—, showing amount of funds and interest, date of bid, and date of action taken by the commissioners.
n. Correspondence with banks and depositories, showing date of correspondence, subjects covered, and signature are correspondent.
o. Opinions of judges on certain tax assessment, and date and opinion of judges approving or disapproving assessment.
p. Poor relief bond resolutions, 1933—, date resolution passed, amount of poor relief bonds to be issued, number of bonds, rate of interest, and maturity date.

q. County officials' bonds, 1926-1929, showing name and address county official, name of bonding company, amount, and date of bond, names of sureties, and signature of parties concerned.
r. Probate fees, 1929-1931, showing date of entry, case number, names of plaintiff and defendant, amount of fees, and date of payment.
s. Aid for blind, 1922-1936, entry 22.
t. Dog warden's reports, 1938—, entry 16.
u. Statistical and financial reports of prosecuting attorney, 1938—, entry 15
All papers of each subject are filed together in a folder. Arranged by subjects and chronologically thereunder by dates reported. No index. Handwritten and typed, some on printed forms. 10.5 x 15 x 26. Commissioners' office.

Aid for the Blind

22. AID FOR BOND
1936—. 1 final box. 1922-1936 in Miscellaneous (to Officers, Bonds, Probate Fees), entry 21-s.
Papers pertaining to blind aid, including applications, showing name and address of applicant, answered questionnaire of personal and case history, date of application, case number, and action county of commissioners; reports of eye examination by physicians on condition of applicant's eyes and recommendation; certificates of awards to accepted cases, showing date and amount of award; social data cards, showing date of first check and date and amount of each check; also includes closed cases, showing date and reason for closing, and applications rejected, showing date and reason. Alphabetical by names of applicants. No index. Handwritten on printed forms 10.5 x 15 x 26. Commissioners' office.

23. ROAD BLANKS, BLIND RELIEF CORRESPONDENCE, RELIEF BUDGETS AND STATEMENTS
1917—. 1 file box.
Correspondence pertaining to blind aid, showing date of correspondence, subjects covered, and signature of the correspondent; list of recipients of blind aid, showing name and address of recipient and amount of monthly payments; statistical reports of probate judge to county commissioners, 1935—, showing number of crippled children and amount of aid granted; relief budgets submitted to commissioners showing date budget submitted, amount of proposed budget, amount passed, and type of relief for which money appropriated; copies of statistical and financial

reports submitted to Ohio Relief commission, 1936—, showing date and amount of report, subjects covered and signature of parties concerned; copies of certificates of award and termination of blind aid, 1936—, showing date and amount of award, names and addresses of persons receiving aid, and termination certificate, showing date and reason for termination of aid; copies of notices of rejection or revision, 1936—, showing name and address of applicant, date of application, remarks, and date and reason for rejection, or date and reason for revision; statement of estimated expenditures and amount of funds made available for relief, 1935—, showing date of statement, total amount of expenditures, original amount of relief fund granted, and balance on hand after expenditures have been deducted; Register of applications for blind aid, 1936—, showing date of reports, name and address of applicant, case number, date investigated, by whom investigated, and date and report of action taken. No road records are kept in this file box. Arranged by subjects and chronologically thereunder by dates reported. No index. Handwritten and typed, some on printed forms. 10 x 15 x 26. Commissioners' office.

Relief Administration
(See also entries 19, 23)

Case Records

24. CASE RECORD

1934—. 4 file boxes.

Case papers of relief clients, including applications, showing date of application, names, address, and ages of all members of household, personal, merit, and military history, action taken, health record, naturalization affidavits, family budgets, and other papers of case. Papers of each case filed together in a folder, showing family name of client. Arranged alphabetically by family names. No index. Handwritten and typed on printed forms. 11 x 16 x 24. Relief Office, Opera House Building, West Main and Center Streets, Ashland, Ohio.

25. CASH HISTORIES–ACTIVE

1934—. 2 File drawer (labeled by contained letters of alphabet).

Records of active relief cases, showing name and address of relief client, case number, date of application for relief, name of relief worker, and complete case history. Papers of each case in individual folder. Arranged alphabetically by names of relief clients. For index, see entry 26. Typed on printed forms. 11.5 x 13.5 x 27. Relief Office, Opera House Building, West Main and Center Streets, Ashland, Ohio.

26. CASE HISTORIES INDEX–ACTIVE

1934—. 1 file drawer.

Card index record to Case Histories–Active, entry 25, showing name and address of relief client, code number, case number, and date of application. Arranged alphabetically by names of clients. Typed on printed cards. 4 x 4 x 17. Relief Office, Opera House Building, West Main and Center Streets, Ashland, Ohio.

27. CASE HISTORIES–INACTIVE

1934—. 7 file drawers (labeled by names of cities and townships).

Complete record of inactive relief cases, showing name and address of relief applicant, case number, marital status, age, nativity, number of dependents, investigation report on application, and date case closed. Arranged numerically by case numbers. For index, see entry 28. Typed on printed forms. 11.5 x 13.5 x 17. Relief Office, Opera House Building, West Main and Center Streets, Ashland, Ohio.

28. CASE HISTORY INDEX–INACTIVE

1934—. 1 file drawer.

Card index record to Case Histories–Inactive, entry 27, showing name and address of client, case number, code number, and date case closed. Arranged alphabetically by names of clients. Typed on printed cards. 4 x 4 x 17. Relief Office, Opera House Building, West Main and Center Streets, Ashland, Ohio.

29. COUNTY–CITY CASES

1934—. 1 file box.

Quick reference cards, showing name and address of client, number in family and minimum and maximum relief allowed; active cases in left side of file drawer; closed cases in right side. Arranged alphabetically by names of clients. No index. Handwritten on printed forms. 6 x 14 x 27. Relief Office, Opera House Building, West Main and Center Streets, Ashland, Ohio.

30. INDIVIDUAL RELIEF POSTING SHEETS
1934—. 1 file box.

Posting sheets, showing name and address of client, date of entry, budgetary deficit, payroll number, amount of food, fuel, utility, clothing, shelter, medical, household necessities, milk, and other relief, total direct relief, and cash payroll. Arranged chronologically by dates entered. No index. Handwritten on printed forms. 11 x 16 x 24. Relief Office, Opera House Building, West Main and Center Streets, Ashland, Ohio.

31. CLOTHING CARDS
1934—. 1 file box.

Record of clothing granted relief clients, showing date of report, case number, name and address of client, and list of articles granted. Arranged alphabetically by names of clients. No index. Handwritten on credit forums. 11 x 16 x 24. Relief Office, Opera House Building, West Main and Center Streets, Ashland, Ohio.

WPA, NYA, and CCC Records

32. CERTIFICATION OF ELIGIBILITY
1935—. 3 file boxes.

Copies of certification for Work Projects Administration and National Youth Administration employment, showing date certified, name of relief agency, names of relief district and county, date of certification, name, sex, and birthplace of client, marital status, and veteran status. Arranged alphabetically by names of certified clients. No index. Handwritten on printed forms. 11 x 16 x 24. Relief Office, Opera House Building, West Main and Center Streets, Ashland, Ohio.

33. CCC [Enrollees]
1932—, 1 file box.

Papers pertaining to Civilian Conservation Corps enrollees, including application for enrollment, showing name and address of applicant, date of application, personal history and other answers to questionnaire, records of salary and amount to allottee, agent's reports, and other records and correspondence. Arranged alphabetically by names of enrollees and chronologically thereunder by dates of papers. No index. Handwritten and typed on printed forms. 11 x 16 x 24. Relief Office, Opera House Building, West Main and Center Streets, Ashland, Ohio.

Miscellaneous

34. RELIEF BILLS
1938— 1 file box.

Copies of bills from vendors for materials and supplies furnished clients, showing date of bill, name of client, name of vendor, list of items, total amount, and date filed. Arranged chronologically by dates filed. No index. Handwritten on printed forms. 11 x 16 x 24. Relief Office, Opera House Building, West Main and Center Streets, Ashland, Ohio.

35. RELIEF DIRECTOR'S FILE
1934—. 1 file box.

File of correspondence and miscellaneous papers pertaining to relief office administration, aid for aged, mother's pensions, employment, surplus commodities, and other related subjects, all showing date of correspondence, name of correspondence or subject, and date filed. Arranged alphabetically by subjects and chronologically thereunder by dates filed. Handwritten and typed, some on printed forms. 11 x 16 x 24. Relief Office, Opera House Building, West Main and Center Streets, Ashland, Ohio.

The office of county recorder, although not unknown as an early English institution for the registration of land titles, developed in colonial America where, because of the mobility and the restless pioneers, changes in land titles were frequent and some system was needed to protect purchasers against previous encumbrances. Public land registers, established in most of the colonies during the colonial period and continued by the states following independence, served as a model of land registration for the territory of which the present state of Ohio was then a part. Thus the office of county recorder was established by an act of the Northwest Territory, effective August 1, 1795. This act, adopted from the Pennsylvania Code, provided for the appointment by the governor of a recorder in each county whose principal duty was the recording of the deeds[1].

When Ohio entered the union in 1803 no constitutional provision was made for the continuance of the office, but the legislature during its first session passed an act providing for a recorder in each county to be appointed by the judges of the court of common pleas for a seven-year term[2]. The recorder continued to be an appointive officer until 1829, when, by an act of the legislature, the office became elected for a three-year term.[3] The tenure of office remained at three years until the constitutional amendment of November 7, 1905, which provided for the election of all county officers in the even numbered years.[4] The term of office was fixed at two years, and so continued until the amendment of 1933, which extended the tenure of the incumbent until January 1937, at which time the recorder elected at the regular election in November 1936 began to serve a four-year term.[5]

The first county recorder was directed by statute to record "all deeds, mortgages and conveyances of lands and tenements," lying within his county, and also all instruments and writings required by law to be recorded.[6] in 1805 he was directed to record all plats and maps of newly laid-out villages.[7]

---

1. Theodore Calvin Pease, ed., *The Laws of the Northwest Territory, 1789-1800* (Illinois State Historical Library, *Law Series*, Springfield, 1925, I), 197-199.
2. *Laws of Ohio*, I, 136.
3. *Ibid.*, XXVII, 65.
4. *Ohio Const. 1851* (Amendment, 1905, Art. XVII, secs. 1,2; *Laws of Ohio* XCVIII, 271.
5. *Laws of Ohio*, CXV, 191.
6. *Ibid.*, I, 137.
7. *Ibid.*, III, 213-215.

In 1835 he was permitted, when authorized by the county commissioners, to transcribe from the records of other counties all deeds, mortgages, and other instruments of writing for the sale or conveyance of lands, tenements, or hereditaments affecting land titles in his county.[8]

Since the establishment of the office many duties besides those of recording land titles have been added. The present practice of recording powers of attorney had its beginning in 1818.[9] Although the mechanics of Cincinnati were authorized to file mechanics' liens with the recorder as early as 1823, it was not until 1843 that the privilege was extended to the laborers of all counties.[10] Successive acts in 1865, 1872, 1881, 1884, 1888, 1904, and 1923 added new duties to the office and the recording of soldiers' discharges,[11] copies of certificates of compliance authorizing insurance companies not incorporated under the law of Ohio to transact business in the state, and certified copies of renewal as granted by such companies to their agents,[12] limited partnership agreements,[13] stallion keepers' liens,[14] oil and gas leases,[15] partition fence records,[16] and federal tax liens.[17] The recording of chattel mortgages and conditional sales began in 1846. Such instruments were to be deposited with the township clerk where the mortgagor was a resident. In the township, however, in which the recorder maintained his office such instruments were to be deposited with him.[18] Since 1906 chattel mortgages have been filed with the county recorder exclusively.[19]

---

8. *Ibid.*, XXXIII, 8; XXXV, 10-11.
9. *Laws of Ohio*, XVI, 155-156.
10. *Ibid.*, XXI, 8-10; XLI, 66.
11. *Ibid.*, LXII, 59.
12. *Ibid.*, LXIX, 32, 148; XCVI, 405.
13. *Ibid.*, LXXVIII, 248.
14. *Ibid.*, LXXXI, 43.
15. *Ibid.*, LXXXV, 179.
16. *Ibid.*, XCVII, 140.
17. *Ibid.*, CX, 252.
18. *Ibid.*, XLIV, 61.
19. G. C. sec. 8561.

It is provided that in order to be valid against subsequent mortgages, the chattel mortgage must be deposited with the county recorder of the county where the mortgagor resides at the time of its execution, and to retain its validity the mortgage must be renewed every three years.[20] In 1936 the legislature passed an act authorizing the recorder to destroy such instruments six years after the time of refiling has expired.[21]

An important extension of the method of recording land titles known as the"Torrens System," was provided by an act of the general assembly in 1896.[22] In 1897 this act was declared unconstitutional by the supreme court of Ohio as being contrary to section 16 of the bill of rights of the state constitution.[23] The act of 1913, amended in 1913 and 1915, provides for the examination of land titles by the recorder and the issuance, if the title proved to be in fee simple, of a certificate of title by the court of common pleas or probate court. The official certificate becomes the title of ownership and is indefeasible. However, in the event an interest is found in the land, after the issuance of the certificate, a claim is allowed to the legal claimant from a fund created for that purpose at the time of registration.[24] This system although adopted by a few counties, including Ashland, is not used as widely as it might be because of the difficulty of replacing the traditional complicated system. Its use was instituted in Ashland County in 1914, but only a few entries were made, and the system was abandoned in less than a year.[25]

The recorder, like other county officials, had been required in earlier years to keep records of the business of his office, but it was not until the middle of the nineteenth century that the legislature, looking forward to some uniformity in land registration, enacted measures prescribing the form and content of such records. Since 1850 the recorder has been required to keep a record of deeds in which is recorded all deeds, powers of attorney, and other instruments of writing for the unconditional sale of land, tenements, or hereditaments.[26]

---

20. G. C. sec. 8565.
21. *Laws of Ohio*, CXVI, 324.
22. *Ibid.*, XCII, 220.
23. *Ohio State Reports* (Cincinnati, 1853), LVI, 575.
24. G. C. secs. 8572-24 - 8572-56; *Laws of Ohio*, CIII, 914-960; CVI, 24; CXV, 443.
25. *See* entries 62, 63.
26. *Laws of Ohio*, XLVIII, 64.

The same year saw the beginning of a record of mortgages in which was recorded all mortgages, powers of attorney, and other instruments of writing by which land, tenements, or hereditaments "shall or may be mortgaged" or otherwise conditionally sold; and a record of plats in which was to be recorded all plats and maps of town lots and of subdivisions thereof, and of other divisions of surveyed lands, in like regular succession according to the priority of their presentation.[27] Since 1851 the recorder has been required to keep a separate record of deeds and mortgages denominated respectively as "Record of Deeds" and "Record of Mortgages."[28] Since 1865 the recorder has been required to keep a separate record of leases.[29] The present practice of keeping a daily register of deeds and a daily register of mortgages has been required by statute since 1896.[30] In Ashland County the register was duly instituted in that year and has been continued to date.[31]

Although indexes had been prepared in earlier years, the present system of indexing had its beginning in 1851 and took practically its present form in 1896.[32] At present the recorder, at the beginning of each day's business, is required to make and maintain a general alphabetical index, direct and reverse, of all names of both parties of all instruments recorded by him. The indexes show the kind of instruments, the date, range, township and section, the survey number and number of acres or lot and sublot numbers and the part thereof, of each track or lot of land described in any such instrument of writing; the name of each grantor is entered in the direct index under the appropriate letter and followed on the same line by the name of the grantee; the name of each grantee is entered in the reverse index under the appropriate letter and followed on the same line by the name of the grantor.[33]

---

27. *Ibid.*, XLVIII, 64.
28. *Ibid.*, XLIV, 1203.
29. *Ibid.*, LXII, 170.
30. *Ibid.*, XCII, 268.
31. *See* entries 40 and 51.
32. *Laws of Ohio*, XLIX, 103; XCII, 268; CII, 288.
33. G. C. sec. 2764.

From 1859 to 1867 the recorder in every county with a population of more than 200,000 was required to maintain sectional or geographical indexes to the records of all real estate in the county. Since 1867 recorders have been required to maintain such indexes in all counties in which the county commissioners have instituted them.[34]

The present duties of the recorder do not differ, in the main, from those prescribed in the middle of the nineteenth century. His records are open to the inspection of the public and are transferred to his successor.

The recorder in Ashland County averages annually the recording of 927 deeds, other conveyances 145, mechanics' liens 19, leases 192, powers of attorney 23, chattel mortgages 6,639, and real estate mortgages 632.[35] The office is self supporting, the total fees amounting to over $5,000 annually, while expenses for all purposes average only $3,689.43 yearly.[36] All fees are paid into the county treasury and salaries and expenses are appropriated by the commissioner's annually. The recorder is under a $2,000 bond[37] and his salary is $133.33 monthly.[38]

---

34. G. C. sec. 2766; *Laws of Ohio*, LVI, 20; LXIV, 256; LXXXVI, 49; CII, 289.
35. Transfer record, 1935-1940, entry 42;Recorder's Annual Reports, 1935-1940, entry 80.
36. Departmental Budgets, 1935-1940, entry 81.
37. Treasurer's Record of Official Bonds, 1941, entry 299.
38. Records of Warrants Issued, 1941, entry 256.

Real Property Transfers

Deeds

36. RECORD OF DEEDS

1814—. 118 vols. (A-E, 1-113).

Copies of deeds to real property in Ashland County, showing names of grantor and grantee, date of deed, dates filed and recorded, consideration, kind of deed, terms of deed, description and location of property, boundaries, range, township, section, and lot numbers, acreage, record of mortgages or other encumbrance, signature of witnesses, and notarization. Also contains; Administrator's and Executor's deeds, 1924—, entry 39; Lease Records, 1846-1865, entry 53; Mortgage Record, 1814-1845, entry 47; Record of Liens, 1814-1845, entry 54; Power of Attorney, 1820-1893, entry 75. Arranged chronologically by dates recorded. 1814-1845, no index; 1846—, indexed alphabetically by name of grantees, showing names of grantors; also separate indexes 1846—, see entries 37, 38. 1814-1846, handwritten; 1847-1920, handwritten on printed forms; 1921—, typed on printed forms. Average 600 pages. 18 x 12 x 3. Recorder's office.

37. INDEX TO DEEDS, GRANTOR

1846—. 9 vols. (A-M, Mc-Z, 2, 3A-G, 3H-O, 3P-Z, 4A-G, 4H-O, 4P-Z).

Titles varies: General Index to Deeds, 1846-1885, 2 vols.

Direct index to record of deeds, entry 36, showing date of deed, names of grantor and grantee, deed number, volume and page numbers of record, description and location of property, consideration, and 1885—, date of release of liens thereon. Arranged alphabetically by names of grantors. Handwritten on printed forms. 2 volumes, average 400 pages. 12 x 12 x 3; 7 volumes average 600 pages. 16 x 12 x 3. Recorder's office.

38. INDEX TO DEEDS, GRANTEE

1885—. 7 vols. (2, 3A-G, 3H-O, 3P-Z, 4A-G, 4H-O, 4P-Z).

Reverse index to Record of Deeds, entry 36, Showing date of deed, name of grantor and grantee, deed number, volume and page numbers of record, description and location of property, consideration, and dates of release of liens. Arranged alphabetically by names of grantees. Handwritten on printed forms. Average 600 pages. 18 x 12 x 3. Recorder's office.

39. ADMINISTRATOR'S AND EXECUTOR'S DEEDS

1899-1923. 1 vol. 1924— in Record Deeds, entry 36.

Copies of deeds executed by administrators or executors of estates, showing name of administrator or executor, name of descendent, names of heirs, lot number, location, appraised value, sale price, court case, number, and date filed. Arranged chronologically by dates filed. No index. Handwritten on printed forms. Average 600 pages. 18 x 12 x 3. Recorder's office.

40. DAILY REGISTER OF DEEDS

1896—. 4 vols. (1-4).

Daily register of deeds filed for recording, showing names of grantor and grantee, consecutive instrument number, date and hour of filing, and remarks. Arranged chronologically by dates filed. Indexed alphabetically by names of grantors and grantees. Handwritten on printed forms. Average 375 pages. 17 x 12 x 2.5. Recorder's office.

41. DEEDS

1916—. 12 file boxes (A-N).

Original papers including guardians', executors', and administrators' deeds, showing name of guardian, executor, or administrator, *writ* of authority to act as trustee to deed issued by probate court, date of instrument, date filed and recorded, and signature of guardian, administrator, or executor. Arranged chronologically by dates of instruments. No index. Handwritten on printed forms. 15 x 4.5 x 9.5. Recorder's office.

42. TRANSFER RECORD

1933—. 2 vols. Title varies; Record, 1940—, 1 vol.

Record of transfers of property, showing name of grantor and grantee, date of entry, kind of instrument, and amount of fees. Arranged chronologically by dates entered. No index. Handwritten on printed forms. 1 volume, 300 pages. 12 x 20 x 1.5; 1 volume, 300 pages. 11 x 14.5 x 1.5. Recorder's office.

Leases

43. LEASE RECORDS

1865—. 32 vols. (1-32). 1846-1865 in Record of Deeds, entry 36.

Copies of leases of lands and machinery, showing date of lease, name of grantor and grantee, description and location of property, terms of lease, and services and goods supplied, includes oil and gas leases and copies of easements given for rights of way for highways and roads. Arranged chronologically by dates of leases. Indexed alphabetically by names of grantees; also separate indexes, entries 44, 45. 1865-1916, handwritten on printed forms. 1917—, typed on printed forms. Average 500 pages. 15 x 11.5 x 3. Recorder's office.

44. GENERAL INDEX TO LEASES–DIRECT

1865—. 2 vols. (1-2).

Index to Lease Records, entry 43, showing date of lease, number of acres involved, name of township, names of grantor and grantee, volume and page number of record, and record of lands released. Arranged alphabetically by names of grantors. Handwritten on printed forms. Average 500 pages. 16 x 12 x 3. Recorder's office.

45. GENERAL INDEX TO LEASE–REVERSE

1923—. 1 vol. Initiated in 1923.

Index to Lease Records, entry 43, showing date of lease, number of acres involved, name of township, names of grantor and grantee, volume and page number of record, and record of lands released. Arranged alphabetically by names of grantees. Typed on printed forms. 500 pages. 16 x 12 x 3. Recorder's office.

46. GAS LEASES

1926—. 1 file box.

Certificates of leases issued by recorder, showing date of issue, names of grantor and grantee, name of county and state, description and location of property, number of acres, terms, and condition of lease. Arranged chronologically by dates issued. No index. Typed on printed forms. 10 x 4.5 x 13.5. Recorder's office.

Mortgages

47. MORTGAGE RECORD

1846—. 73 vols. (1-73). 1814-1845 in Record of Deeds, entry 36.

Copies of mortgages, showing date of mortgage, names of mortgagor and mortgagee, date filed, amount and conditions of mortgage, description and location of property involved and consideration, and cancellations of mortgage on page margins, showing date released or cancelled, and signature of grantee. Arranged chronologically by dates filed. For indexes, see entries 48, 49. Handwritten on printed forms. Average 500 pages. 14 x 10 x 3. Recorder's file room.

48. MORTGAGE INDEX, DIRECT

1846—. 5 vols. Title varies: General Index to Mortgages, 1846-1902, 2 vols. Mortgage Index to, 1902-1935, 2 vols.

Direct index to Mortgage Record, entry 47, showing date of mortgage, names of mortgagor and mortgagee, volume and page numbers of record, date of filing, location and description of property involved, date cancelled, and remarks. Arranged alphabetically by names of mortgagees. Handwritten on printed forms. Average 500 pages. 11 x 14 x 3. Recorder's office.

49. MORTGAGE INDEX, REVERSE

1902—. 3 vols. Title varies: Mortgage Index to, 1902-1935, 2 vols.

Reverse index to Mortgage Record, entry 47, showing date of mortgage, names of mortgagor and mortgagee, volume and page numbers of record, date of filing, location and description of property involved, date cancelled, and remarks. Arranged alphabetically by names of mortgagees. Handwritten on printed forms. Average 500 pages. 11 x 14 x 3. Recorder's office.

50. MORTGAGES, BILLS OF SALE, LEASES

1848—. 48 file boxes.

Original papers of recorder's office including bills of sale, showing instrument number, date of instrument, date of transfer, names of grantor and grantee, date recorded, and value and description of property transferred; leases showing date of lease, instrument number, name of grantor and grantee, conditions of lease, date filed, date recorded, and signatures of witnesses, grantor, and notary; power of attorney, showing name of attorney, name of grantor, type of instrument, enumeration of duties, extent of power, date filed, date recorded, and signatures of witnesses, grantor and notary. Also contains: Original Chattel Mortgages, 1848-1918, entry 71. Arranged chronologically by dates of instruments. No index. Handwritten and typed, some on printed forms. 10.5 x 3.5 x 12. Recorder's office.

51. DAILY REGISTER OF MORTGAGES
1896—. 4 vols. (1-4).

Daily register of mortgages, showing names of mortgagor and mortgagee, consecutive instrument number, date and hour of filing, considerations, and remarks. Arranged chronologically by dates filed. Handwritten on printed forms. Average 200 pages. 17 x 12 x 2. Recorder's office.

52. RECORD OF CERTIFICATES OF DISCHARGE OF MORTGAGES
1892—. 2 vols. (1-2).

Record of certificates of release of mortgages filed for recording, showing name of mortgagor and mortgagee, date, amount, and conditions of mortgage, signatures of mortgagee and witnesses, notarizations, and date of release and discharge. Arranged chronologically by dates discharge. Indexed alphabetically by names of mortgagees. 1992-1907, handwritten on printed forms; 1907—, typed on printed forms. Average 400 pages. 18.5 x 12.5 x 2.5. Recorder's office.

53. CANCELLED REAL ESTATE MORTGAGES
1922— 1 file box.

Original affidavit to obtain mechanics' lien certificate, showing date of certificate, names of state and county, names of parties involved, description of case, amount of fees, name of party claiming leasehold, name and address of owner, and signature of notary public; also construction mortgage and mortgage deed notice received by the recorder to cancel mortgages, showing names and addresses of parties, date of notice, and case number. Arranged chronologically by dates of certificates. No index. Typed on printed forms. 15 x 9.5 x 2.5. Recorder's office.

Liens

54. RECORD OF LIENS

1846—. 6 vols. (1-6), 1814-1845 in Record of Deeds, entry 36.

Copies of mechanics' liens filed, showing date of filing, names of creditor and debtor, amount and date of lien, and detailed statement for labor and material. Arranged chronologically by dates filed. Indexed alphabetically by names of debtors. Handwritten on printed forms. Average 460 pages. 15 x 11.5 x 2.5. Recorder's office.

55. EXCISE AND FRANCHISE LIEN RECORD

1931—. 1 file box.

Original excise and franchise tax lien notices, showing name of delinquent taxpayer, request to file lien, amounts of tax and penalty, total amount of tax, signature of secretary of tax commission, date of filing, and signature of county recorder; also includes notice of payment tax and discharge of lien. Arranged chronologically by dates filed. No index. Handwritten on printed forms. 10 x 4.5 x 13.5. Recorder's office.

56. CORPORATION TAX LIEN RECORD

1931—. 1 vol.

Record of corporation tax liens, showing recorder's file number, date filed, name of corporation, and date of lien; also includes record of discharge of liens, showing date discharged. Arranged chronologically by dates filed. No index. Handwritten on printed forms. 400 pages. 16 x 12 x 2.5. Recorder's office.

57. CORPORATION TAX LIEN AND CANCELLATION

1934—. 1 file box.

Original notice of corporation tax liens and cancellation certificates, showing name of corporation, date of lien, date declared delinquent, date of report, amount of federal tax lien, and date paid and cancelled. Arranged alphabetically by names of corporations and chronologically thereunder by dates incorporated. No index. Typed on printed forms. 10.5 x 4.5 x 13.5. Recorder's office.

58. FEDERAL TAX LIEN AND BANKRUPTCY

1923—. 1 vol.

Record of federal tax lien, showing name and residence of delinquent taxpayer, collector's serial number, consecutive number of lien, date and hour of filing, amounts of tax assessed and penalty, date of refiling, and date of release. Contains no record of bankruptcy. Arranged alphabetically by names of taxpayers and chronologically thereunder by dates filed. Handwritten on printed forms. 260 pages. 18 x 12 x 2. Recorder's office.

59. FEDERAL TAX LIEN

1933—. 1 file box.

Certificate of discharge of federal tax liens, showing name and residence of taxpayer, collector's serial number, consecutive number of lien, date and time of filing, amount of tax assessed, penalty, and date of discharge. Arranged alphabetically by names of taxpayers and chronologically thereunder by dates discharged. No index. Handwritten on printed forms. 10.5 x 4.5 x 13.5. Recorder's office.

60. PERSONAL TAX LIEN RECORD

1930—. 1 vol.

Record of personal tax liens, showing name of debtor, amount of tax, recorder's file number, dates of filing and recording, and years delinquent; also includes certificate and discharge of lien, showing dates of payments, balance unpaid, and penalty. Arranged alphabetically by names of debtors. No index. Handwritten on printed forms. 100 pages. 8 x 14 x .5. Recorder's office.

61. INDEX OF LEAN NOTICES AND DISCHARGES

1930—. 1 vol.

Record of lien notices and discharges of recognizances, showing recorder's file number, from what court issued, names of sureties and defendant, date of issue, date of filing, fee, amount of bond, description of property, and date of cancellation. Arranged alphabetically by names of sureties. Handwritten on printed forms. 200 pages. 16 x 12 x 2.5. Recorder's office.

Registered Lands

62. REGISTERED LANDS- RECEPTION BOOK
1914-1915. 1 vol. (1).

Record of daily receipts and documents affecting registered lands, showing date and time filed, document number, kind of document, from whom, against whom, in favor of whom, date of instrument, terms, amount, date due, rate of interest, description of lands, and certificate numbers. Arranged chronologically by dates filed. Indexed alphabetically by names of owners in front of volume; indexed numerically by certificate numbers in back of volume. Handwritten on printed forms. 400 pages. 16 x 16 x 2.5. Recorder's file room.

63. REGISTERED LANDS–INDEX TO OWNERS

Record of registered lands, showing name of owner, certificate and document numbers, date filed, description of registered lands, date transferred, to whom, date cancelled, and volume and page numbers of Registered Lands–Reception Book, entry 62. Arranged chronologically by dates filed. Index alphabetically by names of owners in front of volume; indexed numerically by certificate numbers in back of volume. Handwritten on printed forms. 400 pages. 16 x 16 x 2.5. Recorder's file room.

Plats and Maps

64. PLAT BOOKS
1850—. 7 vols. (1-7).

Plats of towns, villages, streets, alleys, easements, sewer changes, lot alteration and various surveys, showing name of plat, description and location, lot number, boundary lines, date surveyed, name of surveyor, and date recorded. No index. Record, handwritten; plats hand drawn, black on white. Scales vary. Average 100 pages. 30 x 18 x 1. Recorder's office.

65. PLAT MAPS, CITY OF ASHLAND

1915, 1925. 2 maps.

Plats maps of city of Ashland, showing allotments, subdivisions, lot and section numbers, names of streets, alleys, and routes, corporation lines, and location of institutions, factories, hotels, and cemeteries. Prepared by county engineer. No obvious arrangement. No index. Hand drawn, black on white. 5 x 5. Recorder's file room.

66. TOWNSHIP MAPS

1928-1932. 28 maps. Subtitled by names of townships.

Maps of each township, showing name of township, range and section numbers, acreage of farms, names of landowners, division lines, and names of roads and railways. Prepared by county engineer. No obvious arrangement. No index. Blueprint. Condition poor. 30 x 30. Recorder's file room.

67. ASHLAND COUNTY

1930. 1 map.

Land tenure map of Ashland County compiled from official records and surveys, showing location of farms, number of acres, name of township, size of lots, sections, range, lot numbers, names of owners of farms and lots, location of waterways, highways, and railways. Prepared by county engineer. Hand drawn. Black on white. Scale, 1 inch equals 200 feet. 72 x 42. Recorder's office.

68. ATLAS OF ASHLAND COUNTY

1874. 1 vol.

Atlas of Ashland County, showing original tracks, annexations, new boundaries, and corporation limits by townships. Published by H.J. Toudy and Company, Philadelphia, Pennsylvania. Arranged alphabetically by names of townships. No index. Lithograph and printed. Scale varies. Condition poor. 17 x 14 x 1. Recorder's office.

Personal Property Transfers

69. CHATTEL MORTGAGE INDEX

1875—. 15 vols. (1-15). Title varies: Chattel Register, 1875-1916, 5 vols. Index to Mortgage Record (Chattel), entry 70, and Original Chattel Mortgages, entry 71, showing names of mortgagor and mortgagee, chattel mortgage number, amount of mortgage, date and time filed; also shows date cancelled and to whom delivered, dates of refiling, and remarks. Arranged alphabetically by names of grantors and grantees. Handwritten on printed forms. Average 450 pages. 16 x 12 x 3. 10 volumes, 1875-1922, 1934—, Recorder's office; 5 volumes, 1923-1934, Recorder's file room.

70. MORTGAGE RECORD (CHATTEL)
1906—. 1 vol. Last entry 1936.

Record of chattel mortgages, showing names of mortgagor and mortgagee, amount of mortgage, description of goods conveyed to mortgage insured or not, name of insurance company, beneficiaries in case of loss, condition of mortgage, statement by mortgagor that property is free of other encumbrances, method and dates of payment, date of instrument, signatures of mortgagor, notary public, and recorder, dates filed and recorded, and chattel mortgage number. Arranged chronologically by dates filed. For index, see entry 69. 1906-1948, handwritten; 1919—, typed. 500 pages. 14 x 10 x 3. Recorder's office.

71. ORIGINAL CHATTEL MORTGAGES
1918—. 97 file boxes (labeled by contained instrument numbers). 1848-1918 in Mortgages, Bills of Sales Leases. Entry 50.

Original chattel mortgages, showing names of mortgagor and mortgagee, chattel mortgage number, amount of mortgage, dates filed and recorded, description of goods conveyed, insured or not, by whom insured, name of insurance company, name of beneficiary in case of loss, conditions of mortgage, statement of mortgagor that goods are free of encumbrance, method and dates of payments, date of instrument, and signatures of mortgagee, mortgagor, notary public, and recorder. Arranged numerically by chattel mortgage numbers. For index, see entry 69. Handwritten and typed, some on printed forms. 10 x 4.5 x 13.5. Recorder's file room.

72. CHATTEL MORTGAGES NOT RECORDED
1916—. 12 file boxes (L-W).

Original chattel mortgages not recorded, showing names of mortgagor and mortgagee, amount of mortgage, description of goods conveyed, instrument number and date, and signature of mortgagee. Arranged chronologically by dates of instruments. No index. Typed on printed forms. 15.5 x 4.5 x 9.5. Recorder's office.

Partnerships and Corporations

73. PARTNERSHIP AND TRADER' RECORD

1884-1886. 1 vol. Discontinued, law repealed.

Record of individual partnership traders, showing date agreement filed, kind of business, name and address of business, name and address of each member of firm, Amount of money invested by each, and date a recording. Arranged chronologically by dates filed. No index. Handwritten on printed forms. 500 pages. 18 x 12 x 3. Recorder's office.

74. CHURCH RECORD INCORPORATIONS

1849-1895. 1 vol.

Copies of articles of incorporation of churches, showing name and address of church, date of organization, name of organizers, trustees, and members, copy of charter, and date recorded. Several of these records are written in German. Arranged chronologically by dates recorded. Indexed alphabetically by names of churches. Handwritten. 150 pages. 12.5 x 8 x 1. Recorder's office.

Grants of Authority

75. POWER OF ATTORNEY

1894—. 1 vol. -1820-1893 in Record of Deeds, entry 36.

Copies of grants of authority to act for the grantor in matters set forth in instruments, showing names of grantor and grantee, enumeration of duties to perform, power to sign instruments and legal transactions, date of instrument, signature of grantor and witnesses, notarization, and dates filed and recorded. Arranged chronologically by dates of agreements. Indexed alphabetically by names of grantees. Handwritten on printed forms. 430 pages. 18 x 12 x 2.5. Recorder's office.

76. INDEX TO AGENTS' LICENSES

1916—. 2 vols.

Index record of insurance agents' licenses, showing names of agent and company, date license issued, date filed, and date of cancellation. Arranged alphabetically by names of agents and chronologically thereunder by dates filed. Handwritten. Average 300 pages. 18 x 12 x 2. Recorder's office.

77. CANCELED AGENTS' LICENSES

1930—. 5 file boxes.

Copies of licenses issued by state department of insurance to insurance agents, showing name of company, home office, name and address of agent, date of license, date filed, and date of cancellation. Arranged chronologically by dates filed. No index. Handwritten and typed on printed forms. 10.5 x 4.5 x 13.5. Recorder's office.

78. CERTIFICATES OF COMPLIANCE

1928—. 1 bundle, 2 file boxes.

Certificates of compliance of insurance companies issued by the state department of insurance and filed with the county recorder, showing certificate number, name and address of insurance company, statement of financial status, authorization to practice business for year, date of certificate, date filed, and seal and signature of superintendent of insurance of Ohio. Arranged chronologically by dates filed. No index. Typed on printed forms. Bundle, 12 x 6 x 6; file boxes, 10 x 4.5 x 13.5. Recorder's office.

Fiscal Accounts

79. RECORDER'S RECORD OF FEES

1907—. 12 vols. (1-12).

Daily record of fees received for recording, filing, searching, and registering instruments, showing date of entry, consecutive number of instruments, by whom paid, amount of fees, kind of instrument or service, cancellation, sundries, and total fees. Arranged chronologically by dates entered. No index. Handwritten on printed forms. Average 400 pages. 18 x 12 x 2. Recorder's office.

80. RECORDER'S ANNUAL REPORTS

1933—. 1 bundle.

Recorder's annual reports, showing deeds recorded, consideration transfers recorded, miscellaneous records recorded, mortgages recorded, amount of leases recorded, mortgages cancelled, totals for each instrument, total chattel mortgages filed, total spent for office supplies, total receipts and amount paid into county treasury. Each report is kept in envelopes, showing recorders yearly reports, and year on outside of envelopes. Arranged by years. No index. Typed. 9 x 4 x 6. Recorder's office.

81. DEPARTMENTAL BUDGET
1934—. 1 bundle.
Departmental budgets, showing name of office, head of office or department, expenditure classifications, appropriations for current year, requests for next year, amount approved by commissioners, and appropriation for following year. Arranged by years. No index. Typed on printed forms. 9 x 4 x 6. Recorder's office.

Miscellaneous

82. PARTITION FENCE RECORD
1905—. 1 vol.
Record of assignments of trustees in matter of partition fences, showing names of landowners where partition is disputed, assignments to each landowner of his share of fence upkeep, names of townships, description of land and adjoining lands, dividing lines, and date petition filed and recorded. Arranged chronologically by dates filed. Index alphabetically by names of landowners. Handwritten. 360 pages. 18 x 12 x 2. Recorder's office.

83. RECORD A CONTRACTS AND AGREEMENTS
1901—. 2 vols.
Record of contracts and agreements, showing date of agreement or contract, names of grantor and grantee, amount, name of township, and location of land or property. Arranged chronologically by dates a contracts or agreements. Index alphabetically by names a grantors. Handwritten on printed forms. Average 425 pages. 16 x 11 x 2. Recorder's office.

84. CERTIFICATE COPY- BANKRUPTCY
1932—. 1 file box.
Copies of various certificates and papers in bankruptcy cases, showing name and address of bankrupt, court term, case number, name of judge, and date of instrument. All papers of each case are filed together and a jacket or bundle. Arranged alphabetically by names of bankrupts and chronologically thereunder by dates of instruments. No index. Typed on printed forms. 10 x 4.5 x 13.5. Recorder's office.

85. ORDER OF DISCHARGE; BANKRUPTCY

1936—. 1 file box.

Final papers of adjudication in bankruptcy, showing name of bankrupt, bankruptcy number, city, district, date of final decision, and names of judge and referee and federal court of United States. Arranged alphabetically by names of bankrupts and chronologically thereunder by dates of final papers. No index. Handwritten on printed forms. 10.5 x 4.5 x 13.5. Recorder's office.

86. RECORD OF SOLDIERS' DISCHARGES

1860—. 1 file box.

Record of discharges from the United States army, navy, or marines, a soldiers and sailors enlisted for the War of Rebellion, Spanish American war, Philippine Insurrection, and World War, showing name, rank, company, regiment, and physical description of soldier, sailor, or marine, date, place, and reason for discharge, service record, name of commanding officer, and date of recording. Arranged chronologically by dates recorded. Indexed alphabetically by names of soldiers, sailors, or marines. Handwritten on printed forms. Average 350 pages. 18 x 12 x 2.5. Recorder's office.

87. MISCELLANEOUS RECORD

1938—. 1 vol. (1).

Copies of instruments filed with recorder for which he keeps no separate record, showing names of each party to instrument, data of instrument, date filed, terms or provision of instruments, and kind of instruments. Arranged alphabetically by names of principal parties. No index. 600 pages. 6.5 x 11.5 x 3. Recorder's office.

The office of clerk of courts, an ancient English institution originating before the time of Edward I[1] was transplanted to America during the colonial period. The American Revolution made no radical change to the political heritage derived from England, and the office was continued by the states. The duties of the office were modified in the newer states, however, because of a separation of administrative and judicial functions, which under the English system had been combined.

The section of the Ohio constitution of 1802 creating the judicial system for the state provided for the appointment of a clerk of courts by the judges of the court of common pleas. He was to serve a seven-year term, but was subject to removal by the appointing power for a breach of good behavior.[2] The constitution of 1851 made the office of clerk elective with a three-year term.[3] A constitutional amendment in 1905 provided that the terms of all elective offices should be for an even number of years not exceeding four. In compliance with this amendment, the general assembly passed an act fixing the term of office of the clerk at two years.[4] The term remained at two years until 1936 when it was extended to four years.[5] The remuneration of the office was by fees until 1875, and from 1875 to 1906 by a definite salary based on the population of the county plus a percentage of fees collected. Although the clerk continues to collect fees for the benefit of the county, since 1906 is compensation has been derived from a salary determined on a population basis.[6]

The duties of the clerk of courts, like those of other county officers, are prescribed by statute. In 1853 a code of civil procedure was adopted summarizing the earlier duties and forming the basis for the present ones which are in most respects similar to those prescribed during the earlier years of the office.

---

1. Sir Frederick Pollock and Frederic William Maitland, *The History of English Law Before the Time of Edward I* (Cambridge, 1895), I, 184.
2. *Ohio Const.* 1802, Art. III, sec. 9.
3. *Ohio Const.* 1851, Art. IV, sec. 16.
4. *Laws of Ohio*, XCVIII, 273.
5. *Ibid.*, CXVI, pt. ii. 184.
6. *Ibid.*, III, 53; LXXII, 125; XCVIII, 94, 117.

The clerk of courts was directed to issue all writs and orders for provisional remedies; endorse the date upon all papers filed in his office; keep the journal, record books, and papers appertaining to the court of common pleas and record its proceedings, keeping the appearance docket and the trial docket, as well as a printed duplicate of the trial docket, the journal, the record, and the execution docket.[7] The present practice of preparing an index, direct and reverse, to judgments began in 1866.[8] In 1871 the clerk was made official custodian of the law reports and books furnished by the state for the use of the court and bar, and was made liable in the event of their destruction.[9]

Some of the duties of the clerk as defined by the civil code of 1853 are still effective, others have been added by subsequent legislation. Thus, for example, in 1858 the clerk was directed to receive notary commissions for record.[10] He was required, also, to receive for record special police commissions (1867), timber trademarks (1883), partnership agreements (1894), copies of judgments of federal courts (1898), marks of ownerships [trademarks] (1911), motor vehicle bills of sale (1921), and certificates of judgments to operate as liens (1935).[11] Since January 1, 1938 he has issued certificates of title to motor vehicles.[12] On the other hand, many of the earlier duties of the clerk have been transferred to other departments of the local government or have been abolished. The clerk issued marriage licenses and recorded ministers' licenses until 1852. Since that date the former have been issued and the latter recorded by the probate court,[13] to which court the records have been transferred. Moreover the clerk issued peddlers' licenses until the decade of the sixties, since then they have been issued by the auditor.[14]

---

8. *Laws of Ohio*, LXIII, 10; LXXV, 103; LXXVIII, 88; LXXXII, 33; LXXXVI, 26.
9. *Ibid.*, LXVIII, 109.
10. *Ibid.*, LV, 13; XCIII, 106.
11. *Ibid.*, LXIV, 60; LXXX, 195; XCI, 357; XCII, 25; XCIII, 285; CII, 513-514; CIX, 333; CXVI, 274.
12. G. C. sec. 6290-6.
13. *Laws of Ohio*, I, 31; XXIX, 429; L, 84; *Ohio Const. 1851*, Art. IV, sec. 8.
14. *Laws of Ohio*, LIX, 67.

These records were not found in the inventory. The clerk has been authorized to act as an agent of the state in the sale of hunting and trapping licenses to nonresidents of the state since 1904 and to residents since 1919.[15] He has been authorized also to serve as agent in the sale of fishing licenses to nonresidents since 1919 and to residents since 1925.[16] The practice of recording in the office of clerk, the names of black or mulatto persons to be used as certificates of freedom was, of course, discontinued at the close of the War between the States in 1865.

In 1856 the clerk was directed by the legislature to preserve a list of births, marriages, and deaths as returned to his office by the assessors, and to transmit annually, on or before the first day of June, a copy of such statistics to the secretary of state. These lists are no longer preserved. From these county lists, the secretary of state prepared tabular statements showing the vital statistics in each county. The clerk received 10 copies of the report, one of which he was required to preserve in his office.[17] The clerk was relieved of the task of collecting and preserving vital statistics, when, in1867, such powers and duties were vested in the probate judge.[18]

The clerk of courts was given other duties in addition to those of serving the court of common pleas and receiving documents for record. Since 1850 he has been required to report each year to the county commissioners all fins assessed by the courts in criminal cases, together with the names of the parties to each case, and the amount of money he has paid to the county treasurer.[19] Duplicate copies of these reports have been preserved in the clerk's office. Moreover, since 1867 he has been required to report annually to the secretary of state the number of crimes committed in this county, the number of pending cases, and the amount of fines collected.[20]

---

15. *Ibid.*, XCVII, 474; CVIII, pt. I. 595.
16. *Ibid.*, CVIII, pt. I. 923; CXI, 276.
17. *Laws of Ohio*, LIII, 73-75.
18. *Ibid.*, LXIV, 63-64.
19. *Ibid.*, XLVIII, 66; LVIII, 69; LXXXVI, 239.
20. *Ibid.*, LXIV, 17.

An act of 1927, amending the act of 1867, directed the clerk to report on any matters which the secretary of state might require, and to forward a duplicate copy of his report on crime in his county to the state board of clemency [boards of pardons and parole].[21] The state board of clemency was abolished in 1921 and its duties were assigned to a Board of Pardons and Parole Within the Department of Public Welfare.[22]

The county clerk of courts, like the county prosecuting attorney, is one of the important persons and the judicial system. His significance and influence, however, were not recognized until recent years.

The clerk courts in Ashland County is bonded for $10,000,[23] and receives a salary of $1935 annually.[24] He is assisted by two deputies, also bonded, and one clerk, who receives an annual aggregate compensation of $2,437.90. The office is self-supporting. Fees received during the year 1940 for services rendered to the public totaled $8,849.42,[25] far exceeding the cost of operation.

---

21. *Ibid.*, CXII, 111, 124.
22. *Ibid.*, CIX, 111, 124.
23. Record of Official bonds, 1940, entry 270.
24. Appropriation Ledger, 1940, entry 239.
25. *Ibid.*

Court Proceedings

88. BENCH DOCKET

1894—. 26 vols. (1-26). Titles varies: Trial Docket, 1894-1932, 23 vols. Clerk of courts' docket of cases heard in county courts, showing case number, names of plaintiff and defendant, date case filed, names of attorneys, kind of action, dates of court orders and proceedings of the case, and volume and page number of Appearance Docket, entry 128. Arranged chronologically by date filed. Indexed alphabetically by names of plaintiff and defendants; for separate index, see entry 127. Handwritten on printed forms. Average 500 pages. 10 x 12 x 3. 22 volumes, 1894-1928, basement storage room; 4 volumes, 1928—, Clerk of courts' office.

89. PRAECIPE DOCKET

1879-1893, 1909—. 3 vols. (1, 3, 4).

Docket of orders issued by the clerk of courts, showing case number, date issued, names of plaintiff and defendant, kind of *writ*, names of attorneys, and date of return. Arranged chronologically by dates issued. For index, see entry 95. Handwritten on printed forms. Average 250 pages. 14 x 9 x 2. 2 volumes, 1879-1893, 1909-1935, basement storage room; 1 volume, 1935—, Clerk of courts' main office.

90. BILLS OF EXCEPTION

1883—. 250 documents.

Bills of exceptions, showing notice of filing exceptions, names of plaintiff and defendant, case number, date filed, findings of court as to whether or not new trial shall be granted, entire case as to testimony of both parties and witnesses, signatures of judges, clerk of courts, and court stenographer, order of delivery of personal property, executions, sheriff's return, and list of various exhibits. Arranged chronologically by dates filed. No index. 1833-1910, handwritten; 1910—, typed. Average 50 pages. 14 x 8 x 1. 80 documents, 1883-1926, basement storage room; 170 documents, 1927—, Clerk of courts' private office.

Original Documents

91. CIVIL ACTION AND DIVORCE

1846—. 459 file boxes (labeled by contained case numbers).

Original instruments issued in civil actions in court cases, including petitions, court orders, answers, journal entries, bills and divorce records, 1847—, showing case number, file box number, names of plaintiff and defendant, date case filed, and volume and page number of docket and records where entered. All papers of each case filed together, civil action in white jackets, and divorce papers in green jackets. Arranged chronologically by dates filed. For indexes, see entries 95, 135. Handwritten and typed, some on printed forms. 10 x 4.5 x 13.5. Clerk of courts' private office.

92. CRIMINAL CASES

1846—. 49 file boxes (labeled by contained case numbers).

Original instruments issued in criminal actions and court cases, including charges, indictments, court orders, journal entries, and cost bills, showing case number, file box number, name of defendant, date case filed, charge, and volume and page numbers of dockets where records were entered. All papers of each case filed together and a red jacket. Arranged chronologically by dates filed. For index, see entries 95, 135. Handwritten and typed, some on printed forms. 10 x 4.5 x 13.5.Clerk of courts' private office.

93. PETITIONS- CLOSED CASES

1935—. 62 file boxes (labeled by contained case numbers).

Original petitions, motions, praecipes, summonses, plaintiff's undertakings in replevin, memorandum, affidavits in replevin, inventories and appraisements of personal property, orders for delivery of personal property, and amended petitions. Each case in separate jacket showing case number. Arranged numerically by case numbers. For index, see entry 135. Typed on printed forms. 10 x 18 x 30. Clerk of courts' main office.

Judgments and Executions

94. EXECUTION DOCKET

1846—. 12 vols. (1-12).

Docket of executions to satisfy judgments rendered by county courts, showing name of township, date judgment rendered, name of plaintiff and defendant, date transcript filed, amount of judgment, names of judgment creditor and debtor, date paid, and itemized cost bill. Arranged chronologically by dates of judgments. Indexed alphabetically by names of judgment debtors; For separate indexes, see entries 95, 127. 1846-1912, handwritten; 1912—, typed printed forms. Average 575 pages. 18 x 12 x 3. Clerk of courts' private office.

95. INDEX TO PENDING SUITS, LIVING JUDGMENTS AND EXECUTIONS
1883—. 7 vols. (1-7).
Record of pending suits, showing date case filed, name of plaintiff and defendant, and case number; living judgments, showing date judgment rendered, amount of judgment, and names of judgment debtor and creditor; executions, showing date of execution and sheriff's return; also file box number of Civil Actions and Divorces, entry 91; Criminal Cases, entry 92; Justice of Peace Lien Docket, entry 101; volume and page number of Execution Docket, entry 94; Certificate of Judgment Docket, entry 99; Lien Docket, entry 100; Praecipe Docket, entry 89; and Alimony Record, entry 125. Arranged alphabetically by names of plaintiffs and defendants. No index. Handwritten on printed forms. Average 525 pages. 18 x 12 x 3.3 Clerk of courts' main office.

96. JUDGMENT DOCKET
1846-1875. 1 vol.
Docket of judgments rendered, showing names of plaintiff and defendant, date and amount of judgment, mandates issued for collection of cost, amount of cost for plaintiff and defendant, and amount of fees for clerk and sheriff; also records of appeal of decisions and petitions in error. Arranged chronologically by dates of judgments. Indexed alphabetically by names of plaintiffs; for separate indexes, see entries 97, 98. Handwritten on printed forms. 325 pages. 14 x 9 x 2. Clerk of courts' private office.

97. JUDGMENT INDEX, DIRECT
1846—. 2 vols.
Record of judgment creditors, showing name of judgment creditor and debtor, date of judgment, court term, case number, amount of judgment, and volume and page number of dockets and records where entered, including Judgment Docket, entry 96. Arranged alphabetically by names of judgment creditors. Handwritten on printed forms. Average 600 pages. 18 x 1 x 3. Clerk of courts' main office.

98. JUDGMENT INDEX, REVERSE
1906—. 1 vol.
Record of judgment debtors, showing names of judgment debtor and creditor, date

of judgment, court term, case number, Amount and nature of judgment, and volume and page numbers of dockets and records where entered, including Judgment Docket, entry 96. Arranged alphabetically by names of judgment debtors. Handwritten on printed forms. 625 pages. 18 x 12 x 3. Clerk of courts main office.

99. CERTIFICATE Of JUDGMENT DOCKET

1935—. 1 vol. (1). Initiated in 1935.

Record of certificates of judgment to operate as liens, showing title of action, case number, names of judgment creditor and debtor, amount of judgment and cost, name of court, date of judgment, amount of increased costs, date of accrual, date certificate endorsed and returned from county, date of execution and levy, and volume and page numbers of Common Pleas Court Journal, entry 140. Arranged chronologically by dates of judgments. Indexed alphabetically by names of judgment creditors and debtors; for separate index, see entry 95. Typed on printed forms. 500 pages. 18 x 13 x 3. Clerk of courts' main office.

100. LIEN DOCKET

1875—. 3 vols. (1-3).

Docket of liens, showing title of case, names of plaintiff and defendant, and case number, also includes transcripts from Justice of Peace Lien Docket, entry 101, showing date judgment rendered, amount of judgment and cost, date interest on judgment begins, and date transcript filed; cost bills, showing itemized cost of the case, to whom paid, signature of person receiving fee, assignment of judgments by plaintiff, date execution was issued to sheriff, date returned by sheriff, and date of release of judgment. Arranged chronologically by dates transcripts filed. Indexed alphabetically by names of plaintiffs; for separate index, see entry 96. Handwritten on printed forms. Average 500 pages. 18 x 12 x 3. Clerk of courts' main office.

101. JUSTICE OF PEACE LIEN DOCKET

1931—. 5 file boxes (labeled by container case numbers).

Copies of transcripts for liens from justice of peace courts, showing name of justice of peace, plaintiff, defendant, and attorneys for each party, amount of claim, brief of action and procedure, and case number. Arranged numerically by case numbers. For index, see entry 95. Handwritten and typed, some on printed forms. 4.5 x 10.5 x 13. Clerk of courts' private office.

Jury and Witness Records

102. WITNESS AND JURY DOCKET
1846—. 6 vols. (1-6).
Record of witnesses subpoenaed in criminal and civil cases, showing term of court, names of plaintiff and defendant, case number, volume and page numbers of dockets where entered, date and time of trial, name of witnesses for plaintiff and defendant, date subpoena issued, number of days served, mileage, and total fee; also includes list of petit jurors, showing court term, name of jurors, dates subpoena issued, number of days served, mileage, and total fee. Arranged the chronologically by dates of trials. Indexed alphabetically by names of plaintiffs. Handwritten on printed forms. Average 450 pages. 18 x 12 x 2.5 Clerk of courts' main office.

103. BAR DOCKET
1929—. 1 vol.
Record of grand jurors, showing month and term of court, case numbers, names of grand jurors, name of township, number of days served, mileage, and amount paid. Arranged chronologically by court terms. Indexed alphabetically by names of grand jurors; for separate index, see entry 127. Handwritten on printed forms. 110 pages.7 x 13 x 2. Clerk of courts' private office.

104. GRAND JURY WITNESS SUBPOENA
1933—. 4 file boxes (535-537, 563).
Copies of subpoenas for grand jury witnesses, showing name of court, date issued, signature of clerk, and date witnessed by clerk; this form is used to call witnesses and is presented to the clerk in order to obtain witness fees. Arranged chronologically by dates issued. No index. Typed on printed forms. 12 x 5 x 15. Clerk of courts' private office.

105. SUMMONS FOR PETIT JURY
1935—. 1file box
List of grand and petit jurors drawn for jury duty for each term of court, also special venires; petit jurors, showing term of court, date drawn, name and address of juror, names of townships, city wards, date subpoenaed, petit jury list, title of case, and date of trial. Arranged chronologically by court terms. Indexed alphabetically by names of districts and townships. Typed on printed forms. 300 pages. 14 x 16 x 2. Clerk of courts' main office.

106. ANNUAL JURY LISTS
1931—. 1 vol.

Lists of grand and petit jurors drawn for jury duty for each term of court, also special venires; petit jurors, showing term of court, date drawn, name and address of juror, names of townships, city wards, date subpoenaed, petit jury lists, title of case, and date of trial. Arranged chronologically by court terms. Indexed alphabetically by names of districts and townships. Typed on printed forms. 300 pages. 14 x 16 x 2. Clerk of courts' main office.

Motor Vehicles

107. BILLS OF SALE
1921-1937. 25 file boxes (labeled by contained bills of sale numbers). Discontinued, law revised.

Copies of bills of sale and sworn statements of ownership of new and used motor vehicles, showing date of sale, names and addresses of grantor and grantee, make and description of motor vehicle, name of manufacturer, model, type of body, motor number, horsepower, registration date, and bill of sale number; 1935-1937, showing name and license number of vendor. Arranged numerically by bills of sale numbers. For indexes, see entries 108, 109. Handwritten and typed on printed forms. 12 x 14 x 24. Clerk of courts' main office.

108. INDEX TO MOTOR VEHICLE SALES AND STATEMENT OF OWNERSHIP, GRANTOR DIRECT
1921-1937, 5 vols, Title varies: Index to motor vehicles, Grantors Direct, 1921-1925, 1 vol.; Transfer Binder Index to Motor Vehicle Sales and Statement of Ownership, Grantees Direct, 1926-1928, 1 vol.

Direct index to Bills of Sale, entry 107, showing names of grantor and grantee, date of filing, consecutive bill of sale number, amount of fees, description of motor vehicle, and change of ownership. Arranged alphabetically by names of grantors. Handwritten on printed forms. Average 600 pages. 18 x 15 x 3. 3 volumes, 1921-1934, clerk of courts' private office; 2 volumes, 1934-1937, Clerk of courts' main office.

109. INDEX TO MOTOR VEHICLE SALES AND STATEMENT OF OWNERSHIP, GRANTOR REVERSE
1921-1937. 5 vols. Title varies: Index to Motor Vehicles, Grantee reverse,

1921-1925, 1 vol.; Transfer Binder Index to Motor Vehicle Sales and Statement of Ownership, Grantees Reverse, 1926-1928. 1 vol.

Reverse index to Bills of Sale, entry 107, showing names of grantee and grantor, date of filing, consecutive bill of sale number, amount of fees, description of motor vehicle, and changes of ownership. Arranged alphabetically by names of grantees. Handwritten on printed forms. Average 600 pages. 18 x 15 x 3. 3 volumes, 1921-1934, clerk of courts' private office; 2 volumes, 1934-1937, Clerk of courts' main office.

110. CERTIFICATE OF TITLE

1938—. 4 file boxes (labeled by contained certificate numbers).

Copies of certificates of title to new and used motor vehicles, showing date of certificate, names of purchaser and vendor, description of motor vehicle, record of liens, selling price, amount of sales tax, certificate of title number, and date filed. Arranged chronologically by dates filed and also arranged numerically by certificate of title numbers. For separate index, see entry 111. Typed on printed forms. 12 x 14 x 24. Clerk of courts' main office.

111. CARD INDEX TO CERTIFICATE OF TITLE

1928—. 2 file boxes.

Index to Certificate of Title, entry 110, showing consecutive certificate number, names of purchaser and vendor, date filed, and make and description of new or used motor vehicle. Arranged alphabetically by names of purchasers. Typed on printed forms. 5 x 5 x 12. Clerk of courts' main office.

Commissions

112. RECORD OF JUSTICE COMMISSION

1861—. 3 vols. Title varies: Record of Justice's and Mayor's Oaths, 1861-1863, 1 vol.

Record of justices' commissions, showing name of justice of the peace and township, and date of commission; oaths of justices and mayors, showing date of oath, name of attesting official, amount of bond, names of sureties, and date recorded; also mayor's oath, showing date of election. 1861-1883, arranged alphabetically by names of townships and chronologically thereunder by dates of oaths; 1883—, arranged alphabetically by names of officials. No index. Handwritten on printed forms. Average 425 pages. 14 x 9 x 2. 2 volumes, 1861-

1918, clerk of courts' private office; 1 volume, 1818—, clerk of courts' main office.

113. RECORD OF NOTARIES' COMMISSIONS
1880—. 8 vols. (3-5, 5-9).

Copies of commissions granted by governor of state to notaries, showing date of commission, name and oath of notary, signatures of governor and secretary of state, and date recorded. Arranged chronologically by dates recorded. Indexed alphabetically by names of notaries. Handwritten on printed forms. Average 300 pages. 14 x 8 x 1.25. 6 volumes, 1880-1929, Clerk of courts' private office; 2 volumes, 1929—, clerk of courts' main office.

114. RECORD OF RAILROAD POLICEMAN'S COMMISSIONS
1888—. 2 vols.

Record of commissions granted to appointees by governor of state to act as railroad policemen, showing date of commission, name of railroad, signature of governor, and date recorded. Arranged chronologically by dates of commissions. No index. Handwritten on printed forms. Average 178 pages. 16 x 11 x 1. Clerk of courts' private office.

Licenses

115. EMBALMERS' LICENSE RECORD
1908-1917. 1 vol.

Copies of certificates issued to applicants by state board of embalming examiners, granting license to embalm, showing name and address of licensee, license number, and dates issued and recorded. Arranged chronologically by dates recorded. Indexed alphabetically by names of licensees. Handwritten on printed forms. 200 pages. 16 x 12 x 2. Clerk of courts' private office.

116. RECORD OF HUNTERS' LICENSES
1908—. 5 vols.

Record of hunting licenses issued to resident and nonresident applicants, showing name, age, occupation, and place of residence of licensee, personal description, date of issue, license number, and amount of fee. Arranged alphabetically by names of licensees and chronologically thereunder by dates issued. No index. Handwritten on printed forms. Average 152 pages. 16 x 12 x 1.25. 3 volumes, 1908-1928, clerk of courts' private office; 1 volume, 1928—, Clerk of courts' main office.

117. FISHING LICENSE RECORD
1919—. 1 vol.
Record of fishing licenses issued by clerk of courts, showing date of issue, license number, name, address, age, sex, physical description, and occupation of licensee, and amount of fee paid. Arranged chronologically by dates issued. No index. Handwritten on printed forms. 200 pages. 16 x 12 x 2. Clerk of courts' private office.

118. OPTOMETRISTS' REGISTER
1920—. 1 vol.
Record of licenses granted by the state board of optometry to practice and the state of Ohio, showing names of optometrists, president, and secretary of state board of optometry, and date of filing. Arranged chronologically by dates filed. Indexed alphabetically by names of optometrists. Handwritten on printed forms. 104 pages. 14 x 9 x 1. Clerk of courts' private office.

119. REGISTER Of REAL ESTATE BROKERS
1936—. 1 vol.
Record of licenses granted real estate brokers, showing license number, name and address of licensee, classification for brokers and salesmen, date license issued, date of cancellation, revocation, or suspension, and amount of fee. Arranged chronologically by dates issued. No index. Handwritten on printed forms. 60 pages. 14 x 18 x .5. Clerk of courts' main office.

Partnerships

120. REGISTER Of PARTNERSHIP
1894—. 1 vol.
Register of partners and partnerships, showing names of partners and firm, business address, date of filing, and certificate number. Arranged alphabetically by names of partners. No index. Handwritten on printed forms. 200 pages. 14 x 12 x 1. Clerk of courts' main office.

Coroner's Inquest

121. INQUEST DOCKET
1901—. 1 vol.
Docket of inquest, showing inquest number, date of inquest, name, color, race, sex, nativity, condition of body, and cause of death of decedent, date of post mortem examination, names of coroner holding inques andt examining physician, and amount of fees. Arranged chronologically by dates of inquest. Indexed alphabetically by names of decedents. Handwritten on printed forms. 200 pages. 16 x 11 x 1. Clerk of courts' private office.

Financial Records

122. CLERK'S CASH BOOK
1870—. 26 vols. (1-26).
Record of fines and fees collected by the clerk of courts, showing date received, service rendered, docket number of original entry, case number, name of payer, total amount, and amount due to county, sheriff, witnesses, jury, and sundry fund; also disbursements, showing date paid, name of payee, amount of disbursements, services rendered, check number, and page number of Record of Accrues Fees, 1907-1925. Entry 123. Arranged chronologically by dates received. No index. Handwritten on printed forms. Average 175 pages. 17 x 17 x 1.5. Clerk of courts' main office.

123. RECORD OF ACCRUED FEES
1907-1925. 3 vols.
Record of accrued fees, showing date of accrual, case number, to whom charged, total amount and date of payment, amount due from county, civil and criminal cases, transcripts and copies, certificates, sundries, and date paid and classified as to source. Arranged chronologically by dates accrued, No index .Handwritten on printed forms. Average 200 pages. 18 x 12 x 1.5. Clerk of courts' main office.

124. UNCLAIMED MONEYS
1906—. 1 vol.
Record of unclaimed money paid into county treasury by clerk of courts for unclaimed fees due to witnesses and jurors, showing date of entry, to whom money belongs, amount of money, volumes and page numbers of witness and Jury Docket,

entry 102, date paid into treasury, and date certificate issued to owner for recovery. Arranged chronologically by dates entered. No index. Handwritten on printed forms. Average 275 pages. 14 x 8.5 x 8.5. Clerk of courts' main office.

125. ALIMONY RECORD
1909—. 3 vols.

Clerk of courts' record of alimony payments, showing name of plaintiff and defendant, case number, amount and date of monthly payment, and check number. Arranged chronologically by dates of payments. Indexed alphabetically by names of plaintiffs; for separate index, see entry 95. Handwritten on printed forms. Average 240 pages. 15 x 12 x 2. Clerk of courts' private office.

Miscellaneous

126. RECEIPTS FOR PAPERS
1924—. 1 vol.

Record of court papers which have been removed from files, showing title of case, date and by whom removed, case number, and date returned. Arranged chronologically by dates removed. No index. Handwritten on printed forms. 250 pages. 10 x 12 x 2. Clerk of courts' main office.

The court of common pleas, like many other county institutions, originated in England during the reign of Henry II.[1] Established in America during the colonial period, the office was continued by the states following the War of American Independence.

The Northwest Ordinance of 1787 established a government consisting of a governor, a secretary, and three judges all appointed by congress. The judges were to form a court, known as a general court, which had common law jurisdiction and together with the governor was authorized to draw up a code of civil and criminal law. The territorial act of 1788, establishing the American Colonial policy in the newer West in respect to the judiciary, contained sections authorizing the establishment in each county of a common pleas court to be composed of not less than three nor more than five members. These members appointed and commissioned by the territorial governor, were given jurisdiction in all civil matters.[2] The same act established in each county a primary court called the court of general quarter sessions of the peace to be composed of not more than five nor less than three justices of the peace, appointed and commissioned by the governor.[3] This court, which had limited jurisdiction in criminal matters, was not reestablished by the constitution of 1802 and the jurisdiction which had been exercised by this court was conferred upon the justice of the peace and the court of common pleas.[4]

When a constitution was drafted for Ohio in 1802, preparatory to the entrance of the state into the Union, provision was made for a Continuation of the territorial court of common pleas.[5] The articles of the Ohio Constitution, regarding the courts and judiciary, provide for a court of common pleas in each county to be composed of a president and associate judges. For each county[6] not more than three nor less than two associate judges were to be appointed, with one president for each of the three judicial districts into which the counties were grouped. The associate judges were not as a rule men who had a legal education.[7]

---

1. George Burton Adams, *Constitutional History of England* (New York, 1921), 109, 134.
2. Pease, *op. cit.*, 7.
3. *Ibid.*, 4.
4. *Ibid.*, 5; *Laws of Ohio*, I, 40; II, 235.
5. *Ohio Const. 1802,* Art. III, sec. 1.
6. At this time there were nine counties in the state.
7. Francis J. Amer, *The Development of Judicial System in Ohio from 1787 to 1932* (John Hopkins University, Baltimore, 1932. *Institute of Law Bulletin Number 8*), 17.

The members of the court, appointed by joint ballot of both houses of the general assembly, were to hold court and three judicial districts into which the state was to be divided by legislative action. Their term of office was seven years, "If so long they behaved well."[8]

It was almost half a century before any significant changes were made in the structure of the court. The constitution of 1851 provided that judges of the common pleas court were to be elected for a five-year term. For the purpose of their election the state was divided into nine districts composed of three or more counties. Each district, in turn, was to be subdivided into three parts, in each of which one common pleas judge was to be elected. The court of common pleas was to be held by one or more of these judges in each county in the district.[9] Power was given to the general assembly to increase or diminish the number of districts of the court of common pleas, the number of judges in any district and to change the districts or the subdivisions thereof, whenever two-thirds of the members of the legislature concurred therein.[10] Provisions was also made for the removal of judges by concurrent resolution at two-thirds of the members elected to each house of legislature.[11] An appellate court known as the district court was created, and was to be composed of one supreme court judge and the several common pleas judges of the district. This court was to be held in each county of the district at least once in each year or at least three annual sessions in not less than three places.[12] The district courts were not a success, and after many attempts at revision the circuit courts, staffed by a separate group of elected judges, were adopted by vote of the people in 1883, thus relieving the common pleas judge of this appellate work.[13]

The juvenile court was created in 1904 with jurisdiction and special matters relating to minors and was to be held by a judge of the court of common pleas, court of insolvency, or probate court who should be designated by the judges to hold such court.[14]

---

8. *Ohio Const. 1802*, Art. III, sec. 8.
9. *Ibid.,* 1851, Art. IV, secs, 3, 4.
10. *Ibid.*, Art. IV, sec. 15.
11. *Ibid.*, Art. IV, sec. 17.
12. *Ibid.*, Art. IV, secs. 5, 6.
13. Amer, *op. cit.*, 31-33: *Laws of Ohio,* LXXXI, 168.
14. *Laws of Ohio*, XCVII, 562.

At the opening of the twentieth century sweeping changes in the organization the courts were made. Constitutional amendments adopted in 1912 abolished the divisions and subdivisions of the court of common pleas provided by the constitution of 1851, and authorized the election of one or more common pleas judges in each case.[15] The chief justice of supreme court was given authority to determine the disability or disqualification of any judge of the court of common pleas and also to assign any judge to hold court in any county.[16] Eleven years later the selection of a chief justice of the court of common pleas was authorized. Under an act of March 13, 1923, in counties having two or more common pleas judges, a chief justice was designated by vote of the judges. The justice so designated by his colleagues was to serve in such capacity until the expiration of his term, after which time the office was to be an elective one.[17] The elective section of the act was nullified in effect in 1924 by the supreme court on the grounds that the creation of the new elective office was unconstitutional. Accordingly, in 1927 an amendment was passed eliminating the elective provision of the act.[18]

In recent years attempts have been made to improve the efficiency of the court by imposing stricter qualifications upon those who seek election to the bench. In 1917 an act was passed providing that a common pleas judge shall have been admitted to practice as an attorney at law for a period of six years proceeding his election.[19] More over, the salary of the office was increased to $3,000 per year plus an amount based on the population of the county[20] – thus making the position financially attractive, especially as the term of office is six years.[21] In addition to the regular salaries, common please judges may be paid a per diem allowance and expenses when assigned to special duty by the chief justice of the supreme court in a district not their own. When dockets become crowded or judges are incapacitated or disqualified, such assignments may be made.[22]

---

15. *Ohio Const. 1851*, Art. IV, sec. 3.
16. *Ohio Const. 1851* Art. IV, secs. 3, 6.
17. *Laws of Ohio*, CX, 52.
18. *State ex rel. v. Powell, Ohio State Reports*, CIX, 383; *Laws of Ohio*, CXII, 5; G. C. sec. 1558.
19. *Laws of Ohio*, CVII, 164.
20. G. C. secs. 2251, 2252.
21. G. C. sec. 1532.
22. *Ohio Const. 1851* (Amendment, 1912), Art. IV, sec. 3; G. C. secs. 1469, 1687, 2253.

In the more populous counties, judicial efficiency is promoted by assigning to certain common pleas judges specialized duties such as the hearing of domestic relations and juvenile court cases.

The jurisdiction of the court of common pleas has also been the product of a long period of historical development. The territorial law of 1788 which created the court provided that "the judges so appointed and commissioned ... shall hold pleas of *assizes, scire facias, replevins,* and hear and determine all manner of pleas, actions, suits, and causes of a civil nature, real, personal, and mixed, according to the constitution and laws of the territory."[23] Individually each judge of the court of common pleas was given jurisdiction over contract action not exceeding $5.[24] The probate court was established by an act adopted August 30, 1788, and two other judges of the court by common pleas sat with this judge in ruling on contested points, definitive sentences, and final judgments. Under the laws of 1788 the common pleas had no criminal jurisdiction, and the court of quarter sessions of the peace had no civil jurisdiction. There was no provision for an appeal from one court to another except from the probate court to the general court of the territory.[25]

In 1795 the judicial system underwent the first general revision and this increased the duties of the court of common pleas. Single justice of the peace or judge of the common pleas was given jurisdiction to hear certain civil actions up to $12. Actions under $5 were exclusive with the judges or justices and there was no appeal from their judgment. Actions involving amounts between $5 and $12 could be appealed to the court of common pleas. In 1799 this jurisdiction was raised to $20, and appeals could be taken to the common pleas if the judgment was over $2. If the judgment was for the plaintiff, he could appeal only if the original demand was $4 more than the sum recovered.[26] Appeal from the common pleas to the general court was provided for in 1795, but could not be taken unless the title to land was in question or the amount in controversy exceeded $50.[27]

---

23. Salmon P. Chase, ed., *The Statutes of Ohio and of the Northwest Territory, 1788-1833* (Cincinnati, 1833), I, 94.
24. Pease, *op. cit.*, 8.
25. Chase, *op. cit.*, I, 96.
26. *Ibid.*, I, 143, 233, 307.
27. *Ibid.*, I, 306.

The constitution of 1802 gave the court of common pleas jurisdiction in such common law and chancery cases as should be directed by law. In addition it was given jurisdiction of all probate and testamentary matters, and the appointment and supervision of guardians.[28] Moreover, the court of common pleas and the supreme court were assigned original cognizance of criminal cases as might be provided by law.[29] By statutory provision in 1804 appeals in civil cases might be made to the court of common pleas from the county commissioners, and from the justices of the peace and other inferior courts.[30]

An act of the first general assembly in 1803 provided for the organization of the courts and defined their jurisdiction. The court of common pleas was assigned original jurisdiction in all cases, both in law and equity, when the matter in dispute exceeded the jurisdiction of the justices of the peace of all probate, testamentary, and guardianship matters; and of all criminal matters exceeding the jurisdiction of the justices of peace, except when the punishment of the crime was capital. It was allowed to review certain cases from the justice of peace and also to review the decisions of the county commissioners in highway matters. In addition, the court had the same power to issue the remedial and other process, writs of error and mandamus excepted, as had the supreme court.[31] In 1804 the courts jurisdiction in chancery cases was limited to cases involving less than $500,[32] and in 1805 it was given appellate jurisdiction from the justices of peace in all cases regardless of the amount involved.[33] In 1806 crimes wherein the punishment was capital could be tried in the common pleas court if the accused so elected.[34] In 1807 it was given jurisdiction and all chancery cases and concurred jurisdiction with the supreme court in such cases involving over $500.[35] In 1810 all cases in which the common pleas had original jurisdiction were permitted to be appealed to the supreme court.[36]

---

29. *Ibid.*, Art. III, sec. 4.
30. Chase, *op. cit.*, I, 421, 425.
31. *Ibid.*, I, 355.
32. *Laws of Ohio*, II, 261.
33. *Ibid.*, III, 14.
34. *Ibid.*, IV, 57.
35. *Ibid.*, V, 117.
36. *Ibid.*, VIII, 259.

By this act the right to appeal was established in Ohio and all civil cases. However, the business of the supreme court increased so rapidly that in 1845 the right to appeal of judgment of common pleas court to the supreme court in actions that law was limited. Instead, new trials were allowed "when law and justice required it."[37] Even earlier, appeals to the common pleas for material courts had been limited.[38] The chancery act, adopted in 1824, conferred general chancery powers on the court,[39] and in 1843 it was given concurrent jurisdiction with the supreme court in cases of divorce and alimony.[40]

The constitution of 1851 left the jurisdiction of the court of common pleas to be fixed by law.[41] The jurisdiction conferred on this court by subsequent legislation was essentially the same as that exercised since 1810, with the exception of the jurisdiction which transferred to the probate court,[42] and the addition, in 1853, of exclusive jurisdiction in divorce and alimony cases.[43] The court of common pleas was denied jurisdiction in case of probate, just testamentary, and guardianship matters, but final orders, judgments, and decrees of probate court could be reviewed in common pleas on appeal or by *writ* of *certiorari*.[44] In 1853 the court of common pleas was given original jurisdiction of all crimes and offenses except minor criminal cases, the exclusive jurisdiction of which was vested in the justice of peace or other minor courts.[45]

The creation of criminal, mayors', and police courts also made certain changes in the powers and duties of common pleas courts.[46]

---

37. *Ibid.*, XLIII, 80.
38 *Ibid.*, XXXVIII, 27.
39. *Ibid.*,XXII, 75.
40. *Ibid.*, XLI, 94.
41. *Ohio Const. 1851*, Art. Iv, secs. 3, 4.
42. *Laws of Ohio*, L, 87. Records pertaining to probate matters were to be transferred to the probate court wherever it was possible to separate them from common pleas records. *Ibid..*, 88.
43. *Ibid.*,, 377.
44. *Laws of Ohio*, 84; 145.
45. G. C. sec. 13422-5; *Laws of Ohio*, LI, 474; LII,73.
46. *Laws of Ohio*, L, 90, 240, 246, 251, 253.

The right to appeal from common pleas to the district court was restored in all civil actions in which the common pleas had original jurisdiction,[47] but by an act of 1858 appeals were allowed to the immediate court only in nonjury cases. However, the same act provided for a second jury trial in common pleas as a matter of right in injury cases. This was granted upon demand made by either party at the close of the first trial on condition of his giving bond.[48] The abuse of this privilege led to its abolition1875.[49]

This period witnessed the reestablishment of supreme courts in the state, which were given the same jurisdiction as the courts of common pleas with certain exceptions.[50] At the same time as a superior court was established at Cincinnati, the legislature abolished the criminal court and transferred its jurisdiction to the common pleas court.[51] The criminal jurisdiction of the probate court was transferred to the common pleas court in 1857.[52] A limitation was placed on the right to appeal from probate court to common pleas in 1854.[53] This limitation was repealed, however, in 1856.[54]

For many years there were few changes in the powers of the court of common pleas except in the forms of appeal to higher courts,[55] and such added powers as resulted from the decline in a number of superior courts.[56] In 1906 the probate court was given concurrent jurisdiction with common pleas in all counties in the trial of misdemeanors and all proceedings to prevent crime.[57]

Since 1906 the court of common pleas has had jurisdiction in naturalization proceedings. In that year the federal statute was amended to limit jurisdiction in the granting of naturalization to the United States district courts and state courts having a clerk, a seal, and jurisdiction in matters of law and equity in which the amount of controversy is unlimited.[58]

---

47. *Ibid.*, 93.
48. *Ibid.*, LV, 81.
49. *Ibid.*, LXXII, 34.
50. *Ibid.*, LII, 34; LIII, 38; LIV, 37.
51. *Ibid.*, LII, 107.
52. *Ibid.*, LIV, 97.
53. *Ibid.*, LII, 104.
54. *Ibid.*, LIII, 8.
55. *Ibid.*, LXXXIV, 359; LXXXII, 230.
56. *Ibid.*, LXII, 58; LXXII, 89, 105; LXXXII, 85.
57. *Ibid.*, XCVIII, 49.
58. *United States Statutes at Large*, XXXIV, pt. I, 596.

Constitutional amendments adopted in 1912 had little effect upon the jurisdiction of the court of common pleas, this power being determined by law.[59] In 1911 the juvenile courts were given jurisdiction of all misdemeanors against minors and certain other offenses.[60] Provision was also made for error proceedings from juvenile court to the court of common pleas.[61] The jurisdiction of the common pleas court of today is essentially the same as that of 1913. The few changes that have been made in the judicial system are found in the local, special courts, particularly in the rapidly developing municipal courts.

The court of common pleas has never exercised extensive appointee powers. However, the constitution of 1802 authorized each court to appoint a clerk,[62] and the court was authorized by law in 1803 to appoint a surveyor, a treasurer, and a recorder.[63] An act of 1805 directed the court to appoint a prosecuting attorney.[64] The movement for the extension of the popular election of public officials during the first three decades of Ohio history deprived the court of common pleas of the privilege of appointing the county recorder in 1829, the county surveyor in 1831, and the county prosecuting attorney in 1833, though it continued to appoint the clerk of courts until 1851.[65] As new functions were added to county government the court was again given limited appointee power. Successive acts in 1886, 1891, 1913, 1914, and 1925 authorized the court to appoint a soldiers' relief commission, a jury commission, an assignment commissioner, a conservancy district board, and a probation officer.[66] In 1882 the court was empowered to appoint a board of accounting visitors but this power was transferred to the probate court in 1906.[67]

---

59. *Ohio Const. 1851*, Art. IV, sec. 6.
60. *Ibid.*, CII, 452.
61. *Ibid.*, CIII, 875.
62. *Ohio Const. 1802*, Art. III, sec. 9.
63. *Laws of Ohio*, I, 90, 98, 136. A year later the power of appointing the treasurer was transferred to the county commissioners. *Ibid.*, 154.
64. *Ibid.*, III, 47.
65. *Ibid.*, XXVII, 65; XXIX, 13; *Ohio Const. 1851*, Art. IV, sec. 16.
66. *Laws of Ohio*, LXXXIII, 232; LXXXVIII, 200; CIII, 512; CIV, 13-64; CXI, 423.
67. *Ibid.*, LXXIX, 107; XCVIII, 28.

Other appointments authorized are those of court interpreter and criminal bailiff (1911),[68] inspectors of meetings of corporation stockholders, trustees for county memorial buildings, boards of trustees or endowed libraries, and one member of the metropolitan housing authority in such counties as maintain these agencies.[69] The court may also appoint a court reporter (or reports),[70] and may cooperate with the county commissioners for the establishment of a county department of probation, in which case the court appoints certain probation officers and supervises their work.[71] In case the sheriff is absent, disabled, or disqualified from serving the court's warrant, the judge may appoint temporarily an official for this service.[72] By and large, however, the patronage power of the court of common pleas is a negotiable factor in county government.

Since 1805 the court has been authorized to issue ferry Licenses[73] and tavern keepers licenses.[74] Both ferry and tavern licenses may now be issued by municipal corporation also and the latter by the state fire marshal.[75] From 1803 to 1852 this court also aged licenses to ministers to solemnize marriage ceremonies; this function has since been exercised by the probate court.[76]

The keeping of records of the common pleas court presented no particular difficulties for many decades. However, with the increased number of issues presented to the court in recent years, the problem of judicial administration has become greater. This problem was solved in part by the creation of the office of chief justice of the court of common pleas who has been given the duties of superintending the business of the court, classifying it, and distributing it among the judges. Besides the duties enumerated, the chief justice annually makes a report to the clerk of courts showing the work performed by the court and by each judge in the proceeding calendar year. Moreover, he reports such other data as the chief justice of the supreme court may require.[77]

---

68. G. C. sec. 1541.
69. *Laws of Ohio*, LXXXIV, 115; XCV, 41; CVI, 458; pt. ii, 56.
70. G. C. secs. 1546-1554.
71. G. C. secs. 1554-1 - 1554-6.
72. G. C. sec. 2828.
73. *Laws of Ohio*, III, 96; G. C. secs. 5947, 5949.
74. *Laws of Ohio*, III, 96; XXIX, 310.
75. G. C. secs. 3642, 3672, 843-3 .
76. *Laws of Ohio*, I, 31; L, 84.
77. G. C. sec. 1558.

Judges of the common pleas court are also required to issue an annual order as to the exact time of sessions. The clerk of courts is required to make this information public and to send a copy to the secretary of state. The law sets certain requirements as to the sessions of the court and the power of the judge to call special sessions.[78] The records of the court are deposited for safekeeping with the clerk of courts. The clerk is custodian also of all law reports and books furnished by the state for the use of the court and the bar and is made liable in the event of their destruction.[79]

This court in Ashland County is presided over by but one judge, whose salary is $3806 annually, $806 of which is paid by the county.[80] During the year 1940, this court heard 47 civil cases, 22 criminal cases,[81] 7 petitions for naturalization,[82] and granted 80 divorces.[83] A clerk from the clerk of courts office is usually in attendance, as well as a bailiff.

---

78. G. C. secs. 1533-1539.
79. *Laws of Ohio*, LXVIII, 109.
80. Commissioners' Record, XXVI (1939-1940), 512.
81. Appearance Docket, 1940, entry 128.
82. Naturalization Record–Petition and Record, 1940, entry 133.
83. Appearance Docket, 1940, entry 128.

Civil Cases

127. GENERAL INDEX TO COMMON PLEAS
1846—. 3 vols. (1-3).

General index to Appearance Docket, entry 128; Bar Docket, entry 104; Court Docket, entry 138; Criminal Appearance Docket, entry 134; Motion Docket, 139; Common Pleas Court Journal, entry 140; Treasury Record, entry 131; Law Record, entry 129; Bench Docket, entry 88; and Execution Docket, entry 94 showing names of plaintiff and defendant, case number, and volume and page numbers of record. Arranged alphabetically by names of plaintiffs and defendants. Handwritten on printed forms. Average 600 pages. 18 x 12 x 3.5. Clerk of courts' main office.

128. APPEARANCE DOCKET
1946—. 43 vols. (1-43).

Copies of instruments and proceedings in common pleas court civil cases, showing term of court, names of plaintiff and defendant, case number, date case file, names of attorneys, title of case, dates of instruments, and date of sheriff's return. Also contains Criminal Appearance Docket, 1846-1907, entry 134. Arranged chronologically by dates filed. Indexed alphabetically by names of plaintiffs and defendants; for separate index, see entry 127. Handwritten on printed forms. Average 575 pages. 18 x 12 x 3. Clerk of courts' main office.

129. LAW RECORD
1846—. 80 vols. (1-80).

Final record of civil cases heard in county court, showing case number, names of plaintiff and defendant, title of case, names of attorneys, date in case filed, and complete history of proceedings and disposition; also includes final record in divorce cases, 1847—. Arranged chronologically by dates file. Indexed alphabetically by names of plaintiffs and defendants; for separate index, see entry 127. 1846-1905, Handwritten on printed forms. 1905—, Typed on printed forms. Average 600 pages. 18 x 12 x 3. 10 volumes, 1846-1860, clerk of courts' private office; 70 volumes, 1861—, clerk of courts' main office.

130. COMMON PLEAS COURT RECORD
1847-1852. 1 vol.

Record of cases tried before common pleas court, showing the term of court, case number, names of plaintiff and defendant, kind of case, and date and disposition of case. All cases entered are regarding cognovit and other notes, showing date of note, and amount. Arranged chronologically by court terms. Indexed alphabetically by names of plaintiffs. Handwritten. 100 pages. 12 x 8 x 1. Storage room vault, office, secretary, Ohio State School for Blind, Main Street and Parsons Avenue, Columbus, Ohio.

131. CHANCERY RECORD
1846—. 3 vols. (1-3).
Complete record of chancery cases, showing names of plaintiff and defendant, date case filed, case number, term of court, names of attorneys, dates of hearings, facts presented, amount of cost, from whom due, and disposition of case. Arranged chronologically by court terms. Indexed alphabetically by names of plaintiffs; for separate index, see entry 127. Handwritten on printed forms. Average 600 pages. 18 x 12 x 2.5. Clerk of courts' main office.

Naturalization

132. NATURALIZATION (First Papers)
1818-1911. 3 file boxes.
Original papers and declarations of intentions to become naturalized citizens of the United States, showing names of court, county, and alien, age, occupation, race, complexion, height, weight, color of hair and eyes, and other visible distinctive marks of the applicant, date and place of birth, present address, date arrived in the United States, last foreign residence, marital status, oath of allegiance, and signatures of alien, and clerk of common pleas court. Papers, 1818-1846, are first papers originally filed and those counties the which Ashland was formed. No obvious arrangement. No index. Handwritten on printed forms. 10 x 1.5 x 13.5. 1 file box, 1818-1840, basement storage room; 2 file boxes, 1840-1911, Clerk of courts' private office.

133. NATURALIZATION RECORDS– PETITION AND RECORD
1906—. 2 vols.
Copies of petitions of aliens to become citizens of the United States, showing name of court, county, and alien, place of residence, occupation, dates of petition and birth, marital status, complete personal description, affidavits of citizens of United States affirming petition of aliens, date arrived, oath of allegiance, signatures of aliens, witnesses and clerk of courts. Arranged chronologically by dates petitions

entered. Indexed alphabetically by names of aliens. Handwritten on printed forms. Average 300 pages. 20 x 12 x 1.5. Clerk of courts' main office.

Criminal Cases

134. CRIMINAL APPEARANCE DOCKET

1908—. 3 vols. (1-3). 1846-1907 in Appearance Docket, entry 128.

Docket of criminal cases in common pleas court, showing date case filed, name of defendant, charge, dates and copies of instruments pertaining to case, case number, title of case, and amount of cost. Arranged chronologically by dates filed. Indexed alphabetically by names of defendants; for separate index, see entry 127. Handwritten on printed forms. Average 490 pages. 18 x 12 x 3. Clerk of courts' main office.

135. INDEX TO CRIMINAL AND CIVIL CASES

1846—. 2 vols. (1, 2).

Index to criminal and civil cases, showing case numbers, names of litigants, names of attorneys, court term, case numbers of Criminal Cases, entry 92, and Index to Pending Suits, Living Judgments and Executions, entry 95, kind of action, offense charged, date transcript from magistrate's court filed, date and amount of recognizance, names of sureties, date indictment return, dates of plea, verdict of court, and sentence. Index to Civil Actions and Divorce, entry 91; Criminal Cases, entry 92; Criminal Records, entry 136; Criminal Cases, entry 137; and Petitions–Closed Cases, entry 93. For all details of action taken, see under column headings labeled civil, criminal, or circuit court by case numbers. Arranged alphabetically by names of defendants, showing names of plaintiffs and chronologically thereunder by dates filed. Average 600 pages. 18 x 12 x 3.5. Clerk of courts' private office.

136. CRIMINAL RECORD

1846—. 3 vols. (1-3).

Complete record of criminal cases in common pleas court, showing name of defendant, title of case, case number, date case filed, charge, term of court, history of case, and amount of court costs and fines. Arranged chronologically by dates filed. Indexed alphabetically by names of defendants; for separate index, see entry 135. 1846-1920, Handwritten on printed forms; 1921—, typed on printed forms. Average 500 pages. 18 x 12 x 3. Clerk of courts' main office.

137. CRIMINAL CASES

1931—. 1 file box.

Papers of criminal cases from justice of peace courts, showing case number, name of defendant, charge, plea, and name of justice of peace. Papers include indictments, warrants for arrest to convey, cost bills, and volume and page numbers of criminal appearance docket, entry 134. Arranged alphabetically by names of defendants. For index, see entry 135. Typed on printed forms. 10 x 12 x 30. Clerk of courts' main office.

General Court Proceedings

138. COURT DOCKET

1894-1932. 60 vols. (1-60).

Docket of common pleas court cases, showing case number, kind of case, date of filing, names of plaintiff and defendant, title of case, names of attorneys, date of trial, dates and record of orders issued, volume and page numbers of Bench Docket, entry 88, and Common Pleas Court Journal, entry 140. Arranged chronologically by dates filed and also arranged numerically by case numbers. Indexed alphabetically by names of plaintiffs; for separate index, see entry 127. Handwritten on printed forms. Average 100 pages. 18 x 12 x .5. 1 volume, 1912-1919, clerk of courts' private office; 59 volumes, 1894-1912, 1919-1932, basement storage room.

139. MOTION DOCKET
1889—. 7 vols. (1-7).

Docket of motions in common pleas court cases, showing case number, date of motion, names of plaintiff and defendant, names of attorneys, kind of action, and dates and record of orders of the court. Arranged chronologically by dates of motions. Indexed alphabetically by names of plaintiffs; for separate index, see entry 127. Handwritten on printed forms. Average 150 pages. 16 x 12 x 2. 4 volumes, 1898-1924, basement storage room; 3 volumes, 1924—, Clerk of courts' main office.

140. COMMON PLEAS COURT JOURNAL
1846—. 35 vols. (1-35).

Copies of journal entries in common pleas court cases, showing term of court, case number, names of plaintiff and defendant, title of case, date case filed, names of attorneys, kind of case, and dates and record of court orders. Arranged chronologically by dates filed. Indexed alphabetically by names of plaintiffs; for separate index, see entry 127. 1846-1909, handwritten; 1909—, typed. Average 600 pages. 18 x 12 x 3. Clerk of courts' main office.

The first constitution of Ohio provided for a supreme court consisting of three judges appointed by a joint ballot of the legislature for a seven-year term. This court was required to hold sessions at least once a year in each county.[1] The number of judges, according to constitutional provisions, might be increased to four after a period of five years, in which case the judges were permitted to divide the state into two circuits. Accordingly, in 1808, the membership of the court was increased to four and the state was divided into the requisite number of circuits.[2] Two years later, in 1810, the membership of the court was reduced to three;[3] in 1824 it was again increased to four.[4]

By constitutional provision, this court was given original appellate jurisdiction "both in common law and chancery," in such cases as shall be provided by law.[5] Accordingly, by statutory provision, the court was assigned exclusive cognizance of all cases of divorce and alimony and concurrent jurisdiction of all civil cases both of law and equity where the title to land was in question, or the matter and dispute exceeded $1000; and appellate jurisdiction from the court of common pleas "in all cases respecting the title of lands, or where the matter in controversy exceeds the value of one thousand dollars, and all cases were the proof of validity of wills or the right of administration shall be in question."[6] During the first half century of Ohio history the legislature granted decrees of the divorce. Although the constitution of 1802 did not prohibit the legislature from exercising such jurisdiction, the supreme court prohibited the practice in 1847.[7] The constitution of 1851, Article IV, section 32, contained a prohibiting clause. Moreover, the court was given original cognizance in the trial of capital offenses.[8] All cases in which the title to land or freehold was in question were to be tried in the county where the land was situated. Furthermore, the court was given appellate jurisdiction in the court of common pleas in all cases in which the court of common pleas had original jurisdiction.[9]

---

1. *Ohio Const. 1802*, Art. III, secs. 2, 8, 10.
2. *Laws of Ohio*, VI, 34.
3. *Ibid.*, VIII, 259.
4. *Ibid.*, XXII, 50.
5. *Ohio Const. 1802,* Art. III sec. 2.
6. *Laws of Ohio,* I, 36-37; XIV, 310.
7. *Bingham v. Miller, Ohio Reports*, XVII, 445.
8. *Laws of Ohio*, I, 36-37.
9. *Ibid.*, XIV, 310-354.

In 1831 the supreme court was directed to meet annually in the town of Columbus for the final adjudication of all such questions of law as may have been reserved in any county for decision. This session of the court, known as the court in banc, was required to have its decisions and each case reduced to writing, and transmitted to the clerk of the supreme court in each county in which such question was reserved. The clerk was directed to enter such decisions "on the journal of the said court" and such proceedings were to be taken as if such decisions had been made in the county.[10] Six years later, in 1837, an act was passed providing that the final judgments in the supreme court, held within any county within the state, could be reexamined and reversed or affirmed in the court in banc upon a *writ* of error.[11] This judicial arrangement continued until the adoption of the constitution of 1851, which provided a judicial system modeled upon the federal system existing at that time. The supreme court, as established in 1851, became for the first time in Ohio history, a reviewing court of last resort in the state and ceased to function as a circuit court convening in each county.[12]

The opinions of the supreme court on circuit and the decisions of the court in banc, as transmitted to the clerk of the supreme court and each county, are in the offices of the respective clerks of courts.

---

10. *Laws Ohio*, XXIV, 93-94.
11. *Ibid.*, XXXV, 60-62.
12. G. C. sec. 13422-5; *Laws of Ohio*, LI; LII, 72.

141. SUPREME COURT JOURNAL

1846-1852. 1 vol. (1).

Journal entries of cases heard in supreme court, showing names of plaintiff and defendant, date of entry, cost bill in case, kind of case, and disposition. Also contains District Court Journal, 1851-1852, entry 144. Arranged chronologically by dates entered. Indexed alphabetically by names of plaintiffs. Handwritten. 600 pages. 18 x 12 x 3. Clerk of courts' private office.

142. SUPREME COURT RECORD

1846-1854. 1 vol. (1).

Record of cases heard in supreme court, showing court term, names of plaintiff and defendant, kind of case, date filed, names of attorneys, date of trial and disposition of case. Also contains District Court Record, 1852-1854, entry 145. Arranged chronologically by date filed. Indexed alphabetically by names of plaintiffs. Handwritten on printed forms. 600 pages. 16 x 10 x 3. Clerk of courts' main office.

Until 1851 the judicial power of the State of Ohio in matters of both law and equity was vested in the supreme court, the court of common pleas, and the justices' courts.[1] During the first 50 years of Ohio history the supreme court served as a court of appeals, holding court in each county annually.[2] When a new constitution was adopted in 1851 the judicial system was extended by the creation of district courts composed of one supreme court justice and several common pleas judges in the district. These courts were assigned original jurisdiction in the same matters as a supreme court, and such "appellate jurisdiction" as might be provided by law.[3] Thus by constitutional provision the courts were assigned original cognizance in *quo warranto, mandamus, habeas corpus,* and *procendedo*.[4] In addition to this, in 1852 the legislature authorized the courts to issue writs of error, *certiorari, supersedeas, ne exeat*, and all other writs not specifically provided by statute, whenever such writs were necessary for the exercise of its jurisdiction. The same act gave the courts appellate jurisdiction from the court of common pleas in civil cases wherein the latter court had original jurisdiction.[5]

For the purposes of the district courts the nine common pleas districts were apportioned into five judicial districts. A judge of the supreme court was designated to preside at the sessions of the district courts; in the event that no judge of the supreme court was present, as was often the case, the judge of the court of common pleas in whose subdivision court was being held, was directed to preside.[6]

The district courts failed to function properly. Evidence seemed to indicate that the increasing number of cases coming before the supreme court made it difficult for the justices to attend the meetings of the district courts. Indeed, six years before the creation of the district courts, the supreme court dockets were overcrowded. In 1845 the general assembly found it necessary to afford temporary relief by limiting appeals from the courts of common pleas to the supreme court.[7]

---

1. *Ohio Const. 1802*, Art. III, sec. 1.
2. *See* p. 81.
3. *Ohio Const. 1851*, Art. IV, secs, 5, 6.
4. *Ibid.*, Art. IV, sec. 2.
5. *Laws of Ohio*, L. 69.
6. *Ibid.*
7. *Ibid.*, XLIII, 80.

A similar condition of overcrowding existed in the sixties; so that, in 1865, the supreme court justices were relieved of the duty of attending the meetings of the district courts for that particular year.[8] The judicial system had become slow and cumbersome. The courts declined rapidly after 1865 and were finally abolished.

Following the complete collapse of the district courts an amendment to the constitution, adopted in 1883, made provision for circuit courts. "The circuit courts," stated the amendment, "shall be the successors of the district courts, and all cases, judgments, records, and proceedings pending in said courts, in the several counties, of any district, shall be transferred to the circuit courts." The district courts, however, were to continue in existence until the election and qualification of the judges of the circuit court.[9] The circuit courts were assigned the same "original jurisdiction with the supreme court, and such appellate jurisdiction as may be provided by law." The composition of the courts and the number of circuits were left to the discretion of the legislature. Accordingly, in 1884, an act was passed dividing the states into seven circuits, and providing for the election of three judges in each circuit.[10]

The circuit courts, in addition to the jurisdiction conferred upon them by the constitution,[11] were authorized by the legislature to issue *writs* of *supersedeas* in any case, and all other *writs* not specifically provided by statute when they were necessary for the exercise of their jurisdiction.[12] Moreover, the courts were authorized to make and publish, as they deemed expedient, rules of procedure in their respective circuits, not in conflict with the law or rules of the supreme court. The legislature directed that all cases taken to the circuit courts were to be entered on the docket in the order in which they were commenced, received, or filed, and "to be taken up and disposed of in the same order." However, cases in which persons seeking relief were in prison or were convicted of a felony; cases involving the validity of any tax levy or assessment; cases involving the constitutionality of a statute; and cases involving public right and proceedings in *quo warranto, mandamus, procedendo,* or *habeas corpus,* could be taken up in advance of their assignment or order on the docket.[13]

---

9. *Ohio Const. 1851*, Art. IV, sec. 6.
10. *Laws of Ohio*, LXXXI, 168.
11. *Ohio Const. 1851*, Art. IV, sec. 6.
12. *Laws of Ohio*, LXXXI, 168.
13. *Ibid.*

The judicial system of Ohio was again slightly changed in 1912 when, by constitutional amendment the circuit courts were renamed courts of appeals. "The court of appeals shall continue the work of the respective circuit courts and all pending cases and proceedings in the circuit courts shall proceed to judgment and be determined by the respective courts of appeals." The judges of the several circuit courts were designated as judges of the courts of appeals, and were directed to perform the duties until the expiration of their terms of office. Vacancies caused by the expiration of term of office of the judges were to be filled by the electors of the respective appellate districts. The term of office was fixed at six years.[14]

The jurisdiction of the court of appeals remained much the same as that of the district court in 1851. However, the court was assigned original cognizance in *writs* of prohibition and appellate jurisdiction in the trial of chancery cases.[15] Certain restrictions were imposed upon the court: "No judgment of a court of common pleas, a superior court or other court of record shall be reversed except by the concurrence of all judges of the court of appeals."[16]

At present the court consists of three judges in each of the nine districts into which the state is divided, each of whom shall have been admitted to practice as an attorney at law in the state for a period of six years immediately preceding his election. One court of appeals judge is chosen every two years, and he holds office for six years beginning on the ninth day of February next after his election. The salary of the court of appeals judge, fixed at $6,000 per year in 1913, was increased to $8,000 in 1920 and so continues.[17] The judges hold at least one session of court annually and each county in the district.[18]

Ashland County was assigned to the fifth circuit court district when these courts were established[19] following the constitutional amendment of 1883.[20] It has remained in the fifth district to the present time. As in all counties, a court of appeals holds at least one session in Ashland County each year. The record reveals an average of 13 cases heard annually since 1910.[21]

---

14. *Ohio Const. 1851*, Art. IV, sec. 6.
15. *Ohio Const. 1851* (Amendment 1912), Art. IV, sec. 6.
16. *Ibid.*
17. *Laws of Ohio*, CIII, 418; CVIII, pt. ii, 1301.
18. G. C. sec. 1517.
19. *Laws of Ohio*, LXXXI, 168.
20. *Ohio Const. 1851*, Art. IV, sec. 1, 6.
21. Circuit Court Docket (1910-1915), entry 146; Court of Appeals Docket 1915—, entry 148.

District Court

143. DISTRICT COURT APPEARANCE DOCKET

1852-1893. 1 vol. (1).

Appearance docket of cases heard in district court, showing name of plaintiff and defendant, case number, title of case, date filed, dates petitions and answers, dates *writs* issued, notations of court orders, decisions in cases, itemized cost bill, date cost paid, and by whom. Also contains Circuit Court docket, 1884-1893, entry 146. Arranged chronologically by dates filed. Indexed alphabetically by names of plaintiffs. Handwritten. 400 pages. 18 x 12 x 2.5. Clerk of courts' private office.

144. DISTRICT COURT JOURNAL

1852-1884. 1 vol. (1). In Supreme Court Journal, entry 141.

Journal entries on proceedings in district court, showing date of entry, names of plaintiff and defendant, kind of action, disposition of each case and signatures of witnesses and judge. Arranged chronologically by dates entered. Indexed alphabetically by names of plaintiffs and defendants. Handwritten on printed forms. 600 pages. 18 x 12 x 3. Clerk of courts' private office.

145. DISTRICT COURT RECORD

1854-1884. 2 vols. (1, 2). 1852-1854 in Supreme Court Record, entry 142.

Record of cases heard in district court, showing case number, names of plaintiff and defendant, names of attorneys, kind of action, date filed, and complete record and disposition of case. Arranged chronologically by dates filed. Indexed alphabetically by names of plaintiffs. Handwritten on printed forms. Average 200 pages. 18 x 12 x 1.25. 1 volume, 1854-1870, clerk of courts' main office; 1 volume, 1871-1884, clerk of courts' private office.

Circuit Court

146. CIRCUIT COURT DOCKET

1894-1814. 10 vols. 1884-1893 in District Court Appearance Docket, entry 143.

Docket of cases tried in circuit court, showing case number, kind of action, names of plaintiff and defendant, charge (in criminal action), names of attorneys, date filed, and disposition of case. Also contains Court of Appeals Docket, 1913-1914, entry 148. Arranged numerically by case numbers and chronologically thereunder by dates filed. Index alphabetically by names of plaintiffs. Handwritten on printed forms. Average 200 pages. 10 x 14 x 2. Clerk of courts' private office.

147. CIRCUIT COURT JOURNAL

1884-1912. 2 vols. (1, 2).

Journal entries and record of cases filed in circuit court, showing court term, case number, date of entry, names of plaintiff and defendant, copy of appeal, and copies of petitions, *writs, mandamus* issued, court orders, and decrees. Arranged chronologically by dates entered. Indexed alphabetically by names of plaintiff and defendants. Handwritten on printed forms. Average 600 pages. 18 x 12 x 3. Clerk of courts' private office.

Court of Appeals

148. COURT OF APPEALS DOCKET

1915—. 3 vols. (1-3) 1913-1914 in Circuit Court Docket, entry 146.

Docket of cases tried before court of appeals, showing date filed, names of plaintiff and defendant, case number, copy of appeal, notice of appeal filed, date appeal bond filed, date of motion to dismiss appeal, dates opinions filed, date of reply, and dates journal entry and court costs bill were filed. Arranged numerically by case numbers and also arranged chronologically by dates cases filed. Indexed alphabetically by names of plaintiffs and defendants. Handwritten on printed forms. Average 450 pages. 18 x 12 x 2. Clerk of courts' private office.

149. COURT OF APPEALS JOURNAL
1913—. 3 vols. (1-3).

Journal entries of petitions, answers, *writs* and court orders of cases heard in court of appeals, showing dates entered, names of plaintiff and defendant, title of case, case number, and date case appealed. Arranged chronologically by dates entered. Indexed alphabetically by names of plaintiffs and defendants. 1913-1924, Handwritten on printed forms; 1924—, Typed on printed forms. Average 600 pages. 18 x 12 x 3. Clerk of courts' private office.

150. COURT OF APPEALS RECORD
1913—. 3 vols. (1-3).

Final record of cases filed in appeal from lower courts and heard in court of appeals, showing court term, names of plaintiff and defendant, title of case, case number, date of filing appeal, transcripts of testimony as presented from lower courts, copies of transcript, appeal board, petitions, *demurrers*, answers, motions, amended petitions, decisions, and court orders. Arranged chronologically by court terms and also arranged numerically by case numbers. Indexed alphabetically by names of plaintiffs. Typed on printed forms. 600 pages. 18 x 12 x 3. Clerk of courts' main office.

The probate court, established by an act of the Northwest Territory on August 30, 1788, consisted of a probate judge with jurisdiction in probate, testamentary, and guardianship matters, and two judges of the court of common pleas, who sat with him and ruled on contested points, definitive sentences, and final judgment.[1]

The judicial system established under the first constitution of Ohio in 1802 did not provide for a probate court but vested the court of common pleas with such powers as had been exercised by the court in the territorial period. The constitution of 1851 recreated the probate court and gave it original jurisdiction in "probate and testamentary matters, the appointment of administrators and guardians, the settlement of the accounts of the executors, administrators and guardians, and such jurisdiction in *habeas corpus*.... and for the sale of land by executors, administrators and guardians, and such other jurisdiction,...as may be provided by law."[2] An amendment to the constitution, adopted in 1912, authorized the common pleas judge, when petitioned by 10 per cent of the qualified voters in counties having a population less than 60,000 to submit to the voters at any general election the question of combining the probate court and court of common pleas.[3]

One of the primary functions of the court since its inception has been the settlement of estates. The civil code adopted in 1853 gave the court original jurisdiction in taking proof of wills, and granting letters testamentary, and in settling accounts of executors and administrators.[4] Until 1854 the court had jurisdiction in enforcing the payment of debts and legacies of deceased persons. While the court retains the original jurisdiction regarding estates, new duties have been added in recent years. With the development of inheritance tax laws in 1919 as an added source of taxation the probate court has been required to determine and assess the tax after the county auditor has appraised the decedent's estate.[5]

By constitutional provision the probate court has original jurisdiction in granting marriage licenses.[6] The court also issues licenses to ministers to solemnize marriages.[7]

---

1. Pease, *op. cit.*, 9.
2. *Ohio Const. 1851*, Art. IV, secs. 7, 8.
3. *Ibid.*, Art. IV, sec. 7.
4. *Laws of Ohio*, LI, 167.
5. *Ibid.*, CVIII, pt. I, 561.
6. *Ohio Const. 1851*, Art. IV, sec. 8.
7. *Laws of Ohio*, L, 84.

The former provision was modified by an act adopted in 1931, which requires a lapse of at least five days between the time of application and that of the issuance of marriage licenses. However, power to suspend the operation of the act is vested in the probate judge.[8]

The jurisdiction of the court extends to the state's unfortunates. By the probate code of 1853, reenacted in 1854, exclusive jurisdiction was granted to the court to make inquest respecting insane persons, idiots, and deaf and dumb persons, subject by law to guardianship.[9] In 1856 the court was authorized to commit mentally incompetent persons to state institutions maintained for the care of such persons.[10] Two years later the court was given power to appoint and remove guardians over minors.[11] The act of 1859 authorized the court to render adoption decrees.[12] In 1904 the court was given jurisdiction in trial cases involving neglected, dependent, and delinquent children.[13]

Since the middle of the nineteenth century the probate judge has been required to keep a record of vital statistics. In 1867 the duty of keeping a permanent record of births and deaths, which, in 1856, had been conferred upon the clerk of courts, was transferred to the probate judge.[14] When in 1908, a bureau of vital statistics under the direction of the secretary of state was created the probate judge was relieved temporarily of this task.[15] In 1921 the act of 1908 was amended so as to require the local registrars to transmit to the district health commissioner, who was directed to serve as a state deputy registrar of vital statistics, all certificates of births and deaths received during the preceding month, and a copy of all such certificates to the probate court. Although the general code still requires the probate judge to keep a permanent record of births and deaths and an index to such records[16] neither has been kept in Ashland County since 1908.

---

8. *Ibid.*, CXIV, 93.
9. *Laws of Ohio*, LI, 167; LII, 103.
10. *Ibid.*, LIII, 81-86.
11. *Ibid.*, LV, 54.
12. *Ibid.*, LVI, 82; LXVII, 14.
13. *Ibid.*, XCVII, 561; See also entries 130, 155.
14. *Laws of Ohio*, LXIV, 63-64.
15. *Ibid.*, XCIX, 296-307.
16. G. C. sec. 10501-15

Jurisdiction in naturalization proceedings was exercised by the probate court until 1906 when an amendment to the federal statute vested exclusive jurisdiction and naturalization matters in the United States district courts and all state courts of record having a seal, a clerk, and jurisdiction in action at law and equity in which the amount and controversy was unlimited.[17] The general code still requires the probate judge to keep a naturalization record and an index to the records,[18] but jurisdiction was transferred to the court of common pleas. No naturalization records have been kept since 1905.

During the early years of its existence the court was given limited criminal jurisdiction in cases in which the sentence did not impose capital punishment or punishment by imprisonment. By the code of civil procedure adopted in 1853 the judgments and final decrees of the probate court could be reviewed by the court of common pleas on error.[19] In 1857 the criminal jurisdiction of the probate court was transferred to the court of common pleas,[20] but later acts retain it in certain counties only. Thus in 1858 the probate courts of certain counties, exclusive of Ashland, were granted jurisdiction in all crimes in which the sentence did not impose capital punishment or imprisonment in a penitentiary.[21] This act was repealed in 1878 and the probate courts of certain counties were granted concurrent jurisdiction with the court of common pleas in all misdemeanors and proceedings to prevent crime.[22] Such jurisdiction, however, was not granted to Ashland County until 1883.[23] The probate court continued to exercise such jurisdiction until 1931 when the last vestige of criminal jurisdiction disappeared with the adoption of the probate code.[24]

---

17. *United States Statutes at Large*, XXXIV, pt. I, 596; *see also State of Ohio v. George G. Metzger and Albert L. Irish*, 10 N.P., n.s., 97 *et seq.*
18. G. C. secs. 10501-15, 10501-16.
19. *Laws of Ohio,* LI, 145.
20. *Ibid.*, LIV, 97.
21. *Ibid.*, LV, 186.
22. *Ibid.,* LXXXV, 960.
23. *Ibid.*, LXXX, 48.
24. *Ibid.*, CXIV, 475.

Miscellaneous duties, remotely related to probate and testamentary matters, have been added by legislative action. Since 1888 the court has been required to file a certified list of all unknown depositors as furnished by institutions or persons engaged in lending money for profit.[25] In 1896 the probate court was given concurrent jurisdiction with the court of common pleas in the matter of changing the names of persons who desired it,[26]a matter in which the court of common pleas had exclusive cognizance from 1842 to 1896.[27] Since 1896 the probate court has been required to record certificates of doctors and surgeons, and since 1916 the certificates of registered nurses which authorize them to practice their professions in the state.[28] Since 1913 the court has been vested with the power to grant injunctions,[29] and since 1915 has had concurrent jurisdiction with the court of common pleas in condemnation proceedings for roads.[30]

In like manner the appointive powers of the probate judge have been expanded. In addition to the authority to appoint administrators and guardians he was authorized by the act of 1891 to appoint members of the county board of elections; however this appointive power was abrogated by the act of 1892.[31] Then, too, from 1908 to 1913 the probate judge was authorized to appoint a county blind relief commission[32] comprised of three members each of whom served a three-year term.[33] Since 1906 he has had authority to appoint members of the board of county visitors.[34]

---

25. *Ibid.*, LXXXV, 65; G. C. sec. 9864.
26. *Laws of Ohio*, XCII, 28.
27. *Ibid.*, XL, 28-29.
28. *Ibid.*, XCII, 46; XCIX, 199; CVI, 193.
29. *Ibid.*, CIII, 427.
30. *Ibid.*, CVI, 583.
31. *Ibid.*, LXXXVIII, 449; LXXXIX, 455.
32. *See* p. 229.
33. *Laws of Ohio*,, 56, 60.
34. *Ibid.*, 28, 29; CIII, 173-174.

The probate judge, like other county officials, has been required by statute to keep a record of the business of his office. The present system of records, originating for the most part in 1853 and continued by the probate code of 1931, includes a criminal record, at an administrative docket, a guardians' docket, a marriage record, a record of bonds, a naturalization record, and a permanent record of birth and deaths.[35]

The probate judge has the care and custody of the files, papers, books, and records belonging to the probate office and is *ex-officio* clerk of the court. The probate code, adopted in 1931, directed the probate judge to preserve for future reference and examination all pleadings, accounts, vouchers, and other papers in each estate, trust, assignments, guardianship, or other proceedings, such papers to be properly jacketed and tied together; he is required also to make proper entries and indexes omitted by his predecessors. Certificates of marriages, reports of birth, and similar papers not a part of a case or proceeding are to be arranged and preserved separately in the order of dates in which they are filed.[36]

At present the probate judge is elected for a four-year term.[37] In recent years there has been an attempt to raise the qualification of those seeking election to the office. Accordingly, an amendment to the probate code in 1935 restricted eligibility to the office to a practicing attorney or a person who "*shall have previously served as probate judge immediately prior to his election.*"[38]

The probate judge in Ashland County receives an annual salary of $2409.96[39] and his bond is set at $5000.[40] His office staff consists of a clerk and a deputy, who received an aggregate salary of $2460 and are not bonded. The probation officer receives an annual salary of $720 and is not bonded.[41]

---

35. *Ibid.*, LI, 167; LII, 103; LXXV, 9; CXIV, 324.
36. *Ibid.*, CXIV, 321-322.
37. *Ibid.*, CXIV, 320.
38. *Ibid.*, CXVI, 481.
39. Appropriation ledger, 1940, entry 239.
40. Record of official bonds, 1940, entry 270.
41. Appropriation ledger, 1940, entry 239.

A brief examination of the records of the probate court of Ashland County will serve to show the general nature of its work. From 1852, when the court was established, to 1941, 3337 wills 4795 estates administered, 2391 guardians appointed, and 108 children placed in adopted homes.[42] Seven hundred seventy-four persons were declared insane, 326 feeble-minded, 16 mentally ill, and 54 epileptic.[43] Inheritance taxes were paid upon 804 estates, 25 names were changed, and 14 estates were released from administration because they involved less than $500.[44] Vital statistics were also kept in probate court from 1867 to 1908. During those years 16,900 births and 8299 deaths were recorded.[45] Since 1916, 28 doctors have been issued certificates,[46] 57 nurses have been registered, and 12 limited practitioners have been issued certificates.[47]

---

42. Appearance docket, 1852-1941, *passim*, entry 151.
43. *Ibid.*
44. *Ibid.*
45. Record of Birth, 1867-1908, *passim*, entry 182; Record of Death, 1867-1908, *passim*, entry 183.
46. Physicians' Licenses, 1916-1940, *passim*. entry 186.
47. Record of Registered Nurses and Limited Practitioners, 1916-1940, *passim*, entry 187.

General Court Proceedings

151. APPEARANCE DOCKET
1852—. 22 vols. (1-22).

Record of all cases before probate court, showing title and number of case, names of plaintiff and defendant, or other principal, date case filed, date and kind of *writ* issued, brief proceedings of each case, findings of court, date of sheriff's return on writs, and amount of cost; also includes docket of estates and guardianships, juvenile cases, 1852-1936, criminal cases 1852-1857, 1882-1931,civil docket and court calendar 1853—, and assignment docket, 1853—. Arranged chronologically by dates filed and numerically thereunder by case numbers. Indexed alphabetically by names of plaintiffs, defendants, or other principles; separate index, see entry 152. Handwritten on printed forms. Average 500 pages. 14 x 10 x 3. Probate court office.

152. GENERAL INDEX TO PROBATE COURT RECORDS
1851—. 3 vols. (1-3).

Index to Appearance Docket, entry 151; Original Papers, entry 154; Criminal Record, entry 155; Probate Court Journal, entry 153; Probate Court Record, entry 174; Record of Wills, 156; Record of Administrators' Bonds and Appointments, entry 157; Record of Administrator Bonds and Letters with Will Annexed, *De Bonis Non,* entry 158, Record of Executor's Bond and Appointment, entry 159; Record of Guardians' Bonds and Appointments, entry 160; Notice Record, entry 165; Record of Inventories and Sale Bills, entry 164; Journal of Settlement, entry 171; Guardians' and Administrators' Letters, entry 161; showing names of administrator, executors, guardians, wards, decedents, or other principal, case number, and volume and page numbers of record. Arranged alphabetically by names of administrators, executors, guardians, wards, decedents, or other principles. Handwritten on printed forms. Average 500 pages. 18 x 14 x 3. Probate court office.

153. PROBATE COURT JOURNAL
1852—. 47 vols. (1-47).

Journal entries in all cases in probate court, including juvenile cases, showing date of entry, names of plaintiff, defendant, and other principal, title of case, date case filed, kind of action, case number, and date and copy of court orders and decrees; also includes journal entries for appointments of member of board of county visitors, 1913—, showing date of appointment, name and address of appointee, term of appointment, date certificate of appointment sent to state board of charities, and signature of probate judge; also contains juvenile journal, 1904-1913, entry 197. Arranged chronologically by dates entered. Indexed alphabetically by names of plaintiffs, defendants, or other principles; for separate index, see entry 152. Handwritten on printed forms. Average 430 pages. 18 x 12 x 3. 42 volumes, 1852-1930, basement storage room; 5 volumes, 1930—, Probate court record room.

154. ORIGINAL PAPERS

1852—. 820 file boxes. (labeled by container case numbers).

Original instruments in probate court cases, including papers pertaining to the estates, guardianships, trusteeships, and assignments consisting of appointments, bonds, appraisements, inventories, sale bills, transfers, cost bills, settlements, and other papers of case; wills, showing date of will, provisions of same, signatures of testator and witnesses, and date filed for probate; lunacy and cases of incompetence, showing date complaint filed, medical report, affidavits of witnesses, report of inquest, and amount of cost; juvenile court cases, showing name of delinquent, charge or complaint, disposition of case, and civil cases, and adoption papers. All papers of each case filed together in a jacket, showing date case filed, case number, kind of case, names of plaintiff, defendant, and other principal, and volume and page numbers of dockets and records where entered. Arranged numerically by case numbers. For index, see entry 152. Handwritten on printed forms. 10 x 4.5 x 12.5. 280 file boxes, 1852-1893, basement storage room; 545 file boxes, 1893—, Probate court office.

155. CRIMINAL RECORD

1852-1857. 1 vol.

Record of criminal cases in probate court, showing date case filed, case number, name of defendant, charge, brief history, and disposition of case. Arranged chronologically by dates filed. Indexed alphabetically by names of defendants. For separate index, see entry 152. Handwritten. 600 pages. 18 x 12 x 3. Probate court office.

Estates and Guardianships

(See also entries 151, 153, 154.)

Wills

156. RECORD OF WILLS

1846—. 21 vols. (1-21).

Copies of wills probated, showing date and provision of will, signatures of testator and witnesses, date filed for probate, and date and copy of journal entry approving probation of same. 1846-1851 consists of records filed with probate division of court of common pleas and transferred to probate court. Arranged chronologically by dates filed. Indexed alphabetically by names of testators; for separate index, 1851—, see entry 152. 1846-1908, Handwritten on printed forms; 1909—, typed on printed forms. Average 500 pages. 18 x 12 x 3. Probate court record room.

Applications, Appointments, Bonds, and Letters

157. RECORD OF ADMINISTRATORS BONDS AND APPOINTMENTS

1868—. 13 vols. (1-13).

Copies of appointments of administrators of estates, showing date of appointment, names of administrator and decedent, relationship to descendant, and case number; also includes copies of bonds of administrators, showing amount and date of bond, and names of sureties. Arranged chronologically by dates appointed. Indexed alphabetically by names of decedents; for separate index, see entry 152. 1868-1908, handwritten on printed forms. Average 200 pages. 18 x 12 x 3. Probate court record room.

158. RECORD OF ADMINISTRATORS' BONDS AND LETTERS WITH WILL ANNEXED, *DE BONIS NON*

1926—. 2 vols.

Record of appointments of administrators of estates, showing name of decedent, case number, name of applicant, date of application, names in relationship of heirs-at-law, and estimated value of real and personal property of estates; also includes copies of wills which have been probated; copies of letters of authority issued by court, showing date of appointment, name of appointee, name of decedent, and copy of notice of appointment; copies of bonds filed by administrators, showing date of bond, name of administrator, names of sureties, amount of bond, and date approved.

Arranged chronologically by dates entered. Indexed alphabetically by names of decedents; for separate index, see entry 152. Typed on printed forms. Average 650 pages. 18 x 12 x 3. Probate court record room.

159. RECORD OF EXECUTOR'S BOND AND APPOINTMENT
1861—. 11 vols. (1-11).

Copies of appointments of executors of estates, showing date of appointment, name of executor, name of decedent, degree of kinship to decedent, case number, and estimated value of estate; also includes copies of bonds of executors, showing date and amount of bond, and names of sureties. Arranged chronologically by dates appointed. Indexed alphabetically by names of decedents; for separate index, see entry 152. Typed on printed forms. Average 600 pages. 18 x 12 x 3. Probate court record room.

160. RECORD OF GUARDIANS' BONDS AND APPOINTMENTS
1846—. 12 vols. (1-11).

Copies of applications for appointments as guardians, showing date of application, name of ward, name and address of applicant, date of appearance before probate court, case number, and date of appointment; also includes copies of bonds of guardians, showing date and amount of bond, and names of sureties. 1861—, also shows appraised value of real and personal property with description and location of real property and record of bills of sale. 1846-1851 is record of probate division of court of common pleas, transferred to probate court. Arranged chronologically by dates appointed. Indexed alphabetically by names of wards; for separate index, 1852—, see entry 152. Handwritten on printed forms. 2 volumes average 400 pages. 12 x 8 x 2; 10 volumes average 600 pages. 18 x 12 x 3. 2 volumes, 1846-1860, probate court office; 10 volumes, 1861—, Probate court record room.

161. GUARDIANS' AND ADMINISTRATORS' LETTERS
1862-1871. 1 vol. (1).

Copies of letters of authority granted to guardians and administrators by probate court, showing date of application to act as guardian or administrator, date of appointment, date of order for bond, amount of bond, name of ward or decedent, and name and value of estate. Arranged alphabetically by names of guardians. For index, see entry 152. Handwritten on printed forms. 500 pages. 14 x 12 x 3. Probate court office.

162. RECORD OF TRUSTEES' BONDS AND LETTERS
1888—. 1 vol. (1).

Copies of bonds given by trustees of the estates, showing date of appointment, name of estate, amount and date of bond, and names of sureties and trustees; also includes copies of letters of authority, and oaths and agreements of trustees. Arranged chronologically by dates appointed. Indexed alphabetically by names of trustees. Handwritten on printed forms. 150 pages. 18 x 12 x 2. Probate court record room.

163. NOTICE RECORD
1865—. 3 vols. (1-3),

Proof of publication of notices of appointments of administrators, executors, and guardians, showing date appointed, dates of notices, and name of estates; also includes proof of publication of notices or appraisements, inventories, accounts, and final settlements. Arranged chronologically by dates published. Indexed alphabetically by names of estates; for separate index, see entry 152. Handwritten on printed forms. Average 450 pages. 18 x 12 x 3. Probate court record room.

Inventories, Appraisements, and Sale Bills

164. RECORD OF INVENTORIES AND SALE BILLS
1867—. 26 vols. (1-26).

Copies of inventories of estates, showing name of estates, name of administrator, executor, or guardian, date of inventory, names of appraisers, and itemized appraisement list and date filed; also includes bills of sale for property sold, showing date of sale, description and location of property, appraised value, and date account was filed. Arranged chronologically by dates filed. Indexed alphabetically by names of the estates; for separate index, see entry 152. 1867-1920, handwritten on printed forms; 1920—, typed on printed forms. Average 600 pages. 18 x 12 x 3. 24 volumes, 1867-1931, basement storage room; 2 volumes, 1931—, Probate court record room.

165. INVENTORY AND APPRAISEMENT RECORD

1852—. 26 vols. (1-26). (12 vols. Labeled by contained case numbers; 1-14). Title varies: Inventories of the Estates, Sale Bills and Transfers, 1852-1917, 12 vols.

Copies of inventories of estates, the name of the estate, case number, name of administrator, executor, or guardian, date inventory filed, names of the appraisers, and itemized appraisement list; 1917—, shows amount of indebtedness and amount of inheritance tax; 1852-1917, shows record of sales and transfer of property of estates. 1852-1917, arranged numerically by case numbers; 1917—, arranged alphabetically by names of estates. For index, see entry 152. 1852-1917—, handwritten on printed forms; 1917—, typed on printed forms. Average 600 pages. 18 x 12 x 3. 12 volumes, 1852-1917, probate court office; 14 volumes, 1917—, Probate court record room.

166. INVENTORY AND APPRAISEMENT RECORD, WITH WIDOW

1923—. 7 vols. (30, 32, 34, 38, 40, 43, 44).

Inventory and appraisement of the estates, showing name of decedent, case number, order to appraisers, date of order, waiver of notice, oath of appraisers, personal goods and chattels, with description of articles appraised, and appraised value, bank notes, and total amount of money, stocks, bonds, and securities, serial number, name and post office-address of debtor, kind of claim, date originally payable, rate of interest, and amount collected, real estate assets, property exempted, certificate signed by appraisers, affidavit, signatures of executor or administrator, next of kin, *legatees*, *devisees*, and probate judge. Arranged numerically by case numbers. Indexed alphabetically by names of decedents. Typed on printed forms. Average 600 pages. 18.75 x 13 x 3. 3 volumes, 1923-1932, probate court record room; 4 volumes, 1932—, Probate court office.

167. INVENTORY RECORD, WITHOUT WIDOW

1923—. 9 vols. (31, 33, 35, 36, 37, 39, 41, 42, 45). Title varies: Inventory and Appraisement Record, Without Widow, 1923-1929, 3 vols.

Inventory and appraisement of estates, showing name of decedent, case number, order to appraisers, signature of probate judge, notice of appraisement of the estate of deceased, name of township, date of appraisement, oath of appraisers with signatures of notary public and appraisers, personal goods and chattels, number of items, description of articles appraised, appraised value, deposits, total amount of money, notes and other securities, names and post-office address of debtors, kind of claim, value, date and amount collectible, recapitalization of assets, signatures of executor, appraisers, witnesses, and probate judge. Arranged numerically by case numbers. Index alphabetically by names of decedents. Typed on printed forms. Average 600 pages. 18.75 x 13 x 3. 3 volumes 1923-1929, probate court record room; 6 volumes, 1930—, Probate court office.

168. THE INVENTORY AND SALE BILLS
1871—. 28 vols. (1-24, 24A, 24B, 25, 26). Title varies: Inventory and Sales Bill Record, 1871-1892, 11 vols.

Record of inventories of estates, showing name of decedent, case number, petition to sell personal property, description of articles appraised, appraised value, orders of private sale, and return of report of sale by the administrator bill of sale, showing description of property, appraised value, to whom sold, and journal entry; guardian's inventory, showing personal goods and chattels, number and description of articles, estimated value, statement of notes and other securities for payment, name and post office-address, sum to be collected, all other claims and accounts, recapitalization of assets, and affidavit of administrator. Arranged numerically by case numbers. Indexed alphabetically by names of estates. Handwritten on printed forms. Average 600 pages. 18.5 x 12.5 x 3. 26 volumes, 1871-1930, probate court record room; 2 volumes, 1931—, Probate court office.

Schedule of Debts

169. SCHEDULE OF DEBTS
1932—. 2 vols.

Record of debts of estates, showing case number, date of claim, name of decedent, names and addresses of creditors, nature of claim and how secured, amount of liens, including interest, amount and date of allowance or rejection, amount of interest on allowance, dates of maturity and filing, name of administrator, signature of probate judge, notice of filing of debt schedule, and journal entry. Arranged chronologically by dates filed. Indexed alphabetically by names of decedents; for separate index, see entry 152. Typed on printed forms. Average 600 pages. 18 x 12 x 3. Probate court office.

Cost Bills

170. COST BILLS
(Administrator's Fee Docket), 1846-1857. 4 vols. (1-4).

Record of cost for administering real estate, showing name of decedent, cost of bond, recording will, issuing testamentary letters, recording inventory, filing bill of sale, and recording settlement and fees. Arranged the chronologically by dates entered. Indexed alphabetically by names of decedents. Handwritten on printed forms. Average 200 pages. 12 x 8 x 1.5. 1 volume, 1846-1851, basement storage room; 3 volumes, 1851-1857, Probate court office.

Settlements

171. JOURNAL OF SETTLEMENT
1881—. 8 vols. (1-8). 1852-1880 in Estate Record, Probate Court, entry 172.

Final record of settlement of estates, showing date of filing, name of decedent, minor, or incompetent, name of administrator, executor, or guardian, date account filed, and amount due heirs, in final settlement of estate. Arranged chronologically by dates filed. Indexed alphabetically by names of estates; for separate index, see entry 152. Handwritten and typed on printed forms. Average 500 pages. 18 x 12 x 3. 7 volumes, 1881-1935, basement storage room; 1 volume, 1935—, Probate court record room.

172. ESTATE RECORD, PROBATE COURT
1846—. 46 vols. (1-46). Title varies: Estate Record, Ashland Common Pleas, 1845-1851, 1 vol.

Record of settlement of estates, showing date of entry, name of guardian, trustee, administrator, or executor, and decedent case number, accounts of guardians, administrators, executors, and trustees, distribution of shares, itemized statement of funds, recapitalization, affidavit to account, appraisement of property, inventory of articles appraised, debts owed by the estate, sale bill of property sold by executor, articles as appraised, to whom sold, amount and inventory of estate and property. Also contains journal settlement, 1852-1880, entry 171. Arranged chronologically by dates entered. Indexed alphabetically by names of principles. Handwritten on printed forms. Average 600 pages. 18 x 12 x 3. 42 volumes, 1846-1931, probate court record room; 4 volumes, 1932—, Probate court office.

Inheritance tax

173. INHERITANCE TAX RECORD
1919—. 3 vols.

Record of inheritance tax on estates, showing date of entry, case number, name and address of decedent, date of death, place of birth, name and address of administrator or executor, estimated value of personal and real property, and net value as fixed by probate court. Arranged chronologically by dates entered. Indexed alphabetically by names of decedents. Typed on printed forms. Average 500 pages. 18.5 x 12 x 2.5. Probate court record room.

Final Record

174. PROBATE COURT RECORD
1851—. 26 vols. (1-26).

Complete record of probate court cases including estate matters, showing case number, dates filed, names of plaintiff and defendant or other principles, description of property, name of estate, names of heirs, division of property, claims against estates, appointment, bonds, and compensation of guardian, administrator, executor, or trustee, commitment of epileptic and mental cases, petitions to sell property, and copies of court orders and decrees. Arranged chronologically by dates filed. Indexed alphabetically by names of plaintiffs, defendants, or other principles;for separate index, see entry 152. Handwritten on printed forms. Average 340 pages. 18 x 12 x 3. 22 volumes, 1851-1926, basement storage room; 4 volumes, 1926—. Probate court record room.

Assignments

175. RECORD OF ASSIGNMENT
1867—. 10 vols. (1-10).

Complete record of proceedings and assignments by insolvent debtors, showing date case filed. names of assignor and assignee, and dates of instruments of each case, including orders to appraise, deeds of assignment, orders for sale, bill of sale, assignees' accounts of settlement, and cost bills. Arranged chronologically by dates filed. Indexed alphabetically by names of assignees. 1867-1924, handwritten on printed forms. 1924—, typed on printed forms. Average 625 pages. 18 x 12 x 3. Probate court record room.

Dependents

176. LUNACY RECORD

1882—. 4 vols.

Final record of hearings in lunacy cases, showing name of person filing complaint, name of patient, date filed, warrants of arrests, medical certificates filed by physicians making examinations, proceedings of hearing, warrants to convey to institution, sheriff's return and cost bills, amount of fees, date of admittance to institution, and date of discharge or death. Also contains record of Feeble Minded Youth, 1882-1904, entry 179. Arranged chronologically by dates filed. Indexed alphabetically by names of patients. Handwritten on printed forms. Average 200 pages. 18 x 12 x 2. Probate court record room.

177. COST BILL RECORD, (Lunacy)

1904—. 1 vol.

Record of court costs in lunacy proceedings, showing name of patient, date of hearing, name of physician, amount of physician's fee, amount of fees for hearing, amount of costs and fees for transportation and conveying to institution, and total costs. Arranged chronologically by dates of hearings. Indexed alphabetically by names of patients. Handwritten on printed forms. 300 pages. 18 x 12 x 2. Probate court record room.

178. EPILEPTIC RECORD

1895—. 1 vol. (1).

Copies of applications to probate court for admittance to hospital for epilepsy, showing date of application, name of afflicted person, case number, sex, age, race, nativity, and physical condition, whether insane or epileptic, and cause and duration of condition; also includes copy as sworn statements of witnesses, warrant to arrest, certificate by physician, order to commit to institution, sheriff's return, and cost bills. Arranged chronologically by dates entered. Index alphabetically by names of patients. Handwritten on printed forms. 300 pages. 18 x 12 x 2. Probate court record room.

179. RECORD OF FEEBLE MINDED YOUTH

1905—. 1 vol. 1882-1904 in Lunacy Record, entry 176.

Copies of applications for admittance of feeble-minded youths to institutions, showing names of youth, parents, guardian, and examining physician, and date application filed; also includes copies of medical certificates, affidavits of information, warrant to convey, and sheriff's return. Arranged chronologically by dates filed. Indexed alphabetically by names of patients. Handwritten on printed forms. 230 pages. 18 x 12 x 2. Probate court record room.

180. ADOPTION RECORD
1894—. 3 vols.
Record of petitions and adoption proceedings, showing date of petition, name of applicant, child, and child's parents, and age, sex, nativity of child; also includes reports of investigations on application, and journal entries approving or rejecting application. Arranged chronologically by dates of petitions. No index. Handwritten on printed forms. Average 500 pages. 18 x 12 x 2.5. Probate court record room.

Naturalization

181. NATURALIZATION RECORD
1851-1905. 4 vols. (1-4).
Copies of applications to become citizens of United States, showing date of application, place and date of birth, name and address of applicant, date and place of entry into United States, and statements of witnesses; also includes copies of certificates of citizenship granted. Arranged chronologically by dates of applications. Indexed alphabetically by names of applicants. Handwritten on printed forms. Average 150 pages. 16 x 12 x 2. Probate court record room.

Vital Statistics

Births and Deaths

182. RECORD OF BIRTHS
1867-1908. 3 vols.
Report by physicians and midwives of births, showing date and place of birth, name of child, name of attending physician, child's sex and race, name of father, maiden name of mother, residence of parents, occupation of father, and by whom reported. Arranged chronologically by dates of births. No index. Handwritten on printed forms. Average 220 pages. 18 x 12 x 2. Probate court record room.

183. RECORD OF DEATHS
1867-1908. 2 vols.
Record of deaths as reported by physicians or morticians, showing date reported, name of the decedent, date of death, marital status, age, place of death and birth, occupation, names of parents or next of kin, race, sex, cause of death, late residence, and by whom reported; cases of sudden, accidental, and homicidal deaths, showing coroner's report of findings. Arranged chronologically by dates of deaths. No index. Handwritten on printed forms. Average 280 pages. 18 x 12 x 2. Probate court record room.

Marriages

184. MARRIAGE RECORD
1846—. 16 vols. (1-16).
Record of marriage licenses issued by clerk of courts, 1846-1851, and by probate court, 1852—, showing date issued, names, addresses, ages, and occupations of contracting parties, and name of official or minister, and date ceremony performed. Arranged chronologically by dates issued. Indexed alphabetically by names of contracting parties. Handwritten on printed forms. Average 575 pages. 18 x 12 x 3. Probate court record room.

Licenses and Certificates

185. MINISTERS' LICENSES
1852—. 2 vols. (1, 2).
Copies of licenses granted to ordained ministers to solemnize marriages, showing name of minister, church denomination, state issued, for what country, and name of probate judge. Arranged chronologically by dates issued. Indexed alphabetically by names of ministers. Handwritten on printed forms. Average 400 pages. 14 x 10 x 2. Probate judge's private office.

186. PHYSICIANS' LICENSES
1896—. 1 vol.
Copies of certificates issued to physicians by state board of medical examiners, showing name of physician, date issued , name and address the school attended, date medical degree received, signatures of president and secretary of the examining

board, date recorded, the signature of probate judge. Arranged chronologically by dates recorded. Indexed alphabetically by names of physicians. Handwritten on printed forms. 400 pages. 14 x 10 x 2. Probate judge's private office.

187. RECORD OF REGISTERED NURSES AND LIMITED PRACTITIONERS
1912—. 1 vol.

Copies of certificates issued by state medical board to graduate nurses on passing examinations, showing certificate number, name and address of licensee, date of diploma, name of training school graduated from, date of certificate, and date recorded; also includes copies of certificates issued by state medical board to applicants for limited practitioners, showing certificate number, name and address of licensee, what branch license is for, date of certificate and recording. Arranged chronologically by dates recorded. Indexed alphabetically by names of licensee. Handwritten on printed forms. 150 pages. 14 x 8 x 1.5. Probate court record room.

Financial Records

188. CASH BOOK
1907—. 8 vols. (1-8).

Record of money received by probate court, showing date of receipt, name of payer, amount paid, services rendered and goods supplied; also includes a list of witnesses (payees), showing date of payment, name of payee, and amount of fee; also record of fees collected in juvenile court, 1913—. Arranged chronologically by dates receipts. No index. Handwritten on printed forms. Average 200 pages. 20 x 14 x 1.5. Probate court record room.

189. RECORD OF ACCRUED FEES
1907—. 5 vols. (1-5).

Record of accrued fees, showing date accrued, case number, services rendered, to whom charged, total amount of fee, civil or criminal case, amount due from county and juvenile court for transcripts, copies, and sundries, and date paid. Arranged chronologically by dates of accruals. No index. Handwritten on printed forms. Average 300 pages. 18 x 12 x 1.5. Probate court records room.

190. UNCLAIMED MONEYS

1900—. 1 vol.

Record of unclaimed cost and fees which have been paid into county treasury, showing to whom money is due (payee), amount, volume and page numbers of Appearance Docket, entry 152, case number, date paid in, date certificate for recovery issued, and certificate number. Arranged alphabetically by names of payees and chronologically thereunder by dates entered. No index. Handwritten on printed forms. 160 pages. 14 x 8 x 1.5. Probate court record room.

Miscellaneous

191. RECORD OF UNCLAIMED DEPOSITS

1888—. 1 vol.

Record of unclaimed deposits as reported quarterly by the officials of banks, showing date of report, name and address of bank, name and title of bank official making report, name of depositor, amount credited to account, and date of last credit or debit to account. Arranged chronologically by dates reported. Indexed alphabetically by names of banks. Handwritten on printed forms. 350 pages. 18 x 12 x 2. Probate court record room.

192. CHANGING OF NAMES

1896—. 16 vols. (6-21).

Record of petitions for change of name, showing date of application, date filed, names of attorney and probate judge, and signature of applicants; also includes copies of journal entries of approval, showing name of court, old and new name of applicant, case number, date signed, and signature of probate judge. Arranged chronologically by dates filed. Index alphabetically by former names of applicants, showing new names adopted. Handwritten on printed forms. Average 600 pages. 14 x 12 x 3. Probate court office.

193. RECEIPTS FOR PAPERS WITHDRAWN

1917—. 1 vol.

Record of court papers removed from files, showing case number, title of case, date removed, name of person removing papers, date returned, name of attorney and the estate. Arranged chronologically by dates removed. No index. Handwritten on printed forms. 300 pages. 18 x 8 x 2. Probate court record room.

194. TRANSFER RECORD

1931—. 2 vols. (1, 2).

Copies of applications made by administrators or executors for transfer of real estate to lawful heirs by certificate of transfer, showing date of application, case number, name of the decedent, description and location of property, and names of heirs-at-law; also includes copies of certificates of transfer, showing amount of real estate to be transferred to each heir. Arranged chronologically by dates of applications. Index alphabetically by names of decedents. Typed on printed forms. Average 600 pages. 18 x 12 x 3. Probate court record room.

195. (Miscellaneous) RECORD

1920—. 2 vols. (1, 2).

Miscellaneous record of probate court, including:

a. Inventories and appraisements of estates including appraisements of other counties, showing names of decedents, estate, and heirs, case number, orders to appraisers, return of orders by administrator, date and notice of appraisement, description, value, and inventory list of appraised personal goods and chattel, recapitalization of assets, affidavit of administrator, and true statement of estate and property of decedent.

b. Petition for *writ* of *habeas corpus*, showing date of petition, name of party for whom *writ* is obtained, type of case, case number, and date *writ* served.

c. Changing of names, showing date of entry, name of the person and new name granted by court, and reason for changing name.

d. Land contract, showing date of instrument, names of grantor and grantee, and date recorded.

e. Record of new and additional bonds, showing date of issue, amount of bond, and date of maturity.

f. Dissolution of partnership, showing names of partners, type of business, location, firm name, full names of all owners, residences, date recorded, reasons for dissolving partnership, property settlement, date of dissolution, and signatures of all persons concerned.

g. Determination and statement of heirship, 1932—, showing names of principles, date of instrument, and volume and page numbers of Probate Court Journal, entry 153. Arranged chronologically by dates entered. Indexed alphabetically by names of principles. Typed on printed forms. Average 600 pages. 18.5 x 13 x 3. Probate court office.

The juvenile court, though of uncertain origin, has been generally recognized as an American contribution to the administration of social justice. The establishment of such courts was the logical outcome of the practical philosophy of enlightened public men that child offenders against the law, or conventional social standards, should not be treated as criminals, but as unfortunates needing the help, supervision, and protection of the state.[1] Although the first separate court in the United States for the trial of juvenile offenders was established in 1899, in Cook County, Chicago, Illinois, by an act of the legislature of that state, the juvenile court was an institution of gradual growth. The Illinois experiment gave *impetus* to the movement in the middle west for more enlightened treatment of children.[2]

The Ohio legislature was not slow in seeing the value of the Illinois experiment, and accordingly, in 1902, and act was passed creating the juvenile court in Cuyahoga County. Under this act all counties having a population of over 380,000 and an insolvency court were authorized, under an extension of the jurisdiction of this court to establish children's court. The stipulation of this act excluded Ashland County. It gave the court jurisdiction of the trial of cases involving delinquent and neglected children, defined the terms "delinquent, dependent, and neglected," authorized the appointment of a probation officer, and made it his duty to investigate the facts of cases coming before the court, and to take charge of the offender before and after trial. The clerk of the juvenile court was directed to keep a journal in which were to be recorded the minutes of the case.[3]

Two years after the establishment of the Cuyahoga County juvenile court, the assembly provided by statute for the establishment of juvenile courts in the rural counties of the state which, because of the population requirement, were unable to create the newer agencies under the provisions of the act of 1902. Under the act of 1904 the judges of the court are common pleas, probate court, the insolvency courts (where established), wherein three or more judges held court concurrently, were authorized to appoint one of their members as "juvenile judge."

---

1. Miriam Van Waters, *Youth in Conflict* (New York, 1925), 147, 159, 161.
2. Edwin H. Sutherland, *Principles of Criminology* (Chicago, 1934), 270-272.
3. *Laws of Ohio*, XCV, 785.

The court was given original jurisdiction in all cases involving neglected, dependent, and delinquent children under the age of 16 years; and all children who have been scheduled in the past for trial in a justice of the peace or police court were in the future to be tried before a juvenile judge. As under the act of 1902, the judge was authorized to appoint a probation officer, and the clerk of courts was directed to keep a journal of the minutes of each case.[4] In 1908 the court was given jurisdiction in cases involving minors under 17 years of age, and such children as were brought before the juvenile judge were to become wards of the court until they had attained the age of 21 years. The county commissioners were authorized to provide by lease or purchase, a "detention home" where neglected or dependent children might be detained pending the final disposition of their cases. The clerk of courts was directed to keep not only a journal, but also an appearance docket containing all orders, judgments, and findings of the court.[5] The age jurisdiction of the court was increased to 18 in 1913.[6]

While provisions were being made for the establishment of juvenile courts, the legislature gave the court jurisdiction in cases involving adults charged with committing crimes against children or contributing to the delinquency of dependent children. Thus, in 1906 it was made a misdemeanor to contribute to the delinquency of a child under 17 years of age.[7] Two years later the "lack of parental care" was defined and it was made a misdemeanor to fail to support a minor if able, or to cause him to engage in begging.[8] In 1913 "proper parental care" was defined by statute.[9]

Marked progress has been made in the medical treatment of juveniles. While the act of 1913 authorized the juvenile judge to submit any child sentenced to an institution for correction to a mental test, the act of 1929 authorized him to submit any child coming before the court to a mental and physical test to be made by a physician or psychiatrist.[10]

---

4. *Ibid.*, XCVII, 561.
5. *Laws of Ohio*, XCIV, 192.
6. *Ibid.*, CIII, 869.
7. *Ibid.*, XCVIII, 314.
8. *Ibid.*, XCIX, 193.
9. *Ibid.*, 870.
10. *Ibid.*, CIII, 872; CXIII, 471.

To facilitate the scientific handling of children, the county commissioners were authorized, in the same year, to lease or construct a separate building to be known as the "juvenile court" which should be appropriately constructed, arranged, furnished, and maintained for the convenient and effective translation of the business of the court, including adequate facilities to be used as laboratories, dispensaries, or clinics for the scientific use of specialists attached to the court.[11]

One of the guiding principles of the court has been to make its "custody and discipline" of children approximate as nearly as possible that which should be given by their parents. In the case involving neglected or dependent children not sentenced to state institutions, it has been the policy of judges to assign children to private homes, and make arrangements for their adoption. Many other functions were gradually taken over by the juvenile court, such as administrating mothers' pensions,[12] now known as aid to dependent children.

The juvenile court of Cuyahoga County is the only independent juvenile court in the state, although separate records were not initiated until 1907. There are seven other juvenile courts in Ohio attached to courts of domestic relations. Juvenile court has been held in Ashland County since 1904.[13] The probate judge now serves as judge of the juvenile court under the provisions of the act of April 29, 1937, which repealed the act of 1904.[14]

As in most agricultural counties few juvenile offenders are brought into court, although the number is sufficient to justify the court's functioning. About 60 cases are heard annually. The majority of the culprits are paroled or put on probation in the institution or home best adapted to the offense and offender.

Ashland is provided with a juvenile detention home in the home of the Salvation Army commander, but many children are returned to their own homes where they are kept under observation by the probation officer.[15]

Divorce is here as elsewhere considered a contributing cause to juvenile delinquency, and an average of some 70 divorces are granted here annually.[16]

---

11. *Ibid.*, CXIII, 470.
12. *Ibid.*, CIII, 877.
13. *See* entries 103, 155.
14. G. C. sec. 1639-7.
15. *Laws of Ohio*, XCVII, 561.
16. Appearance Docket, 1935-1940, entry 128.

In 1913 the juvenile court was given the duty of administrating mothers' pensions.[17] With the acceptance of the Federal Social Security act in 1936 the sections of General Code[18] relative to mothers' pensions were repealed and aid for dependent children was provided. The administration of the act in the state is delegated to the state department of public welfare and in the counties to the judge having juvenile jurisdiction.[19]

Under the act of 1941, which amended the act of 1936, children are eligible for aid if they have been deprived of parental support for various stipulated reasons. However, a child over 16 and under 18 may still receive aid if found by the department of public welfare to be regularly attending school. The child must be living with a parent or relative who is a proper person to have charge of the child, and must have adequate own facilities or caring for him.[20] The county administration is empowered to make investigations to determine the eligibility of the applicant and the amount to be awarded which is based on the actual needs of the home.[21] Both the county administration and the department of public welfare are authorized to compel the attendance of witnesses and the production of books and papers.[22] To comply with this act the county is required to provide fifteen-one hundredths of a mill of the tax duplicate in order to participate; the state makes an appropriation to the county in the proportion that the number of children under 16 in the county is to the total in the state, and the federal government contributes one dollar for every two provided by the state and county.[23]

In Ashland County, the division of aid to dependent children is administered by the probate judge, who appoints a secretary and a case worker to investigate the dependency cases. Both are paid by the state department of public welfare. The agency investigated 486 cases in the period from1935 through 1940, extending aid to 81 children annually, the average amount of aid afforded each being $30 a year.[24]

---

17. *Laws of Ohio*, CIII, 877.
18. G. C. secs. 1683-2--1683-10.
19. *United States Statutes at Large*, XLII, 601; *Laws of Ohio*, CXVI, pt. ii, 188.
20. G. C. sec. 1359-32.
21. G. C. secs. 1359-43, 1359-33.
22. G. C. sec. 1359-43.
23. G. C. secs. 1359-36, 1359-37, 1359-38.
24. Appropriation Ledger, 1939-1940, entry 239.

General Court Records

196. JUVENILE APPEARANCE DOCKET

1937—. 1 vol. Initiated in 1937.

Record of juvenile cases in probate court, showing case number, name of delinquent or neglected child, date case filed, name of compliant, charge (if delinquent), dates of proceedings and findings in case, amount of fees, and signature of juvenile judge. Arranged chronologically by dates filed. Indexed alphabetically by names of delinquent or neglected children. Handwritten on printed forms. 300 pages. 16 x 12 x 2. Probate court office.

197. JUVENILE JOURNAL

1913—. 3 vols. 1904-1913 in Probate Court Journal, entry 153.

Journal entries juvenile cases before the probate court, showing date of entry, name and address of delinquent, charge, case history of juvenile, name of institution, date committed, and term of commitment. Arranged chronologically by dates entered. Indexed alphabetically by names of delinquents. Handwritten on printed forms. Average 310 pages. 15 x 12 x 2.5. Probate court record room.

Aid to Dependent Children

198. RECORD OF MOTHER'S PENSION

1913-1936. 2 vols. Discontinued; superseded by Aid to Dependent Children

Record of mothers' pensions, showing name and address of applicant, names and dates of birth of dependent children, date application filed, and remarks; also includes copies of reports on investigation of applicant, showing journal entries approving or rejecting application, amount of award, and record of payments. Arranged chronologically by dates of application. Indexed alphabetically by names of applicants. Typed on printed forms. Average 500 pages. 18 x 12 x 3. Probate court record room.

199. ACTIVE, PENDING, CANCELED, REJECTED, AND CLOSED CASES

1936—. 3 file boxes.

Papers pertaining to aid to dependent children: applications and active cases, showing case number, date of application, and name and address of applicant, complete history of case, verifications of marriage and divorce, birth and death certificates, family budgets, and investigator's report; pending cases, showing that case has been investigated, history compiled, and date submitted to board of public assistance for approval; rejected cases, showing also reason family has failed to qualify for aid, and data rejection; closed cases showing also date case closed and reason. Arranged alphabetically by names of applicants and chronologically thereunder by dates of applications. Handwritten and typed on printed forms. 6 x 6 x 24. Aid to dependents children's office.

200. SOCIAL SERVICE INDEX
1937—. 1 file drawer.

Card index record of other relief granted aid to dependent children families, showing name, address, age, sex, color, race, and occupation of client, names of the agencies that have contacted the individual, date of contact, and kind of aid. Arranged alphabetically by names of clients. No index. Typed on printed forms. 12 x 5 x 26. Aid to dependent children's office.

201. DISTRICT SUPERVISOR'S REPORT, PAYROLLS AND MISCELLANEOUS
1936—. 1 file box.

Copies of monthly statistical reports of district supervisors to bureau of public assistance, including public welfare, blind relief, aid for the aged, and aid to dependent children in accordance with the Social Security Act, showing name of county and agency, date of the report, number of applications for aid, number of cases where aid was granted, number of families, number of children in families, age and sex of children, and date filed; also includes correspondence in regard to relief, copies of statement of monthly payments for aid to dependent children issued by the district supervisor to the county auditor, showing date of statement, name of county, case number, name of recipient, total monthly payment, warrant number, number of children included in payment under 16 years of age, number between 16 and 18 years of age, and date filed. Arranged in file folders by subjects and chronologically thereunder by dates filed. No index. Typed on printed forms. 10 x 12 x 26. Aid to dependent children's office.

Jury commissioners were first authorized for Hamilton and Cuyahoga Counties in 1881.[1] In 1890 provision was made for the appointment of jury commissioners in counties having a city of the first class or of the first grade, second class.[2]

In 1891 the judges of the court of common pleas in counties having a city with a population of not less than 33,000 nor more than 50,000 were authorized to appoint four residents of the county to serve as a jury commission for a term of one year. The limitations of these acts excluded Ashland County. It was the duty of this commission to determine the qualifications and fitness of persons to be selected as jurors.[3] Three years later, in 1894, the provisions of the act were extended to all other counties in the state except Cuyahoga, Franklin, Hamilton, Lucas, Montgomery, and Mahoning.[4] In 1902 the statute was amended to include all counties.[5] In 1913 the number of jury commissioners in each county was reduced to two.[6]

The jury code, which became effective August 2, 1931, provided for a jury commission of the same number and same qualifications previously specified, to hold office at the pleasure of the court, and to meet and select prospective jurors, both grand and petit, for the ensuing year from the list provided by the board of elections.[7] At the beginning of each jury year the commissioners are required to make up a new and complete jury list, known as the annual jury list, arranged alphabetically by precincts, districts, and townships, recording the name, occupation, business address, and residence of each prospective juror, and to prepare an index to this list. A duplicate list is certified by the commissioners and filed in the office of the clerk of court of common pleas.[8]

---

1. *Laws of Ohio*, LXXVIII, 95.
2. *Ibid.*, LXXXVII, 327.
3. *Ibid.*, LXXXVIII, 200.
4. *Ibid.*, XCI, 176.
5. *Ibid.*, XCVI, 3.
6. *Ibid.*, CIII, 513; CVI, 106.
7. *Ibid.*, CXIV, 193-213.
8. *Ibid.*, CXIV, 205.

The jury commissioners selected prospective jurors for civil and criminal cases as well as for the grand jury. It selects jurors for the probate court, juvenile court, and other minor courts.

Ashland County had its first jury commission under the act of 1894. There are, as elsewhere, two commissioners. Each is paid $100 annually and serves during the pleasure of the court.[9] The annual jury list of 300 names is made up accordingly to the uniform method prescribed in the jury code of 1932. Each person listed is investigated by the jury commissioners regarding his fitness to serve before he is summoned.[10] The jury commissioners keep no separate records; for jury list, see entry 106.

---

9. Common Pleas Court Journal, XXIV, 58, entry 140.
10. *Laws of Ohio*, CXIV, 193.

The grand jury, sometimes called the palladium of English liberty, has as its function preliminary examination of persons charged with a capital or other infamous crime. The right, guaranteed by the federal constitution, to an examination by a grand jury, is recognized in the provision of the Ohio constitutions of 1802 and 1851 and in the amendments of 1912.[1]

Under the present system, which does not differ in detail from that inaugurated in the early days of the state's history, the grand jury is composed of 15 members, who are resident electors of the county having "the qualifications of jurors."[2] It is the duty of the grand jury "to inquire of and present all offenses committed in the county in and for which it was empaneled and sworn."[3] The proceedings of the grand jury are secret and each juror is required to take an oath to preserve such secrecy. Moreover, no grand juror may be required to reveal the way he or other grand jurors voted.[4]

The grand jurors are aided in their investigations by the county prosecuting attorney, who, since 1869, has been authorized by statute to present evidence before this body and compel the attendance of witnesses against whom he may institute contempt proceedings if they refuse to testify. The prosecuting attorney must leave the room before the jurors begin the expression of their views or before a poll is taken. The courts have decreed, however, that the mere presence of the prosecuting attorney in the room doing the deliberations is "not sufficient to sustain a plea in abatement."[5] Since 1902 the official court stenographer of the county may take shorthand notes of the testimony and furnish a transcript to the prosecuting attorney at his request. This reporter, like the prosecuting attorney and his assistants, is required to retire from the jury room before the grand jury begins its deliberations.[6]

At least 12 of the 15 jurors must concur and finding an indictment.[7] Indictments found by the grand jury are presented by the foreman to the court and are filed with the clerk of courts[8]

---

1. *Ohio Const. 1851*, Art. I, sec. 10.
2. G. C. sec. 13436-2.
3. G. C. sec. 13436-5.
4. G. C. sec. 13436-16.
5. See *State of Ohio v. William Stichtenoth*, 8 N.P., 297-339.
6. G. C. sec. 13436-8.
7. G. C. sec. 13436-17.
8. G. C. sec. 13436-21.

No grand juror or officer of the court is permitted to disclose that a person has been indicted before such an indictment if filed and the case docketed.[9] Any incarcerated person charged with an indictable offense who has not been indicted during the term of court at which he is held to answer is discharged.[10]

Since 1869 it has been the duty of the grand jury to visit the county jail once at each term of court at which they may be in attendance, examine its state and condition and inquire into the discipline and treatment of prisoners, and return a written report to the court.[11]

The majority of contemporary opinion holds that the grand jury, although still defended as a safeguard against oppressive prosecution, is of little usefulness in the administration of modern criminal justice. It is argued that the grand jury not only delays the prosecution of criminal offenses but also makes it impossible to place responsibility for neglect of duty, and is, in many instances a rubber stamp for the opinions of the county prosecuting attorney.

The grand jury meets in Ashland County three times annually or for each term of court, although special sessions may be called at the request of the county prosecuting attorney. The sessions are short, the indictments few, two terms or sessions in 1941 yielding but 12 indictments and 13 no bills.[12] Of these 12 indictments, only two were for the more serious offenses. Grand jurors receive $3 per day.

The grand jury keeps no permanent records. For grand jury records kept by the clerk of courts, see entries 103, 104, 106.

The grand jury keeps no separate records; for clerk of court's records, see entries 102-104, 106.

---

9. G. C. sec. 13436-15.
10. G. C. sec. 13436-23.
11. G. C. sec. 13436-20.
12. Criminal Appearance Docket, 1941, entry 134.

The petit jury, like the grand jury, had its origin and England during the reign of Henry II.[1] The right of trial by jury, guaranteed by the federal constitution, was included in each of the Ohio constitutions. At any trail, and any court, for the violation of a statute of the State of Ohio, or any ordinance of any municipality, except in cases where the penalty involved does not exceed a fine of $50, the accused is entitled to a trial by jury.[2]

Except in the method of selecting prospective jurors, the petit jury has remained unchanged for over 135 years. The number of jurors drawn for each term of court is fixed by an order of the court.[3] A venire is issued to the county sheriff for persons whose names are so drawn to appear on the day fixed for the trial.[4] From the persons so summoned a jury of 12 is empaneled. The county prosecuting attorney and the defense council may, in capital cases, peremptorily challenge six of the jurors. In other cases, four peremptory challenges are allowed.[5] Other challenges, alternately made, may be made for reasons prescribed by statute.[6]

When the case is submitted, the jury may decide the question before it in court, or retired to deliberate. Upon retiring, the jury members must be kept together at a convenient place by an officer of the court until they agree upon a verdict or are discharged by the court. The court may permit them to separate at night.[7] If the jurors disagree as to testimony, or desire to be further instructed on the law in the case, they may request the officer in charge to conduct them to the court for additional information.[8] In civil actions a jury renders a written verdict upon the concurrence of three-fourths or more of its members. This verdict is signed by each concurring therein.[9]

---

1. Adams, *op. cit.*, 116.
2. G. C. sec. 13443.
3. G. C. sec. 11419-21.
4. G. C. sec. 11419-27.
5. G. C. sec. 13443-4, 13443-6.
6. G. C. sec. 13443-8.
7. G. C. sec. 11420-6.
8. G. C. sec. 11420-6.
9. G. C. sec. 11420-9.

Under the criminal code adopted in 1929 the accused may waive his right to a jury trial in favor of a trial by a judge. This procedure, although criticized by some, is considered by others to be a logical step in the administration of criminal justice in a modern state. In Ashland, as in most counties, petit juries are being waived in favor of the trial judge. From January 16, 1939 to December 19, 1940, there were only 39 jury trials.[10] Petit juries serve for a term of court or until they are discharged from further duty.

The petit jury keeps no permanent records. For jury records kept by the clerk of courts, see entries 102, 105, and 106.

---

10. Witness and Jury Docket (1939-1940), entry 102.

The office of county prosecuting attorney, unlike those of the sheriff and the coroner, is one of the relatively newer agency in the administration of criminal justice. Established in America by the English during the colonial period it offers a striking difference in the development of the American criminal procedure as contrasted with the English procedure where criminal prosecutions were usually instituted by private persons. As developed in recent years, the office of the prosecuting attorney has become one of the state's most important agencies in its defense against modern crime.

The acts of the Northwest Territory place the responsibility for criminal prosecution upon the attorney general, who, and turn, appointed and commissioned persons to *prosecuto* cases in their respective counties.[1]

While the acts of the Northwestern Territory outlined the local institutions for the newer states, the constitution of Ohio contained no provisions for a prosecutor, leaving the creation of the office to the discretion of the legislature. In 1803, during the first session of the legislature, an act was passed authorizing the supreme court to appoint in each county an attorney to prosecute cases in behalf of the state.[2] Two years later, the appointing power was vested in the court of common pleas.[3] The office remained an appointive one until 1833 when the electorate of the county was directed to choose a prosecuting attorney in each county for a two-year term.[4] The act of 1852 let the office elective and a term unchanged, but in 1881 the term of office was set at three years, and in 1906 it was reduced to two years, and in 1936 increased to four years.[5]

Under the present system the prosecuting attorney is elected for four-year term.[6] He is required to get bond of not less than $1000 conditioned for the faithful performance of his duties of his office. If the office becomes vacant the court common pleas is authorized to appoint a successor.[7]

---

1. Chase, *op. cit.*, I, 287, 348.
2. *Laws of Ohio*, I, 50.
3. *Ibid.*, III, 47.
4. *Ibid.*, XXXI, 13-14; Chase, *op. cit.*, III, 1935.
5. *Laws of Ohio*, LXXVIII, 260; XCVIII, 271-272; CXVI, pt. ii, 184.
6. G. C. sec. 2909.
7. G. C. sec. 2911, 2912.

The county prosecuting attorney is authorized to appoint clerks, assistants, and stenographers and to fix their salary subject to the approval of the county commissioners. Since1911 he has been authorized to appoint a secret service agent or officer whose duty it is to aid him in the collection of evidence to be used in the trial of criminal cases and in matters of a criminal nature. The compensation of such officer is determined by the court of common pleas.[8]

Most important among the duties of the prosecuting attorney are those connected with criminal prosecutions. Differing little from those of early days of the office, these duties include the prosecution on behalf of the state of all complaints, suits, and controversies in which the state is a party, and such other suits, matters, and controversies as he is directed by law to prosecute within or without his county, in the probate court, court of common pleas, and court of appeals. In conjunction with the attorney general, he prosecutes cases in the supreme court which originated in his county.[9]

In felony cases, when a complaint is made to the prosecuting attorney, he is required to examine the evidence and determine if it is sufficient for prosecution. If he decides in the affirmative, he prepares the evidence for presentation to the grand jury.[10] If this body returns an indictment the prosecuting attorney prepares to present the evidence in trial court. The court of common pleas may appoint an attorney to assist the prosecuting attorney in criminal cases.[11] In the case of conviction, the prosecuting attorney causes execution to be issued for the fines or costs and pays into the county treasury all moneys so received.[12] Without reference to the grand jury, the county prosecuting attorney may initiate prosecutions in misdemeanor cases in the court of common pleas by information.[13] After prosecution is inaugurated, he may eliminate the case without trial by means of the *nolle prosequi*. Although he is prohibited from enlisting the *nolle prosequi* without leave of the court on good cause shown, his requests are usually granted.[14] After prosecution has begun, it remains with the prosecuting attorney whether the case shall be pressed and steps taken that will lead to conviction.

---

8. G. C. secs. 2914, 2915-1.
9. G. C. sec. 2916.
10. *See* p. 109.
11. G. C. sec. 2918.
12. G. C. sec. 2916.
13. G. C. sec. 13437-34.
14. G. C. sec. 13437-32

Besides prosecution in criminal cases, the prosecuting attorney also acts in civil matters. He may bring suit in the name of the state when he is convinced that public money is being misapplied or is being illegally withheld or withdrawn from the county treasury. Moreover, he may bring suit against persons violating the obligation of contracts of which the county is a party, or when county property is being used or occupied illegally.[15]

In addition to these, his other duties have been prescribed by statute. On the request of the judge having jurisdiction over juvenile cases, he must prosecute individuals for committing crimes against children.[16] Furthermore, when directed by the court of common pleas, he must prosecute persons for keeping a house of prostitution.[17] At the instance of the secretary of state, he must prosecute any officer who refuses to furnish gratuitously statistical information for the use of that office.[18]

The prosecuting attorney has also served in an advisory capacity since 1906.[19] He acts as an advisor to all county boards and officials and to township officers who may require his opinion in writing on matters connected with their official duties.[20] In addition to this, he prepares the official bonds for all county officers.[21]

The prosecuting attorney is required to make an annual report to the county commissioners stating the number of criminal prosecutions completed, the name or names of the party or parties to each, and the amount collected in fines and costs, and the amount of.[22] Moreover, on the demand of the attorney general he must make an annual report on forms provided by the state on all criminal actions prosecuted by indictments in his county.[23]

---

15. G. C. sec. 2921.
16. G. C. sec. 1639-42.
17. G. C. secs. 6212-5, 6212-7.
18. G. C. sec. 174.
19. *Laws of Ohio*, XCVIII, 160-161.
20. *Ibid.*, LXXVIII, 120; G. C. sec. 2917.
21. G. C. sec. 2920.
22. *Laws of Ohio*, LXXVIII, 120; G. C. sec. 2926.
23. G. C. sec. 2925; *Laws of Ohio*, XC, 225.

For the period between January 9, 1939 and December 28, 1940, the Ashland County prosecutor tried 38 offenders of whom 35 were convicted. During the same period 13 cases were suspended, 24 entries of *nolle prosequi* were made, and 62 defendants pleaded guilty.[24] This record indicates a fairly busy criminal department. The civil department was concerned mostly with foreclosure actions for taxes of which there were eight cases.[25] The prosecutor requires but one assistant and keeps his work well up to date, although his services as legal advisor are in considerable demand. His salary is $133.33 monthly and is bond is $1,700.[26]

All records are kept in the prosecutor's office, Wimbliger Block, 23$^{1/2}$ West Main Street, Ashland, Ohio.

---

24. Criminal Appearance Docket, 1939-1940, entry 134; Common Pleas Court Journal, 1939-1940, entry 140.
25. Appearance Docket, 1939-1940, entry 128; Common Pleas Court Journal, 1939-1940, entry 140.
26. Records of Warrants Issued, 1941, entry 256; Record of Official Bonds, 1941, entry 270.

202. PROSECUTING ATTORNEY'S CRIMINAL DOCKET
1936—. 1 vol.
Criminal docket, showing case number, volume and page numbers of court docket, name of court, names of defendant and attorney, offense, dates transcribed and indictment file, plea, recognizance, date trial heard, verdict returned, sentence, fine and costs, court proceedings, papers filed, names of witnesses, and memoranda. Arranged chronologically by dates filed. Indexed alphabetically by names of defendants. Average 300 pages. 9.5 x 14.5 x 1.5.

203. ACTIVE CRIMINAL CASES
1936—. 1 file box.
Papers pertaining to active criminal cases, showing date of court term, names of plaintiff and defendant, name of court, case number, indictment, and signatures of judge, prosecuting attorney, and attorney for defendant; also date of arrest and statement of prisoner taken at sheriff's office or police station. All papers of each case filed together in a folder showing name of defendant. Arranged alphabetically by names of defendants. No index. Handwritten on printed forms. 12 x 8 x 12.

204. COMPLETED CRIMINAL CASES
1936—. 1 file box.
Papers pertaining to criminal cases closed, showing name of defendant, date of court term, name of court, case number, reason for indictment, and final disposition of case; also date of arrest and statements of witnesses and prisoner. All papers of each case are filed together in a folder, showing name of defendant. Arranged alphabetically by names of defendants. No index. Handwritten on printed forms. 12 x 12 x 18.

The office of coroner, next to that of sheriff the oldest county office in America, had its inception in England during the latter part the twelfth century when the coroner kept a record of the activities in the county, especially regarding the administration of criminal justice. At the end of the thirteenth century it was his duty to make inquests whenever there was a sudden death in the shire, and the results were recorded and the coroner's rolls and presented to the justices in *eyre*.[1]

This office, transplanted to America during the colonial period was continued by the state, and was adopted by the territory of which the state of Ohio was then a part. An ordinance of the Northwest Territory published in 1788 authorized the governor to appoint a coroner in each county within the territory. This act, together with a supplementary act of 1795 adopted from the Massachusetts Code, fixed the power and duties of the coroner. He was empowered to do any act which by previous legislation had been delegated to the sheriff, and was given the ancient duty of English coroners in holding the preliminary investigations over the bodies of all persons found within his county, and were believed to have died by violence or casualty.[2]

The Ohio constitution of 1802 continued the historic office, making it elected for a two-year term.[3] A statute of 1805 defined the duties of the authority of the coroner which, in the main were comparable with those prescribed in the territorial code, except that he was denied the privilege of concurrent jurisdiction with the sheriff.[4] The coroner was required to post bond with the county commissioners, which was to be recorded in the record of their proceedings. The act further provided that the coroner should receive his remuneration of fees, and that if the office of sheriff was to become vacant the coroner was to execute temporarily the duties of the sheriff.[5] The latter remained active until its abrogation in 1887.[6]

---

1. Pollock and Maitland, *op. cit.*, I, 519, 571; II, 641.
2. Pease, *op. cit.*, 24-24, 272-275.
3. *Ohio Const. 1802*, Art. VI. sec. 1.
4. *Laws of Ohio*, III, 156-161.
5. *Ibid.*, III, 158-161.
6. *Ibid.*, LXXXIV, 208-210.

The constitution of 1851 and the constitutional amendments of 1912 left the duties of the coroner unchanged and it was not until recent years, when he became an aid in a scientific detection of crime, that laws have been passed which materially affects his office. By the legislative acted of 1921 the coroner was made official custodian of the morgue in counties where a morgue is maintained. The same act provided that only licensed physicians were eligible to the office in counties having a population of 100,000 or more,[7] and in 1937 such restrictions was extended to all counties.[8]

The coroner is required to draw up and subscribe his findings of facts in inquest and autopsies and to report them to the clerk of courts. This record contains a detailed description of the body over which the inquest has been held and a statement of the coroner's findings as to the cause of death.[9] He is required also to return to the probate court an inventory of articles of property found on or about the body and to preserve such property until the proper distribution may be made.[10] All records are open to public inspection.[11] In 1936 the tenure of office of the coroner was extended from two to four years.[12]

He is required to give bond in a sum of not less than $5,000 or more than $50,000 to be determined by the county commissioners, the bond and oath of office are filed with the county auditor.[13] The legal maximum salary in counties of less than 400,000 population, is $5000.[14] The coroner may appoint necessary assistants, and if the population of the county warrants, he may appoint a stenographer-secretary.[15]

---

7. *Laws of Ohio*, CIX, 543-244.
8. *Ibid.*, CXVII, 43.
9. G. C. secs. 2856, 2857.
10. G. C. secs. 2859.
11. G. C. secs. 2856-2.
12. G. C. secs. 2823.
13. G. C. secs. 2823, 2824.
14. G. C. secs. 2866-1.
15. *Laws Ohio*, CIX, 543.

In Ashland County, the absence of a large urban population tends to reduce the work of the coroner to a minimum. There were 28 cases requiring a coroner's investigation in 1939 and 25 in 1940, but criminal prosecutions resulted from none of these.16. The salary of the coroner is made up from an approximation of $175 authorized by the commissioners, together with the income from fees.[17] In the year 1931 to 1940 the fees ranged from a low of $132.70 in 1938 to a high of $251.73 in 1939.[18]

The coroner keeps no separate records; for coroner's records of fees, see entry 20-1, clerk of courts' records, see entry 121; and corner's bonds, see entry 270.

---

16. Inquest Docket, 1939, 1940, entry 121.
17. Commissioners Record, XXVI (1939- 1941), 513, entry 1.
18. (Auditor's) Annual Financial Reports to County Commissioners, 1931-1940, entry 267.

The office of sheriff antedates the Norman Conquest. This official was enjoying great power and importance centuries ago, and was probably brought into the English system after a model which existed in the Roman law. The name comes from the Saxon "shire-reeve" softened to "shireve," "shyrife," and finally to "sheriff." In ancient times he received his commission directly from the king and specifically represented the sovereign. Originally the sheriff in England was a judicial as well as a ministerial officer. He once held court in the shire and exercised no inconsiderable jurisdiction . By the time of Lord Coke (1560-1634), the functions of the English sheriff had become standardized under three general heads: (l) to serve process by which a suit was begun; (2) to execute the decrees of the court; (3) to act as conservator of peace within the county.[1]

The office appeared in America in modified form among the earliest colonial institutions, being created in Virginia in 1634, and in Massachusetts in 1654. This ancient office was continued by the states created after independence.[2] The office assumed a new significance in the latter part of the eighteenth century when a flood of colonists swept across the ineffective Allegheny barrier to establish homes in the Northwest Territory organized by Congress in 1787. In the remote West the pioneers, far removed from the orderly legal processes and courts of the East, were subjected to the machinations of the lawless element prevalent in every new community.

In 1792 the governor and judges of the territory adopted an act providing for the appointment by the governor of a sheriff in each county and defining his duties.[3] This pioneer law clearly established three of the four major duties of the sheriff as they remain today namely: attendance upon the court; execution of writs, warrants, and the like; and policing and the arrest of criminals.

When Ohio entered the union as a state in 1803, the office of sheriff was continued by constitutional provision, and was made elective for a two-year term.[4] Since that time relatively few changes have been made in the structural organization of the office.

---

1. Adams, *op. cit.*, 17-19; William A. Morris, "The office of Sheriff in the Anglo-Saxon period," *English Historical Review*, XXXI (1916), 20-40; Raymond Moley, *The Sheriff and the Coroner* (New York, 1926. *The Missouri Crime Survey,* pt. ii), 59-60.
2. For a comparative study of the Sheriff in England and the Chesapeake colonies, see Cyrus Harreld Karraker, *The Seventeenth-Century Sheriff ...* (Chapel Hill, 1930).
3. Pease, *op. cit.*, 8.
4. *Ohio Const. 1802,* Art. VI, sec. 1.

When a new county was erected the associate judges appointed a day on which the qualified voters met at the temporary seat of justice and elected a sheriff who served until the next general election.[5] Although the constitution of 1851 did not specifically provide for this office, it did declare that no person shall be eligible to the office for more than four in any period of six years.[6] No county officer was to have a longer term than three years,[7] but the matter of removal from office was left to the legislative action.[8] The limitations upon the consecutive terms which a sheriff might serve remained in force until 1933, when it was repealed by an amendment authorizing any county to adopt a charter form of government. The term of office remained at two years until 1936 when it was extended to four years.[9] The sheriff received his remuneration of fees until 1875. From 1875 to 1906 he received a definite salary based upon the population of the county according to the last federal census proceeding his election, plus a percentage of fees collected.[10] Since 1906 the compensation has been derived entirely from a salary determined on a population basis.[11] In 1831, in consideration of the increasing complexity of the duties of the office, the sheriff was authorized to appoint, with consent of the court of common pleas, one or more deputies. These men, like their superior, were required to give bond for the faithful performance of the duties of their office, and the sheriff was made responsible for their neglect of duty or misconduct in office.[12]

The present organization of the office may be briefly summarized; the sheriff is elected for a four-year term,[13] can hold no other elective office at the same time, and may not practice law while in office.[14]

---

5. A.E. Gwynne, *A Practical Treatise on the Law of Sheriff and Coroner with Forms and Reference to the Statutes of Ohio, Indiana, and Kentucky*, (Cincinnati, 1849), 3.
6. *Ohio Const, 1851*, art. X, sec. 3.
7. *Ibid.*, Art. X, sec. 2.
8. *Ibid.*, Art. X, sec, 6.
9. *Laws of Ohio*, CXVI, pt. ii, 184.
10. *Ibid.*, III, 49-51; XXXIII, 18, LII, 86; LXXII, 126.
11. *Ibid.*, XCVIII, 95.
12. *Ibid.*, XXIX, 410.
13. G. C. sec. 2823.
14. G. C. secs. 11, 1706, 2565, 2783, 2910.

He is required to give bond, the cost of which is paid by the county commissioners[15] are also required to provide an office for the sheriff at the county seat, equipment, supplies, and other essentials of the office.[16] The commissioners also appropriate funds for the expenses incurred by the sheriff in carrying out the various duties of his office.[17] The sheriff may appoint a deputy or deputies, but all appointees must be endorsed by the local judge of the common pleas court, the electors of the county, and no deputy may be a justice of the peace or mayor.[18] Deputies are also forbidden to practice law while in office.[19] The sheriff fixes the salaries of the deputies, subject to the budget limitations of the county commissioners,[20] and shares with his deputies certain duties in both civil and criminal cases.[21] In Ashland County the salary of the sheriff, based on a graded scale according to population within a $6,000 per year maximum, is $1,744.92.[22] The office may be vacated by failure to give proper bond, nonacceptance, or death.[23] Vacancies in the office are filled by the county commissioners.[24]

The sheriff may be removed for various financial defalcations,[25] for willfully refusing or neglecting his duty in criminal cases,[26] for malfeasance in office,[27] or for permitting the lynching of a person in his custody.[28] In the latter case the governor conducts the hearing and may remove the sheriff. If for some reason the sheriff is unable to serve a court order the judge of the common pleas court is authorized to make a temporary appointment for the post.[29]

---

15. G. C. sec. 2824.
16. G. C. sec. 2832.
17. G. C. sec. 2997.
18. G. C. secs. 1706, 2830
19. G. C. sec. 1706
20. G. C. sec. 2981
21. Willis A. Estrich, ed., *Ohio Jurisprudence* (Rochester, 1934), XXXVI, 660-672, 669-701.
22. G. C. secs. 2994, 2996, 2997; Estrich, XXXVI, 704-705.
23. G. C. secs. 2827, 12196.
24. G. C. sec. 2828.
25. G. C. secs 3036, 3049.
26. G. C. secs 12850, 12851.
27. *Ohio Const. 1851* (Amendment, 1912), Art. II, sec. 38.
28. *Laws of Ohio*, CI, 109
29. G. C. sec. 2828

The retiring sheriff is required to deliver to his successor all moneys, papers, books, and the like, as well as the custody of all the prisoners.[30]

Aside from his power to appoint deputies, the sheriff has other special powers which are largely the products of historical development. From earliest years the sheriff has been empowered to call to his aid such persons as he deemed necessary to perform his lawful duty and apprehension of criminals.[31] Thus the *posse comitatus* was at his disposal as it is today.[32]

The specific duties of the sheriff were and are prescribed by statute and may be classified under four main divisions; attendance upon the courts; execution of summonses, warrants, processes, and other *writs*; controlling and being responsible for the care of the jail and the courthouse; policing the county and arresting criminals.

The territorial law of 1792 required the sheriff to attend the sessions of court of common pleas and the court of appeals during their sessions,[33] and this requirement has been carried over into the laws of Ohio,[34] the present duties of the sheriff in this respect being survivals for the provisions of this act. He is required to attend the county court of common pleas,[35] the appellate court,[36] and the probate court if required by the judge of that division.[37] The sheriff may adjourn the court of common pleas from day to day upon failure of the judge to appear at regularly scheduled sessions.[38]

The duty of the sheriff to execute all warrants, *writs*, and processes directed to him by the proper and lawful authority has also been operative since territorial period.[39] At present he executes every summons, order, or other process, and makes return thereof as required by law.[40]

---

30. G. C. secs. 2842, 2843
31. *Laws of Ohio,* III, 156-158; XXIX 112-113.
32. G. C. sec. 2833.
33. Pease, *op. cit.*, 8.
34. *Laws of Ohio,* III, 156-158; XXIX, 112; LXXXII, 26.
35. G. C. sec. 2833.
36. G. C. sec. 1530, 2833.
37. G. C. sec. 2833.
38. G. C. sec. 2855.
39. Pease, *op. cit.,* 8; *Laws of Ohio,* III, 156-158; XXIX, 112; LXXXII, 26.
40. G. C. sec. 2834.

He executes processes from the probate, juvenile, common pleas, and appellate courts. Although the jury commission has supplanted the clerk of courts in the manner of selecting names of prospective jurors to the jury wheel, the sheriff's duties in this respect remain much as they were in the earlier years of his office. He also executes warrants issued by the governor of the state,[41] and serves *writs* and subpoenas issued by various state officers and boards.[42] In other words, the sheriff serves all the papers which concerned the county as a unit of government and some for the state as well.

As early as 1805 the sheriff was made official custodian of the county jail.[43] Although the earliest statutes directed the county commissioners to provide dungeons for Incarceration of prisoners, the act of 1847 directed the sheriff to exercise reasonable care for the preservation of the life, health, and welfare of those committed to his care. He was and is authorized to transport prisoners to other counties for safekeeping.[44] Under the direction and control of the county commissioners the sheriff is also given charge of the courthouse.[45]

The sheriff has had extensive and important police power since 1792 when the territorial act authorized him to keep and preserve the peace, and suppress affrays, routs, riots, unlawful assemblies, and insurrections; to apprehend, and confined to jail all felons and traitors; and to return persons who, having committed a crime in his county, had taken refuge in another.[46] During the legislative session of 1805 the general assembly passed an act defining the duties of the sheriff which were in all respects similar to the provisions inherited from the territorial code.[47] In the same year the sheriff was designated as the county's executioner, and was bound to carry out sentences of death by hanging, when imposed by the courts, upon those convicted of murder.[48]

---

41. G. C. sec. 118.
42. G. C. secs. 285, 346, 2709, *et al.*
43. *Laws of Ohio,* III, 157.
44. *Ibid.,* III, 157; XXIX. 112-119; XCIII, 131. For general provisions as to jail duties, *see* G. C. secs. 3157-3176, *passim.*
45. G. C. sec. 2833.
46. Pease, *op. cit.,* 8.
47. *Laws of Ohio,* III, 156-158.
48. Chase, *op. cit.,* I, 442.

Public executions, the general rule during the earlier years, were abolished in 1844.[49] In 1886 the sheriff's duties in this respect were delegated to the warden of the Ohio Penitentiary.[50]

An act of 1831, repealing the act of 1805 redefined the duties of the sheriff as a conservator of the peace in his county,[51] and his present duties in this respect are survivals from the provisions of this act.[52] Although the sheriff is still regarded as a chief peace officer in the county, many of his earlier duties in this respect have been abolished by the development of other agencies of law enforcement, notably the state highway patrol. On the other hand, the powers of the sheriff to suppress affrays, riots, and unlawful assemblies became especially important in times of strikes or threatened riots. On a properly issued warrant he may arrest any person charged with the probability of doing injury to another person or the property of another.[53] Moreover, since 1921 the sheriff has forwarded to the state bureau of criminal identification fingerprints of all persons arrested for a felony,[54] and since 1913 has been authorized to arrest any person violating his parole.[55]

The present police powers of the sheriff are very comprehensive. His jurisdiction is coextensive with the county, including all municipalities and townships, and he is the chief law-enforcement officer of the county. In municipalities the sheriff and mayor stand on an equality as law enforcement officers so far as state laws are concerned, and neither is permitted to cast the burden of action upon the other.[56]

---

49. *Laws of Ohio,* XLII, 71.
50. *Ibid.,* LXXXII, 145.
51. *Ibid.,* XXIX, 112-113.
52. *Ibid.,* LXXXIII, 26.
53. G. C. sec. 12428-1.
54. *Laws of Ohio,* CIX, 548; CX, 5.
55. *Ibid.,* CII, 404.
56. Estrich, *op.. cit.,* XXXVI, 645. For the most important police powers *see* G. C. secs. 2833, 3345, 4112, 12811.

The sheriff has possessed and still possesses many powers and duties which are miscellaneous and nature. As in England, the sheriff, during the earlier years of his office, was required to notify the electors of his county of the time and place of holding elections. He was enjoined to furnish ballot boxes at the expense of the county, hold special elections when so directed by the governor, and deliver the poll books to the secretary of state.[57] Since 1891 these duties have been taken over by the board of elections.[58] The sheriff also has many heterogeneous powers and duties regarding elections,[59] executive orders of the secretary of agriculture,[60] fish and game laws,[61] probation officers,[62] military census,[63] traffic rules and regulations,[64] funds and deposits in court,[65] shanty boats,[66] and executive orders of the governor.[67]

The multiplicate duties of the sheriff have made it necessary to keep many records of the business of the office. The sheriff has been required to keep a foreign execution docket since 1838,[68] a cash book since 1842,[69] and a jail register since 1843.[70] These records for Ashland County are extant only for 1867, 1868, in 1869 to date respectively.[71] Indexes, direct and reverse, to the foreign execution docket were prescribed by the legislature in 1925.[72] Since 1843 he has been required annually to transmit the jail register, and certified copies, to the clerk of courts, the county auditor, and the secretary of state.[73]

---

57. *Laws of Ohio,* II, 88-90; III, 331-332.
58. *See* p. 191.
59. G. C.secs. 4785-124, 4829.
60. G. C. sec. 1110.
61. G. C. secs. 1434, 1441, 1444, 1451.
62. G. C. sec. 1639-19.
63. G. C. sec. 5188-5.
64. G. C. sec. 7251-1.
65. G. C. sec. 11900.
66. G. C. sec. 13403-1.
67. G. C. sec. 118.
68. *Laws of Ohio,* XXXVI, 18; LVII, 6; LXXXIV, 208-209.
69. *Ibid.,* XL, 25; LXV, 115; LXXXIV, 6; LXXXIV, 208-209.
70. *Ibid.,* XLI, 74.
71. *See* entries 205, 209, 210.
72. *Laws of Ohio,* CXI, 31.
73. *Ibid.,* XLI, 74.

Since 1850 he has been required, on the first Monday of September in each year, to submit to the county commissioners a certified statement of all fines and costs collected during the year, and the amount of fees collected and paid to the clerk of courts of common pleas.[74]

Thus the modern sheriff keeps the following records: (1) a case book which is a record of all monies handled; (2) a foreign summons docket which is a record of all summonses from counties other than his own; (3) a foreign execution docket which is a record of executions from counties other than his own; (4) a service record which includes all probate and divorce papers served; (5) an execution register which records all executions handled: (6) an accrued fee record which list fees received; (7) a commission register which records the commissions of all special deputies; (8) a jail register which records all prisoners brought in, the charge, how long detained, and when released.[75] By statute the sheriff is also required to make an annual financial report to the county commissioners.[76]

The sheriff of Ashland County is bonded for $2,000, and receives a salary of $1,744.92 annually.[77] He has three deputies, and is provided with two cars equipped with radios. The present jail, built in 1886,[78] contains cells for ten men and three women and is administered by the sheriff with the assistance of the jail staff of four. It has housed during the past ten years an average of 220 persons annually.[79]

In 1940, 189 traffic accidents were investigated, and 14 sales on foreclosure were conducted.[80] Fees received by the sheriff's office were $1,690.79.[81]

One sheriff, John J. Herzog, has been removed from office in Ashland County. He was arrested and charged with embezzlement on July 14, 1892,[82] and upon his refusal to satisfy a demand for new bond, the office fell vacant.

---

74. G. C. sec. 2744; *Laws of Ohio,* XLVIII, 66.
75. G. C. secs. 2837, 2979, 3045, 3046.
76. G. C. sec. 2844.
77. Record of Official Bonds, 1940, entry 270. County Officer's Statement of Fees and Compensation, 1940, entry 265.
78. The *Ashland Times*, January 27, 1887.
79. Jail Record II, III, years covered.
80. Index to Deeds, Grantor, 1940, entry 37.
81. Record of Accrued Fees, 1940, entry 212.
82. Commissioners' record IV (1882-1893), 383.

Court Orders

205. FOREIGN EXECUTION DOCKET

1867—. 4 vols. (One unlabeled; 1-3).

Record of executions ordered by courts outside Ashland County on property located in Ashland County to satisfy judgments rendered, showing names of plaintiff and defendant, execution and case numbers, from what court, date *writ* received and return, itemized cost bill, copies of orders of sale, name of attorney, and record of sheriff's sale. Arranged chronologically by dates *writs* received. Indexed alphabetically by names of plaintiffs and defendants. Handwritten on printed forms. Average 400 pages. 15 x 10 x 2.5. County jail, sheriff's private office.

206. FOREIGN SUMMONS DOCKET

1933—. 1 vol.

Sheriff's record of summonses issued by courts other than Ashland County on residents of Ashland County, showing from what county and court, names of plaintiff, defendant, and attorney, case number, dates *writ* received, served, and returned, sheriff's costs, fees, and return on *writ*. Arranged chronologically by dates *writs* served. Indexed alphabetically by names of plaintiffs and defendants. Handwritten on printed forms. 250 pages. 16 x 10 x 2. County jail, sheriff's private office.

207. ORDER OF SALE DOCKET

1885-1927. 2 vols.

Record of orders to sell, issued to sheriff by county courts, showing name of court, kind of *writ*, date of order, and names of judgment debtor and creditor. Arranged chronologically by dates of orders. Indexed alphabetically by names of judgment creditors. Handwritten on printed forms. Average 300 pages. 15 x 12 x 2. 1 volume, 1885-1897, county jail, sheriff's private office; 1 volume, 1898-1927. County jail storage room.

208. PARTITION RECORD

1874—. 2 vols. (1, 2).

Record of sales in partition cases, showing docket number of original entry, names of plaintiff and defendant, date of order to sell, date and amount of sale, names of persons to whom sale proceeds were distributed, amount to each recipient, amount of cost, and sheriff's fees. Arranged chronologically by dates of orders. Indexed alphabetically by names of plaintiffs and defendants. Handwritten on printed forms. Average 240 pages. 18 x 12 x 3. County jail, sheriff's private office.

Jail and Identification Records

209. JAIL RECORD

1869—. 4 vols, (1-4). Title varies; Jail Register, 1869-1922, 2 vols.

Register of commitment to county jail showing date of commitment, name, nativity, age, and race of prisoner, number of days in jail, sheriff's cost and fees, by what authority held and discharged, date of discharge, and reason for commitment to jail; also includes record of arrest of parole violators, 1913—. Arranged chronologically by dates of commitments. No index. Handwritten on printed forms. Average 200 pages. 17 x 15 x 2. 1 volume, 1869-1895, county jail storage room; 3 volumes, 1896—, county jail, sheriff's private office.

210. CRIMINAL FILES

1925—. 1 file box.

Photographs and descriptions of suspects wanted by federal bureau of investigation, sheriff, and police departments, showing name, address, and alias of suspect, physical description with fingerprints, and date, place, and description of crime committed. Arranged alphabetically by names of suspects. No index. Typed on printed forms. 8 x 5 x 10. County jail, sheriff's private office.

Financial Records

211. SHERIFF'S CASH BOOK

1869—. 4 vols. (1, 1-3).

Record of cash received, showing case number, names of plaintiff and defendant, by whom paid, date entered, to whom due, amounts for court cost, judgment, sales, and sundries, date distributed, and amount paid. Arranged chronologically by dates entered. No index. Handwritten on printed forms. Average 300 pages. 18 x 12 x 2. County jail, sheriff's private office.

212. OF ACCRUED FEES
1907—. 6 vols. (1-6).

Record of accrued fees collected by sheriff, showing case number, nature of case, names of plaintiff and defendant, date accrued, total cost, amount of fees from county, and foreign *writs.* Arranged chronologically by dates accrued. No index. Handwritten on printed forms. Average 300 pages. 18 x 13 x 2. 4 volumes, 1907-1929, county jail storage room; 2 volumes, county jail, sheriff's private office.

213. UNCLAIMED FEES, UNCLAIMED MONEY
1907—. 1 vol.

Record of unclaimed money and fees, showing name of owner (payee), date of entry, amount of fee, case number, date paid into treasury, volume and page number of record; also certificate of recovery, showing date issued and amount of certificate. Arranged chronologically by dates entered. Indexed alphabetically by names of owners. Handwritten on printed forms. 200 pages. 14 x 18 x 1.5. County jail, sheriff's private office.

The county dog warden, appointed by the county commissioners, has as his duty the enforcement of the provision of the General Code relative to licensing dogs, the impounding and destruction of unlicensed dogs, and the payment of compensation for damages to livestock inflicted by dogs. This officer, like other county officials, is required to give bond conditioned for the faithful performance of the duties of his office. This bond, in the sum of not less than $500 nor more than $200, is filed with the county auditor. His compensation and tenure, like that of his deputies, is determined by the county commissioners.[1]

The warden is required to make a record of all dogs owned, kept, or harbored in his county; to patrol the county; to seize and impound dogs more than three months of age found not wearing a valid registration tag. The latter provisions do not apply, however, to dogs kept in a regularly licensed kennel. Moreover, he is required to make weekly written reports to the commissioners of all dogs seized, impounded, redeemed, and destroyed. Then, too, he is required to report all claims for damages to livestock inflicted by dogs.

The dog warden and his deputies have, in the performance of their legal duties, the same police powers as are conferred by statute upon sheriffs and police. They may summon the assistance of bystanders in performing their duties, serve *writs* and other legal processes issued by any court in the county with reference to enforcing the provisions of the laws relating to dogs.[2]

In Ashland County the duties of dog warden were under the jurisdiction of the sheriff from 1917 to 1927 as provided by the statute.[3] In 1927 an act authorized the commissioners to appoint a county dog warden responsible to the commissioner, under which act the Ashland County dog warden was appointed in September 1927.[4] During the year 1940, 529 dogs were seized. One was redeemed, seven were sold, and the remainder were destroyed. Since 4292 licensees were issued that year[5] for dogs and 41 for kennels the office is self-sustaining, the appropriations for 1940 being $4,967.08.[6] The dog warden is under $500 bond and is paid $142.50 monthly.[7]

---

1. G. C. sec. 5652-7.
2. *Ibid.*
3. *Laws of Ohio,* CVII, 535.
4. *Ibid.,* CXII, 348; Commissioners' Record, XIX (1926-1927), 476.
5. Record of All Licensed Dogs, 1940, entry 214.
6. Appropriation Ledger, 1940, entry 239.
7. Record of Official Bonds, 1940, entry 270; Records of Warrants Issued, 1940, enter 256.

214. RECORD OF ALL LICENSED DOGS

1937—. 1 vol.

List of licensed dogs as applied periodically to auditor by dog warden, showing name and address of owner, age, sex, and description of dog, and tag number. Arranged alphabetically by names of owners. No index. Typed on printed forms. 200 pages. 16 x x12 x 2. Auditor clerk office, dog warden's desk.

215. POUND KEEPERS RECORD

1927—. 7 vols.

Pound keeper's record of impounded dogs, showing date of report, description of dog, including sex, color, hair (long or short), weight, height, and breed, address of owner, keeper, or harborer, date impounded, date disposed of, manner of disposition, date of payment of cost, amount received for sale of dog, name and address of purchaser, and signature of pound keeper. Arranged chronologically by dates reported. No index. Handwritten on printed forms. Average 75 pages. 15 x 9 x .5. Auditor clerk office, dog warden's desk.

216. REPORTS (Dog Warden)

1927—. 3 vols.

Copies of dog wardens report, showing date of report, name of owner, keeper, or harborer, number of dogs kept, name and address of keeper, date seized or impounded, date sold, redeemed, or destroyed, funds collected, and date money is paid into county treasurer. Arranged chronologically by dates reported. No index. Handwritten on printed forms. Average 100 pages. 14 x 10 x 2. Auditor clerk office, dog warden's desk.

217. ANIMAL CLAIM REPORT OF DOG WARDEN

1927—. 15 vols.

Dog warden's record, showing name and address of claimant, date of filing, name of township, number of animals killed or wounded, grade, date of discovery, and signature of dog warden. Arranged chronologically by dates filed. No index. Handwritten on printed forms. Average 35 pages. 4 x 6 x .25. Auditor clerk office, dog warden's desk.

The first Ohio Constitution, adopted in 1802, did not provide for the office of county auditor and it was not until 1820 that the general assembly by joint resolution appointed an auditor in each county for a one-year term.[1] In 1821 the office became elective and the term was fixed at one year.[2] In 1831 the term was set at two years, in 1877 at three years, and 1906 reduced to two years, and in 1919 extended to four years.[3]

The county auditor is required to take oath and give bond for faithful performance of the duties of his office; to preserve all copies of entries, surveys, extracts, and other documents transmitted to his office from the state auditor; and to transfer to his successor all books, records, maps, and other papers pertaining to his office.[4] With the approval of the county commissioners he is authorized to appoint deputies, for whose official acts he and his sureties are held liable; since 1869 the record of these appointments has been required to be filed with the county treasurer.[5] If the office of county auditor falls vacant the county commissioners are authorized to appoint a successor.[6]

The first auditor in each county was required to list all lands in his county subject to taxation. From this list and one submitted to him by the county commissioner and one from the state auditor, the county auditor was directed to make a tax duplicate to be kept in a book for that purpose, and to give a copy of the list to the tax collector.[7] The auditor was also directed to compile from the treasurer's duplicate a list of lands on which taxes were delinquent, and if such lands were sold for taxes, to grant a deed to the purchaser.[8]

---

1. *Laws of Ohio,* XVIII, 70.
2. *Ibid.,* XIX, 116.
3. *Ibid.,* XXIX, 280; LXXIV, 381; XCVIII, 271; CVIII, pt. ii, 1294.
4. *Ibid.,* 116, LXVII, 103; G. C. secs. 2559, 2582.
5. *Laws of Ohio,* LV, 20; LXVI, 35; G. C. sec. 2563.
6. G. C.secs, 2979, 2580, 2990, 2996.
7. *Laws of Ohio,* XVIII, 79.
8. *Ibid.,* XVIII, 82; XIX, 115.

Subsequent legislation expanded and itemized the duties of the auditor regarding taxation. With modifications to meet modern requirements these duties have continued much as they were during the earlier years of his office. During the 1840s the office of county assessor was abolished and provision was made for township assessors whose duty it was to list all taxable property and make a return to the auditor.[9] Since 1874 the auditor is required by statute to keep a book in which he lists additions to and deductions from the amount of tax assessment.[10] In 1915 he was made chief assessing officer of the county.[11]

The county auditor has been a member and served as a secretary of the county budget commission since its beginning in 1911, his duties include keeping full and accurate records of the proceedings of that body. For the purpose of adjusting the tax rates and fixing the amount to be levied each year the commissioners are governed by the amount of taxable property as shown on the auditor's tax list for the current year. He submits to the commissioners the annual tax budget given him by each taxing authority of each subdivision, together with an estimate of any levy prepared by the state auditor, and such other information as a budget commission may request or the state tax commission required.[12]

Tax settlements had been made annually until 1859 when the auditor was required to make semiannual settlement with the treasurer to ascertain the amount of taxes the treasurer is to stand charged.[13] Since 1904 liquor, cigarette, and inheritance taxes have constituted separate funds. All other taxes are credited to the general fund.[14]

Since 1831 the county auditor has kept an account current with the county treasurer showing the payments of moneys into the treasury, listing the date, by whom paid, and to which fund. On receiving the treasurer's daily statement the auditor enters on his account current the amount shown as a charge to the treasurer.[15]

---

9. *Ibid.,* XXXIX, 22-25.
10. *Laws of Ohio,* LXXI, 30.
11. *Ibid.,* CVI, 246.
12. G. C. sec. 5625-19; *Laws of Ohio,* CXII, 402.
13. G. C. sec. 2596, *Laws of Ohio,* LVI, 132; LXXVIII, 226.
14. *Laws of Ohio,* XCVII, 457.
15. *Ibid.,* XXIX, 280-291; LXVII, 103.

Another important function of the county auditor is the approval before payment of bills and other claims against the county. Since 1831 he has been authorized to issue, on presentation of the proper voucher, all warrants on the county treasurer for moneys payable from the county treasury; and to preserve all warrants, showing the number, date of issue, amount for which drawn, in whose favor, and from which fund.[16] County money due the state is paid on warrant of the state auditor. Since 1904 a bill or voucher for payment from any fund controlled by the county commissioners or board of county commissioners or board of county infirmary directors is filed with a county auditor and entered in a book with that purpose at least five days before its approval for payment by the commissioners, and when approved the date is entered opposite the claim.[17]

Besides approving bills and claims against the county, the auditor in 1835 was given the duty of certifying all moneys, except collections on the tax duplicate, into the county treasury, specifying by whom paid and the fund to which such payment is credited. Such moneys he charges to the treasurer, keeping a duplicate copy of the statement in his office. Since 1835 all costs collected in penitentiary cases to be paid to the state have been certified into the treasury as belonging to the state.[18]

In 1902 the legislature provided for a system of uniform accounting and auditing of all public offices, and for the annual examination of their finances, under the direction of a bureau of inspection in the office of the state auditor.[19] Since 1904 the county auditor has been required to report to the commissioners on the state of county finances. On the first business day of each month he prepares in duplicate a statement of the county finances for the proceeding month, compares it with the treasurer's balance, and submits it to the commissioners, who post one copy of it in the auditor's office for 30 days for public inspection.[20]

---

16. G. C. sec. 2570; *Laws of Ohio*, XXIX, 280-291; LXVII, 103.
17. *Laws of Ohio,* XCVII, 25; CVIII, pt. I, 272.
18. *Laws of Ohio,* XXXIII, 44; LXVII, 103.
19. *Ibid.,* XCV, 511-515.
20. *Ibid.,* XCVII, 457.

During the development of the office additional duties in great diversity have been delegated to the county auditor. Since 1833 he has been authorized to discharge prisoners jailed for nonpayment of any fine or amercment due the county when in his opinion the amount is not collectible.[21] In 1838 an act was passed making him county superintendent of schools. He was relieved of this duty in 1848 when a county superintendent of schools was authorized in each county.[22] Since 1846 he has served as the sealer of weights and measures, is responsible for the preservation of the copies of the original standards delivered to his office, and enforces in his county all state laws regulating weights and measures.[23] In 1861 he was authorized to report to the state auditor statistics concerning the deaf, dumb, blind, insane, and idiots in his county, with the names and addresses of their parents or guardians.[24] Eight years later, in 1869, he was authorized to report to the same officer statistics concerning livestock in his county as returned to his office by assessors, and an abstract of the funded and indebtedness of his county, and of each township, city, village, and school district.[25] Since 1827 he has been authorized to issue licenses to traveling public shows and exhibitions, although municipal authorities may impose an additional license.[26] In 1862 he was authorized to issue peddlers' licenses to persons who filed a statement of stock in trade in conformity with a law requiring the listing of such stock for taxation, and since 1917 he has issued dog licenses.[27] The auditor has issued licenses to wholesale and retail dealers in cigarettes since 1892,[28] in brewers' wort and malt since 1933,[29] and has issued cosmetic licenses from August 1, 1933 to June 30, 1936.[30]

---

21. G. C. sec. 2576; *Laws of Ohio,* XXXI, 18; LXVII, 103.
22. *See* p. 195.
23. G. C. sec. 2615; *Laws of Ohio,* XLIV, 55; LVIII, 78, CI, 234.
24. *Laws of Ohio,* LVIII, 40
25. G. C. sec. 2604.
26. Chase, *op. cit.,* III, 1582; *Laws of Ohio,* XXIX, 446; G. C.secs, 6374, 6375.
27. *Laws of Ohio,* LIX, 67; LXXIX, 96; CVII, 534.
28. G. C. sec. 5894-5.
29. G. C. sec. 5545-5.
30. *Laws of Ohio,* CXV, 649; CXV, pt. ii, 83; CXVI, pt. ii, 323.

From 1850 to 1910 the auditor was the official custodian of the reports submitted to the commissioners by the prosecuting attorney, the clerk of courts, the sheriff, and the treasurer; these reports are required to be recorded by the auditor in books kept specifically for that purpose.[31] From 1910— a full-time commissioner's clerk has assumed these duties. The auditor is a member of the County Board of Revision, established in 1825, secretary of the Budget Commission, and serves as a trustee and a secretary of the Board of Trustees of the Sinking Fund, established in 1919.

In Ashland County, the work of the auditor's office is carried on by a staff of five in addition to the auditor himself. The total appraised value of property in the county has shown some increase in recent years, being given as $37,416,050 in 1935, and as $39,881,920 in 1940.[32] In the same period the tax rate for real property has declined, having been set at 3.52 mills in 1935, 3.77 in 1936, but at 2.60 in 1940.[33] The bonded indebtedness of the county has also declined in these years, from $482,410 in 1935 to $248,100 in 1940.[34]

---

31. G. C. sec. 2504; R.S. sec. 886; *Laws of Ohio,* XLVIII, 66.
32. Auditors Duplicate, 1935, 1940, entry 223.
33. County Commissioners' Resolutions, 1935, 1936, 1940, entry 276.
34. Abstract of Indebtedness to State Auditor, 1935, 1940, entry 268.

Property Transfers

218. TRANSFER RECORD (County)

1846—. 11 vols. (1-11).

Record of transfers of titles to real estate, showing date of transfer, to whom, range, township, section, and lot numbers, what part of lot, value, from whom, date of deed, and remarks; include transfer records and affidavits, executor's, administrator's, trustee's, guardian's, warranty, and sheriff's deeds, and transfer record of auditor's deeds, including auditor's deeds for land sold for delinquent taxes, showing name of taxing district, name of original owner, date of sale, name of purchaser, range, township, and section numbers, acreage, description of tract, quantity sold, amount of sale, date deed issued and to whom, and signature of county auditor. Arranged alphabetically by names of townships and chronologically thereunder by dates of transfers. No index. Handwritten on printed forms. 400 pages. 16 x 14 x 3. 5 volumes, 1846-1925, Auditor's clerk office; 6 volumes 1926—, Auditor's main office.

219. TRANSFERS OF CITY AND VILLAGE

1891—. 5 vols.

Record of transfers made of city and village lands and lots, showing date of transfer, to whom transferred, range, township, tract or section, lot number, what part, value, from whom transferred, date of deed, and remarks. Arranged alphabetically by townships and chronologically thereunder by dates of transfers. No index. Handwritten on printed forms. Average 250 pages. 16 x 12 x 2.5. Auditor's clerk office.

Maps and Plats

220. (MAPS AND PLATS)

1849—. 37 vols. (unlabeled; 1-7; 1-15). Subtitled by names of townships. Plats of townships, cities, and towns, showing name of owners, description and lot number; also includes a transfer record, showing letter, date of transfer, to whom transferred, range, township, section, and lot numbers, what part of lot, number of acres, from whom transferred, date of deed, date filed, value of property, and remarks. Arranged chronologically by dates filed. No index. Handwritten on printed forms. Average 50 pages. 16 x 12 x 1. 7 volumes, 1849-1922, recorder's record room; 30 volumes, 1923—, Auditor's main office.

Tax Records

Real property taxes

221. APPRAISEMENTS
1848—. 22 vols. Last appraisement 1935.

Record of appraisement of real estate, showing names of taxing district and owners, description of property, number of acres of land, classified as meadow, pasture, uncultivated, and woodland, value of land and buildings, amounts added and deducted by county and state boards of revision, and total value as equalized; also includes appraiser's account of days worked and money received from auditor, appraiser's oath, and hand drawn physical maps taxing district appraised. These appraisements are made every six years. Arranged alphabetically by names of taxing district and alphabetically thereunder by names of property owners. No index. Handwritten and typed, some on printed forms. Average 200 pages. 9 x 15 x 3. Auditor's clerk office.

222. ASSESSORS' RETURNS
1846—. 15 file boxes.

Record of township assessors' returns on real and personal property; real property, showing name of owner, year, description of land, number of acres, valuation of buildings, improved lands, total value, and remarks; personal property, showing name and address of owner, year, value of livestock, jewelry, musical instruments, moneys, credits, investments, and remarks as sworn or affirmed. Arranged in envelopes by years. No index. Handwritten on printed forms. 5 x 30 x 26. 10 file drawers, 1846-1935, basement storage room; 5 file drawers 1936—, Auditor's main office.

223. AUDITOR'S DUPLICATE
1846—. 132 vols. (Dated). Titles varies: Tax List, 1915-1930, 27 vols. Subtitled by names of townships.

Auditors duplicate of real property assessments, showing year, name of taxing district, name of owner, description and location of property, value of land and buildings, total value for taxation, and total amount of taxes due; tax list, showing assessment certificate number, name and address of taxpayer, and final assessment. Also contains auditor's Delinquent Record, 1846-1869, entry 220. Arranged alphabetically by names of taxing districts and chronologically thereunder by years.

No index. Handwritten and typed, some on printed forms. Average 300 pages. 16 x 14 x 3. 123 volumes, 1846-1931, basement storage room; 9 volumes, 1932—, Auditor's main office.

224. SPECIAL ASSESSMENT DUPLICATE
1906—. 8 vols., 2 file boxes.

Records of assessments for public improvements, showing lot number, acreage, location and description of property, name of owners, quantity of property, amount of assessment, date notice sent out, date paid, receipt number, and total tax. Arranged alphabetically by names of taxing districts and alphabetically thereunder by names of property owners. No index. Handwritten on printed forms. Average 250 pages. 14 x 12 x 2; file boxes, 10 x 4.5 x 13.5. 4 volumes, 1906-1913, basement storage room; 4 volumes, 2 file boxes, 1914—, Auditor's clerk office.

Personal Property Taxes (See also entry 222)

225. RETURNS Of PERSONAL PROPERTY
1869-1932. 672 vols.

Copies of reports of statistics on chattels as returned by township assessors, showing name and address of property holder, name and value of horses, cattle, sheep, hogs, poultry, and mules, value of motor and other vehicles, household goods and furnishings, farm tools and other machinery, farm and agricultural products of all kinds, motor boats and other vessels, office furniture, mining machinery and equipment, stocks, bonds, annuities, and other personal property, grand total, balance for taxation, and total as equalized by board of revision. Arranged alphabetically by townships and chronologically thereunder by dates filed. No index. Handwritten on printed forms. Average 300 pages. 15 x 17.5 x 2. Auditor's main office.

226. PERSONAL TAX RETURNS
1935—. 1 file box, 12 file drawers (labeled by contained letters of alphabet).

Individual personal tax returns, showing year, name of taxing district, name of property owner, itemized tangible and intangible tax, summary and computation of tax, and affidavits. Arranged alphabetically by names of property owners. No index. Handwritten on printed forms. File box, 4 x 8 x 20; File drawer, 10 x 12 x 20. 1 file box, 1935, basement storage room; 12 file drawers, 1936—, Auditor's clerk office.

227. PERMIT FOR EXTENSION OF TIME TO MAKE TAX RETURNS

1932—. 7 file boxes.

Copies of permits, issued by auditor to taxpayers for extension of time to make personal tax returns, showing name of taxpayer, permit number, names of county and township, date of permit, and time granted. Arranged alphabetically by names of taxpayers and chronologically thereunder by dates of permits. No index. Handwritten on printed forms. 10 x 4.5 x 13.5. Auditor's main office.

Delinquent Taxes

228. AUDITOR'S DELINQUENT RECORD

1870—. 7 vols. (1-7). 1846-1869 in auditor's duplicate entry 223.

Record of delinquent land taxes, showing year, tax rate, name of taxing district, names of owner and township, range, section, and lot numbers, acreage, description of property, location, valuation, penalties, and total tax due; also includes list of unpaid personal property taxes, 1870-1904, showing information as in entry 227. Arranged alphabetically by names of taxing districts and chronologically thereunder by years. No index. Handwritten on printed forms. Average 220 pages. 18 x 12 x 2. 4 volumes, 1870-1911, basement storage room; 3 volumes, 1912—, Auditors' clerk office.

229. DELINQUENT PERSONAL TAX

1904—. 5 vols. (1-5), Title varies; Delinquent Record, 1909-1913, 1 vol.

Auditors duplicate delinquent personal taxes, showing name of taxing district, name of property owner, value of property, years delinquent, penalty, total tax unpaid, total tax paid, and date of payment; collected February settlement, unpaid February settlement, the collected August settlement, and the unpaid August settlement. Arranged alphabetically by names of taxing districts and chronologically thereunder by dates of payments. No index. Handwritten on printed forms. Average 350 pages. 14 x 8 x 2. 2 volumes, 1904-1912 basement storage room; 3 volumes, 1913—, Auditor's main office.

230. RECORD OF TAX PAYMENT UNDER WHITTEMORE PLAN

1933—. 1 file box.

Auditors copies of undertakings to pay full amount of delinquent taxes and assessments, less penalties, interest, and other charges in annual installments under Whittemore plan, showing names of property owners, date due, amount of general taxes, names of county and township, amount of municipal assessments, amount of principal, date paid, and contract number. Arranged alphabetically by names of property owners. No index. Typed on printed forms. 12 x 4 x 18. Auditor's main office.

Adjustments

231. ADDITION AND DEDUCTION ORDERS AND CERTIFICATION
1874—. 15 vols. (1-15).

Record of additions to and deductions from tax duplicate, showing name of taxing district, date of order, names of property owner and township, range, and lot number, value, total tax, and amount added or deducted. 1921—, consists of copies of orders. Arranged chronologically by dates of orders. No index. Handwritten on printed forms. Average 400 pages. 18 x 12 x 2.5. 5 volumes, 1874-1920, basement storage room; 10 volumes, 1921—, Auditor's clerk office. Auditor - Tax Record.

232. AUDITOR'S DUPLICATE, ADDITIONS TO, SPECIAL AND MISCELLANEOUS
1855—. 18 vols. Subtitled by names of townships.

Auditor's duplicate of additions to tax duplicates, duplicate of special and miscellaneous taxes, showing date of addition, name of taxing district, name of personal property owner, description and location of property, receipt number for tax paid, total tax, penalties, and remarks. No index. Handwritten on printed forms. Average 350 pages. 18 x 12 x 2.5. 15 volumes, 1855-1933, basement storage room; 3 volumes, 1934—, Auditor's clerk office.

Inheritance Taxes

233. INHERITANCE TAX RECORD
1919—. 4 bundles, 3 file boxes.

Inheritance tax charges, showing name of estate, name of administrator or executor, value of estate, cost of administration, names and relationship of heirs, signature of probate judge, probate court file number, amount of exemption, amount subject to tax, date of accrual, name of taxing district, and date papers filed. Arranged chronologically by dates filed. No index. Typed on printed forms. Bundles, 12 x 4 x 24; file boxes, 12 x 4 x 18. Auditor's main office.

Utility Taxes

234. RAILROAD APPRAISEMENT
1892-1913. 1 vol.

Record of appraisement of railroad property, showing date of appraisement, description, number, condition, and value of buildings, tools, and machinery, total of other property, additions or deductions by state board of equalization, and net value for taxation; minutes of various meetings, showing attendance record of officials at meetings, credits, and estimated value of moneys. Arranged chronologically by dates of appraisements. Indexed alphabetically by names of railroads. Handwritten on printed forms. 150 pages. 18 x 10 x 2. Basement storage room.

Excise Taxes

235. CIGARETTE TAX COLLECTION
1869-1925. 3 vols.

Auditor's record of cigarette taxes collected, showing name of taxing district, name and address of taxpayer, date of collection, and amount collected. Arranged alphabetically by names of taxpayers. No index. Handwritten on printed forms. Average 200 pages. 16 x 12 x 2. Basement storage room.

236. CIGARETTE LICENSE
1931—. 8 vols.

Copies of licenses issued by auditor to traffic in sale of cigarettes, showing date of issue, license number, name of licensee, business address, date effective, date of expiration, amount of tax, penalties, and signatures of auditor and deputy. Arranged chronologically by dates issued. No index. Handwritten on printed forms. Average 250 pages. 6 x 15 x 2. Auditor's main office.

237. COSMETIC LICENSE APPLICATIONS
1933-1934. 1 file box.

Record of applications for cosmetic dealer's licenses, showing date of application, name and address of dealer, date of expiration, and the name of city, village, or township. Arranged alphabetically by names of dealers and chronologically thereunder by dates of applications. No index. Handwritten on printed forms. 10 x 4.5 x 13.5. Auditor's main office.

238. BREWER'S WORT AND MALT DEALER'S LICENSE
1933—. 1 file box, 2 bundles.
Record of applications for brewer's wort and malt dealer's license, showing date of application, name of applicant, business address, kind of business, and date issued. Arranged alphabetically by names of applicants and chronologically thereunder by dates of applications. No index. Handwritten on printed forms. File box, 10 x 4.5 x 13.5; bundles, average 9.5 x 4 x 2.5. Auditor's main office.

Fiscal Accounts
(See also entries 263-268)

Appropriations

239. APPROPRIATION LEDGER
1928—. 12 vols.
Record of appropriations to each county fund and record of disbursements from same, including soldiers' relief and burial commissions, blind relief commission, aid for the aged, aid to dependent children, and mothers' pensions, showing date and amount of appropriation, date and amount paid, to whom paid, for what purpose, purchase order and certificate number, warrant number, total debit to each fund, and amount of unencumbered balance of each fund. Arranged alphabetically by names of funds and chronologically thereunder by dates entered. No index. Handwritten on printed forms. Average 200 pages. 10 x 12 x 2. Auditor's main office.

Settlements

240. ANNUAL SETTLEMENTS
1846—. 14 vols.
Copies of abstracts of the duplicate, sent to the auditor of state, this being a settlement record with the state, showing date of abstract, rate of taxation by taxing district, totals of all state, county, township, district, and other taxes, certification by auditor, value of all property as equalized by board of revision, and amount of delinquencies and forfeitures of other years. Arranged chronologically by dates of abstracts. No index. Handwritten on printed forms. Average 300 pages. 9 x 16 x 3. 10 volumes, 1846-1931, basement storage room; 4 volumes, 1932—, Auditor's main office.

241. SCHOOL FUND SETTLEMENTS
1881—. 4 vols. Title varies: Record of Settlements and Abstracts, 1881-1905, 1 vol.

Record of annual settlements of school funds, showing name of township or school district, signature of auditor, bond of school treasurer, and bond of school clerk; auditor's statement of distributions, showing from what source and amount collected, school apportionment, tuition, bonds and interest, total receipts, total disbursements, balance on hand, and date of statement; also includes a record of certification of funds in hands of school treasurer. Arranged alphabetically by names of school districts and chronologically thereunder by dates of settlements. No index. Handwritten on printed forms. Average 250 pages. 14 x 10 x 2. 3 volumes, 1881-1916, basement storage room; 1 volume, 1917—, Auditor's main office.

242. SEMI-ANNUAL STATEMENTS WITH TREASURER
5 vols., 1 file box, 2 file drawers. Title varies: Record of settlements and Abstracts, 1859-1906. 1 vol.; Settlements and Abstracts, 1906-1928, 2 vols.; Settlement Record, 1906-1928, 2 vols.

Record of settlements of the county auditor with township treasurers, 1859-1927, showing date of settlement, detailed statement of all receipts from real chattel duplicates and from all other sources, amount credited to county, township, town, or corporation, and to schools; also shows expenditures for each taxing district, purpose, total expenditures, and balance. Settlements of real, utility, and personal taxes; 1928—, real and utility settlements, showing original amount of duplicates, names of taxing district, county, township, school, or corporation, total amount of duplicates, also schedule of special assessments, of sub-additions to general duplicates, delinquencies, and forfeitures of former years, remitter's unpaid taxes, unpaid delinquencies, and forfeitures, schedule of auditor's and treasure's fees deducted, refunders, rate used in distributing depository interest, cigarette settlement, inheritance tax collected, certificate of personal fees due in inheritance tax proceedings, schedule of workmen's compensation withheld, schedule of election expenses, schedule of examiner's expenses, board of health expenses, schedule of advanced drafts, special assessments, itemized list of local taxes collected, including schools, townships, corporations distribution of refunding bond fund, abstract of settlements with state auditor, statement of semiannual apportionment of township taxes, cigarette traffic tax settlement, and itemized account of license taxes. Settlements of personal property, showing list of individual tax returns, refunders, classified tax distribution, township distribution, school distribution, corporation, receipts and disbursements, statement, and draft by treasurer. Arranged alphabetically by names of townships and chronologically thereunder by dates of settlements. No index. 1859-1928, Handwritten on printed forms.; 1928—, typed on printed forms. Volumes average 200 pages.10 x 16 x 2; file box, 4 x 18 x 36; file drawer, 4 x 8 x 20. 5 volumes, 1 file box, 1859-1931, basement storage room; 2 file drawers 1932—, Auditor's clerk office.

General Accounts

243. AUDITOR'S LEDGER

1863—. 8 vols. (1-8).

Auditor's fund account ledger; fund credits, showing name of fund, date, source, pay-in order number, and amount; fund debits, showing name of fund, date debited, for services and goods supplied, order number, and amount; also total credit and debit for each thirty day period of funds, including county, general tax, cigarette, inheritance tax, automobile, infirmary, crippled children, and board of education funds. Arranged alphabetically by names of funds and chronologically thereunder by dates entered. No index. Handwritten on printed forms. Average 500 pages. 20 x 14 x 3. 6 volumes, 1863-1919, basement storage room; 2 volumes, 1920—, Auditor's clerk office.

244. AUDITOR'S JOURNAL OF PAYMENTS INTO TREASURY

1904—. 6 vols. -1867-1904 in record of Warrants Issued, entry 256.

Record of payments into treasury, showing date of payment, name of taxpayer, services and goods supplied, number and amount of pay-in order, and names of funds, including general, children's home, dog and kennel, road and bridges, general tax, cigarette tax, and inheritance tax funds. Arranged chronologically by dates of payments. No index. Handwritten on printed forms. Average 230 pages. 18 x 11.5 x 1.5. Auditor's main office.

Special Accounts

245. RECORD OF WORTHY BLIND

1904—. 4 vols. (1-4). Initiated and 1904.

Auditor's record of grants for worthy blind, showing application number, date filed, name and address of applicant, date of application, date approved or rejected, amount of grant and date paid, and complete record of relief payments. Arranged chronologically by dates of payments and numerically thereunder by application numbers. Indexed alphabetically by names of applicants. Handwritten on printed forms. Average 125 pages. 16 x 12 x 1. 2 volumes, 1904-1913, basement storage room; 2 volumes, 1914—, Auditor's clerk office.

246. INDIGENT SOLDIERS' RECORD
1901-1933. 2 vols. (2, 3).

Record of monthly allowances for relief made to indigent soldiers, their wives or widows, showing name of township, date of payment, name of recipient, amount allowed, name of treasurer, and order number. Arranged alphabetically by names of townships and chronologically thereunder by dates of payments. No index. Handwritten on printed forms. Average 110 pages. 14 x 10 x 1. 1 volume, 1901-1915, Basement storage room; 1 volume, 1916-1933, auditor's main office.

247. RECEIPTS SOLDIERS' RELIEF
1910-1927. 4 vols. (labeled by contain receipts numbers).

Itemized list of all disbursements of the soldiers relief and burial commission fund, showing date of entry, to whom and amount paid, and total amount paid out each month; also includes original receipts of recipients for amounts paid monthly for relief of indigent soldiers, showing date of receipt, amount paid, receipt number, name of township, name of recipient, certification of client as eligible for relief, and signature of treasurer and recipient. Itemized list, arranged chronologically by dates entered; receipts, arranged numerically by receipt numbers. No index. Handwritten on printed forms. Average 150 pages. 12 x 8 x 1. Basement storage room.

248. RECORD OF MOTHERS' PENSIONS
1913—. 3 vols.

Record of mothers' pensions, showing name and address of pensioner, names and date of birth of dependent children, date application filed, copy of reports on investigations of application, copy of journal entry approving application, amount of award, and record of payments. No index. Handwritten on printed forms. Average 200 pages. 16 x 12 x 2. 1 volume, 1913-1925, auditor's private office; 2 volumes, 1926—, Auditor's main office.

249. AUDITOR'S FEES

1862—. 6 vols. (1-3). Titles varies: Fee Book, 1862-1906, 3 vols. Record of licenses and fees for peddlers' licenses, 1862—, showing date license issued, license number, name and address of licensee, brief military history of soldier or sailor, territory to be covered, and amount of fee; includes record of fees received for transfer, settlement, and sundries, 1907—, showing date and amount of payment, name of payer, and services and goods supplied. Arranged chronologically by dates of payments. No index. Handwritten on printed forms. 3 volumes, average 200 pages. 12 x 8 x 2; 3 volumes, average 285 pages. 16 x 12 x 2. 3 volumes, 1862-1906, basement storage room; 3 volumes, 1907—, Auditor's main office.

Bills and Claims

250. RECORD OF BILLS FILED – COMMISSIONERS

1904—. 14 vols. (1-14).

Record of bills filed, showing date of bill, consecutive bill number, name of person claiming bill, services of rendered or goods supplied, date of filing, date and amount approved, date of payment, and number of warrant. Arranged chronologically by dates filed and numerically thereunder by consecutive bill numbers. No index. Handwritten on printed forms. Average 150 pages. 16 x 12 x 2. 6 volumes, 1904-1918, basement storage room; 4 volumes, 1919-1928, auditor's clerk office; 4 volumes, 1928—, Commissioner's office.

251. RECORD OF BILLS (Infirmary)

1904—. 2 vols. (1, 2).

Record of bills filed for payment from county home fund, showing date filed, name of creditor, number and amount of bill, services rendered or good supplied, and date approved. Arranged chronologically by dates filed and numerically thereunder by consecutive bill numbers. No index. Handwritten on printed forms. Average 300 pages. 18 x 12 x 2.5. 1 volume, 1904-1907, basement storage room; 1 volume, 1908—. Auditor's main office.

252. RECORD OF BILLS ALLOWED

1883—. 3 vols.

List of bills allowed by county commissioners, including road, ditch, contract, and miscellaneous, showing name and address the creditor, services rendered or goods supplied, and date, number, and amount of bills allowed; also volume and page number of Commissioners' Record, entry 1. Arranged alphabetically by names creditors. No index. Handwritten on printed forms. Average 300 pages. 18 x 12 x 2.5. Auditor's clerk office.

253. ANIMAL CLAIM RECORD
1917—. 2 vols. (1, 2).

Record of claims as presented by trustees of the various townships to the county commissioners and approved by them for payment of damages done by dogs, for killing or injuring animals, showing number, kind, grade, quality, and value of animals, nature of injury, name of township, amount claimed, names and addresses of owners and witnesses, date of claim, date approved, and auditor's record of payment, showing date of payment and warrant number. Arranged chronologically by dates of claims and numerically thereunder by warrant numbers. No index. Handwritten on printed forms. Average 125 pages. 14 x 8 x 1.5. Auditor's main office.

254. RENTS AND LEASES
1869—. 8 file boxes.

Record of money due county from the townships for rent or lease of county owned property, showing name of township, date of receipt, date due, description of property, and total amount. Arranged chronologically by dates of receipts. No index. Handwritten on printed forms. 10 x 4.5 x 13.5. Auditor's main office.

Pay-in Orders and Warrants

255. PAY-IN ORDERS
1921—. 9 vols.

Record of pay-in orders issued by auditor authorizing treasurer to receive payments into treasury and credit same to certain funds, showing consecutive pay-in order number, date of issue, name of person making payments, amount, Fund credited, and services and good supplied. Arranged chronologically by dates issued and numerically thereunder by pay-in order numbers. No index. Handwritten on printed forms. Average 250 pages. 14 x 12 x 1.5. 2 volumes, 1921-1925, basement storage room; 7 volumes, 1926—, Auditor's clerk office.

256. RECORDS OF WARRANTS ISSUED

1846—. 23 vols. (Five unlabeled; 1, 2, 1-16). Title varies: Title illegible, 1846-1866, 2 vols. ; Records of Orders and Receipts, 1867-1904, 5 vols.

Record of general warrants issued, showing date and number of warrant, name of payee, amount, services and goods supplied, and name of fund. Also contains Auditor's Journal of Payment into Treasury, 1867-1904, entry 244. Arranged chronologically by dates of warrants and numerically thereunder by warrant numbers. No index. Handwritten on printed forms. 7 volumes average 300 pages. 18.5 x 11.25 x 1.5; 16 volumes average 375 pages. 14 x 10 x 2. 7 volumes, 1846-1903, basement storage room; 16 volumes, 1904—, Auditor's main office.

257. AUDITOR'S RECORD (Court Warrants)

1878—. 4 vols. (1-4).

Record of court warrants issued, showing date and number of warrant, name of payee, service rendered, goods supplied, including petit and grand jury witnesses and jurors, witnesses in lunacy and epilepsy cases, and witnesses and jurors in minor courts, and for coroner's inquests. Arranged chronologically by dates of warrants and also arranged numerically by warrant numbers. No index. Handwritten on printed forms. Average 275 pages. 18 x 12 x 2. 2 volumes, 1878-1890, basement storage room; 2 volumes, 1891—, Auditor's main office.

258. CANCELED WARRANTS

1904—. 20 file boxes.

General and court warrants which have been redeemed, showing date and number of warrant, name of payee, amount, services and good supplied, name of fund, and date canceled or redeemed. Arranged chronologically by dates redeemed and numerically thereunder by warrant numbers. No index. Handwritten on printed forms. 15 x 10 x 15. 8 file boxes, 1904-1932, basement storage room; 12 file boxes, 1933—, Auditor's clerk office.

Licenses

(See also entries 236-238)

259. DOG LICENSE APPLICATIONS

1917—. 12 file boxes.

Auditor's copy of dog licenses issued, showing name and address of owner, license number, date issued, name of township, description of dog as to age, sex, color hair, and breed if known, fee paid, penalty, effectively spayed, name of former owner if purchased outside of Ohio, tag number assigned, and signatures of auditor or notary public and owner. No index. Handwritten on printed forms. 6 file boxes, 12 x 12 x 30; 6 file boxes, 10 x 4.5 x 13.5. 6 file boxes, 1917-1934, basement storage room; 6 file boxes, 1935—, Auditor's main office.

260. VENDOR'S LICENSE

1935—. 21 vols. (Labeled by contain license numbers).

Copies of license issued to vendors by auditor, showing names of county and state, license number, date issued, name and address and applicant, type of business, code number, penalties, and signature of auditor or deputy. Arranged chronologically by dates issued and numerically thereunder by license number. No index. Handwritten on printed forms. Average 200 pages. 5 x 6 x 1. Auditor's main office.

261. MOTOR VEHICLE LICENSES

1935—. 24 file boxes.

Record of motor vehicle licenses issued, showing registration number, number of horsepower, amount of fee, name and address of owner, name of taxing district, year, make and type of car, number of cylinders, serial or factory number, model, new or used car, date of purchase, clerk of courts' file, number on bill, sworn statement of ownership or certificate of title, where filed, signature of notary, and date license issued. Arranged numerically by registration numbers. No index. Typed on printed forms. 5 x 8 x 22. Auditor's main office.

Enumerations and Statistics

262. SCHOOL ENUMERATIONS

1873—. 1 carton, 1 bundle, 1 file box.

Abstracts of enumeration of youths between the age of 5 and 18 years residing in Ashland County, showing names of school districts, total number of boys and girls between the age of 5 and 15 years, total number of boys and girls between the ages 16 and 17 years, total number of boys and girls between the age of 5 and 18 years, number of youths in school and number of youths out of school with working permits; handicapped youths between the age of 1 and 21 years, classified as boys and girls between the age of 1 and 4, 5 and 15, 16 and 17, 18 and 21, with nature of handicap; also includes a grand total of each group, signature of auditor, and date filed. Arranged chronologically by dates filed. No index. Handwritten on printed forms. 1 carton, 1873-1914, basement storage room; 1 bundle, 1 file box, 1915—, Auditor's main office.

263. MONTHLY STATEMENT OF MEALS
1875—. 10 vols.
Sheriff's monthly statement of county commissioners and auditor, of number of meals served to prisoners, showing number of prisoners, names of prisoners and other persons, date of entry, date prisoner received, date of last report, date discharge, number of meals served, total number of meals, and total monthly cost; including requisitions and purchase orders for supplies, showing county commissioners' approval, signatures of auditor and sheriff, account code number, and amount allowed. Arranged chronologically by dates entered. No index. Handwritten on printed forms. 5 x 5 x 12. 7 volumes, 1875-1930, basement storage room; 3 volumes, 1931—, Auditor's main office.

264. STATEMENT OF FINES (Mayor's and Justice of Peace)
1927—. 1 file box.
Original monthly statements to county auditor by mayor's and justice of the peace courts of fines and fees collected and paid into county general fund, showing date of report, names of county and township, case number, docket and page numbers, names of plaintiffs and defendants, amount of fines and fees, date collected, and name of justice of peace or mayor. Arranged alphabetically by names of justices or mayors and chronologically thereunder by dates reported. No index. Typed on printed forms. 12 x 12 x 25. Auditor's clerk office.

265. COUNTY OFFICER'S STATEMENT OF FEES AND COMPENSATION
1850—. 1 carton, 1 bundle, 1 file box.
Original reports of county commissioners, clerk of courts, sheriff, treasurer, and prosecuting attorney of amount of fees and salaries, showing name of county, date filed, amounts of salaries and expenses paid or due for the year, fees earned during the year, name of office, salaries of officers, other compensations, salaries of assistants, deputies, and clerks, expense of maintenance of vehicles, other expenses, total general fees, inheritance fees, total fees earned, and signature of auditor to sworn statement. Arranged chronologically by dates filed. No index. Handwritten

on printed forms. Carton, 6 x 12 x 12; bundle, 4 x 12 x 24; file box, 4 x 12 x 18. 1 carton, 1850-1900, basement storage room; 1 bundle, 1 file box, 1901—, Auditor's clerk office.

266. MONTHLY FINANCIAL REPORTS TO COUNTY COMMISSIONERS
1928—. 3 file boxes.

Copies of monthly financial statements of auditor to county commissioners, showing name of ending month, date filed, names of various funds, balance brought forward from preceding month, overdraft at end of month, and balance forward; also includes daily statement of treasurer, showing date of statement, balance at close of business on previous day, amount in treasury, amount in depository, and total; number of pay-in orders, amount of general personal tax, classified personal tax, amount checked from depository, total, balance, at signature of treasurer. Arranged chronologically by dates filed. No index. Handwritten on printed forms. 10 x 12 x 24. Auditor's main office.

267. (Auditor's) ANNUAL FINANCIAL REPORTS TO COUNTY COMMISSIONERS
1928—. 11 vols.

Copies of auditor's annual financial statements to county commissioners, showing date of report, receipts and disbursements of general fund, and special fund, including county road and bridge, state road and bridge, motor vehicle and gas tax, maintenance and repairs, dog and kennel, sewer and water district, county home, bond retirement, sinking funds, emergency relief, aid to dependent children, undistributed tax, and trust funds belonging to other governmental units, county board of education and county health funds, and transfers of funds. Arranged alphabetically by names of funds. No index. Handwritten on printed forms. Average 50 pages. 12 x 10 x .25. Auditor's main office.

268. ABSTRACT OF INDEBTEDNESS TO STATE AUDITOR
1869—. 2 bundles.

Copies of reports by county auditor to state auditor regarding the county indebtedness, showing purpose for which debt was created, amount of outstanding indebtedness, amount paid off, balance, rate of interest, date of maturity of loan, amount of cash on hand and amount anticipated to take care of indebtedness, date and report, signature of county auditor, and date filed. Arranged chronologically by dates filed. No index. Handwritten on printed forms. Bundles average 10 x 10 x 36; file box, 4 x 12 x 18. 1 bundle, 1869-1900, basement storage room; 1 bundle, 1 file box, 1901—, Auditor's main office.

Bonds

269. OFFICIAL BONDS
1898—. 1 vol.
Register of official bonds, showing date filed and approved by prosecuting attorney, name of official, date and amount of bond, names of sureties, and signature of prosecuting attorney. Arranged chronologically by dates filed. Indexed alphabetically by names of officials. Handwritten on printed forms. Average 300 pages. 8 x 12 x 1.25. Auditor's main office.

270. RECORD OF OFFICIAL BONDS
1897—. 2 vols. (1, 2).
Copies of surety bonds filed with county auditor by all elected county officials, including treasurer, sheriff, coroner, prosecuting attorney, clerk of courts, and probate judge, showing names of principal and sureties, name of office, date of bond, date filed, copy of oath of office, and date of expiration of term; also includes bonds of depositories of county funds, showing conditions of obligations, names of bondsmen, prosecuting attorney's certificate of approval, and oath. Arranged chronologically by dates filed. Indexed alphabetically by names of persons bonded. Handwritten on printed forms. Average 175 pages. 18 x 12 x 2.25. Auditor's clerk office.

271. REGISTER OF BONDS
1915—. 1 vol. (2).
Record of bonds, showing amount of bond, when due, dates of payment, issue, and sale, amount of interest, purpose, and date coupon was redeemed. Arranged chronologically by dates issued. No index. Handwritten on printed forms. 100 pages. 12 x 17 x 2. Auditor's clerk office.

272. REDEEMED BONDS AND COUPONS
1925—. 11 FILE BOXES.
Original bonds, showing date of issue, maturity, rate of interest to be paid, for what services, to whom paid, kind of bond, total amount of bonds and coupons, bond

number, and date payable. Arranged chronologically by dates issued and numerically thereunder by bond number. No index. Handwritten on printed forms. 10 x 4.5 x 13.5. Auditor's clerk office.

Weights and Measures

273. SEALER OF WEIGHTS AND MEASURES
1912—. 1 vol.

Copies of monthly reports of the county sealer made to county auditor, showing date of inspection, name and address of firm, individual, or corporation, kind of business, types of weight and measuring devices tested, kinds of commodities re-measured, numbers found correct, incorrect, and whether over or under weight; also includes record of orders issued to owners of weighing and measuring devices. Arranged chronologically by years and alphabetically thereunder by names of months. No index. 150 pages. 16 x 13 x 1.5. Auditor's clerk office.

Miscellaneous

274. REPORT OF EXAMINATION
1874—. 24 bundles, 2 file boxes.

Reports of examination of county funds by state examiners and county commissioners, showing date of report, period covered by report, financial statistics, and date report filed. Arranged chronologically by dates filed. No index. Handwritten and typed, some on printed forms. Bundles, 12 x 14 x 4; file box, 12 x 14 x 30. 24 bundles, 1974-1913, basement storage room; 2 file boxes, 1914—, Auditor's main office.

275. RECORD OF DISTRIBUTION OF FEES FOR AUTO LICENSES
1925-1932. 4 vols. (1-4).

Daily report of auditor concerning distribution of motor vehicle license fees to subdivision, showing date of report, name of county, district of registration, number of cars, type of car, amount of fees, commercial dealer's license, additional fees to correct errors, refunds and totals, and date filed; also includes monthly reports, showing names of municipalities, motor vehicles, registration for month, including date of daily report, total license fees for the month, and date filed. Arranged chronologically by dates filed. No index. Handwritten on printed forms. Average 500 pages. 12 x 15 x 3. Auditor's main office.

276. COUNTY COMMISSIONERS' RESOLUTIONS
1846—. 12 file boxes, 3 bundles.

Copies of resolutions as adopted by county commissioners in matters pertaining to budgets, tax rates, and levies, showing date of resolution and subject covered; also includes copies of resolutions of board of education pertaining to the issuance of bonds, showing date and subject of resolution. Arranged chronologically by dates of resolutions. No index. File box, 10 x 4.5 x 13.5; bundles, 9.5 x 3 x 4. 12 file boxes, 1846-1934, basement storage room; Th3 bundles, 1935—, Auditor's clerk office.

277. CITY ORDINANCES AND COURT ORDERS
1924—. 1 file box.

Copies of ordinances passed by the city of Ashland, showing effective date, ordinance number, and provision of same; also includes copies of court orders in regard to board of education matters, showing document number, name of court, docket and page references, names of plaintiff and defendant, and date issue. Arranged chronologically by dates of ordinances of court orders. No index. Typed on printed forms. 10 x 4.5 x 13.5. Auditor's clerk office.

The office of county treasurer was established by an act of the Northwest Territory in 1792 and continued by the state of Ohio.[1] Although the constitution of 1802 made no provision for the office of county treasurer, it was created by the legislative act of 1803.[2] The treasurer, appointed by the associate judges in 1803 and by the county commissioners in 1804, was required to take an oath and give bond for the faithful performance of the duties of his office, and was subject to removal by the appointing power.[3] The treasurer remained an appointive official until 1827 when the office became an elected one by popular vote in the county.[4] Although it did not specifically create the office, the constitution of 1851 stated that no person shall hold the office of treasurer for more than four years in any six. This provision was repealed in 1933 by an amendment authorizing any county to adopt a charter form of government.[5] Interpreting the constitutional provision, the legislature fixed the term of office at two years in 1859.[6] The term of office continued at two years until 1936 when it was extended to four years.[7] The remuneration of the office was by fees until 1875, and from 1875 to 1906 by a definite salary based on population plus a percentage of the fees collected. Since 1906 the treasurer's compensation has been derived entirely from a salary determined on a population basis.[8]

The duties of the treasurer were defined by statute in the earlier period and specified in detail by the act of 1827 and 1831 repealing previous acts. The provision of the latter act, although subject to amendment and repeal, furnish the basis for subsequent legislation and laid the basis for the present duties of the treasurer, which do not differ greatly from those prescribed by the earlier statutes.

In 1803 the treasurer was given his present duty of giving public notice of the tax duplicate. On receiving from the county auditor a duplicate of the taxes assessed upon the property of the county, the treasurer prepares and post notices in three places in each township including the place in which elections are held; and inserts the notice for six consecutive weeks in the newspaper having the greatest circulation in the county.[9]

---

1. Pease, *op.cit.,* 68-69.
2. *Laws of Ohio,* I, 97.
3. *Ibid.,* I, 97-98; II, 154.
4. *Ibid.,* XXV, 25-32.
5. *Ohio Const. 1851,* Art. X, sec. 3 (Amendment, 1933).
6. *Laws of Ohio,* LVI, 105.
7. *Ibid.,* CXVI, pt. ii, 184.
8. *Ibid.,* III, 49-51; LXXII, 126; XCVIII, 89.
9. *Ibid.,* I, 98; XXIX, 291; LII, 124.

He receives money in payment of taxes levied for the county, for the state, and for other purposes, and gives the payer a receipt.[10] In the early years of the office the treasurer was required to give announcement of the time he would be in the respective townships of the county and in his office at the seat of justice to receive tax collections. Since 1858 the treasurer has been authorized to prescribe the time of semiannual payment of taxes or assessments levied upon real estate or upon delinquent real estate taxes or assessments.[11] Moreover, since 1908, the commissioners have been authorized to extend the time for paying taxes to not more than 30 days after the time fixed by law.[12]

After each semiannual collection of taxes, the treasurer is required to report to the auditor showing the amount of taxes received in each taxing district in the county since the last settlement. Since 1904 the semiannual settlements have been made under the heads of liquor, cigarette, inheritance, delinquent, personal, road, and general taxes. The treasurer keeps his accounts in books which enable him to compile such reports.[13]

After the taxes are collected and immediately after each settlement with the county auditor, the county treasurer, upon the presentation of the proper warrant from the auditor, pays to the township treasurer, city or village treasurer, the treasurer of the school district, or treasurer of any "legally constituted board authorized by law to receive the funds or proceeds of any special tax levy," or other officers delegated with the authority to receive such funds, all money in the treasury belonging to such boards and subdivisions.[14] In addition, after the treasurer has made each settlement with the county auditor, he is required to pay to the state treasurer, on warrant from state auditor, "the full amount of all sums" found by the latter to belong to the state.[15]

---

10. G. C. sec. 2650; *Laws of Ohio,* XXIX, 292; LXXVI, 70; LXXXV, 327.
11. *Laws of Ohio,* LV, 62; LVI, 101.
12. *Laws of Ohio,* XCIV, 435; CXIV, 730; CXV, pt. ii, 226.
13. G. C. sec. 2643; *Laws of Ohio,* XXIX, 296; XCVII, 458.
14. G. C. sec. 2689; *Laws of Ohio,* LVI, 101.
15. *Laws of Ohio,* LVI, 101; CXIV, 732.

Another function of the county treasurer, which had its inception in the earlier years of the office, is a collection of delinquent taxes. It was and is his duty to assess a penalty on a tax duplicate for nonpayment of taxes –which penalty when collected, is paid to the treasurer's fund. If the treasurer is unable to collect the delinquent taxes, he is authorized to apply to the clerk of court of common pleas, who serves notice to show cause why such taxes were not paid. The court may enter a rule against the delinquent taxpayer for the payment and cost and enforce it by attachment.[16]

During the last decade provision has been made for the installment payment of delinquent taxes without interest or penalty. In 1931 it was provided that delinquent taxes, assessments, and penalties charged on the tax duplicate against any entry of real estate might be paid in installment during five consecutive semiannual taxpaying periods "whether such real estate had been certified as delinquent or not."[17] The Whittemore Act, passed as an emergency measure in 1933, provided for the collection in installments, without interest or penalty, of delinquent real estate assessments. Anyone electing to pay such delinquent real property taxes and assessments in installments pursuant to this act may, at any installment period, pay the entire unpaid balance, in which event no interest shall be charged or collected on the amount so paid. In 1934 the benefits of the act were extended to include delinquent personal and classified taxes.[18] With slight alterations the law was reenacted in 1935 and again in 1936.[19] An act was passed in February 1937 and continued by legislation in 1938 and 1939 providing for the settlement of taxes delinquent prior to 1936 without interest or penalty in one payment or in 10 annual installments.[20]

The county treasurer has charge of the funds collected by taxes, and also other funds belonging to the county. Although earlier acts made provision for storage vaults in the county treasury for county deposits, the commissioners have been authorized, since 1894, to receive sealed bids for the deposit county funds; and the banks or trust companies offering the highest rates of interest are selected as a county depositories.[21]

---

16. G. C. sec. 2660; *Laws of Ohio,* LVI, 175; XCIX, 435.
17. G. C. sec. 2672; Laws of Ohio, CXIV, 827.
18. *Laws of Ohio,* CXV, 161-164; CXV, pt. ii, 230, 332.
19. *Ibid.,* CXVI, 199, 468; CXVI, pt. ii, 14-21.
20. *Ibid.,* CXVII, 32, 832; CXVIII, 70.
21. *Laws of Ohio*, XCI, 403; CII, 59; CXV, pt. ii, 215.

The treasurer is required to keep an account current with the county auditor, a practice which originated in 1831. Each day the treasurer makes a statement to the county auditor for the previous day's business, showing the amount of taxes received on auditor's drafts, the amount received from other sources, together with the amount of money deposited in the depository, the total amount paid out by check and by cash, and the balance in the treasury.[22]

The treasurer, as well as the sheriff, the prosecuting attorney, and the clerk of courts, has been required since 1850 to report annually to the county commissioners.[23] Since 1874 the county auditor and county commissioners have been required to make a thorough examination of all books, vouchers, accounts, moneys, bonds, securities, and other property in the treasury at least every six months.[24] Besides being under the supervision of the county commissioners and county auditor, the treasurer is subject to the supervision of the state auditor. In 1902 an act was passed providing for a uniform system of accounting and auditing for all public offices in the state, under the direction of a bureau of inspection in the office of the state auditor, and for the annual examination of the finances of all public offices.[25]

The treasurer is a member of the budget commission and the county board of revision, and serves as a trustee of the sinking fund.[26] Since the early days of the office the treasurer has been the official custodian of the bonds furnished to the state by the county auditor, county commissioners, and other officials. Since 1869 he has been required to record and preserve a record of the deputies appointed and removed by the county auditor.[27]

---

22. G. C. sec. 2642; *Laws of Ohio,* XCVII, 457.
23. G. C. sec. 2504.
24. *Laws of Ohio,* LXXXI, 137. This law was repealed by implication by the act creating the bureau of inspection and supervision of public offices. Ohio Attorney General, *Opinions*, 1934, 3506.
25. G. C. sec. 2641; *Laws of Ohio,* CXIV; 728; XCV, 511-515.
26. G. C. secs. 5625-19, 2976-18, 5580. *See* also pages 181, 183, 188.
27. G. C. sec. 2563; *Laws of Ohio,* LXVI, 35.

Like other county officials, the treasurer is required at the expiration of his term to turn over to his successor all books, papers, moneys, and records appertaining to his office.[28]

In Ashland County, there are three on the treasurer's staff, one a deputy treasurer. The treasurer's salary is $200.83 monthly and his official bond is fixed at $50,000.[29] Taxes may be paid either at the courthouse office or at certain banks with which arrangements have been made by the treasurer.[30] Until the advent of the Whittemore bill, taxes were paid semiannually, but since the passing of this act, the treasurer, on his own authority and as a convenience to the property owner, accepts monthly payments on delinquent taxes, which are held and credited on the tax duplicates twice a year at the regular tax collection periods, a practice which has resulted in a noticeable decrease in delinquent taxes. Ashland's treasurer uses four depositories for public funds. They are in Loudonville, Ashland, and Polk.[31]

---

28. G. C. sec. 2639.
29. Records of Warrants Issued, 1940, entry 256; Treasurer's Record of Official Bonds, 1940, entry 299.
30. Treasurer's Ledger, 1941, entry 295.
31. *Ibid.*

Tax Records

Real Property Taxes

278. TREASURER'S DUPLICATE
1846—. 672 vols. (Labeled by names of townships and dated). Title varies: Tax duplicate of real property, 1846-1930, 576 vols.

Treasurers tax duplicate, showing names of taxing district and township, receipt number, names and address of property owner, description of property, number of acres, value of property, valuation by board of revision, total tax and dates of payment during year, amount delinquent, amount of semiannual taxes, amount delinquent and date paid for each half, penalty, amount delinquent brought forward, and remarks; also includes personal property taxes from 1846-1931. Arranged alphabetically by names of townships and alphabetically thereunder by names of property owners. 1846-1928, handwritten on printed forms; 1928—, typed on printed forms. Average 250 pages. 17 x 15 x 1.5. 592 volumes, 1846-1930, basement storage room; 80 volumes, 1931—, Treasurer's main office.

279. TAXES RECEIVED
1846—. 1 bundle. 8 file boxes, 57 vols.

Carbon copies of individual tax receipts, showing date and number of receipt, name of property owner, kind of tax, volume and page numbers of tax duplicates, where entered and amount, reclassification, name of township, description of property, valuation, amount of delinquencies and penalties, special assessments, and total amount due. Arranged alphabetically by names of property owners. No index. Handwritten on printed forms. Bundle, 10 x 5 x 10; file boxes, 10 x 5 x 18; Volumes average 200 pages. 18 x 12 x 1. 57 volumes, 7 file boxes, 1 bundle, 1846-1936, basement storage room; 1 file box, 1937—, Treasurer's main office.

280. RECORD Of TAX COLLECTIONS (Real and Personal)
1914-1936. 12 vols.

Record of both real and personal tax collections, showing date of tax collection, names of taxing district and property owner, property value, receipt number, real estate and public utility taxes, special assessments, delinquent and classified personal tax, Total for each taxing district, and total amount collected. Arranged alphabetically by names of taxing districts and alphabetically thereunder by names of property owners. No index. Handwritten on printed forms. Average 300 pages.

14 x 10 x 2. 6 volumes, 1914-1924, basement storage room; 6 volumes, 1925-1936, Treasurer's main office.

281. TREASURER'S SPECIAL DUPLICATE
1908—. 15 vols.

Duplicate of special tax assessments for public improvements, showing certificate number, name of taxpayer, lot number, description of property, total tax due, amount paid, delinquencies and amount paid, semiannual taxes paid, delinquencies, penalties, and total amount paid for year. Arranged alphabetically by names of townships and alphabetically thereunder by names of taxpayers. No index. Handwritten on printed forms. Average 75 pages. 16 x 12 x 1. 6 volumes, 1908-1925, basement storage room; 9 volumes, 1925—, Treasurer's main office.

Personal Property Taxes (See also entry 280)

282. TREASURER'S CLASSIFIED TAX DUPLICATE
1932—. 3 vols. (1-3).

Treasurer's classified tax duplicate, showing assessment certificate number, name and address of taxpayer, names of township and corporation; productive investments, showing tax rate, final assessments, and amount of tax; unproductive investments, showing tax rate, final assessments and amount of tax, deposits, credits; moneys and other taxable intangibles, showing final assessments and amount of tax, tax rate, total tax for the year, amount of tax due, advanced payment, amount and date paid, unpaid taxes for the year, and remarks. Arranged alphabetically by names of taxpayers. Indexed alphabetically by names of taxing districts. Typed on printed forms. Average 450 pages. 17 x 19 x 2. Treasurer's main office.

283. TREASURER'S PERSONAL DUPLICATE
1932—. 3 vols. (1-3).

Treasurer's personal duplicate, showing name of taxing district, tax rate, assessment certificate number, name and address of taxpayer, final assessments, total tax for the year, advanced payment, tax due, amount and date paid, unpaid taxes for the year, and remarks. Alphabetically by names of taxpayers. Indexed alphabetically by names of taxing districts. Typed on printed forms. Average 200 pages. 18.5 x 17 x 1. Treasurer's main office.

284. RECORD OF TAX COLLECTIONS (Personal)

1937—. 1 vol. (1).

Treasurer's record of personal taxes collected, showing date of collection, name of taxing district and taxpayer, receipt number, dog and road tax, special assessments, other taxes, and total collected. Arranged alphabetically by townships and numerically thereunder by receipt numbers. No index. Handwritten on printed forms. 350 pages. 16 x 14 x 3. Treasurer's main office. For other records, 1914-1936, see entry 280.

Delinquent Taxes

285. TREASURER'S DELINQUENT TAX DUPLICATE

1846—. 16 vols. Title varies: Delinquent Record, 1846-1906. 10 vols.

Duplicate of delinquent real and personal property taxes, showing name of taxing district, date of entry, name and address of taxpayer, location, description, property value, amount of taxes assessed, years delinquent, amount of delinquencies and penalties, and total amount due. Arranged alphabetically by names of taxing districts and chronologically thereunder by dates entered. No index. 1846-1905, handwritten; 1906—, typed on printed forms. Average 200 pages. 18 x 12 x 2. 14 volumes, 1846-1925, basement storage room; 2 volumes, 1925—, Treasurer's main office.

286. TREASURER'S CUMULATIVE DELINQUENT DUPLICATE

1935—. 1 vol. Initiated in 1935.

Treasurer's cumulative delinquent duplicate, showing taxes other than those on real estate or specific type, name of taxing district, page number of duplicate of original entry, year, amount of tax, penalty, total amount due, date paid and name and address of taxpayer. Arranged alphabetically by names of taxpayers and chronologically thereunder by dates paid. No index. Typed on printed forms. 700 pages. 12 x 10 x 5. Treasurer's main office.

287. UNDERTAKINGS

1933—. 2 vols.

Record of undertakings paid to full principal amount of delinquent taxes and assessments on real property, less penalties, interest, and other charges, in annual installments, showing date due, name of property owner, date of undertaking, general taxes, county, township, and municipal assessments, and totals. Arranged alphabetically by names of taxing districts and chronologically thereunder by dates of undertakings. No index. Handwritten on printed forms. Average 250 pages. 15 x 16 x 2.5. Treasurer's main office.

288. TRIENNIAL LAND TAX CERTIFICATES
1919—. 1 vol.

Triennial land tax certificate of delinquent tract of land, city or town lot, showing names of taxpayer and township, description of property, valuation, general taxes, special assessments, settlement, total, fees for making delinquent land list, and grand total. Arranged alphabetically by names of taxpayers. No index. Typed on printed forms. 170 pages. 18 x 15 x 1.5. Treasurer's main office.

Adjustments

289. ADDITIONS AND DEDUCTIONS
1874-1887, 1908-1921. 2 vols. (One unlabeled; 1).

Additions and deductions in Ashland County, 1874-1887, showing year, name of owner, range, township, section, lot numbers, description of property, number of acres, value of real estate and personal property, amount of additions and deductions, and remarks; 1908-1921, showing year, name of owner, description and value of property, amount of tax, name of township, corporation or school district, and remarks. Arranged chronologically by years. No index. Handwritten on printed forms. 1 volume, 479 pages. 14 x 9 x 2; 1 volume, 236 pages. 18 x 13 x 1.25. Basement storage room.

Excise Taxes

290. RECORD OF DOW AND CIGARETTE COLLECTIONS
1904-1910 1 vol.

Treasurer's record of liquor and cigarette tax collections, showing date paid, name of taxpayer, receipt number, municipal corporations, civil townships, and total collections. Arranged alphabetically by names of taxpayers. No index. Handwritten on printed forms. 200 pages. 16 x 12 x 1. Basement storage room.

291. CIGARETTE TAX RECORD

1931—. 2 vols.

Treasurer's daily report of cigarette tax stamps received and sold, showing date of report, amount of stamps received and sold, name and address of purchaser, receipt, check or sales report number, total amount of sales, amount credited to general fund, and total net amount. Arranged chronologically by dates of reports. No index. Handwritten on printed forms. Average 300 pages. 12 x 14 x 3. Treasurer's main office.

292. CIGARETTE TAX RECORD

1904—. 16 vols.

Stubs of cigarette tax receipts, showing names of county and state, to whom issued, ownership of business property where cigarette license is used, date and number of receipt, amount of tax, and signature of treasurer. Arranged numerically by consecutive receipt numbers. No index. Handwritten on printed forms. Average 100 pages. 6 x 16 x 1. 1 volume, 1904-1912, basement storage room; 15 volumes, 1913—, Treasurer's main office.

293. SALES TAX RECEIPTS

1935—. 3 FILE BOXES.

Daily record of sales tax stamps received and sold, showing denominations, quantity, amount, total gross amount, date of sale, and name and address of purchaser. Arranged chronologically by dates of sales. No index. Handwritten on printed forms. 8 x 8 x 30. Treasurer's main office.

Fiscal Accounts

General Accounts

294. DAILY CASH BALANCE

1846—. 27 vols. (1-27). Title varies: Cash Book, 1846-1903, 11 vols.

Record of cash received and disbursed, receipts, showing balance on hand, from whom received, total receipts and date entered; disbursements, showing date received, and total disbursements; also shows balance forwarded. Arranged chronologically by dates entered. No index. Handwritten on printed forms. Average 200 pages. 14 x 10 x 2. 4 volumes, 1846-1918, basement storage room; 23 volumes, 1919—, Treasurer's main office.

295. TREASURER'S LEDGER
1904—. 10 vols. (1-10).

Treasurer's fund ledger, showing date and amount of receipts, from whom received, credited and debited to each fund, showing date and amount of disbursements, services and goods supplied, date entered, and balance of each fund for every 30 day period; also includes record of collections of liquor, cigarette, and inheritance tax, debited to county treasurer and credited to account of each taxing district, showing dates of each tax collection and settlement period, date entered, and amount of warrants redeemed against each fund. Arranged chronologically by dates entered. No index. Handwritten on printed forms. Average 475 pages. 18 x 12 x 3. 2 volumes, 1904-1920, basement storage room; 8 volumes, 1921—, Treasurer's main office.

296. SETTLEMENT SHEETS
1846—. 1 file box, 12 vols. Title varies: Auditor settlement, 1846-1875, 2 volumes; Record of Abstracts and Settlements, 1875-1897, 2 volumes; Treasurers Settlements, 1897-1904, 1 volume; School fund Settlements, 1904-1928, 3 vols.

Statement of receipts and disbursements of school funds, showing name of school district, year, signature of treasurer, balance at last settlement, amount of township school funds, amount accrued from sales and state common school fund, amount paid for tuition, fuel, building repairs, janitor's salary, and balance on hand, certifications by county auditor regarding examination of accounts of township treasurer and finding of amount received from county treasurer, total balance, and date filed. Arranged chronologically by dates filed. No index. Handwritten on printed forms. File box, 4 x 24 x 40; volumes average 250 pages. 16 x 12 x 1. 12 volumes, 1846-1928, basement storage room; 1 file box, 1928—, Auditor's clerk office.

Warrants

297. TREASURER'S JOURNAL OF WARRANTS AND RECEIPTS
1904—. 17 vols. Title varies: Treasurer's Journal of Warrants and Receipts into Treasury, 1904-1928, 8 volumes; Treasurer's Journal of Warrants Redeem and Receipts into Treasury, 1928-1931, 2 vols.

Treasurer's journal of payments into county treasury, receipts, showing date of receipt, name of payee, service and goods supplied, and number of pay-in order;

debit treasurer, showing date of entry, amount of pay-in order, credit general fund, children's home fund, dog and kennel fund, county and state road funds, bridge fund, auto license and gas tax fund, undivided general tax and undivided tangible personal property tax funds, undivided intangible personal property tax fund, credit undivided cigarette license fund, undivided inheritance tax fund, undivided auto license tax fund, credit miscellaneous funds, names of funds, and amount. Receipts arranged chronologically by dates of receipts; no index. Handwritten on printed forms. Average 250 pages. 18.5 x 13 x 1.5. 8 volumes, 1904-1928, basement storage room; 9 volumes, 1928—, Treasurer's main office.

298. TREASURER'S RECORD OF COURT WARRANTS REDEEMED
1904—. 1 vol. (1).

Treasurer's record of warrants redeemed, showing number and date of warrant and name of payee, names of common pleas court petit jurors, grand jurors, and witnesses; names of probate court jurors, witnesses in criminal, lunacy, and epilepsy cases, fees for witnesses, and names of jurors and coroner's and other minor courts, and total. Arranged numerically by warrant numbers. No index. Handwritten on printed forms. 400 pages. 18 x 12 x 2. Treasurer's main office.

Bonds

299. TREASURER'S RECORD OF OFFICIAL BONDS
1846—. 4 vols.

Copies of bonds filed by elected county officials, showing date and amount of bond, name of official, date elected, name of office, signatures of principles and witnesses, names of sureties, and approval of county commissioners, certificate of prosecuting attorney, signature of probate judge, copy of oath of office, and date filed. Arranged chronologically by dates filed. Indexed alphabetically by names of officials. Handwritten on printed forms. Average 250 pages. 16 x 12 x 2. 1 volume, 1846-1899, basement storage room; 3 volumes, 1900—, Treasurer's main office.

300. BONDS OF COUNTY OFFICIALS
1937—. 1 file box.
Original bonds filed by elected county officials, showing date of bond, names of principles, to what office elected, names the sureties, amount of bond, date filed, and date approved by county commissioners. Arranged chronologically by dates filed. No index. Handwritten and typed on printed forms. 5 x 5 x 10. Treasurer's main office.

301. CLERKS' BOND RECORD, TOWNSHIPS
1927—. 2 vols. (1, 2).
Copies of bonds filed by township officers, showing date and amount of bond, names of officials and office held, names of sureties, date approved by township trustees, date filed, and copy of oath of office. Arranged chronologically by dates filed. Indexed alphabetically by names of officials. Handwritten on printed forms. Average 100 pages. 14 x 8 x 1. Treasurer's main office.

302. CLERKS' ORIGINAL BOND RECORDS, TOWNSHIPS
1846—. 1 carton, 1 file box.
Original bonds filed by township officers, showing information as in entry 301. Arranged chronologically by dates filed. No index. Handwritten on printed forms. Carton, 8 x 12 x 18; file box, 5 x 5 x 10. Basement storage room.

A budget commission functions in Ashland County under an act of 1911 which authorized the establishment of such an agency in each county, to be composed of the county auditor, the mayor of the largest municipality, and the prosecuting attorney.[1] In 1915 the county treasurer replaced the mayor as a member of the commission.[2] It was not until after the World War, when county expenditures steadily increased, that the importance of improved methods of finance were forcibly brought to the attention of the legislature. This need was met in 1927 by enlarging the powers and minutely prescribing the duties of the budget commission.[3] Under the present law, passed in 1927, the commission, consisting as before of the county auditor, the county treasurer, and the county prosecuting attorney, received and examines the annual budget of the county, municipal, township, school authorities, with an estimate of the amount to be raised for state purposes in each subdivision.[4] If the total amount exceeds the sum authorized to be raised, the commission adjusts the amount to be raised and may change and revise the estimates. The commission may reduce all items in the budget, but it is prohibited from increasing the total of any budget or any Item.

The adjusted budget is certified to the taxing authority in each subdivision. If the work of the commission is satisfactory, each taxing authority by ordinance or resolution authorizes the necessary tax levies and certifies them to the county auditor. On the other hand, the taxing authority in any subdivision may appeal, through its fiscal officer, from the decision of the budget commission to the state tax commission of Ohio, which is empowered to adjust the estimates of revenues and balances in fixing the tax rate.[5]

The county auditor, as secretary to the commission, is required to keep a full and accurate record of the proceedings of the commission.

---

1. *Laws of Ohio,* CII, 271.
2. *Ibid.,* CVI, 180.
3. *Ibid.,* CX, 469. Under the provision of this act elected commissioners might be substituted for *ex-officio* members, at the option of the electors of the county.
4. *Ibid.,* CXII, 399.
5. G. C. secs. 5625-25, 5625-28.

303. BUDGET COMMISSION RECORD

1927– in Board of Revision (Minutes).

Minutes of budget commission, showing date of meeting, names of members present property valuation for each taxing district, anticipated operating expenses and tax rate for each district, total property valuation, real and personal, commissioner's budget for each fund for each district, record of motions made, votes, and disposal of all cases presented for the attention of the commission.

The county board of revision was established by the general assembly in 1825 for the purpose of correcting some of the defects and inequalities in tax assessments. The first board of revision, or board of equalization as it was sometimes called, was composed by the county commissioners, the county auditor, and the assessor. The board was authorized to meet at the seat of justice on the first Monday in June annually "to hear and determine the complaint of any owner of property listed and valued by the assessor... and shall correct any list valuations made by the assessor, either by adding or deducting from his valuation."[1] The act of 1831, repealing the act of 1825, left the duties and personnel of the board unchanged.[2]

In 1859 the legislature made provision for two county boards of equalization. One board, composed of the county auditor and the county commissioners, was directed to meet annually for the purpose of equalizing real and personal property assessments, and moneys and credits in the county. The other board, composed of the county auditor, the county surveyor, and the county commissioners, was authorized to meet sexennially for the same purposes.[3]

The act of 1863 amending the act of 1859, left the personnel and duties of the annual county board unchanged. The second county board, although continuing without alterations and compensation or duties, was directed to meet decennially, rather than sexennially.[4] The legislative act of 1868, amending the act of 1863, left the membership of the annual and special boards, as well as their duties, practically unchanged.[5]

---

1. *Laws of Ohio,* XXIII, 64.
2. *Ibid.,* XXIX, 278.
3. *Ibid.,* LVI, 193-194.
4. *Ibid.,* LX, 57, 59.
5. *Ibid.,* LXV, 168-170.

The annual and special boards of equalization were abolished, when, in 1913, the state tax commission of Ohio was given the task of supervising the assessment of real and personal property in the state.[6] Under this arrangement each county constituted a district. In each district containing less than 60,000 inhabitants, by which stipulation Ashland County was included, there was to be appointed by the governor one state tax commissioner. In all other districts there were appointed, in the same manner, two state deputy tax commissioners. In each district there was appointed a district board of complaints. This board, appointed by the state tax commission with the consent of the governor, took over the duties and powers formerly vested in the boards of equalization. The county auditor, made secretary to the board of complaints, was required to be present at each meeting in person or by deputy, and kept an accurate record of their proceedings to be kept in a book for that purpose.[7] Moreover, the board was directed to take full minutes of all evidence given before it and might have such evidence taken in shorthand and extended into typewritten form. The auditor was required to preserve in his office separate records of all minutes and documentary evidence offered in each complaint.[8]

This arrangement, after being in operation for two years, was abrogated by the legislature in 1915. In that year the county auditor, under the supervision of the tax commission of Ohio, became the chief assessing officer in the county. The county treasurer, the county prosecuting attorney, the probate judge, and the president of the county commissioners were to serve as a board for the purpose of appointing three members to constitute a board of revision. Again the county auditor was made secretary of the board and was directed to keep a record of their proceedings and to preserve in his office a separate record of all minutes and documentary evidence offered in each complaint.[9]

Under the present system, inaugurated in 1917, the county treasurer, the county auditor, and the president of the county commissioners constitute a board of revision. This board organizes annually, on a second Monday in June, by electing a chairman for the ensuing year. The county auditor serves as secretary of the board.[10]

---

6. *See* pp. xli, xlii, xiiv.
7. *Laws of Ohio,* CIII, 791.
8. *Ibid.,* CIII, 794.
9. *Ibid.,* CVI, 254-258.
10. G. C. sec. 5580.

The county board of revision may, with a consent and approval of the tax commission of Ohio, employ experts, clerks, and other employees.[11]

The duties of the board, not differing in detail from those prescribed in 1825, include the hearing of all complaints relating to valuation or assessments of both real and personal property as it appears upon the tax duplicates of the "then current year." The board is authorized to investigate all complaints and may increase or decrease any valuation or correct any assessment complained of or may order a reassessment of the original assessing official.[12] No valuation is increased, however, without giving notice to the person in whose name the property affected is listed.[13] The board of revision in all respects, is governed by the law relating to the valuation of real property and makes no change of any valuation "except in accordance with such laws."[14]

On the second Monday in June, annually, the county auditor lays before the board of revision the statements and returns of assessments of any personal property for the current year, and the board proceeds to review the returns. On the first Monday in July, annually, the auditor lays before the board of returns of assessments of any real property for the current year. The board of revision reviews the assessments and certifies its action to the county auditor, who corrects the tax list and duplicate according to the additions and deductions ordered by the board. The auditor is prohibited by statute for making up his tax list and duplicate until the board has completed its work and has returned to him all the returns laid before it with revisions.[15] But in the event the tax duplicate has been delivered to the county treasurer, the auditor is required to certify such corrections to him and enter such corrections in his tax duplicate.[16]

In its investigations the board may examine, under oath, persons as to their or others' real property. In the event witnesses fail to appear or refuse to testify, the board through its chairman is authorized to make a complaint in writing to the probate judge, who, by statute, is directed to institute proceedings against them.[17]

---

11. G. C. sec. 5587.
12. G. C. sec. 5597.
13. G. C. sec. 5599.
14. G. C. sec. 5596.
15. G. C. sec. 5605.
16. G. C. sec. 5602
17. G. C. sec. 5596.

The decisions of the board are subject to appeal to the tax commission of Ohio within thirty days after a decision is served.[18]

The secretary of the board is required to keep "an accurate record of the proceedings of the board in a book to be kept for that purpose."[19] The county auditor, as in 1913, is required to preserve in his office separate records of all minutes and documentary evidence offered in each complaint.[20] The records of the board are open to the inspection of the public.[21]

Ashland County seems to have had a board of revision since government was organized in the county, although records of such a body would not found for the years prior to 1915. Only two appeals from the board's decision have been taken to the state tax commission since the appraisement of 1937.[22] In 1940, 56 complaints were investigated.[23]

---

18. G. C. sec. 5610.
19. G. C. sec. 5592.
20. G. C. sec. 5603.
21. G. C. sec. 5591.
22. (Board of Revision– Original Documents), 1937-1941, entry 305.
23. Board of Revision (Minutes), 1940, entry 304.

304. BOARD OF REVISION (Minutes)

1913—. 3 vols. (1-3). Title varies: Board of Review, 1913-1914, 1 vol.

Minutes of meetings of the board of revision to consider complaints on appraisement or re-appraisement of property, showing date of meeting, names of members present, names of property owner and taxing district, record of adjustment made on taxation values of real and personal property, and signatures of president and secretary of board. Also contains (Budget Commission Record), 1927—, entry 303. Arranged chronologically by dates of meetings. No index. Typed. Average 120 pages. 10 x 8 x 1.5. 2 volumes, 1913-1927, basement storage room; 1 volume, 1927—, Auditor's main office.

305. (BOARD OF REVISION– ORIGINAL DOCUMENTS)

1915—. 1 file box.

Original complaints filed by property owners on values for taxation, showing name and address of complainant, name of owner of property, names of county and taxing district, complaint number, name of attorney, amount assessed, changes requested, number of acres, lot number, assessed value, amount of increase or decrease, date property was purchased, amount paid, complete description of property and buildings, fences and roads about the property, affidavit of cost, and signature of auditor; certificate of correction valuation on complaints, showing certificate number, date filed, names of property owner and taxing district, description of property, amount of complaint on valuation, increased or decreased valuation fixed by board of revision, lot number, location, amount of assessment, reasons for revision, and action of board of revision on complaint. Arranged chronologically by dates filed. No index. Typed. 12 x 5 x 12. Auditor's main office.

The board of trustees of the sinking fund, composed of the prosecuting attorney, auditor, and treasurer, was organized in 1919 in Ashland County and in each county owing a bonded debt. The county prosecuting attorney serves as president of the board and the auditor as secretary. It is the duty of the trustees to provide for the payment of all bonds issued by the county and the interest maturing thereon.[1]

From 1919 all bonds issued by the county were required to be recorded in the office of the trustees of the sinking fund, to bear a stamp containing the words "Recorded in the office of the sinking fund trustees," and to be signed by the secretary before they became valid in the hands of any purchaser. In 1921 the act was amended to allow such recording and authenticating to be performed by the county treasurer and in 1935 such provisions were abrogated by the legislature.[2]

On or before the first Monday in May of each year, the trustees certify to the county commissioners the rate of tax necessary to provide a sinking fund both for the payment and maturity of bonds heretofore issued by the county and for the payment of interest on the bonded indebtedness. The amount certified by the trustees is set forth without diminution in the annual budget of the commissioners.[3] Then, after each semiannual settlement of taxes and assessments, the county auditor reports to the trustees the amount of money in the treasury of the county charged to the credit of the sinking fund. Money is drawn from the county treasury for investment or disbursement by the issuance of a voucher signed by all the members of the board and directed to the county auditor. The trustees are directed, by statute, to invest all moneys subject to their control in United States bonds, Ohio bonds, or bonds of a municipal corporation, school district, township, or county in the state.

The board members are required to keep "a full and complete record of their transactions, the complete record of the funded debt of the county specifying the dates, purposes, amounts, numbers, maturities, and rate and maturities of interest and installments thereof, and where payable, and an account exhibiting the amount held in the sinking fund for the payment thereof."[4]

The meetings of the trustees are open to the public. All questions relating to the purchase or sale of securities for the payment of bonds or interest are decided by a yea or nay vote, which is recorded in their journal.

---

1. G. C. secs. 2976-18, 1976-19.
2. *Laws of Ohio,* CIX, 16; CXVI, 442.
3. G. C. sec. 2976-26.
4. G. C. sec. 2976-24.

306. SINKING FUND TRUSTEES' RECORD
1919—. 1 vol. (1).

Minutes of meetings of sinking fund trustees, showing date of meeting, order of business, record of bonds issued or sold, maturity dates of bonds, bond numbers of each issue, and interest dates when coupons were due; also record of resolutions presented, showing details of resolutions, number of resolutions adopted or rejected, and date of resolution. Arranged chronologically by dates of meetings. No index. Typed on printed forms. 500 pages. 18 x 12 x 3. Auditor's main office.

The responsibility for supervising and conducting elections in the county is delegated to state deputy supervisors of elections–the county board of elections. This board, created by the legislature in 1891 and consisting of four qualified voters in the county, is appointed for a four-year term by the secretary of state, who, by virtue of his office, is the chief election official of the state.[1] On the first day of March in the even-numbered years, the secretary of state appoints two board members, one of whom is from the political party which polled the highest number of votes in the state for the office of governor at the last preceding state election, and the other from the political party which polled the next highest vote at such election.[2] The board members may be removed by the secretary of state for the neglect of duty, malfeasance, misfeasance in office, for willful violation of the election laws, or for other good and sufficient causes.[3] The compensation of the members is determined by the basis of population of the county and is paid by the county.[4] Similarly the expenses of the county board are paid from the county treasury, "in pursuance of appropriations by the county commissioners," in the same manner as other expenses are paid.[5]

The persons so appointed by the secretary, meeting five days after their appointment, select one of their members as chairman and a resident elector of the county who is not a member of the board as clerk.[6] The board is vested with the authority to establish, define, and provide election precincts; to fix places of registration; to provide for the purchase, preservation, and maintenance of voting booths, ballot boxes, books, maps, flags, blanks, cards of instruction, and other equipment used in registration; and to issue rules, regulations, and instructions not inconsistent with the law or contrary to the rules and regulations as established by the chief election official.[7]

---

1. *Laws of Ohio,* LXXXVIII, 449.
2. G. C. sec. 4785-8. For the method of appointment when the term of each of the four members of the board expires on the same date, *see* G. C. sec. 4785-8a.
3. G. C. sec. 4785-11.
4. G. C. sec. 4785-18.
5. G. C. sec. 4785-20.
6. G. C. sec. 4785-10.
7. G. C. sec. 4785-13.

Besides providing places of voting and equipment, the board is authorized to appoint clerks and other officers of Elections. On or before the first day of September before each November election, the board by a majority vote, is authorized, after careful examination and investigation as to the qualifications, to appoint for each precinct six "competent persons, four as judges and two as clerks, who shall constitute the election officers of such precinct." Not more than two other judges and one other clerks, states the law, "shall be members of the same political party." Precinct election officers, appointment for one year term, may be removed by the board for neglect of duty, malfeasance, or misconduct in office.[8]

Finally, the board is empowered to investigate irregularities, nonperformance of duty, or violation of election laws by election officials. For the purpose of conducting investigations they may administer oaths, issue subpoenas, summon witnesses, and compel the presentation of books, papers, and records in connection with any investigation and report the facts to the prosecuting attorney.[10]

The secretary of state, in 1930, ruled that the members of the various boards of elections were to be considered as state officials. This ruling had reference to appointments made under section 4785-8a of the General Code.[11]

In Ashland County the board supervises elections in 50 precincts in which at the latest registration there were 16,717 voters.[12] A clerk and part-time assistant clerk are employed by the board. The board members receive $29 monthly, but the total appropriations for the board vary from year to year with the number and importance of the elections to be held. In the last five years the sums spent have ranged from $7,000 in 1936 to $16,198 in 1940. The appropriation for 1941 was $8,057.[13.]

All records are located in the board of elections office.

---

8. G. C. sec. 4785-25.
9. G. C. sec. 4785-13.
10. G. C. sec. 4785-13.
11. *See* George C. Trautwein, ed., *Supplement to Page's Annotated General Code, 1926-1935* (Cincinnati, 1935), note on page 688.
12. Poll Books and Tally Sheets, 1940, entry 308.
13. (Auditor's) Annual Financial Reports to County Commissioners, 1936-1941, entry 267.

Minutes

307. MINUTE BOOKS

1899—. 4 vols. (1-4).

Minutes of meetings of board of elections, showing date of meeting, name of members present, business transacted, financial statements, and appointment of officers. Arranged chronologically by dates of meetings. No index. Handwritten on printed forms. 300 pages. 12 x 8 x 2.

Elections

308. POLL BOOKS AND TALLY SHEETS

1925—. 1280 vols. Subtitled by names of voting districts.

Poll books of registered voters, showing name, address, and signature of voter, voting district and political party; tally sheets, showing date of election, names of candidates, issues, and number of votes received by each candidate or issue. Poll books arranged by voting district and alphabetically thereunder by names of voters; tally sheets arranged in order of offices and issues. No index. Average 35 pages. 26 x 16 x .25.

309. BALLOTS

1940. 50 cardboard boxes.

Original ballots cast in primary election held in May 1940, showing date of election, voting district, names of candidates, and office sought. The ballots are destroyed after 90 days. Arranged by voting districts. No index. Handwritten on printed forms. 6 x 12 x 20.

310. CERTIFIED ABSTRACT OF VOTES

1930—. 1 folder.

Record of all votes cast as shown by poll books and tally sheets, showing date of election, voting district, total number of votes for each candidate, and for each proposal or bond issue. Arranged chronologically by dates of elections and thereunder by voting districts. No index. Handwritten on printed forms. 30 x 20 x .5.

311. REGISTER OF ABSENT VOTERS

1917—. 2 vols. (1, 2).

Record of applications to vote by absentee ballot, showing name, address, and sex of voter, date of election, place of voting, ballot number, date of receipt of returned envelope, and date delivered. Arranged chronologically by dates of elections and numerically thereunder by ballot numbers. No index. Handwritten on printed forms. Average 50 pages. 8 x 14 x .5.

The county board of education, a modern administrative and supervisory agency developed during the last two decades, supplanted the smaller education units, which, established during the early period of Ohio history, became inefficient and unable to meet the modern requirements as demanded by real communities.

During the earlier period of Ohio history, educational administration, because of the newness of the state, the sparseness of the population, and the undeveloped means of transportation was, by necessity, local in character. For 14 years after the accession of Ohio to statehood, though the constitution stated means of education should be encouraged by the general assembly, no legislation was enacted for public schools.[1] It was not until 1817 that the legislature authorized six or more people to form associations to build school houses and to be incorporated for educational purposes.[2]

The first permanent law for the organization of schools in Ohio was passed in 1821. Under the provision of this act, the electors of the township were authorized to vote on the proposition of dividing the townships into school districts. If the proposal carried, there were to be elected three school commissioners, who, in turn, were authorized to select a clerk and a collector who should act as a treasurer. They were instructed also, to levy taxes for the support of schools and to hire teachers.[3]

As education began to advance in the early years of the nineteenth century, some kind of state control was needed. Accordingly, in 1837, the office of state superintendent of schools was established.[4] A year later an act was passed making the county auditor *ex-officio* county superintendent of schools, and in each township the clerk became superintendent of the smaller unit. The county superintendent was made responsible to the state superintendent in all educational affairs. In the same year each incorporated city, or borough not regulated by a charter was made a separate school district. The voters and each division were authorized to elect three directors.[5] The effectiveness of this organization was destroyed in 1840, however, when the legislature abolished the office of state superintendent and the secretary of state took over his functions of tabulating and transmitting school statistics.[6]

---

1. *Ohio Const. 1802,* Art. VII, secs. 3, 25, 27.
2. *Laws of Ohio,* XV, 107.
3. *Ibid.,* XIX, 52.
4. *Ibid.,* XXXV, 82.
5. *Ibid.,* XXXVI, 21.
6. *Ibid.,* XXXVIII, 130.

Seven years later, 25 counties, exclusive of Ashland, were allowed to have county superintendents,[7] and in 1848 the provisions of the previous act were extended to Ashland and all other counties in the state.[8]

Although marked changes were made in the curricula of the schools, the history of education in Ohio from 1850 to the early part of the twentieth century were largely one of the gradual transference of power from districts to townships, and from townships to county in the interest of a better system of education. It was not, however, until within the last three decades that the county became the unit for educational administration.[9]

Although the county superintendent was known as early as 1838, the first permanent law for the establishment of the county board of education was enacted in 1914. Under this act the school districts were classified, and provision was made for a county school district, exclusive territory embraced in any city or village having a population of 3,000 or more desiring exemption. The county district was to be under the supervision of five board members elected by the presidents of the village and rural school boards. The members were to hold office for one, two, three, four, and five years respectively, and each year thereafter one member was to be selected to serve for a 5-year term.[10]

The county board of education was authorized to change school district lines; to provide transportation for children living more than two miles from a schoolhouse; to appoint a county superintendent; and to certify annually to the county auditor the number of teachers and superintendents employed, their salaries, and the amount apportioned to each school district for the payment of the salaries of the county and district superintendents. The county superintendent, acting as secretary of the board, was required to keep in a book provided for the purpose a full record of the proceedings of the board, properly indexed. Each motion, together with a name of the person making it and the vote thereon, was to be entered on the record.[11]

---

7. Laws of Ohio, XLV, 32.
8. *Ibid.*, XLVI, 86.
9. *Ibid.*, LXX, 195, 242; XCVII, 354.
10. *Ibid.*, CIV, 133.
11. *Ibid.*, CIV, 133; CVIII, pt. I, 704.

The county was divided into administrative divisions containing one or more villages or rural school districts. Each district was to be under the supervision of a district superintendent, who was required to visit the schools in his charge, direct and assist teachers in the performance of their duties, and classify and control promotion of pupils. He was required also to report annually to the county superintendent on matters under his charge, and to assemble teachers for the purpose of conferring on curricular matters, discipline, and school management.[12]

Changes were made by the act of 1921, under which the board members became elective by popular vote. They were authorized to appoint one or more assistant county superintendents for a term of three years. The board was authorized also to publish, with the advice and consent of the county superintendent, a minimum course of study to serve as a guide to local board members. The same act abolished the office of district superintendent.[13]

The county organization has placed the rural schools on a plane of equality of the city schools. The consolidation of the smaller units has eliminated the small, ill-equipped schools, and provides under one roof facilities and instruction suited to the needs of the rural children under the supervision of educational specialists.

Ashland County's board was organized in 1914 immediately after the passage of the authorizing legislation. Its centralized direction of educational activities in the county has had the effect of consolidating the 57 one-room grade schools and 13 two to eight-room high schools existing in 1916 into11 modern grade schools and eight modern high schools.[14] These were administered in 11 districts by a personnel consisting of seven superintendents receiving annual salaries of $2,000, four principles receiving annual salaries of $1,400, and 460 teachers receiving annual salaries of $1,260. About 2,400 pupils attend the county schools, and 2,000 of them receive free transportation, each of the 11 districts financing its own bus service.[15]

The tax rate for county schools and recent years has ranged from 5.41 to 8.9 mills. Loudonville and Ashland are the only two communities having separate school systems, all other schools in the county being under the jurisdiction of the county board of education.

All records are located and board of education office.

---

12. *Ibid.,* CIV, 133-145.
13. G. C. secs. 4728-1, 4729; *Laws of Ohio,* CIX, 242.
14. Annual statistical Report of Public Schools, 1916, 1940, entry 320.
15. *Ibid.,* 1940.

Minutes
(See also entering 323-c)

312. COUNTY BOARDS RECORD BOOK
1914—. 1 vol.
Minutes of board of education, showing date of meeting, names of members present and absent, resolutions passed or rejected, oaths of officers, and date and signature of notary administering the oath. Arranged chronologically by dates of meeting. No index. Typed. 400 pages. 16 x 10 x 2.5.

Teacher's Records
(See also entries 323-d, 323-e)

313. SCHOOL EXAMINER'S RECORD
1893-1935—. 2 vols.
Record of examinations for teachers certificates, showing date of examination, names of examiners present, amount of examination fees, name, post office address, nativity, age, and experience of applicants, number of applicants re-examined, and per cent of correct answers in various subjects. Arranged chronologically by dates of examinations. No index. Handwritten on printed forms. Average 380 pages. 18 x 12 x 2.5.

314. TEACHER'S APPLICATIONS
1937—. 1 file box.
Applications for teaching positions, showing date of application, name, address, telephone number, personal description, weight, height, general health and church affiliation of applicant, and complete records of training, including grade school, high school, normal school, and college, and degree or certificate granted by each institution. Arranged alphabetically by names of applicants. No index. Handwritten on printed forms. 12 x 17 x 30.

315. TEACHERS' CERTIFICATES

1922—. 1 file box.

Certificate of qualifications to teach in Ohio schools deposited by teachers, showing date filed, name and address of teacher, name of state board of school examiners, and name of director of education. Arranged alphabetically by names of teachers in chronologically thereunder by date file. No index. Handwritten on printed forms. 7 x 5 x 17.

316. CREDIT RECORDS

1920—. 1 file box.

Credit record of teachers, showing name of teacher, date filed, years of high school and college work, and professional training; also record of semester credits and date obtained. Arranged alphabetically by names of teachers and chronologically thereunder by dates filed. No index. Typed. 12 x 17 x 30.

Pupil's Records

(See also entries 323-f--323-j).

317. SCHOOL CENSUS SHEET

1922—. 3 file boxes.

School census sheets of pupils, showing names of teacher and school, date of census, name of township, name, address, grade, sex, and date of birth of pupil, and name, address, and occupation of parent or guardian. Arranged alphabetically by names of townships and alphabetically thereunder by names of pupils. No index. Handwritten on printed forms. 12 x 17 x 30.

318. WORKING CERTIFICATES

1919—. 1 file box.

Work certificates of pupils under compulsory age limit leaving school for employment, showing date of certificate, name and age of pupil, name of parent or guardian, name and address of employer, nature of employment, and pledge of employer. Arranged alphabetically by names of pupils and chronologically there under by dates issued. No index. Handwritten on printed forms. 7 x 5 x 17.

Statistics
(See also entry 323)

319. SCHOOL ENUMERATION
1930—. 1 file box.
Enumeration of all youths between the age of five and eighteen, showing name of school, date filed, name, date, and place of birth of child, names and addresses of parents or guardian, last school attended, grade or place of employment (if employed), and age on current May first. Arranged alphabetically by names of schools and chronologically thereunder by dates filed. No index. Handwritten on printed forms. 12 x 17 x 30.

320. ANNUAL STATISTICAL REPORT OF PUBLIC SCHOOLS
1914—. 10 bundles. 3 file boxes.
Copies of statistical reports of superintendent of county schools to state department of education, showing name of county, city, or exempted village, date of report, name and address of board members, date of expiration, number and names of school children, location and type of school, including kindergarten, elementary, junior, and senior high, and total net enrollment, average daily attendance, number of school days for given year, teaching and supervising personnel, number of tuition pupils and rates of tuition, number of colored and foreign pupils, number of pupils spending more than one year in any one grade including high schools, list of the exceptional pupils, number of school buildings occupied for that year, date of additions to schools and new buildings, details concerning part time and evening schools, and length of sessions; also financial report, showing date of report, amount of funds at end of year, amount and source of receipts, amount for service or goods supplied, tuition fund, contingent fund, and state aid; expenditures, showing itemized account, including teaching, supervision, transportation of pupils, and janitor, or school upkeep, and totals of paid and unpaid indebtedness. Arranged chronologically by dates reported. No index. Handwritten on printed forms. Bundles, 5 x 10 x 1. File boxes, 12 x 17 x 30.

Financial Records

(See also entry 323-p)

321. PURCHASE ORDERS

1930—. 1 file box.

Copies of purchase orders, showing appropriation, code, amount, date of order, name of vendor, place of delivery, to whom delivered, terms of discount, quantity, unit, description, unit price, amount, and signature of superintendent of schools. Arranged alphabetically by names of vendors and chronologically thereunder by date ordered. No index. Handwritten on printed forms. 12 x 17 x 30.

322. BOOK INVOICES

1937—. 1 file box.

Record of books purchased, showing appropriation, code, amount, place of delivery, terms, quantity, unit, description, price for each unit, amount, name of township, date filed, and signature of clerk. Arranged alphabetically by names of townships and chronologically thereunder by date filed. No index. Handwritten on printed forms. 12 x 17 x 30.

Miscellaneous

323. STATISTICS

1922—. 1 file box.

a. List of Ashland County school bus drivers, 1932-1933, showing name and address of bus driver, date filed, kind of vehicle used, and name of school district.

b. Papers pertaining to transfer of land from one school district to another, including description of land to be transferred, petitions of electors, plats of district, and opinions of attorney general, 1927-1934, showing dates of petition and transfer, location and description of school district, amount of land transferred, and signatures of interested parties.

c. Original minutes of board of education, 1929—, showing date of meeting, names of members present, resolutions presented and passed, record of voting on petitions, and signature of president and clerk.

d. Papers pertaining to teachers, including school examiner's record of teachers' examinations, 1925-1935, showing name of county, city, or town, names of members of board, date filed, number of examinations held, number of applicants, sex, number of applicants denied, number of certificates issued, and subject credits.

e. Program of meetings of teachers' institute, 1929-1936, showing subjects, names and addresses of members, appointments of committees, election of officers, representative instructors from State Teachers' Association of Columbus and County Teachers' Association of Ashland and method of teaching.

f. Examination papers of elementary school pupils, 1929, showing date of paper, name of county, school district, and city or village, signature of pupil, date of examination, and average grade.

g. Eighth grade test, 1929-1936, showing names and addresses of the eighth grade graduates, place of exercise, and distribution of diplomas and certificates.

h. Ashland county annual eighth grade commencement programs, 1933-1934, showing address where program was held, presentation of diplomas, class color, motto, and flower.

i. List of eighth grade graduates, showing names of pupil and township, street address, school, age, and yearly average.

j. Record of contest held in spelling, music, oratory, and athletics, showing date of contest, names of contestants, kind of contest, and names of winners.

k. Eligibility list and certificates of Ohio High School Athletic Associations 1926-1938, showing list of players eligible under the rules of the Ohio High School Athletic Association to represent the high schools in basketball games to be played at Ashland County on date of tournament that year, showing contestants name and birth record, name of school attended last semester, date of enrollment present semester, number of semesters enrolled, number of recitation periods passed last semester, and signature of principal of high school.

l. Statistics of numeration returns to county auditor, 1928-1929, showing name of school district, city, village, or rural, date of return, number of pupils, number school age, sex, total number of youths enumerated in the Connecticut Western Reserve, and United States Military District, and name of township.

m. Attendance officer's monthly report, 1936—, showing name and age of minor, name of parent or guardian, relation to minor, address, school district, and date visited, number of miles, amount due officer, and signature of officer.

n. Annual report of school attendance department, 1930—, showing occupation and industry entered, age accepted, grade completed, age, sex, race, total grades, date and certificate, and investigation of absent and reasons.

o. Annual statistical report of public schools, 1929—, showing name of county, date and report, certification of county school superintendent, names, addresses, and term of members of board of education, net enrollment for all schools, average attendance by day, number of teaching positions at end of session, total aggregate number of school days, number teachers and principals, education, number of children promoted, number failed, number of failures by subject, number of graduates for year, description and value of buildings and equipment, reports on finance and music, and instructions of rural and village Schools.

p. Copies of certification of board of education to county auditor of salaries and other expenses of county school teachers, 1922-1934, showing rural and village school district, number teachers, amount of salary of county superintendent, teachers, and attendance officer, traveling expenses, grand total, date of certification, and date filed.

All papers of each subject filed together and a folder. Arranged alphabetically by subjects and chronologically thereunder by dates filed. No index. Handwritten on printed forms. 12 x 17 x 30.

324. COUNTY MAP

No date. 1 map.

County map, showing names and location of schools in each township of the county, and symbols designating type of school, whether village, rural, or centralized. Prepared by county engineer. Mimeograph. 8 x 14. Hanging on the wall.

The general health district, or county health department, is one of the recent developments in county health administration. An act of the legislature in 1919 provided that townships and municipalities in each county, excluding any city with 25,000 or more population, should constitute a general health district; cities with 25,000 or more population a municipal health district; municipalities of not less than 10,000 nor more than 25,000 population, and maintaining a board of health meeting the qualifications of the legislative act, were authorized after examination by the state health department to continue operation as separate health district.[1]

An amendment in December 1919 made each city a health district. The townships and villages in each county were combined into a general health district, and a city and general health district might combine for administrative purposes. The mayor of each municipality not constituting a city health district, and the chairman of the trustees of each township, are authorized to meet at the seat of justice and by selecting a chairman and the secretary organize a district advisory council which selects and appoints a district board of health composed of five members, one of whom must be a physician, who serves without compensation.[2]

Within 30 days after their appointment the members of the district board of health–the county board of health–organize by appointing one of their members president and another president *pro tempore.* The board is authorized to appoint as district health commissioner a licensed physician who serves as secretary to the board. This official is designated deputy state registrar of vital statistics and is required to report monthly to the state registrar a vital statistics.[3]

On recommendation of the district health commissioner, the board appoints a full-time public health nurse, a clerk, and such additional public health nurses, physicians, and others as may be necessary for the proper conduct of its work. The board studies the prevalence of disease, and particular communicable diseases, provides for treatment of venereal diseases, and is authorized to make any and all regulations it deems necessary for the prevention or restriction of disease, and the prevention, abolition, or suppression of nuisances. It provides for inspection of public charitable, benevolent, correctional, and penal institutions; and may provide inspection at dairies, stores, restaurants, hotels, and other places where food is manufactured, handled, stored, sold, or offered for sale.

---

1. *Laws of Ohio,* CVIII, pt. I, 236.
2. *Ibid.,* CVIII, pt. ii, 1085.
3. G. C. sec. 1261-32; *Laws of Ohio,* CVIII, pt. I, 238-242.

The board is authorized to carry on necessary laboratory test by establishing a laboratory or contracting with existing laboratories, and all state institutions supported in whole or in part by public funds must furnish such laboratory service to a county board of health under the terms agreed upon.[4]

The health department is financed by public taxation. The district board of health annually estimates in itemized form the amount needed for the fiscal year, and these estimates are certified to the county auditor and submitted by him to the county budget commissioners who may reduce any item but cannot increase any item or the aggregate of all items. The total amount fixed by the budget commissioners is apportioned by the county health department on the basis of taxable valuations in the townships in the municipalities composing the district.[5]

In Ashland County the board of health carries on its work with one county nurse, an assistant nurse, a clerk, and a sanitarian, all under the supervision the state health department. Laboratory tests of water and milk, or for typhoid, diphtheria, syphilis, undulant fever, bangs disease are made for the district at the Ohio State University. Rabies treatment serum is available at the local office at all times, and the state health department provides free treatment of syphilis when application is properly made through the local office. The annual budget of the board amounted in 1940 to $6,940.60 of which the state health department contributed $1,000.[6]

Tuberculosis clinics, supported by the county commissioners as authorized by law[7] have been conducted semiannually by the board of health since 1924.[8] Complete X-ray files and case records are kept in its office.[9] Since Ashland County maintains no sanitarium, it sends its indigent patients to one of three institutions, the Ohio State and Avalon Sanitariums at Mt. Vernon in Knox County, and Oak Ridge Sanitarium at Green Springs, in Sandusky County. In 1940 the commissioner's appropriated for this purpose $10,062.88, supporting nine patients at one or another of these institutions.[10]

All records are located in the board of health main office.

---

4. *Laws of Ohio,* CVIII, pt. ii, 1088, 1089.
5. *Ibid.,* CVIII, pt. ii, 1091.
6. Record of Minutes and Proceedings, 1940, entry 325.
7. *Laws of Ohio,* CVII, 495.
8. Record of Minutes and Proceedings, 1924, entry 325.
9. *See* entries 331-355.
10. Appropriation Ledger, 1940, entry 239.

Minutes

325. RECORD OF MINUTES AND PROCEEDINGS
1919—. 2 vols. (1, 2).

Minutes of board of health, showing dates of meetings, names of members present, and business transacted, including reports of committees and health commissioner, resolutions approved or rejected, record of agreements of clerk of health commission, agreements of nurses to carry out duties to best of their ability, bills presented for payment, and record of monthly and yearly salaries of officials and employees. Arranged chronologically by dates of meetings. No index. Handwritten on printed forms. 260 pages. 14 x 8 x 1.5.

Case Records

326. ACTIVE FAMILY RECORDS AND DISMISSED FAMILY RECORDS
1921—. 2 file boxes.

Card record of active and closed cases, showing name of township, name and address of patient, date of birth, history of illness, diagnosis of disease, names of attending physician and nurse, reported condition of patient, medical advice given, referred to clinic or discharge, sex, race, and date of first and final examinations. Arranged alphabetically by names of townships and alphabetically thereunder by names of patients. No index. Handwritten on printed forms. 10 x 18 x 36.

327. FAMILY FOLDERS
1936—. 1 file box.

Card record of families, showing date of report, Name and address of patient, age, sex, race, name of township, county, and city, and by whom reports were made. Arranged chronologically by dates reported. No index. Handwritten on printed forms. 10 x 18 x 36.

328. CAMP PERMITS (Inspection)
1937—. 1 file box.

Original record of camping permits issued, showing date of inspection, to whom issued and address, name and location of camp, number of enrollees, accomplishments of each camp, grades, Individual progress record, and signature of director of health and district health commissioner. Arranged chronologically by dates inspected. No index. Handwritten on printed forms. 10 x 10 x 36.

329. PRESCHOOL CLINIC RECORDS
1923—. 1 file box.

Original record of activities of clinics held for children of preschool age entering school the following semester, showing name of child, names and address of parents, sex, race, date of birth, name of family physician, physical condition of parents, health record of child, and date of clinic examination. Arranged alphabetically by names of children. No index. Handwritten on printed forms. 10 x 18 x 36.

330. SCHOOL HEALTH RECORDS
1919—. 1 file box.

Record of periodic examinations of school children, showing names of township and school, date of the report, name and address, date of birth, race and sex of child, age, height, weight, posture, eyes, grade, whether or not the child is retarded; report on hearing, teeth, tonsils, various glands, skin, heart, lungs, orthopedia, and signature of nurses and physicians. Arranged alphabetically by names of townships, alphabetically thereunder by names of pupils, and chronologically thereunder by dates reported. No index. Typed on printed forms. 10 x 18 x 36.

331. DIAGNOSTIC CHEST CHARTS
1924—. 1 file box.

Chest charts, showing date of record, name and address of person examined, name and address of parents of minors and adults, age, sex, color, nativity, number of dependents, names and addresses of physician and employer (if working), education, length of residence in county, life insurance, family history, personal history, habits, army service (if any), diseases, operations, home and work environment, present illness and duration, physical examination and results, and diagnosis. Arranged alphabetically by names of persons examined. No index. Typed on printed forms. Approximately 450 sheets. 14 x 11.5 x 26.5.

332. TUBERCULOSIS TEST PRINTS
1924—. 1 file drawer.

Test prints of school children, showing name of school, grade, room, name and address of pupil, signature of parents or guardian, name of teacher, and date tested.

Arranged alphabetically by names of schools and alphabetically thereunder by names of pupils. No index. Typed on printed forms. Approximately 1,500 cards. 4 x 5.5 x 19.

333. CHEST X-RAY PICTURES
1924—. 3 file drawers.

X-ray films, showing date and number of X-ray and chest exposures; each X-ray filed in envelope, showing date and number of x-ray and name and address of patient. Arranged alphabetically by names of patients. No index. Approximately 150 X-rays. 16 x 19 x 26.

334. CARD INDEX (Tuberculosis Records)
1924—. 1 file drawer.

Index record cards of active and closed cases, showing name and address of patient, sex, color, marital status, date and place of birth, nationality of father and mother, occupation, diagnosis, names of physician and nurse, date of first and last visit, number of visits, conditions, and remarks. Arranged alphabetically by names of patients. No index. Typed on printed forms. Approximately 1,500 cards. 4 x 5.5 x 19.

Communicable Diseases

335. COMMUNICABLE DISEASE RECORDS
1920—. 1 file box.

Record of reported communicable diseases, showing name of disease, name and address of patient, date of report, age, sex, race, names of township, county, and city, date of onset, and report of case. Arranged alphabetically by names of townships and alphabetically thereunder by names of patients. No index. Handwritten on printed forms. 10 x 18 x 36.

Vital statistics

336. BIRTH CERTIFICATES

1921—. 1 file box.

Copies of birth certificates, showing date of birth, name of township, name of infant, names and address of parents, mother's maiden name, date and place of birth, signature of attending physician, sex, race, weight, height of infant, and occupation of father. Arranged alphabetically by names of townships and alphabetically thereunder by names of families. No index. Handwritten on printed forms. 10 x 18 x 36.

337. DEATH CERTIFICATES

1922—. 1 file box.

Copies of death certificates, showing name of the decedent, age, date and place of birth, cause and date of death, name of township, sex, race, name and address the nearest relative, coroner's report (if any), and names of mortician, physician, or person reporting death. Arranged alphabetically by names of townships and alphabetically thereunder by names of decedents. No index. Types of printed forms. 10 x 18 x 36.

By the provisions of the legislative act of 1816, the county commissioners were authorized to build a "poor house," and to appoint annually seven persons to constitute a board of directors. This board, a corporate body, was authorized to make such rules and regulations as were necessary for the management of the institution, and to appoint a superintendent, who might receive only persons who had the required order from the township trustees. He was directed to keep a book listing the name and age of every person admitted, together with the date of admission.[1] The board of directors, or a committee of that body, was required to visit the "poor house" to examine the condition of the paupers and to make a report on such matters as the food, clothing, and treatment of the inmates. Moreover, they were required to inspect the books and accounts of the superintendent. The board was required to report annually to the county commissioners the "state of the institution" with a full and correct account of all their proceedings, contracts, and disbursements; and the expenses of establishing and supporting the institution were to be paid on the order of the county commissioners out of the money in the treasury not otherwise appropriated.[2]

By a legislative act of 1831, the membership of the board was reduced to three. This board, like its predecessor, was authorized to appoint a superintendent. It was his duty, upon the order of the board, to discharge from the poorhouse any person who had been admitted because of illness when he had sufficiently recovered. The directors were further authorized to remove paupers to their legal place of residence,[3] and any pauper rejected by the board of directors could be turned over to the township overseers to be cared for by contracting with the lowest bidder.[4]

In 1850 the name "county poorhouse" was changed to that of "county infirmary."[5] Fifteen years later, in 1865, the board of the infirmary directors, consisting of three resident electors, was made elective by the voters of the county for a three-year term. The board was still authorized to appoint a superintendent, and was still required to make inspection visits, and to report its finding to the county commissioners.[6]

---

1. *Laws of Ohio,* XIV, 447.
2. *Ibid.,* XIV, 499.
3. *Ibid.,* XXIX, 319.
4. *Ibid.,* XXIX, 321-322.
5. *Ibid.,* XLVIII, 62.
6. *Ibid.,* LXII, 24-25.

Although reports have been required of the infirmary management in previous years, it was not until the decade of the seventies that the legislature enacted measures looking to really systematic management of this ancient institution. Accordingly, in 1872, an act was passed which required each infirmary director, as well as a superintendent, to give bond conditioned for the faithful performance of the duties of his office.[7] Under this act the directors were required to report semiannually to the county commissioners the condition of infirmary, number of inmates, and such other information as the county commissioners believed proper. Furthermore, the board of directors was required to file a full account "of all moneys received and paid out, together with the vouchers ... from whence received, to whom and for what paid out" with the county commissioners, who, after examining it, entered the report in the minutes of their proceedings. This report, as well as the vouchers, was to be filed in the auditor's office, and must be "safely preserved" by that officer.[8]

The county infirmary served also as a place for the confinement of children, the mentally ill, and persons afflicted with epilepsy. Although the state assumed responsibility for the mentally ill in the early years of the nineteenth century, it was not until 1898 that it was made unlawful to confine the adult insane and epileptics in and the county home.[9] Previously, in 1884, the legislature had prohibited the housing in the county infirmary of children who were eligible to the county children's home or to some other charitable institution, unless separated from adults.[10] Exceptions were made, however, in the case of insane, idiotic, and epileptic children.[11] The latter provision is still in effect in Ohio.[12]

By an act of May 31, 1911, effective January 1, 1913, the board of infirmary directors was abolished and the powers formerly exercised for this body were transferred to the county commissioners and the infirmary superintendent.[13]

---

7. *Laws of Ohio,* LXIX, 120-121.
8. *Ibid.,* LXIX, 121-122.
9. *Ibid.,* XCIII, 274.
10. *Ibid.,* LXXXI, 92.
11. *Ibid.,* CIII, 890.
12. G. C. sec. 3089.
13. *Laws of Ohio,* CII, 433.

The superintendent is still required to keep a record of the inmates, as prescribed by statute and to report annually to the county commissioners. This report, the acceptance of which is evidence by an entry and the minutes of the commissioner's journal, is filed with the county auditor and by him preserved.[14] In 1919 the name county infirmary was changed to that of county home.[15]

The county commissioners still make provision for the establishment and maintenance of the county home, appoint a superintendent, and make regular inspection visits. Since December 1, 1932, the superintendent has been appointed from a list of names of persons eligible under civil service regulations,[16] and is authorized to appoint a matron and other employees.[17] Since 1882, the commissioners have been authorized to appoint an infirmary physician, who, like the superintendent, is required by statute to report to the county commissioners. This report, made quarterly, includes such information as the nature and extent of medical services rendered, to whom, and the character of the disease treated.[18]

Although there is some relation between the old age pension system and the county home, the newer form of aid is merely supplementary to the institution. As always, the county home cares for those whose condition is such that they cannot be satisfactory cared for except in an institution.[19] The benefits granted by the division of aid for the aged have somewhat reduced the number of inmates of the county home in Ashland County, as those who are able to do so leave the home upon receiving a pension.[20]

The contract for the Ashland County Infirmary was let in 1849 by the county commissioners[21] under authority of the act of 1816.[22] Before this time Ashland County commissioners were especially permitted by law to send paupers to Richland County.[23]

---

14. G. C. sec. 2535.
15. *Laws of Ohio,* CVIII, pt. I, 68.
16. Ohio Attorney General, *Opinions,* III, 2021.
17. G. C. sec. 2522.
18. G. C. sec. 2546; *Laws of Ohio,* LXXIX, 90; CII, 436; CVIII, pt. I, 269.
19. The Reorganization of County Government in Ohio, 132, 135.
20. (Minutes) Infirmary Record, 1936-1841, *passim,* entry 338.
21. Commissioners' Record, I (1846-1963), 78.
22. *Laws of Ohio,* XIV, 447.
23. *Ibid.,* XLVI, 53-54.

The Ashland County Home has given refuge to about 1,640 persons in the past quarter century. They have ranged in age from babyhood to the nineties. While a few of the inmates pay all or part of the cost of their care, by far the greater number do not. In 1940 the commissioners appropriated $14,352 for the maintenance of the home. The eight resident members of the staff received an average salary of $4,428.[24]

Physical care is given within the limits of the resources of the institution. Cases of severe illnesses, however, requiring special attention, are cared for at the cost of the county at the city hospital in Ashland as are other indigent patients.[25] A preacher is retained by the commissioners to provide religious services once a month.[26]

All records are located and the superintendent's office at the county home, Hayesville Road, Ashland, Ohio, unless otherwise specified.

---

24. (Auditor's) Annual Financial Reports to County Commissioners, 1940, entry 267.
25. Annual Appropriation Resolutions, 1940, In Commissioners Record, XXVII, (1940—). 510.
26. (Minutes) Infirmary Record, 1940, entry 338.

Minutes

338. (Minutes) INFIRMARY RECORD
1849—. 3 vols. (1-3).

Record of minutes of meetings of board of infirmary directors, 1849-1913, and county commissioners sitting as board of directors, 1913—, showing names of directors present, date of meeting, names of township and trustees, bills submitted and paid, date and number of bill, goods supplied or services rendered, amount of bill, and name and address and creditor. Arranged chronologically by dates of meetings. No index. Handwritten. Average 450 pages. 12 x 18 x 2.5.

Case Records

339. APPLICATIONS
1849—. 2 file boxes, 1 bundled.

Copies of accepted applications for admission to county home, showing date of application, name and address of applicant, age, race, color, sex, marital status, number in family, description of property owned by applicant, name of nearest relative, length of the residence in county or township, former residence, date of last public relief, cause of indigence, nature of relief needed, probable duration of relief, physical condition at present time, present legal residence, and signatures of Commissioners. Arranged chronologically by dates of applications. No index. Handwritten on printed forms. File box, 10 x 12 x 18; bundle, 4 x 4 x 12.

340. INFIRMARY RECORD
1849—. 2 vols. (1, 2).

Register of admissions to county infirmary, showing date of admission, name of inmate, age, nativity, marital status, length of residence in county, state, and township, and whether insane, epileptic, idiotic, or deformed; also record of discharges, showing date and reason for discharge, and record of deaths, showing date and cause of death. Arranged chronologically by dates of admissions. No index. Handwritten on printed forms. Average 150 pages. 12 x 18 x 2.

341. ARTICLES OF AGREEMENT
1880—. 1 vol.

Articles of agreement between infirmary board and inmate, showing names of directors, name of inmate, date of agreement, itemized list of goods disposed of by public sale, and amount received for goods, and transferred to poor fund with name of article, quantity, and total amount. Arranged alphabetically by names of inmates. No index. Handwritten on printed forms. 100 pages. 12 x 8 x 1.

Financial Records

342. INFIRMARY DIRECTORS' DIARY
1892-1901. 1 vol. 1902— in expenditures and receipts, infirmary fund, entry 344.

Infirmary directors' diary, showing date of entry, cost of labor and supplies, and number of inmates admitted. Arranged chronologically by dates entered. No index. Handwritten. 90 pages. 12 x 4 x 1.

343. JOURNAL
1897—. 2 vols.

Journal record of cash, showing date of entry, balance on hand, amount of debits, credits, and balance. Arranged chronologically by dates entered. No index. Handwritten. 480 pages. 8 x 14 x 2.5.

344. EXPENDITURES AND RECEIPTS, INFIRMARY FUND
1892—. 3 vols.

Record of expenditures, showing date of entry, name and number of item, salaries of superintendent and matron, wages of other employees, total amount of salaries and wages, expenses for groceries, provisions, fuel, light, clothing, footwear, drugs, medicine, liquor, tobacco, livestock, hay, grain, vehicles, tools, implements, machinery, repairs, furniture, burial expenses, and total expenses; receipts, showing date of entry, moneys received by infirmary for sale of farm produce, stock, cream sold to dairy, insurance, donation of inmates and friends for care and keep of inmates for a limited time, and from insurance company for damage to home. Payments are made to county treasurer. Also contains Infirmary Directors' Diary, 1902—, entry 342. Arranged chronologically by dates entered. No index. Handwritten on printed forms. Average 200 pages. 14 x 18 x 2.5.

345. RECEIPTS
1888—. 4 file boxes.

Original receipts issued by county treasurer for grain, hay, and other produce sold, showing date of receipts, signatures of treasurer and superintendent of infirmary, sale price of produce, to whom sold, and amount of sale; also receipt for taxes paid to treasurer by infirmary director of property taken from inmates, showing amount of taxes, date paid, and location and description of property. Records are contained in folders. Arranged chronologically by dates of receipts. No index. Handwritten on printed forms. 10 x 12 x 18.

346. BILLS
1893—. 4 file boxes.

Original bills for equipment and supplies, including freight, groceries, gas, oil, and funeral bills, showing date of filings, itemized list of purchases, name of purchaser, from whom purchased, total amount and date of each bill, number and weight of packages, freight rates, and total for each; funeral bills, showing name of decedent, date of death, itemized account of expenses, name of funeral director, and place of burial. Records are contained in folders. Arranged chronologically by dates filed. No index. Handwritten on printed forms. 10 x 12 x 18.

Miscellaneous

347. ORDER OF TRANSPORTATION
1888—. 1 file box.

Copies kept in infirmary office of expense accounts of infirmary directors regarding transportation, showing starting place, destination and return, also cost of ticket or traveling expense, with signature of ticket agent, and name of purchaser of ticket; also includes infirmary directors account for services rendered to the infirmary (gas, light, and water), showing date, place, and total. Arranged chronologically by dates filed. No index. Handwritten on printed forms. File box, 10 x 12 x 18.

348. INVENTORY AND SETTLEMENTS OF PAYING PAUPERS
1878-1908. 1 vol.

Inventory of property belonging to inmates, showing date of inventory, name of inmate, itemized list of quantity, kind of article, and price, and signature of sale clerk and superintendent of infirmary. Contains no record of settlements. Arranged chronologically by dates of inventories. No index. Handwritten. 400 pages. 12 x 7 x 1.5.

349. PAUPERS STATISTICS
1849—. 1 file box.

Copies of statistics submitted by county auditor to state department, including costs and expenditures of keeping patients in the home and keeping patients outside the home, showing numbers supported by each method, total supported, date report submitted, signatures of superintendent of home and board of directors. Records are contained and folders. Arranged chronologically by dates reported. No index. Handwritten on printed forms. 10 x 12 x 18.

350. DIVISION OF CHARITIES
1937—. 1 file box, 1 bundle.

Record copies of monthly reports of superintendent of county home to the state division of charities, showing date of report, number of male and female inmates at beginning of each day, number received during day, number discharged, died, or ran away during day, number continuously present for the entire month, number of persons received for the first time, number of persons received who were former inmates, number of deaths, and average number of inmates cared for during month. Arranged chronologically by dates filed. No index. File box, 10 x 4.5 x 13.5; bundle, 14 x 8 x .25.

351. VISITORS REGISTER
1877—. 1 vol.

Record of visitors to county infirmary, showing date of visit, name and address of visitor, number of meals served, and remarks. Arranged chronologically by dates of visit. No index. Handwritten on printed forms. 500 pages. 10 x 12 x 3. Reception hall.

352. SUMMONS IN PROBATE COURT
1904—. 1 file box.

Copies of petitions to sell real estate belonging to infirmary inmates, showing date of filing, name of person summoned, reason for sale, and signature of probate judge. Arranged chronologically by dates filed. No index. Handwritten on printed forms. 10 x 12 x 18.

353. MISCELLANEOUS FILE

1887—. 2 file boxes.

Copies of agreements for care of inmates by relatives, list of articles sold at public auction, papers of surrender of child to children's home by inmates of county infirmary, indentures of apprenticeship; agreements for care of inmates by relatives, 1896—, showing date, names of inmate and relative, place of residence, agreement as to amount relative must pay towards care of inmates, and description of case; articles sold at public auction, 1896—, showing name of article, quantity, amount paid, name of inmate, name of clerk, and date of sale; surrender of child, 1896—, showing date of commitment, names of child and inmate, age of child, sex, signature of superintendent, and date to be released; indenture of minors, 1896-1905, showing date of indenture, and name of inmate, name of family or business where apprenticeship is to be served, title of position to be held, and signatures of superintendent and guardian or parents; copies of abstracts of title and deeds turned over by inmates, 1887—, showing history of title, location of property, rightful owner, names of grantor and grantee, date filed, and term of agreement. Records are contained in folders. Arranged alphabetically by subjects and chronologically thereunder by dates filed. No index. Handwritten on printed forms. 10 x 12 x 18.

354. WELFARE (Miscellaneous Correspondence)

1898—. 2 file boxes (labeled by contained letters of alphabet).

Correspondence between superintendent of infirmary and department of public welfare regarding reports on daily movement of inmates for current month, showing date of correspondence, to whom, subject matter, and signature of correspondent. Records are contained in folders. Arranged chronologically by dates of correspondence. No index. 1898-1917—, handwritten; 1917—, typed. 10 x 12 x 18.

Although the legislature made provisions for institutional care of the county's indigent as early as 1816, it was not until after the middle of the nineteenth century, when hundreds of Ohio children were left homeless by the scourge of Civil War, that the legislature enacted measures for the care of dependent children. Previous to this time the Ohio statutes relative to the care of children had been taken from the territorial code, which authorized the overseers of the poor, and later the trustee of the "poor house," to apprentice the children of the indigent, boys until 21 and girls until 18 years of age.[1] The fact that this system was not only inhuman but entirely unsatisfactory, is evidenced by the innumerable advertisements for runaway apprentices appearing in the press.

In 1865 the legislature authorized the county commissioners to receive request for orphans' asylums, and, when funds accumulated in sufficient quantities, to construct such a home, and appoint a board of directors consisting of six persons who were given the task of managing the institution, subject to the rules and regulations of the county commissioners. This board, electing a president and a treasurer from its own number, was required annually to make a report of the receipts and disbursements of the asylum, together with the number of orphans received into and discharged from the institution. This report was to be published by the commissioners in a newspaper having a general circulation.[2]

A year later, in 1866, the commissioners were authorized, when in their judgment the best interest of the wards of the county would be served, to establish children's homes, and to provide by means of taxation, funds to be used for the purchase of a site, to construct buildings, and to maintain such charitable institutions.[3] In 1874 an act was passed authorizing counties to the combine for the formation of children's home districts.[4] Then, in 1876, an act was passed which repealed all previous legislation and established the present duties of the county commissioners, trustees, superintendent, and matron in respect to children's homes. The act authorized accounting commissioners to appoint a board of trustees and a superintendent of each children's home.[5]

---

1. Pease, *op. cit.*, 219; *Laws of Ohio*, III, 176; VIII, 223-224; XXIX, 318.
2. *Laws of Ohio,* LXII, 97.
3. *Ibid.,* LXIII, 45.
4. *Ibid.,* LXXI, 60.
5. *Ibid.,* LXXIII, 67.

The board of trustees consists of five members appointed for a five-year term. The trustees, besides appointing a superintendent, hold monthly meetings at which time they examine all accounts presented for payment, examine into the condition of the property and the manner of care offered to the wards. Annually or oftener, they are required to file with the state board of charities a detailed account giving the whereabouts of each child and the physical condition of each ward under their care.[6]

The superintendent, operating under the rules and regulations of the trustees, has entire charge and control of the home and its wards. He may appoint a matron, assistant matron, and other necessary employees, subject to the approval of the board of trustees. It is the duty of such employees to care for the residents of the home, direct their employment, and give suitable physical, mental and moral training. Under the direction of the superintendent, the matron has general management and supervision of the household duties of the home. The matron, like other employees, receives such salary as the trustees may direct and may be removed by the superintendent or at the pleasure of a majority of the trustees.[7]

The county children's home serves as a refuge for children under 18 years of age who have resided in the county for one year and who are, in the opinion of the trustees, eligible to admission by reason of orphanage, abandonment, or neglect by parents, or the inability of parents to provide for them.[8] Children are admitted to the home on order of the juvenile court or on the order of the majority of the board of trustees. Since 1876 each child committed to the children's home must be accompanied by a statement of the facts setting forth his name, his age, his birthplace, and his condition. These facts, recorded by the superintendent in a book kept for that purpose, are confidential and open to inspection only at the discretion of the board of trustees.[9] All wards of the children's home who have been committed to the institution by the juvenile court because of abandonment, neglect, or dependency, or who have been voluntarily surrendered by their parents, are under the exclusive jurisdiction, guardianship, and control of the trustees until they have become a lawful age.[10]

---

6. G. C. sec. 3082-1.
7. G. C. sec. 3085.
8. G. C. sec. 3089.
9. G. C. sec. 3090; *Laws of Ohio,* LXXIII, 64; LXXXIII, 196; XCIX, 187; CIII, 889.
10. G. C. sec. 3093.

The county commissioners may, subject to the approval of the division of charities of the department of public welfare, after an opportunity has been given to the electorate to demand a referendum on the proposition, abandoned the children's home. If the home is discontinued, they may sell the site and building and use the funds for care and neglected and dependent children, providing that the wards in the children's home who are placed in foster homes and those who are under the guardianship of the trustees are legally committed to the guardianship of the division of the charities.[11]

Ashland County was indebted to the philanthropic generosity of a local woman, Mrs. Jonas Freer, for the establishment of its children's home. Deeply interested in child welfare, as evidenced by the fact that she reared nine orphan children, Mrs. Freer willed to the county a 94-acre farm and a spacious house which on October 17, 1907 was opened as the county children's home.[12] More recently the home benefitted from another generous request by an Ashland woman, a gift of $8,343.31 by Mary Sloan.[13]

During the first 20 years of its history the home cared for 408 children.[14] In recent years the number of children at the home has tended to increase, 48 being housed at one time during 1941.[15]

The cost to the county for operating the home is approximately 60 cents a day for each child. From 1936 to 1941 the annual appropriations ranged from $10,020 to $11,000.[16] In 1934 and 1935 the commissioners also appropriated $29,151.60 for additions, improvements, and new equipment.[17]

All records are located in the superintendent's office at the children's home, 1204 South Center Street, Ashland, Ohio.

---

11. G. C. sec. 3092-1.
12. Duff, William A. ed., *Ashland, The City of Progress and Prosperity* (Ashland, 1915), 95-97.
13. Commissioners' Record, XXVI, (1939-1941), 240, entry 1.
14. Commitment Record, 1907-1927, entry 356.
15. *Ibid.,* 1941.
16. Commissioners' Record, (1935-1937), 83, 421; XXV (1937-1939), 113, 423; XXVI (1939-1941), 171, 513.
17. *Ibid.,* XXIII (1934-1935), 22, 314.

Minutes

355. TRUSTEES' JOURNAL
1907—. 2 vols.
Minutes of board of trustees children's home, showing date of meeting, motions and resolutions adopted and rejected, and record of paid and unpaid bills. Arranged chronologically by dates of meetings. No index. Handwritten on printed forms. Average 240 pages. 12 x 18 x 3.

Case records

356. COMMITMENT RECORD
1907—. 1 vol.
Record of admission to children's home, showing name of child, date of birth, date committed, names of township, county, and state, by whom and date brought to home, date returned to parent or guardian, and whether parents are living or dead. Arranged chronologically by dates of commitments. Indexed alphabetically by names of children. Handwritten on printed forms. 110 pages. 8 x 12 x .5.

357. JOURNAL ENTRY
1907—. 2 file boxes.
Case records of family and personal history of child, showing parents names, whether living or deceased, name of county, date and place of birth of child, school grade or occupation, mental and physical condition, birth dates of parents, nationality, religion, length of residence in state, naturalized or not, date and place of parents marriage, Previous marriage (if any), and divorce (if any), and date record filed. No index. Handwritten on printed forms. 12 x 12 x 30.

Financial Records

358. APPROPRIATION SCHEDULE
1932—. 2 file boxes.
Record of appropriations resolutions, showing date of board meeting, location, names of members present, adoption or rejection of resolutions, vote and signature of each member present. Arranged chronologically by dates of meetings. No index. Typed on printed forms. 3 x 4 x 12.

359. CHILDREN'S HOME LEDGER, ASHLAND COUNTY

1907—. 2 vols. Title varies: Trustees' Ledger No. 1, 1907-1926, 1 vol.

Record of quarterly allowance by board of trustees of children's home, for fuel, forage, clothing, officers' and employees' salaries, repair and improvement of building and grounds, books, stationary, furniture, transportation, and livestock, showing name and number of account, amount of budget estimate, date of entry, name, services rendered and goods supplied, bill number, receipt number, amount received, fund credited, and balance; in back of volume, appropriation ledger, 1926—, showing fund, name of account, code, sheet number date of entry, vendor or payee, services rendered and good supplied, purchase order and warrant numbers, and amount of warrant; fund credited, under appropriation or authorization, showing debit certification, credit adjustment, and unencumbered balance. Indexed alphabetically by subjects. Handwritten on printed forms. 1 volume 400 pages. 16 x 11 x 2; 1 volume 500 pages. 14 x 12 x 2.5.

360. CLASSIFICATION OF EXPENDITURES FROM CHILDREN'S HOME

1917—. 1 vol.

Expense record of maintenance of children's home, including salaries of superintendent and physician, wages of other employees, fuel and light, wearing apparel, dry goods, drugs, medicines, education, recreation, motor vehicles, repairs, and replacement of machinery, showing date of entry, to whom paid, and number and amount of warrant. Arranged chronologically by dates entered. No index. Handwritten on printed forms. 250 pages. 12 x 18 x 3.

361. RECEIPTS OF BILLS PAID

1924—. 1 file box.

Paid bills and receipts for money paid out, showing date of payment, date filed, Amount of bill or receipt, name of payee, and name of fund. Arranged chronologically by dates filed. No index. Handwritten on printed forms. 3 x 4 x 12.

The board of county visitors, an agency for the examination and inspection of county institutions supported wholly or in part by county or municipal taxation, was created by an act of the general assembly in 1882. Under this act, the judge of the court of common pleas was authorized to appoint five persons, three of whom were to be women, who were to visit periodically such county institutions as the county infirmary, county jail, municipal prisons, and children's home, and file annually a report of their proceedings and recommendations for changes with the clerk of court, and to forward a copy to the state board of charities. The members, appointed for an indefinite period, were to serve without compensation.[1]

By the act of 1892 the personnel of the board was increased to six persons, three of whom were to be women, and not more than three to have the same political affiliation. Furthermore the act made it the duty of the probate judge, whenever proceedings were instituted in his court to commit a child under 16 years of age to the boys' industrial home or to the girls' industrial home, to have notice given to the board of such proceedings; and it was made the duty of the board of visitors to attend the meetings of the court, as a body or as a committee, to protect the interest of the child.[2]

While the provision of the act of 1892 were redefined by the act of 1898 and 1900, these acts did not, in the main, affect the duties of the board.[3] The letter act, however, made the board a continuous body with two members of the first board appointed thereafter serving for one year, two members serving for two years, and two members serving for three years. In addition to this, the board was allowed a minimum expense schedule for their services.[4] Six years later the power of appointment of board members was given to the probate judge. The board was authorized to recommend to the county commissioners measures for the more economical administration of county institutions. Their report, together with their recommendations, was to be filed each year with the judge of the probate court and with the county prosecuting attorney.[5]

---

1. *Laws of Ohio,* LXXIX, 107.
2. *Ibid.,* LXXXIX, 161.
3. *Ibid.,* XCIII, 57; XCIV, 70.
4. *Ibid.,* XCIV, 70.
5. *Ibid.,* XCVIII, 28.

Under an act of 1913 the juvenile judge, like the probate judge under the act of 1892, was authorized to notify the visitors when any proceedings were instituted in his court for the commitment of any child to a state institution or correction.[6] The practice of annually filing reports of the board with the probate judge, prosecuting attorney, and state board of charities has been continued.[7]

In Ashland County the board makes its inspections of the county institutions at intervals of six months. The board makes its annual reports according to the requirements a state law to the county commissioners.

The board of county visitors keep no separate records; for reports, see miscellaneous (To Officers, Bonds, Probate Fees), 1907—, entry 21e, and Record of Appointments, 1913—, entry 153.

---

6. *Ibid.,* CIII, 173-174, 888.
7. G. C. sec. 2976.

The soldiers' relief commission was established by an act of the legislature passed May 19, 1886, entitled "An act to provide for the relief of indigent Union soldiers, sailors, and marines, and the indigent wives, widows and minor children of indigent or deceased Union soldiers, sailors and marines." Under the provisions of this act the commissioners of each county were authorized to levy a specified tax for the purpose of creating a fund for the relief of such beneficiaries; and the judge of the court of common pleas was authorized to appoint three county residents, at least two of whom were honorably discharged Union soldiers, to serve for a term of three years as members of the commission, which was organized by the selection of a chairman and a secretary.[1]

An amendment passed on March 4, 1887, provided that the councilman of the city wards, as well as the board of trustees of the townships, certify to the soldiers' relief commission the names of those requiring and entitled to aid under the act.[2]

By an act of the legislature, passed April 28, 1890, the soldiers' relief commission was required to appoint annually a committee of three in each township and a committee of three in each ward in any city in the county, whose duty it was to receive all applications for aid and to certify them to the soldiers' relief commission. The commission after receiving from the auxiliary committees reports on the financial status of each applicant for relief is empowered to increase, decrease, or discontinue any allowance and certify their findings to the auditor.[3]

The commission is authorized to grant relief to soldiers, sailors, and marines, and their indigent parents, wives, widows, and minor children; including widows of soldiers, sailors, and marines, who have remarried, but again have become indigent widows, who reside in such township or ward, and including the soldiers, sailors, and marines, of the Spanish-American War and the World War, and their wives, widows, indigent parents, minor children, and wards, who have been bona fide residence, of the state for one year and of the county six months.[4]

---

1. *Laws of Ohio,* LXXXIII, 232.
2. *Ibid.,* LXXXIV, 100.
3. *Ibid.,* LXXXVII, 325.
4. G. C. sec. 2934.

Section 2930 of the General Code was amended in 1941 changing the membership of the commission in each county to three persons, residents of the county to serve for three years. Whenever possible one member is to be a member of the United Spanish War Veterans, one a member of the American Legion, and one a member of the Veterans of Foreign Wars or of the Disabled American Veterans of the World War.[5]

The Ashland County commissioners appropriate funds each year for this commission and each member is allowed $100 annually as compensation.[6] The aid granted varies from year to year; in 1938 the average monthly award was $71.16; in 1939 it dropped to $54.16; and in 1940 it was still for the reduced to $47.16.[7]

All records of soldiers' relief commission are located in the secretary's office, 229 Union Street, Loudonville, Ohio.

362. MINUTES OF SOLDIERS' RELIEF COMMISSION AND RECORD OF GRANTS
1905—. 2 vols.

Minutes of soldiers' relief commission, showing date of meeting, number and names of members present, amount awarded for relief, cancellation of relief, action taken by the commissioners on various cases, and signature of the secretary and members; record of grants, showing date of entry, name and address of indigent soldier, child, and wife or widow; amount of grant to be paid, and date of authorization of payments by the commission. Arranged chronologically by dates entered. No index. Handwritten and typed, some on printed forms. Average 150 pages. 14 x 10 x 1.

---

5. *Laws of Ohio,* CXIX, S. B. 293.
6. Commissioners Record, XXVI (1939-1940), 514.
7. Records of Warrants Issued, 1938, 1939, 1940, entry 256.

Provision for the relief of the indigent was made in 1805, but it was not until 1898 that the legislature provided separate relief for the indigent blind. The act authorized the township trustees to certify to the county commissioners an amount not to exceed $100 a person annually for such relief, the certification to be made a record listing the name of the beneficiary and the amount required, and directed the county commissioners to levy on the townships to the amount certified, this amount to be paid into the county treasury and thence to the township treasurer to be used for blind relief.[1]

Six years later, in 1904, certification authority was transferred from the township trustees to the probate judge, who was required to register the name and address of beneficiaries and to issue to each a certificate giving his name, address, and the amount to be drawn. Persons eligible for relief were blind males over 21 and blind females over 18 years of age, without property or means of support. Not less than two county citizens, one a physician selected by the court, were required to testify that the applicant had been a resident of the state for five years and a resident of the county for one year immediately preceding the filing of an application for relief as a condition for granting aid.[2]

The act of 1904 was declared unconstitutional on the ground that it required the spending public funds raised by taxation for a private purpose.[3] Hence, in 1908, an act was passed authorizing the county commissioners to levy a stipulated tax to create a fund for relief of the needy blind, the maximum benefit not to exceed $150 a person annually to be paid quarterly; and authorizing the probate judge to appoint a blind relief commission consisting of three members to serve for a three-year term, directed to meet annually in the office of the county commissioners to examine applications recorded in order of their receipt in a book furnished by the county commissioner. This record was required to be kept open for public inspection.[4]

The blind relief commission was abolished by legislature in 1913 and its powers and duties were transferred to the county commissioners.[5]

---

1. *Laws of Ohio,* XCIII, 270.
2. *Ibid.,* XCVII, 392-394.
3. *Auditor of Lucas County v The State, Ohio State Reports,* LXXV, 114-137.
4. *Laws of Ohio,* XCIX, 56-58.
5. *Ibid.,* CIII, 60.

363. BLIND RELIEF COMMISSION RECORD
1908-1913. 1 vol.

Minutes of blind relief commission, showing date and place of meeting, names of members present, applications considered, approved or rejected, reason for rejection, amount granted accepted applicants, certification of award to county auditor, and signatures of secretary and president of the board; statistical reports for each year, showing number of males and females on the roll at the time of the last report, number of applications received during year, number of applications granted, rejected, or pending, number receiving maximum amount granted, number withdrawn from roll by death, moved from county, other causes, and dismissed from roll by action of commissioners, number on roll at end of year, total amount paid for relief during year, age of each person on roll at end of year, certification by secretary of blind relief commission that report is correct, name and address of members of commission, and date of expiration of term of each. Arranged chronologically by dates of meetings. No index. 50 pages. 12 x 8 x 1. Basement storage room.

The "Old Age Pension" law proposed by initiative petition, was adopted by the people of Ohio in the general election of 1933.[1] The act, as amended in 1941, provides that any person 65 or more years of age may upon certain stipulated conditions, receive a pension, providing his total income does not exceed $480 annually. The applicant must be a citizen of the United States, and must have resided in Ohio not less than five years of the nine prior to making application for aid, nor less than one year continuously in the county in which application is made. He must be unable to support himself, and have no claim on any legally responsible person who is able to support him. In addition, the net value of all property of the unmarried applicant, less encumbrance, must not exceed $3,000; if the applicant is married, the combined property of husband and wife must not exceed $4,000 in value.[2]

Such property may be transferred to the division of aid for the aged to be held in trust. An amendment in 1937[3] made this transfer of property optional, and not as originally ruled, a requirement to be compiled with before aid maybe granted. Upon the death of the recipient of aid, this property, as well as life insurance over $250, less deductions for funeral expenses, claims of administrators, doctors, widow, and children, is used to defray in part or wholly the expense to the state of such aid as has been allowed. A bill for the amount of the aid is presented to the estate. If no funds are available for funeral expenses, the state allows up to $200 for burial expenses.[4]

The division of aid for the aged was set up as a part of the state department of public welfare in 1933 for the purpose of administrating the old age pension law. In each county, however, the commissioners might operate as a local board if they so desire. If they declined to serve in this capacity, the chief of the division of aid for the aged was authorized to appoint, with the consent of the director of public welfare, a board of three or five members of the community who served without compensation. The board was required to keep complete records, and might employ, subject to the approval of the division, such agents and other assistance as proper administration of the act required.[5]

---

1. *Laws of Ohio,* CXV, pt. ii, 431-439.
2. *Ibid.,* CXVI, pt. ii, 216-221; CXVIII, 740; CXIX, S. B., 157.
3. G. C. sec. 1359-6.
4. G. C. sec. 1359-6, 1359-7, 1359-7b.
5. *Laws of Ohio,* CXV, pt. ii, 431-439.

Since 1937 the chief of the division has been required to appoint such a board in each county.[6]

Each case is thoroughly investigated, but the board is advised to make its inquiries not in a strictly formal way, but in the matter which seems "best calculated to conform to substantial justice." Its decision may be appealed to the division.[7] After a case has been investigated, the applicant, if considered eligible, is granted a certificate of aid which is then passed on by the division,[8] and once accepted by the division, need not be renewed.

Under the Federal Social Security Act, the federal government contributes all administrative expenses and 50 per cent of the amount contributed as aid to the aged, within a maximum of $20 a month for each person aided.[9] The remainder of money is supplied by the state.

The local board has been operating since 1934. A subdivision manager is appointed directly by the state welfare department and works under the supervision of a district supervisor who directs work in ten counties. The administrator is appointed by the chief of Ohio Division of Aid to the Aged.[10] The manager has a staff of four. From 1937 to 1941, 2,300 persons were receiving aid from his agency;[11] the grant for this period is $580,000.[12]

All records for board of aid for the aged, are located in the secretary's office, 122 West Main Street, Ashland, Ohio.

---

6. G. C. sec. 1359-12.
7. *Laws of Ohio,* CXV, pt. ii, 431-439.
8. *Ibid.,* CXVII, 319.
9. *United States Code Annotated*, XLII, 303.
10. *Laws of Ohio,* CXV, pt. ii, 431-439.
11. Monthly Statistical Reports, 1937-1941, entry 371.
12. *Ibid.*

364. REGISTER OF APPLICATIONS RECEIVED – OLD AGE ASSISTANCE

1934—. 3 vols.

Record of applications for aid for the aged, showing name of county, date and number of application, name and address of applicant, sex, marital status, date case assigned, to whom assigned, date investigation was completed, action taken, date application was sent to state office, date action taken, and decision. Arranged chronologically by dates of applications and also arranged numerically by application number. No index. Handwritten on printed forms. Average 60 pages. 12 x 16 x .5.

365. CASE RECORD

1934—. 1 File box.

Card record to all old age assistant records, showing name and address of applicant or client, names of city or town and county, date of birth, number of persons in immediate household, and application number; accepted cases, showing certificate of award number, date certified, and amount of aid granted; application denied, showing date and reason for denial; cases closed, showing date and reason for closing, total amount paid, and total period for which aid was extended. Arranged alphabetically by names of applicants or clients. No index. Types of printed forms. 11 x 12 x 30.

366. DENIALS

1934—. 1 file box.

Case papers of rejected applications, including application for aid, case history, report of investigator, and correspondence, showing name and address of applicant, application number and date of application, date and reason for rejection. Arranged alphabetically by names of applicants or clients. No index. Typed on printed forms. 12 x 12 x 18.

367. INVESTIGATOR'S CASE CARDS

1934—. 5 file boxes.

Complete record of active cases including application, investigator's record, case history, and certificate of award; applications, showing name of county, application number, name of applicant, date of first application, date and place of birth, citizenship, present address, married or single, living conditions and expenses, amount of income, number of dependents, amount of insurance, and real property; investigator's record, showing dates and reports of visits; certificates of awards, showing certificate number, date aid began, and amount granted; property record, showing date trust deed was filed, amount of mortgage and interest, name of council or plaintiff, and volume and page number of record; also includes record of closed cases, showing in addition to the usual case history the reason and date case was closed; certificates of cancellation, showing date of certificate and reason for cancellation; case paper of deceased recipients, showing date of death and date of amount of aid paid. Arranged alphabetically by names of clients. No index. Typed on printed forms. 12 x 12 x 18.

368. ACTIVE (And Closed) CASES

1934—. 1 file box.

Card record of active and closed cases; active cases, showing name and address of the recipient, date and place of birth, date aid began, application number, and certificate of aid number; closed cases, showing also date and reason closed, and total amount of aid given. Arranged alphabetically by the names of clients. No index. Handwritten and typed on printed forms. 11 x 12 x 30.

369. DEATH CASES

1934—. 2 file boxes.

Card record of deceased recipients, showing date and number of application, date and number of certificate of award, total amount of aid received, date of death, and cost of undertaker's services. Arranged alphabetically by names of decedent. No index. Typed on printed forms. 5 x 6 x 12.

370. TRANSFERS

1934—. 1 file box.

Case papers pertaining to cases transferred to another county, showing information as in Investigator's Case Cards, entry 367, date of transfer, and name of county. Arranged alphabetically by names of clients. No index. Handwritten and typed on printed forms. 12 x 12 x 18.

371. MONTHLY STATISTICAL REPORT

1934—. 1 file box.

Copies of monthly statistical reports to bureau of public assistance, showing name of county, date filed, signature of person making report, number of applications pending from previous month, number received and disposed of doing current month, total received and disposed of, total number of cases, and number pending at end of month. Arranged chronologically by dates filed. No index. Typed on mimeograph form. 12x x12 x 18.

The office of county surveyor, another English institution transplanted to America during the colonial period became an important office in frontier Ohio where land titles and boundary lines were often in dispute. The office is entirely a product of statute, there being no constitutional provision for its establishment.

The first act of general assembly pertaining to the surveyor was passed during the first legislative session of 1803. Under this act the court of common pleas was authorized to appoint a person well qualified to act as a county surveyor. He received his commission from the governor, was required to give bond conditioned for the faithful performance of the duties of his office, and was directed to survey all lands which were sold or were to be sold for taxes, and was authorized to appoint chainman or markers whose function it was to establish corners. The surveys made by the surveyor or his deputies were the only ones to be accepted as legal evidence in any court of law or equity. For remuneration, the surveyor was permitted to retain all fees collected by him in the operation of his office.[1]

Although it made no fundamental change in the duties of the surveyor, the act of 1816 fixed his term of office at five years; authorized him to appoint deputies, and made him responsible for their official acts; and liable to suit by persons believing themselves damaged by his negligence or that of his deputies.[2] A year later, in 1817, provision was made for the appointment of a successor in the event the office became vacant because of death, resignation, or removal.[3]

---

1. *Laws of Ohio,* I, 90-93.
2. *Ibid.,* XIV, 424-431.
3. *Ibid.,* XV, 64.

The act of 1831 consolidated the previous acts, redefined the duties of the surveyor, increased the amount of his bond, and authorized him, when directed by the county commissioners, to procure the surveyor general's office a "certified plat, together with the field notes of corners, and bearing trees to each section, quarter section, lot, or original survey in his county, and cause the same to be preserved in a book by him provided for that purpose; which shall be deposited in the county auditor's office, for the use of the landowners and the county." It provided further, that the surveyor should keep "a fair and accurate record of all official surveys made by him or his deputies," in a suitable book to be kept by him for that purpose, and that he should number his surveys progressively. More significant, however, was the fact that the office was made elected for a three-year term by the act of 1831. The term remained at three years until 1906, when it was reduced to a two-year period; by the act of 1927, effective with the term of the surveyor elected in 1928, the term was increased to four years.[4]

During the years of the development of the office other duties have been delegated to the surveyor. In 1842 he was given the duty of ascertaining and reporting trespassing of public lands.[5] Twelve years later he was given the same powers as the justice of the peace to take and certify deeds, mortgages, powers of attorney, and other instruments affecting real estate, to administer oaths, and to take and certify affidavits.[6] In 1867 he was given authority, when directed by the county commissioners, to transcribe any and all dilapidated maps, records of plats, and field notes of surveys and other counties.[7] Similarly, in 1881 he was authorized to procure from any office in the state a certified plat together with the field notes of corners, quarter sections, lots, or original surveys and place them in a book provided for that purpose. Certified copies from his book were to be taken as evidence.[8]

---

4. *Ibid.,* XXIX, 399; XCVIII, 245-247; CXII, 179.
5. *Laws of Ohio,* XL, 57.
6. *Ibid.,* LII, 70.
7. *Ibid.,* LXIV, 216-217; LXXVIII, 285.
8. *Ibid.,* XXIX, 399; LXXVIII, 285.

With the increase in modern means of transportation, there developed a growing need for more efficient methods of road construction and maintenance. Accordingly, in 1906, the surveyor was directed to act, whenever the services of an engineer were required, in the capacity of an engineer with respect to roads, turnpikes, bridges, or ditches, except in cities of the first grade.[9] He was directed by statute to perform all duties in his county which would be done by a civil engineer or surveyor, to prepare all plans, specifications, and estimates of cost, and to submit forms for contracts for construction and repair of all bridges, culverts, roads, draws, ditches, and other public improvements (except buildings) over which the county commissioners had authority. At the same time, he was made responsible for the inspection of all public improvements, and was directed to keep a complete list of all estimates and bids received for such work, as well as contracts awarded for improvements.[10]

Similarly, another major enacted in 1919 increased the duties of the surveyor regarding road construction and road maintenance. Under this act the surveyor was authorized to designate one of his deputies as maintenance engineer. This engineer, under the direction of the surveyor, was to have charge of all "road maintenance and repair work" in his county. Furthermore, when authorized by the county commissioners, the surveyor was to appoint a maintenance supervisor or supervisors to have charge of the maintenance of improved highways within a district or districts established by the commissioner or the surveyor, and containing not less than 10 miles of improved county roads.[11] In 1923 the surveyor was delegated to assist the county planning commissioner wherever such commission was established.[12]

---

9. *Ibid.,* XCVIII, 245-247.
10. *Ibid.*
11. *Ibid.,* CVIII, pt. I, 497.
12. *Ibid.,* CX, 312.

Thus the general responsibility of planning and directing county road construction is vested, by statute, in the county surveyor. Because of this increased responsibility placed on this office there has been an attempt to raise the general qualifications of those seeking election to it. Accordingly, in 1935, an act was passed changing the title of the office to that of "county engineer," and eligibility to that office was restricted to "*a registered professional engineer and registered surveyor licensed to practice in the state of Ohio.*"[13] This act was amended in 1935 to prevent the incumbent to continue in office upon re-election, even if he lacked these qualifications.[14]

In Ashland County, the staff of the engineer's office includes, in addition to the engineer himself, a maintenance engineer, a maintenance supervisor, two highway engineers, and a tax map draftsman. There is a permanent maintenance force of 60 men, which in the busy summer session is enlarged with temporary workers.[15] This staff maintains 795 miles of county and township roads, and about 5,500 bridges and culverts.[16] In 1939 expenditures for construction, maintenance, and repairs amounted to $142,687.70; in 1940 this sum rose to $180,997.33[17]Funds are appropriated by the commissioners entirely from the county's income in gasoline and motor vehicle taxes.

All records are located in the engineers drafting room.

---

13. *Laws of Ohio,* CXVI, 283.
14. *Ibid.,* CXVI, pt. ii, 152.
15. Payrolls, 1940, entry 408.
16. Highway Map of Ashland County, current, entry 387.
17. (Auditor's) Annual Financial Reports to County Commissioners, 1940, entry 267.

Surveys

372. RECORD OF SURVEYS
1846—. 4 vols. (A-D).

Record of surveys, showing volume and page numbers of Field Books, entry 374, number and location of lot, key to plat, date and number of survey, part surveyed, name of owner, by whom surveyed, township, area of tract, signature of surveyor, boundary lines, length of each boundary line, streams, roads, and location of landmarks; also includes plat sketch of survey. Arranged chronologically by date surveyed. For index, see entry 373. Handwritten. Average 400 pages. 12 x 8 x 1.

373. (Index) RECORD OF SURVEYS
1846—. 1 vol.

Index to Record of Surveys, entry 372, showing volume and page numbers of record, name of township, range, section, lot, and tract numbers, date of survey, name of surveyor, and for whom surveyed. Arranged numerically by lots or tract number. Handwritten on printed forms. 450 pages. 16 x 12 x 2.

374. FIELD BOOKS
1846—. 195 vols. (1-195).

Surveyors' field notes on surveys for bridges, sidewalks, roads, and ditches, showing date of entry, name of surveyor, name of township, detailed sketches of depths, grade elevations, and type of ground on each job; also exact location of projects with photograph of project attached. Arranged chronologically by dates energy. For index, see entry 375. Handwritten and hand drawn. Average 175 pages. 6 x 10 x 1.5.

375. INDEX TO FIELD BOOKS
1846—. 1 vol.

Index to Field Books, entry 374, showing volume and page number of record, location of tract, number of bridge, sidewalk, ditch or road, quarter section numbers, names of townships, range or lot number; also names of projects and surveyor, for whom surveyed, and date of survey. Arranged alphabetically by names of projects. Handwritten on printed forms. 100 pages. 8 x 5 x .5.

376. UNITED STATES SURVEYS
1806-1862. 1 vol.

Record of early United States government surveys, showing name and number of township, range number, number of chains and links, length and width of tract, record and date of survey, by whom surveyed, certification by secretary of state that surveys of townships and parts thereof of Ashland County, south of Connecticut Reserve, have been correctly copied from records deposited in office of secretary of state, and date of testimony. Arranged chronologically by dates surveyed. Indexed numerically by townships and range numbers. Handwritten. 350 pages. 12 x 8 x 2.5.

Plats and Maps

377. SURVEY PLATS, ASHLAND CITY
1907—. 1 file box.

Plats of surveys of city of Ashland, showing date of survey, for whom surveyed, type of corner markers, lot numbers, frontage, alleys, amount and identification of private property taken over or purchased for public use, certified by county engineer, approved by platting commissioner, accepted by city clerk, transfers by city auditor, signature of recorder, and recording date. Prepared by county engineer. No obvious arrangement. No index. Hand drawn, black on white. Scale, 1 inch equals 50 feet. 200 plats in file box, 3 x 24 x 36.

378. TOWNSHIP–CITIES AND TOWNS
1909—. 6 vols. (1-6).

Plats of townships, cities, and towns, showing plat key, date of plat, description of property, number of acres, and name of owner; also transfer record on each page directly under plat with letter to correspond with plat, showing to whom and from whom transferred, lot number, number of acres, dates of deed and transfer, and remarks. Arranged chronologically by dates of plats. Indexed numerically by lot numbers. Handwritten on printed forms. Average 100 pages. 18 x 18 x 1.

379. TOPOGRAPHY AND BUILDING LOCATIONS IN ASHLAND AND SURROUNDING COUNTY
1911—. 1 file drawer.

Plats and topographical maps of city of Ashland and surrounding territory, showing plans of churches, bank buildings, schools, post office, old courthouse, armory,

Ashland College, stadium, Ashland Hospital, factory buildings, and sewers. Prepared by county engineer. No obvious arrangement. No index. Tracing and blueprints. Scale 1 inch equals 50 feet.100 plats in file drawer, 3 x 24 x 36.

380. MISCELLANEOUS PLATS
1896—. 1 file box.
Plats of allotments and surveys of villages around city of Ashland, showing detailed description of schools, cemeteries, street improvements, sidewalks, filling stations, town additions, industrial surveys, parks, and sewers. Prepared by county engineer. No obvious arrangement. No index. Hand drawn, black on white. Scale, 1 inch equals 50 feet. 150 plats in file box. 3 x 24 x 36.

381. LOTS IN TOWNSHIPS OF ASHLAND COUNTY
Current. 2 file boxes.
Reference card file of all lots in each township of Ashland County, showing names of townships and property owners, description of property, record of transfers, name of street and lot number, and remarks. Arranged alphabetically by names of townships. No index. Handwritten on printed forms. 6 x 6 x 14.

382. LOTS NORTH OF ASHLAND,
Current. 1 file box.
Reference card file of lots immediately north of city of Ashland, showing names of owner and street, number of lot, description of property, record of transfer, and remarks. Arranged numerically by lot numbers. No index. Handwritten on printed forms. 6 x 6 x 14.

383. LAND TAKEN PLATS
1930—. 1 file box.
Plats of land for roadways in Ashland County, showing amount of land secured from each landowner, name of landowner, value of land, price paid by county for right of way, and name of township. Prepared by county engineer. No obvious arrangement. No index. Hand drawn, black on white. Scale, 1 inch equals 400 feet. 200 maps in file drawer, 3 x 24 x 36.

384. MAP OF ASHLAND COUNTY
1861. 1 map.
Map of Ashland County, showing names of townships, range, lot, and section numbers, names of property owners, acreage, names of towns, railroads, and streams; towns. showing lot numbers and names of property owners, distance between certain points, sectional pictures of points of interest, and list of sponsors for publication. Published by John McDonnell, Philadelphia, Pennsylvania. Engraved and colored. Scale, 1.5 inches equal 1 mile. 60 x 60. Framed.

385. TOPOGRAPHICAL MAP OF ASHLAND COUNTY
1920. 1 map.
Topographical map of Ashland County, 1914, edited and engraved, resurveyed and reprinted in 1920, showing contours, contour intervals, railroads, schools, rivers, lakes, streams, and general view of entire county. Prepared by United States geographers and topographers, department of interior and artists. Published by the United States Geological Survey, Washington, District of Columbia. Scale, 1 inch equals 62,500 feet. Contour interval, 20 feet. 60 x 36. Mounted.

386. COUNTY MAPS
1935. 1 file box.
Communication maps of Ashland County, showing types of roads, number of miles in each highway, township through which highways run, mileage in each township, and total mileage for county, legend, approval of director of highways, and certificate of county commissioners. Prepared by county engineer. No obvious arrangement. No index. Blueprint. Scales vary. 3 x 24 x 36.

387. HIGHWAY MAP OF ASHLAND COUNTY
Current. 1 map.
Map of highways in Ashland County by townships, showing each township, mileage by townships, scale of miles, legend of state and county highways, names, or route numbers, type of roads, bridges, and culverts under construction, and those completed. Prepared by county engineer. Hand drawn, black on white. Scale, 2 inches equals 1 mile. 72 x 48.

388. FARM ACREAGE OF ASHLAND COUNTY

1912—. 1 file drawer.

Land tenure maps of farms in Ashland County, showing boundary lines of each section, location by degree and minutes, length in chains, section and range numbers, names of owner and township, acreage, date survey, and signature of county surveyor. No obvious arrangement. No index. Hand drawn, black on white. Scales vary. 200 maps in file drawer, 3 x 24 x 36.

389. TOWNSHIP MAPS

1927, 1938. 3 file drawers.

Land tenure maps of townships in Ashland County, showing name of owner, number of acres, range and section numbers, and name of township. Prepared in 1927 and revised in 1938 by county engineer. No obvious arrangement. No index. 11 maps hand drawn, black on white; 60 maps, blueprints. Scale, 4 inches equals 1 mile. 71 maps and file drawer, 3 x 24 x 36.

390. MAP OF ASHLAND CITY

1925—. 1 map.

Map of city of Ashland, showing names of allotments and subdivisions, lots, names and locations surrounding territory, churches, schools, industries, and streets, lot numbers, and names of owners of lots. Data revised to date. Prepared by R. L. Williams, Ashland city engineer, and revised by county engineer. Index attached, showing names of allotments and subdivisions, locations of same, and lot numbers. Hand drawn, black on white. Scale 1 inch equals 200 feet. 72 x 72. Mounted.

391. CITY MAPS

1936. 1 file drawer.

Maps of towns and cities of Ashland County, showing name of town or city, name and widths of streets, territory occupied by city, lot numbers, foot frontage, names of owners of farms immediately surrounding town or city, and acreage. Prepared by county engineer. No obvious arrangement. No index. Hand drawn, black on white. Scale, 1 inch equals 50 feet. 36 maps and file drawer, 3 x 24 x 36.

392. SCHOOL DISTRICT MAPS
1915—. 1 file drawer.

Maps of school districts in Ashland County, showing section and range numbers, names and numbers of townships, names of owners of land immediately surrounding school district, location of district and township, and signature of county surveyor. Prepared by county engineer. No obvious arrangement. Hand drawn, black on white. Scales vary. 200 maps and file drawer, 3 x 24 x 36.

393. VILLAGE TRACINGS
1936, 1938. 1 file drawer.

Tracing maps of various villages in Ashland County, showing names of villages, locations of schools, cemeteries, and streets, name of township where located, section and range number, and foot frontage. Prepared by county engineer. Arranged by townships. No index. Hand drawn, black on white. Scale, 1 inch equals 50 feet. 23 maps and file drawer, 3 x 24 x 36.

394. ATLAS OF ASHLAND COUNTY, OHIO
1874. 1 vol.

Maps of Ashland County, showing names of towns, townships, and railroads; also photographs of industrial plants and of several leading citizens and their residence or farms, business directory of various towns, bibliographies of leading early settlers, historical sketch of Ashland County, election statistics, and table of airline distances, and population. Published by J. A. Caldwell, Condit, Ohio. Artists, C. Gasche and H. G. Howland. Printed by H. J. Towdy and company, Philadelphia, Pennsylvania. Engraved by Worley and Bracher, Philadelphia, Pennsylvania. Arranged alphabetically by names of townships and towns. No index. Table of contents. Printed, lithographed, and engraved. 125 pages. 14 x 14 x 1.

395. MISCELLANEOUS
1926—. 1 file box.

Miscellaneous maps including plans of allotments, showing lots, additions, subdivisions, lot numbers, boundary lines, and foot frontage; plans and tracing of culverts, catch basins, and sections of state roads; drawings of Work Projects Administration improvements, showing place and type of proposed improvement, estimate of cost, and bids, including trucking bids; plans for schools, showing specifications, estimate of cost, and proposed location; also maps of gas and oil surveys. Prepared by county engineer. No obvious arrangement. No index. Hand drawn, black on white. Scales vary. 400 items in file drawer, 3 x 24 x 36.

Public Improvements
(See also entry 411)

Roads

396. TRANSCRIPTS FROM RICHLAND COUNTY (Road Records)
1814-1845. 1 vol.

Transcripts from road records of Richland County, showing names of petitioners, date petition submitted to board of county commissioners, viewers' and surveyors' reports, exact location of road, section and range numbers, names of township, name or number of road, and bridges and culverts constructed along roadway. Transcribed in 1937. Arranged chronologically by date submitted. No index. Typed. 200 pages. 18 x 12 x 1.5.

397. ROAD RECORD
1846—. 4 vols. (1-4).

Record of surveys of proposed roads and highways in Ashland County, showing date of entry, location of proposed road, name of township, quarter section, range, and line numbers, road notice, copy of affidavit of printer of said notice, names of petitioners, and final action taken, also data on elevation, grades, bridges, and general description of road. Arranged chronologically by dates entered. For index, see entry 398. Handwritten on printed forms. Average 475 pages. 18 x 12 x 3.

398. GENERAL INDEX TO ROAD RECORD
1846—. 1 vol. (1).

Index to road record, entry 397, showing name of road, volume and page numbers of record, names of principal petitioners and viewers, date petition filed, date viewers appointed, and report of viewers, whether road petition was rejected or established, vacating of lands through which road must pass, damages allowed, to whom paid, and name of township. Arranged alphabetically by names of roads. No index. Handwritten on printed forms. 575 pages. 18 x 12 x 3.

399. TOWNSHIP ROAD DATA AND RESOLUTIONS–ROAD PROJECTS

1934—. 1 file box.

Copies of various original papers regarding road construction in township, including resolutions, showing proposal for public road improvement, name of village or city concerned, date of resolution, names of township and county, name or number of road, location where road is to begin and end, length of road to be improved, names of members of board of township trustees, how they voted on resolution, date adapted, signature of clerk of board of trustees, and date filed; attached to resolution is surveyor's estimate of cost, showing name of township, number or name of road, place where improvement begins and ends, cost of material and grading, total cost, signature of county surveyor, trustees' resolution to proceed with project, name of township, and clerk's certificate and signature; Work Projects Administration proposals, 1935—, showing work proposed or roads, bridges, and culverts in various townships, names of township and county, number and name of county road, section, length of proposed project by miles and feet, number of laborers and their classifications, number of days estimated necessary to complete project, daily wages, amount of total wages, engineering and inspection cost, superintendent and foreman cost, rental of equipment, cost of materials, and date filed; insurance and compensation certificates, 1934—, showing correspondence with insurance regarding claims, certificates of premiums, and payments for workman's compensation; correspondence between county engineer and Public Works Administration regarding roads, and their construction and materials; reports of test of materials, showing county engineers test of sampled materials, name of county in which material is used, name of contractor using them, kind, size, and number of sample, by whom sampled, brand of material and name of manufacturer, proposed use of tested material, date sent to laboratory, date filed, and result of tests; certified transcript of public works administration payroll, 1938—, showing amount of labor performed, amount paid for labor and material, and total amount of payroll, and date filed. Arranged alphabetically by names of townships and chronologically thereunder by dates filed. Handwritten and typed, some on printed forms. 12 x 12 x 18.

400. COUNTY AND STATE ROAD PLANS
1930—. 1 file box.

Plans of proposed roadways in Ashland County, showing obstructions to be removed, specifications, grading to be done, names of owners of land along proposed road, number of acres, names of townships, and numbers of section and range through which road would pass. Prepared by county engineer. No obvious arrangement. No index. Hand drawn, some tracings and some blueprints. Scale, 1 inch equals 50 feet. 100 plans and file drawer, 3 x 24 x 36.

401. PHOTOGRAPHS OF ROADS
No date. 1 file box.

Photographs of roads, bridges, and ditches, showing where repair work is proposed, and where work is completed; also photographs of locations where work is needed. No obvious arrangement. No index. 300 photographs, 6 x 3 in file box, 12 x 12 x 18.

Bridges and Culverts (See also entry 407).

402. STANDARD BRIDGE IN CULVERT
1921—. 1 file drawer.

Bridges and culverts, showing name of improvement and detailed specifications. Prepared by county engineer. No obvious arrangement. No index. Blueprint. Scale, 1 inch equals 50 feet. 50 plans and file drawer, 3 x 24 x 36.

403. BRIDGE AND CULVERT TRACINGS
1934—. 1 file drawer.

Tracings of bridge and culvert plans, showing designs, type of material used, dimensions, name of bridge or culvert, names of township and road, date signed, and signature of county engineer. Prepared by county engineer. No obvious arrangement. No index. Hand drawn, black on white. Scale, 1 inch equals 50 feet. 50 tracings and file drawer, 3 x 24 x 36.

Ditches

404. OLD AND NEW DITCH PLANS
1912—. 1 file drawer.

Plans of ditches, showing names of owners of land traversed or adjoining, number of acres, section and range numbers, names of townships, and specifications of ditches as to depths, grade, and length; also relocation or division of creeks, typical sections, and excavation of channels and dams. Prepared by county engineer. No obvious arrangement. No index. Hand drawn, some tracings and some blueprints. Scale, 1 inch equals 50 feet. 400 plans and file drawer, 3 x 24 x 36.

Grade Crossings

405. RAILROAD PROPERTIES AND CROSSING PLANS
1911—. 1 file drawer.

Plans of railroad properties and crossings in Ashland County, showing railroad rights of way in each township, number of tracks, and frequency of use; crossings, showing specifications for construction and general view of grades eliminated. Prepared by county engineer. No obvious arrangement. No index. Hand drawn, black on white. Scales vary. 100 plans and file drawer, 3 x 24 x 36.

Estimates, Contracts, and Specifications

(See also entry 411-g)

406. CONTRACTORS' ESTIMATES AND SPECIFICATIONS
1930-1932. 1 file box.

Preliminary surveys and estimates on proposed dams in Ashland County, including plans of proposed dams, correspondence between contractor and commissioners regarding this work, and certain tests of samples of material used, showing date sent to laboratory, date of approval, result of test, name of manufacturer of material, name of contractor, and date filed. Prepared by county engineer. Arranged chronologically by dates filed. No index. Hand written and typed, some on printed forms; plans, hand drawn; blueprint. 12 x 12 x 18.

407. CONTRACTS, ESTIMATES, AND SPECIFICATIONS
1930—. 1 file box.
Copies of papers regarding construction of roads and bridges, including contracts, showing name of contractor, type of work, name of township, date of contract, signature of auditor, amount of bond of contractor, and signatures of board of county commissioners; estimates, showing type of work, number of road or name of bridge, acknowledgment of estimate by county commissioners, amounts for labor and material, and total estimate; specifications, showing itemized list of work to be done, material to be used, size and specification of various items used in construction, signatures of surveyor and county commissioners, and date filed. Arranged chronologically by dates filed. No index. Typed on printed forms. 12 x 12 x 18.

Financial Records

408. PAYROLLS
1938—, 1 file drawer.
Daily pay rolls, showing date of pay roll, name of employee, kind of service, name of job, classification, and rate of pay. Arranged chronologically by dates of pay rolls. No index. Handwritten on printed forms. 3 x 24 x 36.

Miscellaneous

409. COUNTY BUILDINGS
1916—. 1 file drawer.
Plans of public buildings in Ashland County, showing size, dimensions, location of buildings, floor plans, and position of rooms and windows. Prepared by county engineer. No obvious arrangement. No index. Blueprint. Scale,1/16 inch equals 1 foot. 200 plans in file drawer, 3 x 24 x 36.

410. INVOICES AND CORRESPONDENCE
1935—. 5 file boxes.
General correspondence regarding business transactions of engineer in purchasing supplies, and awarding contracts, showing date filed, and name of correspondent; also includes statements and bills for companies furnishing materials for roads and bridges in county, showing date files, name of vendor, and itemized statement or bill.

Arranged alphabetically by subjects and chronologically thereunder by dates filed. Hand written and typed, some on printed forms. 12 x 12 x 18.

411. COUNTY ROADS, BRIDGES, DITCHES,
1923—. 1 file box.

Miscellaneous file of road, bridge, and ditch records, including:

a. Lincoln -way road reports of road foreman concerning wages of workers and other expenses for building road, 1932, showing date filed, names of employees, and particular job assigned, rate of pay, total hours worked, and total amount of pay due.

b. Itemized list of other expenses for Lincoln-way road, showing amount due, to whom payable, supplies and services rendered, and signature of foreman.

c. Copies of resolutions passed by board of county commissioners authorizing construction or repair accounting and inter-county roads, highways, bridges or ditches, and engineer's estimate of cost of proposed work, showing name of improvement and date resolution filed.

d. Bills of lading, 1932—, of materials used on roads, bridges, and ditches, showing name of railroad, date and amount of bill, date delivered, weight of material, and date bill filed.

e. Contracts for painting county bridges, 1928—, showing date filed, name of contractor, and names of sureties.

f. County inspectors' weekly progress reports of painting done on county bridges, showing name of bridge and date report filed.

g. Estimate of ditches, which is final report of surveyor, showing total cost of ditch, total cost assessed, prorated assessment, grand total, and date filed. Arranged by subject and chronologically thereunder by dates filed. No index. Handwritten and typed on printed forms. 12 x 12 x 18.

BOARD OF DIRECTORS OF THE CONSERVANCY DISTRICT

The legislature at its 1914 session, following disastrous floods of the previous year, made provision for the establishment of conservancy districts in Ohio the objects of which were to prevent floods, to protect cities, villages, farms, and highways from inundation. This act, authorized by the constitutional amendment of 1912,[1] was upheld by the courts as a valid exercise of the police power of the state.[2] The conservancy districts, according to the act, may be established not only to prevent floods but to regulate streams, reclaim overflowed lands, provide irrigation, regulate the flow of streams, or divert water courses.

The court of common pleas of any county in the state or any judge in vacation is authorized, after a petition signed either by five hundred freeholders or by a majority of freeholders has been filed with the clerk of courts, to establish a conservancy district which might be within or without the county where the court is located. The court, after conducting hearings on a petition as to the purpose of the district, may declare the district organized and give it a corporate name. The clerk of court, within thirty days after the district has been declared a corporation by the court, transmits to the secretary of state, and to the county recorder in each county having lands in the district, copies of the finding and the decree of the court incorporating the district which, according to the statute, is considered a political subdivision.

Within thirty days after the decree of incorporation the court is authorized to appoint three persons, at least two of whom are freeholders in the district, to serve as a board of directors of the district to serve three, five, and seven years respectively. After the expiration of their terms the tenure of office is five years. The board of directors, after taking an oath that they "will not be interested directly or indirectly in any contract let by the district," organize by selecting one of their members as president and some person, not a member of the board, as secretary. The board is authorized to employ a chief engineer who may be an individual, copartnership, or corporation, an attorney; and such other engineers and attorneys as may be necessary for carrying on the work. The board may provide for their compensation, which, with other necessary expenditures, shall be taken as a part of the cost of improvement. While the chief engineer prepares plans and specifications of work, all contracts which exceed $1,000 are let by competitive bidding.

---

1. *Ohio Const. 1851,* Art. II, sec. 36.
2. *County of Miami v Dayton, Ohio State Reports.* XCII, 223-224, 236.

The board, or its agents, is authorized to enter upon lands within or without the conservancy district for the purpose of making surveys. They are authorized to exercise the right of eminent domain; condemn property, after appraisal, for the use of the district; make regulations to protect their work by prescribing the method of building roads, bridges, or fences; to remove bridges, cemeteries, or other structures impeding their work; and to cooperate with the federal government, with persons, railways, corporations, the state government of Ohio or other states, for assistance for drainage, conservancy, or other improvements.

To finance such improvements the board is authorized to levy upon the property of the district with tax not to exceed three-tenths of a mill on the assessed valuation. This tax is certified to the county auditor, and to the various treasurers of the counties within the district and is used to pay the expenses of organization, surveys, and plans. The commission is authorized further to borrow money at a rate not to exceed six per cent annually and levy assessments for a bond fund.[3]

The board is required to "keep in a well-bound book a record of all its proceedings, minutes of meetings, certificates, contracts, bonds given by employees and all corporate acts, which shall be open to the inspection of all owners of property in the district, as well as to all other interested parties. The secretary, who may serve also as treasurer, is designated as the "custodian of the records of the district and its corporate seal."[4]

Ashland County is in the Muskingum Valley Conservancy District with headquarters in New Philadelphia where the records are located.

---

3. *Laws of Ohio,* CIV, 13-64.
4. *Ibid.,* CIV, 18.

County agricultural societies in Ohio were provided for by statute as early as 1833, and on February 28, 1846 the legislature passed an act authorizing the forming of such societies and making provisions for their aid by the counties,[1] and it was under this act that the Ashland society was formed in 1850. On February 15, 1853, the legislature declared such societies to be bodies corporate and politic, capable of suing and being sued, and capable of holding in fee simple such real estate as they might purchase for sites whereon to hold fairs, the same to be paid by the county commissioners.[2]

By an act of legislature passed February 20, 1861, county agricultural societies were required to report annually to the state board of agriculture, and to meet with the state board at Columbus once each year.[3] In 1883 the legislature provided for the organization of district or county agricultural societies. The act making this provision stipulated that 30 or more persons, residents of any county or district embracing two counties, organized themselves into an agricultural society, under the rules and regulations of the state board of agriculture, the county might aid such society with a grant not to exceed $400 a year.[4] By act of April 21, 1896, provision was made for representation in a county society of 30 or more residents of any county or district embracing two or more counties.[5] In 1900 the legislature extended the amount of county aid to $800 a year.[6] Later, on May 6, 1902, the legislature passed an act authorizing 30 or more residents of a county or of a district embracing one or more counties, to organize themselves into an agricultural society.[7]

1. *Laws of Ohio,* XXX, 28, 29; XLIV, 70.
2. *Ibid., LI, 333.*
3. *Ibid., Ibid*, 22.
4. *Ibid.*, LXXX, 142.
5. *Ibid.*, XCII, 205.
6. *Ibid.*, XCIV, 395.
7. *Ibid.*, XCV, 403.

On April 17, 1919, the legislature provided for the organization of county and independent agricultural societies, authorized the payment of class premiums, defined the duties of persons competing for premiums, prescribed the publication of treasures' accounts and the list of awards by societies, designated condition of membership in a county agricultural society, authorized the society to elect a board of directors consisting of eight members, and prescribe the term of office and the manner of their election. The act further stipulated how such societies might obtain state aid, and authorize the county commissioners to insure all buildings belonging to agricultural societies.[8]

The legislature in 1921 passed an act stipulating that the total amount of county aid to county agricultural societies should equal 100 percent of the amount paid by the society in regular class premiums but should not exceed $800.[9] By act of March 27, 1925, the county commissioners were authorized to purchase or to lease, for a term of but not less than 20 years, real estate whereon to hold fairs under the management of county agricultural societies, and to erect thereon suitable buildings.[10] On March 10, 1927, the legislature authorized the county commissioners to appropriate annually on the request of the agricultural society a sum not less than $1,500 nor more than $2,000 from the general fund for the purpose of "encouraging agricultural affairs."[11]

In Ashland County interest in agricultural society activities was shown very early, and a society was formed at Hayesville and 1850, only four years after the legislature first authorized financial aid to such organizations. The first fair was held at Hayesville in 1851, and others were held there each year until 1887, when the annual event was moved to Ashland. The county seat was the scene of the fair until 1908 when the event was discontinued. The society was reorganized in 1929 and a fair has been held at Ashland annually.[13]

---

8. *Ibid.*, CVIII, pt. I, 381-385.
9. *Laws of Ohio*, CIX. 240.
10. *Ibid.*, CXI, 238.
11. *Ibid.*, CXII, 84.
12. *Ibid.*, CXVI, 47.
13. Ohio Department of Agriculture. *A Summary of the Activities of the Ohio Department of Agriculture... for 1936* (Published by state authority, 1937), 27.

Since then the society has been a vital organization, and in recent years has increased the scope and interest of its fairs. Improvements and new buildings, including the grandstand and a special junior fair building, have increased the attractiveness of the fair site. Further evidence of revived interest is found in the fact that all townships in the county are now represented among the 30 members of the society's board of directors. A junior fair board which conducts its own phase of the annual three-day program now enlist participation of the youth of the county in a society's activities.

412. ANNUAL REPORT OF AGRICULTURAL SOCIETY
1939—. 3 vols.

Annual report of agricultural society, showing list of exhibits and premiums, amount of premiums paid, gate receipts, and signature of secretary. This report is made in duplicate and one copy is sent to Columbus, Ohio. No obvious arrangement. No index. Handwritten on printed forms. Average 12 pages. 8 x 12 x 12.5. Mr. James Atterholt, secretary, 613 Heltman Avenue, Ashland, Ohio.

In 1914 the federal government passed an act providing for cooperative agricultural extension service between the state agricultural colleges and the United States Department of Agriculture. The purpose of the extension service was to give instructions and practical demonstrations in agriculture and home economics to persons not attending college, and to give such information through field demonstrations, publications, and other means. The funds for such work were to be supplied in part by the federal government and in part by the state.[1]

A year following the federal legislation, the Ohio legislature accepted the provisions of the act by providing that when twenty or more residents of a county organized themselves into a "farmers institute society for the purpose of teaching better methods of farming, stock raising, fruit culture and business connected with agriculture," accepted a constitution and bylaws conforming to the rules and regulations prescribed by the trustees of Ohio State University, and elected proper officers, the institute could be a corporate body. The Ohio State University was required to furnish speakers for their annual meeting. At the close of the session the trustees were authorized to publish the lectures in pamphlet or book form.

Besides maintaining an institute, the society was authorized to maintain a county experiment farm, Furthermore the county commissioners were authorized to select a county agent subject to the approval of the dean of the college of agriculture of the Ohio State University. It is the duty of the agent to inspect and study the agricultural conditions in his county, distribute agricultural literature, cooperate with United States Department of Agriculture and the college of agriculture of the Ohio State University. In the event the commissioners failed to make such an appointment, the electorate could require them to do so on a referendum vote.[2]

---

1. *United States Statutes at Large,* XXVIII, pt. I, 372-374.
2. *Laws of Ohio,* CVI, 356-359.

In 1919 the original legislation was amended so as to authorize the employment of a home demonstration agent. An act of 1929, which is still effective, empowered the trustees of Ohio State University to employ boys' and girls' club agents as well as agricultural and home demonstration agents. The county extension agent was given the additional duty of carrying the teachings of the college of agriculture of Ohio State University in agriculture and home economics to the residents of his county through personal visits, bulletins, and practical demonstrations. Furthermore it was his duty to render educational service not only in relation to agricultural productions, but also in relation to economic problems, including marketing, distribution, and the utilization of farm products.[3]

The initial legislation contained a clause which required the county commissioners to appropriate annually $1,000 if they wished to obtain the services of an agricultural agent. This amount was to be matched by the state. Under the present system the commissioners are empowered to levy a tax and to appropriate from the proceeds thereof or from the general fund of the county not in excess of $3,000 for each agent, to be paid to the state treasury to the credit of the agricultural extension fund. Amounts in excess of $3,000 must have the unanimous consent of the commissioners.[4]

The extension service began in Ashland County in 1919, and in its early years was closely related to and financially supported by the Ohio Cooperative Farm Bureau. At the present time the county commissioners make an annual appropriation of $2,100 and other funds are derived from federal and state sources. Since 1927 there has also been a home demonstration agent in charge of women's work and 4-H clubs for girls. The service sponsors and assists 377 boys' and girls' 4-H clubs in the county with a membership of 600.

All records of agricultural extension agents are located in the agricultural society office unless otherwise specified.

---

3. *Ibid.,* CVIII, pt. I. 364; CXIII, 82-83.
4. *Laws of Ohio,* CXIII, 82-83.

413. [Agricultural Adjustment Association], WHEAT REDUCTION PROGRAM

1933—. 1 file box.

Record of wheat curtailment, showing name and address of farm operator, terms of wheat allotment contract, names of state and county, certificate and proof of compliance, map of farm, threshers' certificate, and record of wheat sown on land not under contract. Arranged alphabetically by names of farm operators. No index. Typed on printed forms. 11 x 16 x 24.

414. INDIVIDUAL AGRICULTURAL RECORDS

1937—. 1 file box.

Record of test and analyses of individuals, showing type of work, name and address of individual, and dates and results are various tests and analyses. Arranged alphabetically by names of individuals. No index. Typed on cards. 11 x 16 x 24. Basement storage room.

415. POULTRY SCHOOL ENROLLMENT

1937—. 1 file box.

Register of pupils in poultry school, showing name and address of person enrolled, date of enrollment, and in what particular branch enrolled. Arranged alphabetically by names of pupils. No index. Typed. 11 x 16 x 24. Basement storage room.

416. TUBERCULOSIS RECORDS

1932—. 2 file boxes.

Record of tests for tuberculosis, showing name of county and township, dates first and second tests started, dates test completed, number of herds and cattle tested, number of reactors, number of tags used, test refused, herds not tested, number of infected herds, signature of veterinarian or inspector, and date filed. Arranged chronologically by dates filed. No index. Handwritten on printed forms. 11 x 16 x 24.

417. BANGS TESTS

1937—. 1 envelope, 1 file box.

Results of bangs disease tests, showing name of state and county, exact location of farm, name of owner of cattle, date of bleeding, number of purebreds and others, total number of the herd, tag numbers of reactors and date filed, questionable cattle, and signature of veterinarian. Arranged chronologically by dates filed. No index.

Typed on printed forms. Envelopes, 10 x 4 x .5; file box, 11 x 16 x 24. Basement storage room.

418. 4-H SECRETARY RECORD BOOK
1926-1932. 2 vols.
Record of minutes of meetings of 4-H clubs, showing resolutions adopted or rejected, committee reports, election of officers, appointment of committees, dates of meetings, and expenditures of club. Arranged chronologically by dates of meetings. No index. Handwritten. Average 50 pages. 6 x 4 x .5.

419. 4-H ENROLLMENT CARDS
1938—. 1 file box.
Applications for enrollment into 4-H clubs, showing name and address of applicant, name of township, names of parents, and statement concerning desire to join club. Arranged alphabetically by names of applicants. No index. Typed. 11 x 16 x 24.

420. BOYS–GIRLS
1934—. 1 file box.
Record of 4-H club members, showing names and addresses of boy and girl members, name of township, date of birth, name of parent or guardian, date enrolled, size of project, project completed or not completed, and reason for not completing. Arranged alphabetically by names of members. No index. Typed. 11 x 16 x 24.

421. INACTIVE RECORDS
1924—. 4 file boxes.
Miscellaneous papers of statistics and reports pertaining to animal husbandry, treatment of rodents, insects, and weeds, 4-H club, horticulture, poultry, credit management, and rural economics, showing date of reports and subjects covered. No obvious arrangement. No index. Typed on printed forms. 11 x 16 x 24.

Archival Materials and Printed Documents

Abstract of Indebtedness to State Auditor, 1869—, Two bundles, entry 272.

Acts of General Assembly, 1803-1941 (119 volumes, published annually by state authority).

Ashland College, Publication, *Ashland College bulletin 1941-1942* (Published annually by the college, Ashland).

[Auditors] Annual Financial Reports to County Commissioners, 1928—,11 volumes, entry 271.

Annual Statistical Report of Public Schools, 1914—, 10 bundles, entry 320.

Appearance Docket, 1852—, 22 volumes, entry 152.

Appropriation Ledger, 1928—, 12 volumes, entry 244.

Auditor's duplicate, 1846—, 132 volumes, entry 224.

Baldwin, William Edward, ed., *Throckmorton's Ohio code annotated* (certified ed., Banks-Baldwin Company, Cleveland 1936).

Board of Revision [Minutes]. 1913—, 3 volumes, entry 304.

[Board of Revision - Original Documents], 1915—, 1 file box, entry 305

Burial Record–Indigent Soldiers, 1884—, four volumes, entry 10.

Carter, Clarence Edwin, ed. and comp., *The Territorial Papers of the United States* (8 volumes, Government Printing Office, Washington, 1934, in progress).

Case Histories–Active, 1934—, two file drawers, entry 25.

Case History Index– active, 1934—, 1 file drawer, entry 26.

Chase, Salmon P. Ed., *The statutes of Ohio and of the Northwest Territory ... 1738-1883* ... (3 volumes, Corey and Fairbank, Cincinnati, 1883-1835.

Circuit Court Docket, 1894-1914 10 volumes, entry 147.

Commissioners' Record, 1846—, 26 volumes, entry 1.

Commitment Record, 1907—, 1 volume, entry 356.

Common Pleas Court Journal, 1846—, 35 volumes, entry 139.

County Commissioners' Resolutions, 1846—, 12 file boxes, 3 bundles, entry 276.

County Officers' Statements of Fees and Compensation, 1850—, 1 carton, 1 bundle, 1 file box, entry 264.

Court of Appeals Docket, 1915—, 3 volumes, entry 149.

Criminal Appearance Docket, 1908—, 3 volumes, entry 133.

Curwen, Maskell E. ed. *The Public Statutes at large of the State of Ohio* ... (4 volumes, published by the author, Cincinnati, 1853-1854).

Departmental Budget, 1934–, 1 bundle, entry 87.

Hammond, Charles, William Lawrence, Edwin M. Stanton, and others, eds., *Reports of Cases Argued and Determined in the Supreme Court of Ohio in bank* ... (20 volumes, Robert Clarke & Company, Cincinnati, 1821-1852.

Highway Map of Ashland County, current, entry 387.

Index to Deeds, Grantor, 1846—, 9 volumes, entry 37.

Infirmary Record, 1849—, 2 volumes, entry 340.

Inquest Docket, 1901—, 1 volume, entry 122.

Jail Record, 1869—, 4volumes, entry 210.

Laning, Jay F. Comp., *Revised Statutes and Recodified Laws of the State of Ohio* ... (2d ed. 3 volumes, The Laning Company, Norwalk, Ohio, 1907).

Laws of the Territory of the United States Northwest of the River Ohio (3 volumes, published by authority, Philadelphia and Cincinnati, 1792-1796).

"The Legislature of the Northwest Territory, 1795," *Ohio State Archaeological Historical Quarterly*, XXX (1921), 13-53.

McCook, G. W. Emilius O. Randall, J. L. W. Henney, and others, *Reports of Cases Argued and Determined in the Supreme Court of Ohio* (New Series, 137 volumes, various publishers, Columbus, New York, and Cincinnati, 1853—).

Monthly Statistical Reports, 1934—, 1 file box, entry 371.

Naturalization Records–Petition and Record, 1906—, 2 volumes, entry 141.

Ohio Attorney General, *Opinions,* 1846-1940 (Published annually by state authority, 1904-1940). Title varies: *Reports.*

Ohio, Constitution of, 1802.

Ohio, Constitution of, 1851.

Ohio Department of Agriculture, *A Summary of the Activities of the Ohio Department of Agriculture* ... for 1936 (published by state authority 1937).

Ohio Department of Commerce, Division of Banks, *Annual report* (published annually by state authority).

Ohio Department of Education, Division of Statistics, Files for 1942.

Ohio Department of Industrial Relations, Division of Labor Statistics, Files for 1940.

Order Book [Supreme Court of Ohio]. 1852—, 36 volumes. Titled Journal, 1903-1942, 18 volumes.

Page, William Herbert, and John J. Adams, *The Anointed General Code of the State of Ohio* (7 volumes, W. H. Anderson Company, Cincinnati, 1912).

Payrolls, 1938—, 1 file drawer, entry 408.

Pease, Theodore Calvin, ed., *The Laws of the Northwest Territory,* 1788-1800 (Trustees of the Illinois State Historical Library, *Law Series,* Springfield, 1925), I.
Physicians' License, 1896—, 1 volume, entry 188.
Poll Books and Tally Sheets, 1925—, 1280 volumes, entry 308.
Poore, Benjamin Parley, *Federal and State Constitutions and other Organic Laws of the United States* (2 Parts, Government Printing Office, Washington, 1877).
Record of Accrued Fees, 1907—, 6 volumes, entry 213.
Records of All Licensed Dogs, 1937—, 1 volume, entry 215.
Record of Births 1867-1908, 3 volumes, entry 184.
Record of Death, 1867-1908, 2 volumes, entry 185.
Record of Minutes and Proceedings, 1919—, 2 volumes, entry 325.
Record of Official Bonds, 1897—, 2 volumes, entry 263.
Record of Registered Nurses and Limited Practitioners, 1912—, 1 volume, entry 189.
Recorder's Annual Report, 1933—, 1 bundle, entry 86.
Records of Warrants Issued, 1846—, 23 volumes, entry 257.
Register of Bonds, 1915—, 1 volume, entry 264.
Sayler, J. R., comp. *The statutes of the State of Ohio* (4 volumes, Robert Clarke & Company, Cincinnati, 1876).
Shepherd, Vinton R., ed. *The Ohio NISI PRIUS REPORTS* (New series, 32 volumes, Ohio law Reporter Company, Columbus and Cincinnati, 1904—).
Smith, J. V., *Official reports of the Debates and Proceedings of the Ohio Convention ... held at Columbus, Commencing May 6, 1950, and at Cincinnati, Commencing December 2, 1850* (Scott and Bascom, Columbus 1851).
Transfer Record, 1933—, 2 volumes, entry 42.
Trautwein, George C., ed., *Supplement to Page's Annotated General Code, 1926-1935* (W. H. Anderson Company, Cincinnati, 1935).
Treasurer's Ledger, 1904—, 10 volumes, entry 296.
U. S. Bureau of the Census, *Fifteenth Census of the United States, 1930, Agriculture* (4 volumes, Government Printing Office, Washington, 1931-1932).
U. S. Bureau of the Census, *Fifteenth Census of the United States, 1930, Population* (6 volumes, Government Printing Office, Washington 1931-1933).
U. S. Bureau of the Census, *Religious Bodies,* 1926 (2 volumes, Government Printing Office, Washington, 1929-1930).

U. S. Bureau of the Census, *Sixteenth Census of the United States, 1940, Agriculture,* Ohio, First Series (Government Printing Office, Washington, 1941).

U. S. Bureau of the Census, *Sixteenth Census of the United States,1940, Manufacturers,* First Series (Government Printing Office, Washington, 1941).

U. S. Bureau of the Census, *Sixteenth Census of the United States, 1940, Population,* First Series, Number of Inhabitants (Government Printing Office, Washington, 1941).

United States Code Annotated (65 volumes, Editorial staffs of Edward Thompson Company, Northport, Long Island, New York and West Publishing Company St. Paul, 1927—).

U. S. Comptroller of the Currency, *Individual Statements of Conditions of National Banks, December 31, 1940* (Government Printing Office, Washington, 1941).

United States Statutes at Large, 1789-1941 (54 volumes, United States Government Printing Office, Washington, 1848-1941).

Witness and Jury Docket, 1846—, 6 volumes, entry 103.

Diaries and Memoirs

Burnet [Jacob], *Notes on the Early Settlement of the Northwest Territory* (Derby, Bradley and Company, Cincinnati, 1847).

General Histories and Reference Works

Adams, George Burton, *Constitutional History of England* (Henry Holt and Company, New York, c1931).

Ayer, N. W. And Son, *Directory of Newspapers and Periodicals* (N. W. Ayer And Son, Inc. Philadelphia, 1940).

Gwynne, A. E., *A practical Treaties on the Law of Sheriff and Coroner with Forms and References to the Statutes of Ohio, Indiana, and Kentucky* (H. W. Derby and Company Cincinnati, 1849).

Hodgkin, Thomas, *From the Earliest Times to the Norman Conquest*, in William Hunt and Reginald Poole, *The Political History of England* (12 volumes, Longsmans, Green, and Company, New York and London, 1905-1910.

Karraker, Cyrus Harreld, *The seventeenh Century Sheriff: A Comparative Study of the Sheriff in England and the Chesapeake Colonies, 1607-1689* (University of North Carolina Press, Chapel Hill, 1930).

Pollock, Sir Frederick, and Frederic William Maitland, *The History of English Law before the Time of Edward I* (Two volumes, Cambridge University press, Cambridge, Eng., and Little, Brown & Company, Boston, 1895).

Rand McNally and Company, comp., pub., *Commercial atlas and marketing guide 1942* (72d ed. New York, Chicago, San Francisco, 1942).

Sutherland, Edwin H., *Principles of Criminology* (J. B. Lippincott and Company, Chicago, 1934).

Van Waters, Miriam, *Youth in Conflict* (Republic Publishing Company, New York, 1925).

Willoughby, W. F., *Principles of Judicial Administration* (The Brookings Institution, Washington, 1929).

Regional and Local Histories, Treaties, and Monographs

Amer, Francis J., *The Development of Judicial System in Ohio from 1787 to 1932* (Institute of Law Bulletin, Number 8, Johns Hopkins press, Baltimore, 1932).

Baughman, A. J., *History of Ashland County, Ohio* (S. J. Clarke Publishing Company, Chicago, 1909).

Bond, Beverley W., Jr., *The civilization of the Old Northwest: A study of Political, Social, and Economic Development, 1788-1812 (*Macmillan Company, New York, 1934*)*.

Burns, James Jesse, Educational History of Ohio ... (Historical Publications Company, Columbus, 1905).

Caldwell, J. A., *Atlas of Ashland County, Ohio* (J. A. Caldwell, Condit, Ohio, 1874).

Duff, William A., ed., *Ashland, the City of Progress and Prosperity* Ashland Centennial Homecoming Association, Ashland, 1915).

Estrich, Willis, A., ed., *Ohio Jurisprudence* (43 volumes, Lawyers Cooperative Publishing company, Rochester, New York, 1928-1938).

Geological Survey of Ohio, *Report* (second series, 6 volumes, published by state authority, 1873-1893).

Heiges, R. E., *The Office of Sheriff in Rural Counties of Ohio* (Published by the author, Findlay, Ohio, 1933).

Hill, George W., *History of Ashland County, Ohio* (Williams Brothers, Cleveland, 1880).

Hooper, Osman Castle, *History of Ohio Journalism, 1793-1933* (Spahr and Glenn Company, Columbus, 1933).

Howe, Henry, *Historical Collections of Ohio* (2 volumes, published by state authority, Norwalk, Ohio, 1896).

Kennedy, Aileen Elizabeth, *The Poor Law and Its Administration* (Sophonisba P. Breckinridge ed., Social Service Monographs, Number 22, University of Chicago Press, Chicago, 1934).

Knapp, H. S., *History of the Pioneer and Modern Times of Ashland County* (J. B. Lippincott and Company, Philadelphia, 1863).

McCarty, Dwight G., *The Territorial Governors of the old Northwest: A Study in Territorial Administration* (State Historical Society of Iowa, Iowa City, 1910).

Mills, William C., *Archaeological Atlas of Ohio* (Ohio State Archaeological and Historical Society, Columbus, 1914).

Moley, Raymond, "The sheriff and the Corner." The Missouri Association for Criminal Justice, *The Missouri Criminal Survey,* pt. ii (Macmillan Company, New York, 1926).

The Ohio Tax Commission, *Financing State and Local Government in Ohio, 1900-1932* (published by state authority, 1934).

The Reorganization of County Government in Ohio: Report of the Governor's Commission on County Government (n. pub., n. p., submitted to the governor. December 1934).

Riddle, Samuel, *History of Ashland County, Pioneer Historical Society* (Brethren Publishing House, Ashland, 1888).

Roseboom, Eugene Holloway, and Francis Phelps Weisenburger, *A History of Ohio* (Prentice-Hall, Inc., New York, 1934).

Articles in Periodicals

Atkinson, R. C., "County Home Rural Development in Ohio," *National Municipal Review.* XXIII (1934). 235.

Atkinson, R. C., "Ohio–County Charter Elections," *National Municipal Review.* XXIV (1935). 702-703.

Atkinson, R. C., "Ohio–Optional County Legislation," *National Municipal Review.* XXIV (1935). 228.

Downes, Randolph Chandler, "Evolution of Ohio Boundaries."*Ohio State Archaeological and Historical Quarterly,* XXXVI (1927). 340-477.

Dykstra, C. A., "Cleveland's Effort for City-County Consolidation," *National Municipal Review,* VIII (1919). 551-556.

Gates, Charles M., "The Administration of State Archives," *The Pacific Northwest Quarterly,* XXIX (1938), Number 1; also in *The American archivist* I (1938), 130-141.

Haley, W. D., "Johnny Appleseed, a Pioneer Hero," *Harper's New Monthly Magazine,* XLIII (November 1871). 830-836.

Kaplan, H. Eliot, "A Personal Program for County Service, "*National Municipal Review,* XXV (1936). 596-600.

Morris, William A., "The Office of Sheriff in the Anglo-Saxon Period." *English Historical Review,* XXXI (1916), 20-40.

Stone, Donald C., "The Police Attack Crime, *National Municipal Review,* XXIV (1935), 39-41.

Newspapers

The *Ashland Times,* 1887.
The Ohio State Journal, 1840, 1933.

ROSTER OF COUNTY OFFICIALS*
1846-1942**

Commissioners***

Abner Crist	1846-1847
Edward S. Hibbard	1846-1851
Josiah Thomas	1846-1849
Aldrich Carver	1847-1850
James M. Hammett	1849-1852
Christian Newcomer	1850-1853
Luke Selby	1851-1857
George McConnell	1852-1858
Amos Hilburn	1853-1856
Hervey Fenn	1856-1859
William S. Strickland	1857-1860
Jacob Emrick	1858-1864
John Berry	1859-1865
Daniel Pocock	1860-1863
Robert Cowan (Resigned)	1863-1865
John Van Nest	1864-1870
Henry Wicks	1865-1871
John Berry (Vice Robert Cowan)	1865-1866
William Cowan	1866-1872
James Dunlap	1870-1876
John P. Smalley	1871-1877
William M. Crowner	1872-1878
Stephen Barrick	1876-1882
McClure Davis	1877-1883
John J. Wolf	1878-1884
James Wheston	1882-1885
Nathan J. Crosson	1883-1889
John Martin	1884-1890
James Warton	1885-1891
Jacob Kettering	1886-1895
William Hess	1890-1896
George Brubaker	1891-1897
Charles T. Baker	1895-1901
Wilbert Sharick	1896-1902
William L. Noggle	1897-1903
George W. Walter	1901-1907
Christian H Snyder	1902-1905
Theodore W. Hunter (Died in office)	1903-1906
Lewis A. Funk	1905-1909
William Shidler (Vice Theodore W. Hunter)	1906-1909
George W. Emerick	1907-1911
William Shidler	1909-1911
Frank P. Stine	1909-1911
Oscar W. Crone	1911-1915
Joseph E. Gongwer	1911-1915
David F. Hay	1911-1915
Wesley Brubaker	1915-1919
J. Henry Greshner	1915-1919
Charles Kahl	1915-1919
G.E. Goard	1919-1921
J.J. Whitmore	1919-1921
W.V. Shafer	1919-1925
B.F. Zercher	1921-1923
J.W. Ogden	1921-1925

*Compiled from: Ohio Secretary of State *Annual Report*, 1836-1936 (some volumes titled: *Ohio Statistics*); General Record-Governor's Office, 1803-1856, 9 volumes.
**Ashland County was organized in 1846. *Laws of Ohio*, XLIV (local laws) 172-175.
***The board of county commissioners, with three members each sefving a three-year term was established in 1804 (*Laws of Ohio*, II, 1500). In 1906 it was increased to four years, and so remains (*Laws of Ohio*, CVIII, pt. ii, 1300).

J.W. Davidson	1923-1931	George W. Tugend	1931-1939
D.V. Peterson	1925-1929	Clarence R. Keener	1933-1941
R.L. Kreiling	1925-1929	Clayton I Harmon	1937—
Fremont Wallace	1929-1933	Tom J. Spence	1939—
W.W. Barnhill	1929-1937	H.F. Wallett	1941—

Recorders*

Asa S. Reed	1846-1847	Amos M. Kohler	1890-1896
Asa S. Reed	1847-1856	Lorin P. Riddle	1896-1899
Robert Scott	1856-1859	Benjamin F. Paulin	1899-1905
George Johnston	1859-1865	Seth M. Gongwer	1905-1911
George W. Urie	1865-1874	Henry J. Schultz	1911-1915
John P.M. Goodman	1874-1886	Charles H. Bryan	1915-1919
Edwin S. Bird (Died in office)	1886-1889	Fred Sherer	1919-1923
		Cloyd M. Moneysmith	1923-1927
Amos H. Kohler Vice Edwin S. Bird until successor qualified)	1889-1890	Carl J. Harry	1927-1933
		J.W. Maffett	1933-1937
		Ralph H. Maffett	1937—

Clerks of the Court of Common Pleas**

Daniel W. Brown (Appointed to serve at the pleasure of the common pleas court)	1846-1847	Jacob O. Jennings (Appointed to serve at the pleasure of the common pleas court)	1847-1852

*Under the law of 1803, the associate judges of the court of common pleas appointed the recorder for a seven-year term (*Laws of Ohio*, I, 136). The office became elective for a three-year term in 1829, a two-year term in 1905, and a four-year term in 1936. (*Laws of Ohio*, XXVII, 65; *Ohio Const. 1851*, Art. XVII, sec. 2; *Laws of Ohio*, CXVI, pt. ii, 184).

**Called prothonotary under the laws of the Northwest Territory and appointed by the governor. Under the Ohio Constitution of 1802 the court appointed its own clerk for a seven-year term (Art. III, sec. 9). The constitution of 1851 made the office elective for a three-year term (Art. IV, sec. 16). Under the constitutional amendment of 1905, the term was changed to two years and to four in 1936 (*Laws of Ohio*, XCVII, 641; CXVI, pt. ii, 184).

Clerks of the Court of Common Peas (continued)

John Sheridan 1852-1855
Jacob O. Jennings 1855-1858
Henry S. See 1858-1864
William G. Heetman 1864-1865
(Election contested)
Seth M. Barber 1865-1864
(Unexpired term of William G. Heetman)
Edwin T. Drayton 1867-1870
William C. Frazee 1870-1876
John E. McCray 1876-1882
Cloyd Mansfield 1882-1888
Milton Winbigler 1888-1894
Irvin W. Thomas 1894-1900
Charles C. Chapman 1900-1906
Joseph A. Shearer 1906-1911
(Resigned)
Amos M. Kohler 1911-1912
(Part of year; Vice Joseph A. Shearer)
Frank A. Baker 1912-1915
Herbert E. Eckelberger 1915-1921
R.S. Sloan 1921-1923
Cloyd M. Scott 1923-1927
Tully C. Fox 1927-1933
Charles A. McBride 1933—

Judges of the Court of Common Pleas*

President judges under the constitution of 1802 in District XI, which included Ashland County

Jacob Parker 1846-1848
Levi Cox 1848-1852

Associate judges under the constitution of 1802 in District XI, which included Ashland County

John P. Reznor 1846-1847
(Resigned)
Edmund Igmand 1846-1852
George H. Stewart 1846-1852
Daniel W. Brown 1847-1848
(Temporary appointment; Vice John P. Reznor)
Bela B. Clark 1848-1849
(Temporary appointment; Vice D.W. Brown, Vice J.P. Reznor)
John C. Myers 1849-1852
(Appointed to fill vacancy)

*The president and associate judges under the first constitution were appointed for seven-year terms by joint ballot of both houses of the general assembly (*Ohio Const. 1802* Art. III, sec. 8). The constitution of 1851 made the office elective for five-year periods and required the incumbent to be a resident of the district in which elected (*Ohio Const, 1851*),

Art. IV, sec. 12). The amendment of 1912 changed the term to six years, required the election of at least one judge for each county, who must be a resident of the county in which elected (Art. IV, sec. 12, as amended Sep. 3, 1912).

Judges of the common pleas court under the constitution of 1851

James Stewart 1852-1857
George W. Geddes 1857-1866
(Resigned in October)
William Given 1859-1864
William Osborn 1866-1867
(Vice George W. Geddes)
William Osborn 1867-1872
George W. Geddes 1869-1873
(Resigned in November)
Darius Dirlam 1872-1876
(Resigned in September)
Judson A. Beebe 1873-1874
(Vice George W. Geddes; died in office)
Thomas J. Kenny 1874-1875
(Vice J.A. Beebe)
Thomas J. Kenny 1875-1882
(Died in office)
Andrew K. Dunn 1876-1877
(Vice Darius Dirlam)
Moses R. Dickey 1877-1882
(Resigned in February)
John W. Jenner 1882-1883
(Vice M.R. Dickey)
Thos. E. Duncan 1882-1883
Vice T.J. Kenny)
Manuel May 1883-1892
Jabez Dickey 1883-1889
Henry L. McCray 1889-1894
Norman L. Wolfe 1892-1902
Thomas E. Duncan 1894-1899
Robert M. Campbell 1899-1909
Darius Dirlam 1902-1907
Edwin Mansfield 1907-1915
William T. Devor 1909-1915

Resident judges under the constitutional amendment of 1912

D. Homer Graven 1915-1927
Charles C. Chapman 1927-1939
H.C. Culbertson 1939—

ROSTER OF COUNTY OFFICIALS*
1846-1942**

Judges of the Probate Court*

Albert L. Curtis	1852-1858
Collins W. Bushnell (Part of year, died in office)	1858
John D. Jones (Vice C.W. Bushnell)	1858-1861
John D. Jones	1861-1864
William A.G. Emerson (Part of year; election contested)	1864
Edmund Ingman (Vice W.A.G. Emerson; died in office)	1864-1865
Tully C. Bushnell (Vice E. Ingman)	1865-1867
Tully C. Bushnell	1867-1870
Daniel W. Whetmore	1870-1876
John Taylor	1876-1882
James Alberson	1882-1888
Emanuel Finger	1888-1894
Benjamin Myers	1894-1900
Floyd Mansfield	1900-1906
Samuel G. McAdoo	1906-1913
Frank P. Whitman	1913-1925
Benjamin C. McCray	1925-1937
Stanton H. Boffenmeyer	1937—

*The probate court, established under the laws of the Northwest Territory in 1788, consisted of a probate judge and two judges of the court of common pleas (Pease, *op. cit.,* 9). Under the constitution of 1802, it lost its identity completely in the court of common pleas. It emerged with its present form and functions in 1852, with a single judge serving a three-year term, under the constitution of 1851. (*Ohio Const. 1851*, Art. IV, secs. 7, 8). On Sept. 3, 1912, the term was changed to four years as at present (*Ohio Const. 1851*, Art. IV, sec. 7, amendment of 1912).

Prosecuting Attorneys*

Nicholas M. Donaldson	1846-1847
John S. Fulton	1847-1849
Bolivar W. Kellogg	1849-1853
Alexander Porter	1853-1855
John S. Fulton	1855-1857
Thomas J. Kenny	1857-1859
John J. Jacobs	1859-1861
William F. Johnston	1861-1863
George W. Hill	1863-1867
Albert L. Curtis	1867-1869
John J. Jacobs	1869-1871
John T. McCray	1871-1875
Byron Stilwell	1875-1879
George B. Smith	1879-1883
E.U. Harvnot	1883-1886
Frank C. Semple	1886-1892
Harry A. Mykrantz	1892-1895
Frank N. Patterson	1895-1898
Harry A. Mykrantz	1898-1901
William T. Devor	1901-1907
George J. Frey (Resigned)	1907-1912
Frank N. Patterson (Appointed; Vice G.J. Frey)	1912-1913
Thomas H. Moore	1913-1917
C.C. Chapman	1917-1921
J.F. Henderson	1921-1925
H.E. Culbertson	1925-1933

Howard S. Lutz	1933-1937	A. Ross Siverling	1937—

*At first appointed by the supreme court and later (1805) by the court of common pleas a law passed Jan. 23, 1833, made the office of prosecuting attorney elective for a term of two years (*Laws of Ohio*, XXXI, 13). In 1881 the term was increased to three years; in 1906 reduced to two, and in 1936 increased to four (*Laws of Ohio*, LXXVIII, 260; XCVIII, 271; CXVI, pt. ii, 184).

Coroners*

Jacob Miller	1846-1847	Daniel Ambrose	1880-1888
Michael Riddle	1847-1849	William H. Reinhart	1888-1892
Justus Wetherbee	1849-1851	Joseph M. Bittinger	1892-1898
Charles Chaney	1851-1853	Chambers A. Levering	1898-1899
John G. Brown	1853-1855	(Resigned)	
John Woodburn	1855-1858	Jerome H. King	1899-1900
George W. Crozier	1858-1862	(Vice C.A. Levering)	
S.P. Crozier	1862-1863	Jerome H. King	1900-1906
(Election contested)		Ray C. Ash	1906-1911
John Woodburn	1863-1864	George W. Jacoby	1911-1919
(Vice S.P. Crozier)		F.V. Dottenveich	1919-1921
William J. Vermilya	1864-1866	R.C. Ash	1921-1923
Israel Markle	1866-1868	T.S. Sims	1923-1929
Alexander Emerick	1868-1872	George Riebel	1929-1935
Daniel Ambrose	1872-1876	George M. Emery	1935—
Frank H. Wilson	1876-1880		

*Established in 1788, the county coroner was appointed for a two-year term by the territorial governor (Pease, *op. cit.,* 24, 25). The Ohio Constitution of 1802 made the office elective without changing the term, which remained at two years until 1936, when it was increased to four years (*Ohio Const. 1802*, Art. VI, sec. 1; *Laws of Ohio*, CXVI, pt. ii, 184).

ROSTER OF COUNTY OFFICIALS* 1846-1942**

Sheriffs**

James Doty
James Doty
Isaac Gates
John D. Jones
John J. Hootman
James McCool
John G. Brown
Levi H. Kiplinger
William O. Porter
John J. Winbigler
Joseph Moore
Isaac Gates
Randolph F. Andress
John G. Herzog
Samuel R. Jones
John P. Jones
Amos Homan
William F. Conrad
Joseph B. Beninghoff
r.A. Davis
Ora Beard
Charles R. Baar
(Resigned)
F.P. Whitmore
(Appointed Vice C.R. Baar)
Charles R. Baar
Fred E. Ducomb
Clem V. Hassinger
Earl Kiser
H.F. Wallett
(Resigned)
L. Dale Hammond
(Vice H.L. Wallett)
L. Dale Hammond

**Under the territorial government the sheriff was appointed by the governor from the time the office was created in 1792 (Pease, *op. cit.,* 8). Under the first constitution the office was made elective for two-year terms and was not changed until 1936, when the term was increased to four years (*Ohio Const. 1802*, Art. VI, sec. 11; *laws of Ohio*, CXVI, pt. ii, 184).

ROSTER OF COUNTY OFFICIALS*
1846-1942**

Auditors*

Hugh Burns	1846-1847	William F. Alberson	1875-1877
Hugh Burns	1847-1851	Elias J. Crosscup	1877-1885
Aldrich Carver	1851-1853	Samuel L. Arnold	1885-1891
Isaac Gates	1853-1857	Cloyd W. McCool	1891-1897
James Swineford	1857-1861	Edson W. Westover	1897-1903
Johnson Oldroyd	1861-1863	James F. Welty	1903-1909
Isaac Gates	1863-1867	H.C. Westover	1909-1913
Robert M. Campbell	1867-1870	J. Freer Bittinger	1913-1917
(Resigned)		Seth Gongwer	1917-1923
Emanuel Finger	1870-1871	J.P. Hunter	1927-1935
(Vice R.M. Campbell)		Floyd E. Wicks	1935—
Emanuel Finger	1871-1875		

*Office established by legislative act Feb. 18, 1820 (*Laws of Ohio*, XVIII, 70). At first appointive, it was made elective annually by an act of Feb. 2, 1821, the person elected taking off ice March 1, each year (*Laws of Ohio*, XIX, 116). In 1831 the term was set at twop years, in 1877 at three years, in 1906 at two years, and in 1919 at four years (*Laws of Ohio*, XXIX, 280; LXXIV, 381; XCVIII, 271; CVIII, pt. ii, 1294).

Treasurers*

George W. Urie	1846-1847	Joseph Stofer	1883-1887
George W. Urie	1847-1851	James W. Brant	1887-1889
James W. Boyd	1851-1855	Thomas C. Harvey	1889-1893
Jacob Crall	1855-1857	Jacob Saal	1893-1897
John Jacobs	1857-1858	William Shidler	1897-1901
(Died in office)		C.A. Levering	1901-1905
F.S. Jacobs	1858-1859	Amos M. Kohler	1905-1909
(Vice John Jacobs)		Floyd Mansfield	1909-1913
F.S. Jacobs	1859-1861	B.F. Paullin	1913-1917
Rueben N. Hershey	1861-1865	Seth Gongwer	1917-1921
Henry B. Hershey	1865-1867	Charles H. Bryson	1921-1923
William G. Heltman	1867-1871	Hugh Paxton	1923-1925
Guttelius I. Yearick	1871-1875	H.E. Echelberger	1925-1929
Michael Miller	1875-1877	T.O. Deibler	1929-1931
George A. Ullman	1877-1883		

Guy B. Murray	1931-1935	Karl K. Kick	1939-1941
Henry O. Faber	1935-1939	(Vice Henry O. Faber)	
(Resigned)		Karl K. Kick	1941—

*Omitted from the constitution of 1802, the office of treasurer was crated by legislative act in 1803 (*Laws of Ohio*, I, 98). Appointive, by the associate judges in 1803, and annually, by the county commissioners from 1804 to 1827 when the office became elective for two-year terms (*Laws of Ohio*, I, 98; II, 154; XXV 25-32). The constitution of 1851 provided that no person should hold the office for more than four years of any six (Art. X, sec. 3). In accordance with the constitution of 1851 and an act of the general assembly in 1859 the term remained two years (*Laws of Ohio*, LVI, 105). In 1936 it was increased to four years, as at present (*Laws of Ohio*, CXVI, pt. ii, 184).

Infirmary Directors**

Joseph McCorners	1850-1853	Joseph Strickland	1872-1873
John Scott	1850-1853	(Filling vacancy; resigned)	
Elias Ford	1850-1853	Clark A. Barton	1873-1875
Joseph H. Miller	1853-1854	(Vice Joseph Strickland)	
David Bryte	1853-1856	George Myers	1873-1876
George Boldorf	1853-1855	Andrew Jackson	1874-1877
Patrick Kelley	1854-1857	(Resigned)	
Hugh McGuire	1855-1858	Clark A. Barton	1875-1878
Henry Hough	1857-1860	John M. Ritchie	1877-1879
Joseph Strickland	1858-1860	(Vice Andrew Jackson)	
(Resigned)		George Smith	1878-1884
D.K. Hull	1859-1864	Thomas Miller	1879-1885
(Resigned)		Benjamin McGuire	1880-1886
Holliday Ames	1860-1863	Christian K. Fike	1884-1890
Johnson S. Martin	1860-1861	Louis P. Yeater	1885-1891
(Vice Joseph Strickland)		George Honeberger	1886-1892
Johnson S. Martin	1861-1866	Samuel C. Boyd	1890-1893
William Craig	1864-1866	Frederick Remy	1891-1897
(Unexpired term D.K. Hull)		John C. Wolf	1892-1898
James McVance	1864-1867	William F. England	18936-1899
William Craig	1866-1872	(Appointment extension)	
James McNaull	1867-1868	Davis Wertman	1897-1903
(Filling vacancy)		Milton C. McClain	1898-1904
Moses Latta	1867-1873	Samuel P. Ely	1899-1905
William G. Galloway	1868-1874	Edward H. Ingman	1903-1906

John W. Harvey	1904-1907	Randolph F. Andress	1911-1913
James L. Crone	1905-1911	Peter Arch McClure	1911-1913
Jacob Myers	1906-1911	John C. Wolf	1911-1913
Andrew R. Paxton	1907-1911		

**This office was authorized by a legislative act in 1816, providing for the appointment by the commissioners of seven directors to have charge of the county infirmary and choose its superintendent (*Laws of Ohio*, XIV, 447, 448). By an act of 1831 the membershp of the board was reducred to three, and in 1842 the members were made elective for terms of three years (*Laws of Ohio*, XXIX, 317; XL, 35). The board was abolished by law in 1913, and its powers and duties were transferred to the board of county commissioners and the infirmary superintendent (*Laws of Ohio*, CII, 433).

Surveyors*

John Keene, Jr.	1846-1847	John B. Weddell	1888
John Keene, Jr.	1847-1850	(Resigned)	
Orlow Smith	1850-1856	Lucian Rust, Jr.	1888-1889
John Keene, Jr.	1856-1859	(Vice J.B. Weddell)	
Orlow Smith	1859-1862	Lucian Rust, Jr.	1889-1892
George W. Ryall	1862-1865	(Resigned)	
John Keene, Jr.	1865-1867	C.W. McCool	1892-1893
(Died in office)		(Vice Lucian Rust, Jr.)	
George W. Ryall	1867-1868	Francis L. Neiderheiser	1893-1902
(Vice John Keene, Jr.)		Elvin L. Berry	1902-1909
Henry Pifer	1868-1871	Tracy Brindle	1909-1915
George W. Ryall	1871-1874	Ralph Scantleburry	1915-1919
John B. Weddell	1874-1883	Tracy Brindle	1919-1921
Lewis M. Wolf	1883-1887	Gus W. Otter	1921-1925
(Resigned)		Howard H. Fetzer	1925-1929
John B. Weddell	1887-1888	W.M. Spreng	1929-1933
(Vice Lewis M. Wolf)		L.G. Shenberger	1933-1935

*From 1803 to 1831 the surveyor was appointed by the court of common pleas and commissioned by the governor (*Laws of Ohio*, I, 90-93). From 1831 to 1906 he was elected for a three-year term from 1906 to 1928 for a two-year term and since 1928 for a four-year term (*Laws of Ohio*. XXIX, 399; XCVII, 245-247; CXII, 179).

Engineers*

L.G. Shenberger 1935—

*An act of 1935 changed the title of surveyor to engineer (*Laws of Ohio*, CXVI, 283).

All addresses refer to Ashland, Ohio, unless otherwise noted

Auditor
142 W. 2nd Street
https://www.ashlandcounty.org/auditor/

Board of Education
1407 Claremont Avenue
https://ashlandcityschool.org/district/board-education

Board of Elections
110 Cottage Street
https://www.boe.ohio.gov/ashland/

Clerk of Courts
142 W. 2nd Street
https://www.ashlandcounty.org/clerkofcourts/

Commissioners
110 Cottage Street
https://www.ashlandcountyoh.us/about-ashland-county/commissioners

Common Pleas
142 W. 2nd Street
https://ashlandcommonpleas.com/

Coroner
1207 East Main Street
https://www.ashlandcounty.org/coroner/

County Engineer
1511 Cleveland Avenue
https://www.ashlandcounty,.org/engineer/

Dog Warden
1740 Baney Road
https://www.ashlandcountyoh.us/county-services/ashland-county-dog-shelter

Health Department
1211 Claremont Avenue
https://www.ashlandhealth.com/

Recorder
142 W. 2nd Street
https://www.ashlandcounty.org/recorder/

Sheriff
1205 E. Main Street
https://www.ashlandcountysheriff.org/

Treasurer
142 W. 2nd Street
https://www.ashlandcounty.org/treasurer/

Other websites:

FamilySearch.org, a free site, has listings for court records, naturalization and citizenship, probate records, taxation, and vital records.

Ashland County Historical Society, 420 Center St., Ashland, OH 44805 **https://www.ashlandhistory.org/** may have original volumes for selected offices, but not necessarily for consecutive years, but also transcribed local records.

Ashland Public Library, 224 Claremont Ave., Ashland, OH 44805 **https://ashland.lib.oh.us/** has a genealogy section which contains county histories as well as transcribed records.

Ohio History Connection 800 E. 17th Ave., Columbus, OH 43211 **https://www.ohiohistory.org/** has Ashland County information, but is not online.

University of Akron, Polsky Building, Room LL10, 225 South Main Street, Akron, OH 44325-1702 **https://www.uakron.edu/libraries/archives/** houses some local government records Ashland County.

Western Reserve Historical Society, 10825 East Blvd, Cleveland, OH 44106, **https://www.wrhs.org/** the library has transcribed information which is not online.

Heritage Books by Jana Sloan Broglin:

Additions and Corrections to the W.P.A. Inventory of Adams County, Ohio: West Union

Additions and Corrections to the W.P.A. Inventory of Allen County, Ohio: Lima

Additions and Corrections to the W.P.A. Inventory of Ashland County, Ohio: Ashland

Additions and Corrections to the W.P.A. Inventory of Fulton County, Ohio: Wauseon

Additions and Corrections to the W.P.A. Inventory of Lucas County, Ohio: Toledo

Hookers, Crooks and Kooks, Part I: Hookers

Hookers, Crooks and Kooks, Part II: Crooks and Kooks

Lucas County, Ohio, Index to Deaths, 1867–1908

Mason County, Kentucky Wills and Estates, 1791–1832, Second Edition

www.ingramcontent.com/pod-product-compliance
Lightning Source LLC
Chambersburg PA
CBHW071831270326
41929CB00013B/1960

9780788427671